HOW TO BE DISABLED IN A PANDEMIC

How to Be Disabled in a Pandemic

Edited by
Mara Mills, Harris Kornstein,
Faye Ginsburg, *and* Rayna Rapp

NEW YORK UNIVERSITY PRESS
New York

NEW YORK UNIVERSITY PRESS
New York
www.nyupress.org

© 2025 by New York University

This work is licensed under the Creative Commons Attribution-NonCommercial-NoDerivs 4.0 license (CC BY-NC-ND 4.0). To view a copy of the license, visit https://creativecommons.org/licenses/by-nc-nd/4.0.

Please contact the Library of Congress for Cataloging-in-Publication data.

ISBN: 9781479830831 (hardback)
ISBN: 9781479830855 (paperback)
ISBN: 9781479830909 (library ebook)
ISBN: 9781479830886 (consumer ebook)

This book is printed on acid-free paper, and its binding materials are chosen for strength and durability. We strive to use environmentally responsible suppliers and materials to the greatest extent possible in publishing our books.

Manufactured in the United States of America

10 9 8 7 6 5 4 3 2 1

Also available as an ebook

CONTENTS

Foreword: Into the Pandemic's Disability Hinterlands   vii
Ed Yong

Introduction: How to Be Disabled in a Pandemic   1
Mara Mills, Harris Kornstein, Faye Ginsburg, and Rayna Rapp

PART I. LIVING WITH "DISPROPORTIONATE RISK":
POLICIES, INSTITUTIONS, AND CONGREGATE SETTINGS

1. "We Were Sick, and They Punished Us Even More": Living through COVID-19 in New York State Prisons   45
   Tommaso Bardelli, Aiyuba Thomas, and Dylan Brown

2. Second-Class Noncitizens: The Impact of the COVID-19 Pandemic on Immigrants with Disabilities in New York City   63
   J.C. Salyer

3. Housing as Health Care: Shelter and Safety across Decades   81
   Salonee Bhaman

4. From Inaccessibility to Pathologized Mobility on New York City's Public Transit: Finding Affordances in a Pandemic   100
   Yan Grenier

5. Vent: Making and Debating the New York State Ventilator Allocation Guidelines   120
   Mara Mills

6. High Stakes Schooling: Risk, Protection, and the Education of Disabled Children in a Pandemic   151
   Alexandra Freidus, Rachel Fish, and Erica O. Turner

7. Care Work, Creativity, and Unplanned Survival in the Time of COVID   167
   Faye Ginsburg and Rayna Rapp

PART II. DISABILITY COMMUNITIES: EXPERTISE, ACTIVISM, AND SOLIDARITY

8. When Postviral Goes Viral: Myalgic Encephalomyelitis, Long COVID, and Pandemic Déjà Vu 191
   Harris Kornstein and Emily Lim Rogers

9. Blind New Yorkers, Online and Offline, during the Pandemic 214
   Bojana Coklyat and Chancey Fleet

10. The Everyday Lives of *Qilao* during the Pandemic 228
    Shuting Li

11. "We Want Cop-Free Communities": Reflections on Anti-Asian Violences and Safety 251
    Mon Mohapatra, Heena Sharma, Yves Tong Nguyen, and Rachel Kuo

12. Mental Health and Black Futurity: Life, Birth, and Caregiving in Double Pandemics 271
    Nadia Mbonde

13. Disability Justice, Material Needs, and Mutual Aid: Lessons from Autistic Communities during the Pandemic 289
    Cara Ryan

14. Making Art in Bed 308
    Emily Watlington

15. Reflections on Being a Disability Reporter during the Pandemic 319
    Amanda Morris

Coda: Toward a Disability Future 325
Judith Heumann

Appendix A. New York City Pandemic and Disability Activism Timeline 329

Appendix B. Keywords from the Pandemic: A Disability Glossary 335

Acknowledgments 357

About the Editors 361

About the Contributors 363

Index 369

Color insert follows page 180

FOREWORD

Into the Pandemic's Disability Hinterlands

ED YONG

Some people who get COVID-19 recover within a few weeks. Others lose their lives to the infection. But between these outcomes exists a vast hinterland, full of millions of people who neither recover nor die and instead grapple with months, years, and perhaps even a lifetime of disability. Some might carry increased risks of heart disease or diabetes. Others suffer from the long-term consequences of a stint in an intensive care unit. And yet others suffer from Long COVID, defined by the World Health Organization as "the continuation or development of new symptoms 3 months after the initial SARS-CoV-2 infection." Millions of people in the US alone currently have Long COVID, which has, for good reason, been described as a "mass disabling event."

But several publications have questioned that narrative. In June 2022, a piece in *The Atlantic* noted that since the start of the pandemic, the number of disability claims made to the federal government had not gone up; in fact, it had *dropped* by 10 percent. A Harvard professor of healthcare policy was quoted as saying, "It's just not a mass disabling event from that perspective." That quote and that claim were cited the following year by a piece in *Slate*, which also noted that Long COVID accounted for a minuscule fraction of the disability claims administered by the New York State Insurance Fund.

The logic seemed sound: if there had indeed been a mass disabling event, there should have been a rise in disability claims, and the absence of the latter surely refutes the existence of the former. But when I ran that reasoning past Laura Mauldin, a sociologist at the University of Connecticut who specializes in disability, she was, to put it mildly, not convinced. "That argument is absolutely hilarious," she told me. Jennifer Senior, a writer and former colleague who has Long COVID, was even more scathing. "That's f**king horseshit," she said.

Mauldin and Senior, because of their expertise and lived experiences, saw clearly what the authors of the skeptical pieces did not. Absent any public education campaign about Long COVID, a long-hauler might not even know that they have the condition. Even if they do, they have every incentive to hide their illness from their employers or even from themselves. Their symptoms probably fluctuate, casting the beguiling illusion that recovery is just around the corner. This kind of episodic disability holds back the seismic identity shift that one must undergo to even consider making a disability claim. "If you take disability, you're declaring yourself a sick person, which is highly disruptive to your self-conception," Senior told me. At the time, she had yet to file a claim herself.

To make a claim, long-haulers also need thorough medical documentation, and most struggle to find doctors who will even believe their symptoms are real, let alone know which tests to order. Applicants must then navigate a bureaucratic labyrinth that can befuddle even healthy individuals—and most long-haulers have fatigue or brain fog. These factors all show why the use of plateauing or declining disability claims to refute the existence of a mass disability event is profoundly flawed. But more than that, they show why such an argument is *obviously and straightforwardly flawed* after even brief conversations with disabled people or disability scholars—who know all too well the difficulties of reconciling disability as an identity with its more restrictive legal definitions. Hence the indignation and irritation in Mauldin's and Senior's comments.

Over four long years of covering the pandemic as a journalist, I found disabled people to be among my most important sources. When the new coronavirus started spreading through the US, disabled people with chronic illnesses like myalgic encephalomyelitis (also known as chronic fatigue syndrome or ME/CFS) predicted that the novel pathogen would lead to a wave of disability, well before most biomedical scientists and clinicians realized that such an outcome was even possible. When much of the US lamented the unfamiliar world of lockdowns and social distancing, disabled people shared hard-won insights about dealing with spatial confinement, working flexibly, coping with restless impermanence, and building community from a distance—familiar challenges all.

Disabled scholars repeatedly noted how the ableist disregard for disabled lives, the capitalist equating of productivity with worth, and the historical and continuing acceptance of eugenicist ideas explain so many unfathomable aspects of the pandemic: how the US normalized more than one million deaths; why long-haulers face dismissal and gaslighting despite overwhelming evidence about the physiological reality of their condition; and how the needs of immunocompromised people and other at-risk groups were shrugged off when the majority of Americans became eligible for vaccination. Their perspectives were essential, illuminating, and always grounded in humanity and history. They were fonts of knowledge and, more importantly, wisdom.

Long-haulers, too, were the wisest and savviest sources on Long COVID. I always centered them in my reporting. I used their terms, prioritized their stories, and relied on their expertise. This patient-centric approach is sometimes dismissed as advocacy, which is positioned as antithetical to journalism. In fact, it is simply good journalistic practice to give weight to the most knowledgeable sources. I treated long-haulers as the experts on their own condition—because they are. The Patient-Led Research Collaborative had published research on its own community *before* much of the medical establishment even realized that COVID symptoms could persist for months. Many are patient experts who have read the scientific literature on Long COVID and ME/CFS more deeply than most doctors because they are highly motivated to do so. Others are meta-experts who thoroughly understand the community's desires, needs, history, and rifts and can distinguish reliable voices from grifters. Their perspectives are the ground truth against which all other sources of Long-Covid data must be understood.

But disabled voices were rarely centered in this way. As awareness of Long COVID grew, long-haulers became fodder for anecdotal ledes, to be gawked at before the mic was passed to credentialed academics. Disabled voices were rarely consulted on pandemic policy or quoted in pandemic journalism, even on the subject of their own lives. Those lives were often cast aside, too. Pundits and self-professed public health experts who argued in favor of lifting COVID restrictions occasionally gestured at the problem of Long COVID, or the higher risks still faced by immunocompromised people, before moving on, relegating entire groups of vulnerable people to throwaway clauses. Said voices sometimes reassured the public that only the elderly and the immunocompromised were succumbing to COVID. Disabled people were variously cast as impediments to the pandemic's end, objects of pity whose burdens are the acceptable costs of a "normal" world, or outliers whose plights, though tragic, are rare enough to be ignored.

These frames are both morally unacceptable and false. Between Long COVID, immunosuppression, chronic illness, mental health problems, and more, disability is not an outlier but the norm. Meeting the needs of disabled people is not a side quest of pandemic preparedness but part of its main arc. The Centers for Disease Control's own description of what public health is makes this responsibility clear: it includes a graphic of ten core responsibilities, arrayed as the spokes of a wheel that has, at its center, equity. That means equitable access to vaccines and medications and public spaces with better ventilation and other infection-control measures. It means paid sick leave and flexible working policies. It means universal health care. The kinds of policies that prioritize disabled lives would leave everyone better prepared for the pandemics to come, instead of the US's current approach of ineffectually throwing biomedical countermeasures at the threat, in the absence of the social supports that are necessary for those countermeasures to work. Shunting disabled people to society's sidelines during a pandemic is a moral travesty and ultimately a self-defeating one.

This book offers a crucial counterpoint to that intolerable sidelining, offering a view of the pandemic through the perspectives of disabled New Yorkers and the researchers who have catalogued their experiences. Its first set of essays show how the US makes things easier for a fast-spreading virus by cramming some of its most vulnerable citizens into densely packed and poorly resourced settings, highlighting COVID's ability to seep into every existing crack in our society, exposing it and widening it. These chapters place pandemic risk at the intersection between disability and other sources of marginalization, including immigration status, incarceration, being unhoused, and having intellectual and learning disabilities. The spreading virus also revealed long-standing flaws in protocols for allocating lifesaving technology, public transit and public education infrastructures, and the accessibility of technological tools and networks—flaws that harmed disabled New Yorkers but that occasionally led to ingenious solutions.

The second part of the book reminds us that pandemics are collective problems and that if political leaders ignore the mutualistic approaches necessary to protect their citizens, then communities will create those approaches themselves. These essays show how Long COVID cast a spotlight on and found solidarity with the similar (and similarly neglected) illness ME/CFS; how a center for elderly Chinese immigrants created a community space amid a miasma of anti-Asian sentiment; how Asian communities pushed for community-based alternatives to violent policing; how Black mothers individually navigated mental health struggles amid the effects of "double pandemics"; how autistic New Yorkers turned to mutual aid to weather COVID's economic devastation; and how artists reminded us about the radical power of rest.

Collectively, these chapters document stories of immense adversity, unfair burdens, and disproportionate suffering—what happened and what did not need to happen. But they also offer stories of adaptability, creativity, and community. They expand our moral imagination, offering us a model of preparedness that centers disabled needs, disabled expertise, and disabled voices—a model that we should heed if we want to better withstand the plagues to come.

Introduction

How to Be Disabled in a Pandemic

MARA MILLS, HARRIS KORNSTEIN,
FAYE GINSBURG, AND RAYNA RAPP

New York City is an archipelago, a cluster of islands turned into a metropolis on a blueprint of disability and illness management. As elevated trains connected the boroughs, and the first skyscrapers and electric advertising signs began to transform the island of Manhattan in the late nineteenth century, the smaller islands in the rivers and the sound were largely delegated the infrastructures of confinement: infectious disease hospitals, sanatoria, quarantine facilities, psychiatric institutions, drug rehabilitation centers, orphanages, reformatories, migrant detention centers, prisons, and "paupers' graves." The city is significantly patterned by past and present epidemics, including yellow fever, cholera, typhus, smallpox, influenza, and HIV/AIDS. Each new epidemic activates old policies and urban spatial politics, latent and ongoing activism, and traumatic public memories.

When reports began surfacing in late 2019 about a new virus that was causing a pneumonia outbreak in Wuhan, China, most New Yorkers hardly paid attention, with little thought to its potential to spread globally or impact their own lives. In January 2020, however, the Centers for Disease Control and Prevention (CDC) announced that the virus was rapidly spreading in nursing homes in Washington State. By February 29, when the first case was officially confirmed in Manhattan, thousands of New Yorkers had already fallen sick without diagnosis.

American politicians, including then-president Donald Trump, dubbed this new coronavirus the "Wuhan" or "Chinese virus," summoning tropes of pandemic xenophobia. The *New York Times* published interactive graphics that modeled the virus spreading from Hubei Province to New York, even as researchers at Mount Sinai Hospital pointed to Europe as the source of most early infections in the city (Wu et al. 2020; Gonzalez-Reiche et al. 2020). The emerging narrative in the United States seesawed between B-movie horror—fomenting panic about an unanticipated, racialized contagion—and clinical detachment, with scientists and journalists "reassuring" audiences that "only the most vulnerable need to worry" (Martens 2020). Elderly and disabled people, especially residents of hospitals and institutions on New York's "other islands," were those expected to die.

Disability justice activists were among the first to acknowledge the impending threats of what came to be called SARS-CoV-2, or COVID-19, demanding that risks be taken seriously (see a more detailed timeline at the end of this book). They were also the first to argue that disabled people were being disproportionately impacted by city and national policies, work and housing conditions, ableist stigma, racism, and other forms of structural violence as much as by the virus itself. Calling attention to pandemic ableism (Hill 2022) and other viral inequalities, they challenged the neo-eugenicist views of public officials, media personalities, and even friends and family members who routinely dismissed them as disposable.

New York City's infection rate was initially five times higher than the rate in the rest of the country; in mid-March 2020, roughly one-third of all total confirmed US cases were in the metropolitan area (CDC 2020). Before a global pandemic had officially been declared by public health or government officials, disability activists began organizing mutual-aid networks and knowledge-sharing projects, using a range of tools including webinars and Zoom meetings, social media, podcasts, listservs, Google Docs, digital cash payments, DIY crafting, and socially distanced meet-ups. This was hardly surprising, given the extensive individual and communal "disability expertise" (Hartblay 2020) achieved through years of navigating, protesting, and reinventing the numerous political, health, media, and other social systems that exhibit neglect or open hostility toward disabled people. Many of these interventions were remote or public examples of what activist Mia Mingus (2011) calls "access intimacy," the relational process of meeting another's needs through knowledgeable improvisational care.

On March 7, 2020, a coalition of organizations in New York City hosted a webinar for nearly one thousand participants titled "COVID-19 (Coronavirus) Preparation for People Living with Chronic Illnesses in the U.S.," with information and strategy sessions rooted in "herbal remedies, Clorox, western medicine, anarchist DIY brilliance, and poetry" (Davids 2020). Two days later, a group of disabled and chronically ill artists organized Crip Fund, a mutual-aid campaign to pool donations and distribute money, food, medicine, and other aid to disabled, ill, and immunocompromised people "in need of in-home care," prioritizing at-risk queer and trans people of color. Nevertheless, Mayor Bill de Blasio did not declare a state of emergency until March 12. The same day, Governor Andrew Cuomo limited gatherings to fewer than five hundred people, still leaving hospitals, schools, the subway, and many businesses exempt. As disability organizations launched teach-ins and fund-raisers, mainstream news reporting remained incredulous, running headlines like, "Broadway Goes Dark."

Throughout early March 2020, disability activists around the world compiled and distributed syllabi, crip survival guides, and other informational resources, combining practical information with political education. For example, Leah Lakshmi Piepzna-Samarasinha's rapidly updated Google Doc "Half Assed Disabled Prepper Tips for Preparing for a Coronavirus Quarantine," posted on March 9, offered practical suggestions on everything from food preparation to home sterilization to accessing medication (Piepzna-Samarasinha 2020). Many groups also quickly set up mitigation projects by distributing homemade sanitizer and masks to disabled, unhoused, and other uniquely at-risk communities (Kopit and Yi 2022; Green 2020). Activists also launched impactful social media campaigns such as #HighRiskCovid19, in which first-person testimony educated the public about the unique threats of infection for immunocompromised people.

New York City public schools turned to remote learning on March 23, and four days later, the exponential spread of the pandemic had already led to over twenty-three thousand confirmed cases and 365 deaths in the city. Infections continued to escalate with fierce velocity. #DisabledPeopleToldYou began circulating on Twitter, underscoring examples of disability expertise for a broad audience regarding chronic illness, quarantine, and remote work. In the words of disability activist Imani

Barbarin (2020), the pandemic would also be a "mass disabling event"—and those who were affected by COVID and post-COVID conditions had a community ready to advocate for them. Andrew Pulrang (2021) summarized these insights for the decidedly conventional readership of *Forbes* magazine: "While we were at higher risk, it sometimes felt like we were better equipped to handle the pandemic than people without disabilities." He continued, "Disabled people sometimes half-jokingly refer to ourselves as 'oracles' or 'canaries in the coal mine.' As disabled people, we often encounter new problems and threats before most people notice them or truly recognize their potential scale." Similar stories of pandemic ingenuity appear across the chapters of this volume, and we refer to this bifurcated experience as the "disability dialectic": faced with the enormous threats and terrible consequences of the pandemic, disabled people have manifested remarkable creativity and resistance.[1]

Despite this important work, many disabled people remained uniquely vulnerable, isolated, or silenced. Many held jobs as "essential workers," exposed to constant risk through food and mail delivery or working in markets, hospitals, and pharmacies. Others were incarcerated or otherwise confined, with little access to public health information, care, or the means for isolation, mitigation, and communication. Many suffered as a result of interruptions to health care, and far too many died.

The initial impact of the virus in New York was scaffolded by deeply entrenched inequalities, in particular, racial ableism—the racialization of oppression related to disability (Ben-Moshe 2016). The news platform *The City* aptly characterized the New Yorkers who were buried in the potter's field on Hart Island in the first year of the pandemic: "Most were elderly from nursing homes; Black and Hispanic frontline and essential workers from low-income neighborhoods who risked losing a paycheck if they didn't work during the pandemic's peak; and residents of The Bronx and Queens, where life expectancy has long been lower than other boroughs amid a lack of access to health care" (Stabile Center 2021).[2] Such realities serve as a stark reminder that, as much as the pandemic offers examples of disability efficacy in times of crisis and transformation, disabled New Yorkers—especially those who are multiply marginalized or institutionalized—continue to experience extreme precarity. Mass debilitation and death, moreover, are not the occasion for what Michele

Friedner calls "feel-good disability studies."[3] The *feelings* of expertise, like that of resistance, are often grief and anger.

New York City: Hierarchy, Carewashing, and Pandemic Cultural Production

How to Be Disabled in a Pandemic gathers history, ethnography, and first-person accounts of disabled life during the first four years of the COVID-19 pandemic in New York City. With our title, in one sense, we gesture to the many forces of disablement under crisis conditions: if pandemics themselves are mass disabling events, so too are pandemic protocols that create debilitating or deadly conditions of illness exposure, work and housing precarity, and lack of health resources for certain people. In another sense, our title cheekily conjures the genre of self-help, valuing disability and disabled life in and beyond pandemic times: disability sociality, protest, and epistemologies of pandemic survival. Across fifteen chapters, we move beyond the rhetoric of the pandemic's disproportionate impact on a monolithic group of disabled people.

Our focus on one city has allowed us to compare disability experiences that differ with regard to factors like neighborhood, age, race, housing, and carceral status, while situated within a similar geographic location, set of legal constraints, and public health regime.[4] Throughout the pandemic, the authors of *How to Be Disabled in a Pandemic* mostly stayed in the city, researching our own or neighboring communities and recording stories that generally failed to make it into the papers or onto the television. We write about prisons, migrant detention centers, subways, shelters, the New York Public Library, a Chinatown senior center, digital advocacy spaces, racial justice organizing, the homes of single parents, and the work of disability artists. We write about a hybrid city: online, outside, and behind closed apartment or institution doors. As a multi-year endeavor, this book sustains attention to disability experience from the early fraught and chaotic moments of the pandemic in spring 2020 to the illusory "post-pandemic" calm of 2023 and 2024. We collectively track shifts in pandemic experiences and politics from the launch of shelter-in-place orders to the introduction of vaccines, various claims of "reopening," discourses of Long COVID, and the "post-pandemic rollbacks" of access gains. Pandemic profiteering by drug companies, Big Tech, and mask hoarders has made us think critically about the rush of academic "pandemic projects" and plan a response that was longer term but still necessarily incomplete.

Each chapter offers its own distinct argument about the experience of the pandemic in a particular disability world. Yet across the different boroughs and groups of people we spoke to, several patterns also emerge.

First, there is a *hierarchy of disability "vulnerability"* in New York, as in other cities. The phrase "hierarchy of disability" has often been used in disability studies to describe privilege and inequality within the disability rights movement (e.g., early leadership by white men with physical disabilities), with "hierarchy of disablement" used in health circles to refer to "severity," stigma, or capacity for assimilation (Schalk 2020; Deal 2010). With the phrase "hierarchy of disability 'vulnerability,'" we acknowledge the differential likelihood of people to become disabled, as well as the differential likelihood of disabled people to be protected during the pandemic as a result of other elements of social status.

We take a critical approach to the term "vulnerability," which is an often-unexamined part of the jargon of health care, human rights, and many other fields. "Vulnerable" suggests increased susceptibility to harm, but it can also refer to a person in need of care and protection—usually as a result of age or disability. The use of the term "vulnerable" in public health is often patronizing and disenfranchising, signaling a population that seemingly requires management. As such, the word has been critiqued by disability ethicist Adrienne Asch, among others (Bergstresser 2014). We are interested in the ways people have structurally been made vulnerable to the effects of the pandemic. In New York City, we note that people with similar disabilities have been differently susceptible to infection, death, and social inequality on the basis of age, gender, race, class, job, neighborhood, immigration status, and other factors (Mizner 2020; Landes, Finan, and Turk 2022; Gawthrop 2022). And when certain disabled New Yorkers were deemed vulnerable to COVID-19, they were left to their own devices, even as others were granted social protections and services.

Across our chapters, we see an implicit vulnerability calculus taking place in institutions across the city, whereby some disabled people were abandoned in nursing homes and left to die and others were seen as vectors or safety threats and confined. Some nondisabled people, like health-care and essential workers, were disproportionately exposed to illness and trauma; and some neighborhoods were broadly debilitated through lack of access to resources. This hierarchy of disability "vulnerability" underscores who is unprotected during a pandemic, who is considered a threat, and who is given priority for care.

Second, and deeply related to this first pattern, we witnessed *disability and "care" deployed as population management tools* during the pandemic; this was often done in the name of public health and safety but did not serve disabled populations. That is, whether disability is positioned as a metaphor or reality, it has often served as a rationale for policy decisions, such as locking up certain people or diverting resources away from them. Disability is a key element of urban biopolitics, utilized as a justification for medical triage, restricting civil rights, or isolating groups of people in various institutions. As disability activist Marta Russell pointed out regarding the nursing home industry, disability can be a source of profit, and disabled people are sometimes treated as commodities in health-care settings (1998, 98). In allotting health care and other resources, disability is also often a proxy for race, for age, for weight, for lack of citizenship, for neighborhood—from mortality risk measures to definitions of "preexisting conditions" to critiques of individual behaviors and cultural practices. In some cases, city officials publicly described certain groups as "disabled" (e.g., unhoused people) to justify managing them "for their own protection"—a phenomenon known as "carewashing" (Chatzidakis and Littler 2022). Carewashing is often applied to corporations or government institutions that "commodify care" through branding to obfuscate their more harmful activities. Thus, while "care" is an important ethic within disability activism (Piepzna-Samarasinha 2018), it also became a co-opted keyword in many industries and fields during the pandemic. Following Michelle Murphy's call for tactics of "unsettling care" (2015), we have found countless examples of what might be called "the care con"—leveraging the language, logic, or promises of care to administer a population in unwanted or even harmful ways.

Finally, throughout this book, we also document abundant examples of *crip pandemic cultural production* (following Alexandra Juhasz and Theodore Kerr's work on "AIDS cultural production" and "pandemic media"; Juhasz and Kerr 2023; Juhasz 2023). Crip pandemic cultural production includes social practices as well as disability art, media, and aesthetics. Indeed, a primary motivation of this project has been to archive ephemeral evidence of this important cultural work, much of which circulates widely but informally through events, social media, zines, and other formats that are at risk of being lost to longer-term collective memory. Importantly, we note myriad affects expressed by disabled people across this cultural work—ranging from frustration to hope, despair to relief—including many ambiguities, ambivalences, and contradictions. We have also seen new and broad audiences taking up the already-existing insights and methods of chronically ill and disabled activists and scholars, extending their wisdom to the current pandemic. Our chapters describe disability expertise as lay expertise, as artistry, and as conventional scholarly and bioethics expertise.

The two parts of our book—"Living with 'Disproportionate Risk': Policies, Institutions, and Congregate Settings" and "Disability Communities: Expertise, Activism, and Solidarity"—also point to a gap with regard to *which* disabled people have found platforms, audiences, and the means to set or influence policy. Those in permanent "lockdown" in various congregate settings faced the greatest amount and intensity of pandemic constraints and consequences, while others who experience more physical and social freedoms were able to push the boundaries of disability activism.

Pandemic Theorizing and the Most Impacted

Our title, *How to Be Disabled in a Pandemic*, invokes two canonical texts for theorizing the cultural politics of AIDS: Douglas Crimp's article "How to Have Promiscuity in an Epidemic" (1987) and Paula Treichler's book *How to Have Theory in an Epidemic* (1999). These scholars point to the urgency of theorizing a viral pandemic in real time, in both the temporalities of its emergence and as it becomes increasingly endemic. In 1987, Crimp insisted on reframing AIDS expertise as grounded in queer life and epistemology, countering an onslaught of homophobic discourse by arguing that "the gay movement is responsible for virtually every positive achievement in the struggle against AIDS during the epidemic's early years," including not only political and medical victories but also social practices like the development of safe sex techniques

Figure 1.1. "Masks" (2020). Brothers Sick (Ezra Benus and Noah Benus). (Image courtesy of Brothers Sick)

(1987, 250). In conversation with Crimp's work, Treichler noted that "scientists, physicians, and public health authorities [have] argued repeatedly that AIDS represented 'an epidemic of infectious disease and nothing more.'" She instead theorized the crisis as also an "an epidemic of meanings" and political decision-making (1999, 1). Despite these important contributions, we note that these earlier works lacked a theoretical framework that connected AIDS to disability studies and activism. This gap has increasingly been narrowed in the intervening years by scholars and activists working at these intersections, especially in the context of COVID-19 (McRuer 2002; Hrynyk 2021; WWHIVDD Collective 2020a; Schalk 2022; Bhaman, chapter 3 in this volume). By invoking these titles, we not only center the experiences of those who have been most impacted but also underscore the many strands of history, theory, and activism that have converged in the COVID-19 pandemic and enable the analyses in this volume.

Disability is not a homogeneous category or a single "movement"; as an experience, identity, or political affiliation, it is also shaped by vectors such as race, gender, class, and citizenship. Our focus on disability further reveals the term to be in a constant state of negotiation, especially in the collective experience of a public health emergency. Borrowing from disability activist Patty Berne (2015), cofounder of the arts organization Sins Invalid, we have worked with a capacious definition of disability that includes "people with physical impairments, people who identify as 'sick' or are chronically ill, 'psych' survivors and those who identify as 'crazy,' neurodiverse people, people with cognitive impairments, people who are a sensory minority," and people with various experiences of aging, injury, and addiction. We also note the complex and at times contested nature of identifying as disabled. For many, the label offers a strong source of community and identification and may help validate experiences that are not recognized in traditional medicalized settings (such as those seeking support for Long COVID). Some discuss a slow process of coming to identify as disabled through the sequelae of illness. For others, it can still be viewed as a source of stigma or liability, particularly for those whose experiences of disability are rooted in physical and structural violence (such as police brutality, incarceration, and addiction), those whose cultural upbringings disavow or stigmatize disability, and those who have historically been excluded from mainstream US disability rights activism. Authors and interlocutors in this book use varied terminology to describe their identities, including more specific terms to describe experiences or impairments; many use "crip" as a proud reclamation of the term's origins as a slur (McRuer 2006). Among the authors in this book who identify as disabled, there has been no singular experience of the pandemic.

One of Crimp's most forceful arguments, that "anything said or done about AIDS that does not give precedence to the knowledge, the needs, and the demands of people living with AIDS must be condemned" (1987, 240), resembles a slogan of the disability rights movement: "nothing about us without us" (Charlton 2000). To the same end, we insist that there is no adequate theory of the pandemic that is not a disability theory. However, this ethos sits uneasily with the current state of "pandemic theorizing" (Patsavas and Danylevich 2022). If older people and those living in nursing homes or other congregate settings, especially in certain zip codes, have been at the greatest risk of infection and death from COVID-19 in the US, they have hardly featured at all in popular journalism, academic publishing, or even disability media, much less spoken for themselves (Mizner 2020). The editors of a 2022 special issue of *Lateral: Journal of the Cultural Studies Association*, titled "Crip Pandemic Life: A Tapestry," call attention to this gap in disability pandemic studies more generally: "The present installment of our tapestry-archive lacks—and desires—more voices from Black disabled folks; scholars, artists, and thinkers from the global south; incarcerated and/or institutionalized people; refugees; indigenous voices; those disabled by war and climate crisis; and those newly disabled from Long-COVID. The silences and gaps of those disabled and chronically ill lives lost and those too sick, too isolated, too pained, or too fatigued to actively offer their accounts, experiences, and wisdom to this collective project also demand acknowledgement" (Patsavas and Danylevich 2022).

How to Be Disabled in a Pandemic is an open-ended proposition. Too many disabled New Yorkers exist to be represented in one collection, but by convening a large, mixed-background group, we have prioritized a breadth of pandemic narratives—while acknowledging that several gaps remain. Our collection includes researchers with a wide range of disability expertise that has grown from our work *as* and *with*: autistic adults, people living with chronic illness, blind accessibility experts,

Figure I.2. Photograph of a mural painted by artist Chella Man, depicting illustrated hands spelling out the message "Black Disabled Trans Lives Matter" in American Sign Language. The *a* letters in the words "black," "disabled," and "trans" are all connected. The hands are colored using the colors of the Progress Pride flag. (Photo by Faye Ginsburg, taken on August 21, 2020, on MacDougal Street in Greenwich Village)

Black pregnant people experiencing mental health challenges, people with mobility impairments, adults with intellectual and developmental disabilities and their supporters, antiracist activists, and incarcerated and unhoused disabled people.[5] In doing so, we attend to the particularities of individuals and communities, while also documenting cross-disability and cross-issue collectives. We also foreground the structural logics of death and survival that become apparent during pandemics, following the work of the writer/activist Steven Thrasher, who cautions about the unequal tolls of COVID, like HIV/AIDS, on a "viral underclass" (Thrasher 2022).

Many of us write from a place of unwellness, employing what Melissa Kapadia (2020) calls "illness methodology": "the application of ill lenses and ways of knowing to the practice of research." Throughout our collective process, we also kept in mind Mimi Khúc's "pedagogy of unwellness," which critically decenters wellness by insisting that "we are all differentially unwell. . . . We are unwell in different ways at different times, in relation to differentially disabling and enabling structures, so we need differential care at all times" (2021, 370). Moreover, the specific qualitative methods used on our team were eclectic, reflecting different disciplinary backgrounds and social positions. They range from participant observation (online and face-to-face) to interviews, legal analysis, archival research, oral histories, and art criticism. Some of our authors engage remote ethnography as a long-standing practice of disability sociality and research, publicized by the pandemic but also preceding it (Rogers 2023). We have also invited conversations among activists and practitioners.

"Lockdown" versus Lockdown: Two New Yorks

New York City was one of the major global epicenters of the pandemic, particularly in early spring 2020, when infection and death rates skyrocketed and information and mitigation strategies were barely emerging. The city has also been a test bed for national policies like ventilator and vaccine allocation protocols. As Governor Cuomo put New York State "on pause" beginning on March 22, 2020 (see figure I.3), his national broadcasts became immensely popular, providing updates on COVID cases in the state, directives to stay at home, and a bracing sense of determination to fight this unknown virus together (despite a frequent failure to translate this ethos into equitable policies).[6]

Yet disabled people experienced two starkly different New York Cities during the COVID-19 pandemic: the metropolis for the unconfined, and the outer boroughs, islands, and institutions of the confined. Disabled and nondisabled people living in jails, prisons, migrant detention centers, group homes, nursing homes, and other institutions lived and died in pandemic conditions intentionally distinct from disabled and nondisabled New Yorkers on the outside, part of the disability "vulnerability" calculus of city planning.[7] The mother of one of our early collaborators, the New York University bioethicist Arthur Caplan, died of COVID in a nursing home in spring 2020. Caplan, who like many people was only able to wave at his mother through the window as she was dying, calls nursing homes "forgotten institutions" where "we let the elderly go," along, too often, with their care workers (Mathews 2020).[8]

In addition to the checkerboard map of COVID-19 deaths by zip code (see figure I.4), the city can be divided according to those who have

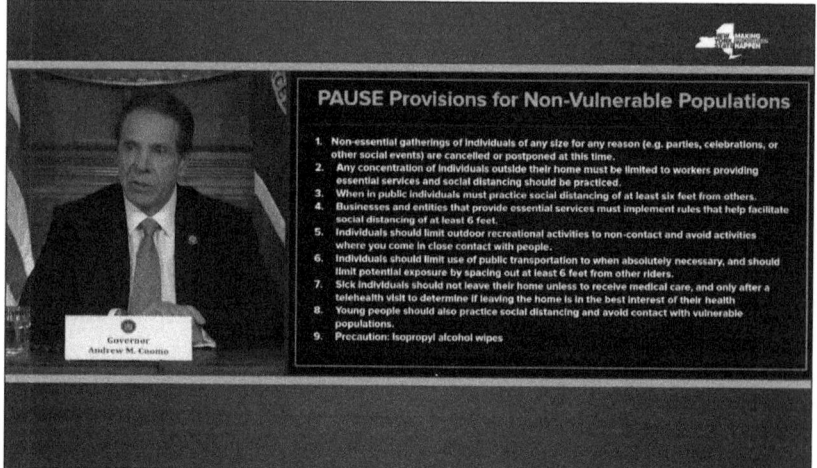

Figure 1.3. Governor Cuomo unveils the New York State PAUSE plan, effective March 22, 2020. (New York State Governor 2020)

freedom of movement and access to the internet, even under so-called lockdown conditions, and *disability inmates*, the rapidly growing segment of New Yorkers who are confined in various settings. The term "lockdown" as colloquially applied to the New York State "PAUSE" program for social distancing or quarantining among the general public was little more than cruel hyperbole, as incarcerated and formerly incarcerated people were quick to point out (Metcalf 2020). "Lockdown" is a North American word coined in the 1970s to refer to a confinement within a confinement, a form of punishment for people incarcerated in prisons and psychiatric hospitals: "the confinement of prisoners to their cells for an extended period of time, usually as a security measure following a disturbance" (*Oxford English Dictionary*). Illness from COVID-19 became a reason for literal lockdowns in carceral settings, and the pandemic itself became a rationale for the increased institutionalization of those who seemed to pose public health or safety risks, especially those with mental disabilities.

In New York City, the pandemic eroded many of the post-1960s gains of the global deinstitutionalization movement and civil rights for people with mental disabilities. Former police captain Eric Adams won the 2021 New York City mayoral election in year two of the pandemic with a "war on crime" campaign that has often manifested itself as a war on unhoused and disabled people. Many were forced into parks and streets as a result of subway closures for overnight disinfection, leading to public anxieties about increased homelessness (with actual numbers difficult to measure).⁹ As Metropolitan Transit Authority ridership rebounded in 2021, fears regarding transit crime, including a few high-profile incidents of violence by people labeled mentally disabled, led Adams to announce large-scale police patrols of the subway system shortly after he was sworn in on January 1, 2022. On November 29, 2022, the mayor additionally announced an eleven-point "Psychiatric Crisis Care Legislative Agenda" that would allow unhoused and/or disabled people to be involuntarily hospitalized, with New York Police Department and Department of Health (DOH) teams deployed in subways to remove "those appearing to have serious mental health issues" (Office of the Mayor 2022). The language of care in this agenda signaled carewashing to many disability

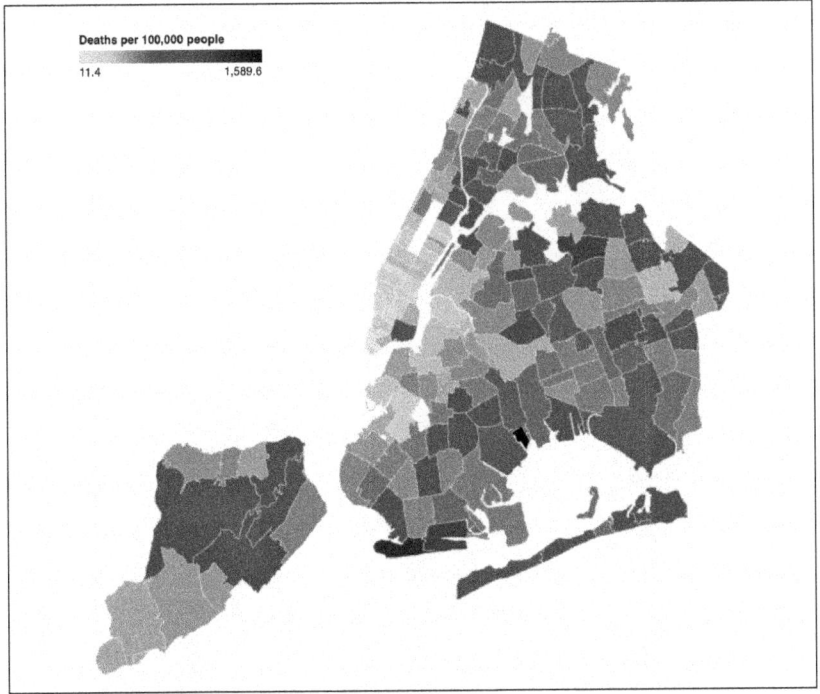

Figure I.4. COVID-19 data by zip code: deaths per one thousand people. (New York City Department of Health and Mental Hygiene n.d.)

activists, who responded by pointing out the lack of hospital space and, more importantly, lack of economic and social supports for housing, work, and health care in the city.

If disability is often used as justification for confinement, that same confinement has also exacerbated injury, illness, and other impacts of COVID-19, with the worst congregate settings effectively functioning as kill shelters. Even city planners with the best intentions to reform nursing homes and other institutions have failed to follow through with any notable improvements. Our research confirms that most congregate settings are not "medically appropriate housing" for older and disabled people; this is an artifact as much of history and policy as of individual physiology or the nature of group living (Bhaman, chapter 3 this volume). Instead, institutionalized disabled people have been widely written off as "acceptable losses," a situation that activists have repeatedly decried as neo-eugenics (Kukla 2020). At the same time, as part 1 of our volume attests, congregate settings and their residents are not all identical, even if the category is often used in a blanket way by politicians, public health workers, and even disability activists. For noncitizens, incarcerated people, and those assigned by the courts to guardianship and conservatorship, the impacts of the pandemic have been dire in highly specific ways, with few opportunities for creative or public response (Bardelli, Thomas, and Brown, chapter 1 this volume; Salyer, chapter 2 in this volume). That is, for disabled people subject to carceral forms of control, *disability expertise* unfortunately does not always translate into *disability autonomy* or *disability authority*.[10]

The Disability Dialectic

A dialectic of risk and resistance also threads through the chapters that follow: among those who survived, among those with means, amid networks of mutual support and care, and among disabled artists who demonstrated time and again that "disability is an ingenious way to live" (Neil Marcus, in Ehrlich 2006, 58). In documenting moments of struggle, insight, and improvisation, however, we resist the impulse to romanticize precarity. As anthropologist Liliana Gil has shown, too many theories of "innovation from below"—whether linked to disability, poverty, or culture—propose that "experiences of precarity contain a valuable repertoire of techniques." These theories entail a number of pitfalls: the "bourgeois fantasy" of subaltern resourcefulness; the co-optation of precarious ingenuity "for its entrepreneurial potential"; and the forwarding of this ingenuity "as a scalable solution for global challenges. A temporary disguised as a structural solution" (Gil 2022, 30, 49). We note that the abundance of theories of design and innovation in disability studies have largely failed to engage with anthropological and decolonial critiques of innovation rhetoric or the neoliberal logic of individuals "making do" in the absence of governmental concerns for social welfare.

A disability dialectic—with often precarious gains or ephemeral cultural forms—has played out in many different arenas of public life and discourse during the COVID-19 pandemic, especially as disabled people contest institutions and policies that are both overtly and more insidiously ableist. When CDC director Rochelle Walensky, a top public health leader in the US, apparently claimed that it was "encouraging news" that the majority of COVID-19 deaths were among those "who were unwell to begin with," it prompted massive protest (Hubrig 2022; Ruiz-Grossman 2022). #MyDisabledLifeIsWorthy, a hashtag launched by Imani Barbarin in January 2022, directly countered Walensky's comments and reasserted the value of disabled life (Barbarin 2022). #MyDisabledLifeIsWorthy sparked wide-ranging conversations about neo-eugenics in government policies, and within a week, on January 14, Walensky met remotely with a group of disability activists to apologize for her comment, promising regular meetings going forward (CDC 2022b). Despite this seeming win, these regular meetings did not happen, and biases in public health policy effectively became self-fulfilling prophecies, requiring an ongoing, iterative series of protests.

Ableist sentiments were further translated into a range of policies that directly threatened many disabled people's health and ability to participate in public life. One major form of injustice that emerged in spring 2020 centered around medical triaging and the rationing of lifesaving treatments that deprioritized or outright denied care to people with a variety of disabilities, judging that their lives were "too expensive" or "lost causes." For example, a 2021 report by the National Council on Disability found that "people with intellectual or developmental disabilities, and medically fragile and technology dependent individuals, faced a high risk of being triaged out of COVID-19 treatment when hospital beds, supplies, and personnel were scarce" (National Council on Disability 2021, 1). In the earliest days of the pandemic, access to ventilators was notably limited, leading to state- and hospital-based rationing proposals for withholding or withdrawing lifesaving equipment from certain groups of disabled people (Mills, chapter 5 this volume). Similarly, when vaccines became available to select groups, many disabled people who were at increased risk were nonetheless not included on the initial lists for priority access in New York State, as only a limited number of "comorbidities" were considered. Unsurprisingly, people whose conditions were not listed protested their longer waits, while activists in other states contested policies that failed to recognize disabled people at all (New York State Governor 2021; Miller 2021; Sharp 2021). The pandemic underscored the endemic ableism of health-care allocation and the stark irony that those who need care the most often cannot access or afford it in the highly stratified privatized US health system. At the same time, as supply chains faltered at different moments, disabled authors shared their unsentimental expertise about how to self-ration when unable to access or afford drugs and medical supplies, offering advice about things like sharing insulin and other hormones or crowdsourcing catheters (Trowe 2022; Mills, chapter 5 in this volume).

Disabled people have organized creatively against any number of structural and legal barriers to health care, education, and information, transforming architecture, city streets, and digital media in the process. During the pandemic, activists were pleased to see expanded options for telemedicine, for which they had long been advocating (and which was temporarily expanded by Medicare and most private insurance under pandemic emergency orders). Yet they also expressed frustration at seeing "ableds accommodating themselves with the accessibility . . . disabled people fight for every day," exemplified by the hashtag #AccessibilityForAbleds (McWilliams 2020). The pandemic revealed just how easy it could be to provide certain accommodations—such as remote access to work, school, and therapy—that disabled and chronically ill people had been demanding, unsuccessfully, for years (Acton and Hamraie 2022).[11]

With the prioritization of urgent COVID-19-related care, necessary in-person appointments were frequently delayed or canceled as medical resources were reconfigured or facilities deemed too risky (Akobirshoev et al. 2022; Moore et al. 2022). Moreover, as care professionals, especially at-home care workers, became ill, refused vaccines, or left the profession, many disabled people found it increasingly difficult to receive basic services; the National Council on Disability notes that this left "some at risk of losing their independence or being institutionalized" (2021, 2). This complex situation highlights the overlapping precarities of the pandemic: the majority of nursing assistants and home-care and direct-care workers are women of color, who earn less than white men and who also experienced higher rates of death than average from COVID-19 (Campbell 2017). Under these seemingly impossible conditions, disabled people and their families demonstrated "ingenuity and creativity . . . to make home accessible" using a range of improvised hacks. Laura Mauldin (n.d.) documents these in her research on "disability at home," accompanied by a photo website where people share images and stories of how they have created access on their own.

Many blind and Deaf people also faced specific barriers to information and treatment for COVID-19 as a result of inaccessible websites, the limited availability of captioning and interpreters, or a lack of materials in Braille and other accessible formats (Coklyat and Fleet, chapter 9 in this volume). For instance, many forms of COVID testing have been inaccessible to blind people, from drive-through testing sites to home tests that rely on visual instructions and displays (Morris 2022; Smith 2022). Some apps, such as Be My Eyes, founded by the visually impaired inventor Hans Jørgen Wiberg, have allowed blind people to video-call sighted people for assistance with visual tasks such as reading rapid test results. Frustrated by the slowness and potential COVID exposure of in-person testing sites, Mark Riccobono, president of the National Federation of the Blind (NFB), wrote to President Biden on January 3, 2022, on behalf of the thousands of NFB members to demand that the free COVID tests provided by the federal government include versions accessible to blind people (Riccobono 2022). He followed up with the Food and Drug Administration (FDA) commissioner shortly after, requesting that kit instructions on the FDA site be posted as accessible PDFs. In response, in June, the US Postal Service temporarily provided what it called "more-accessible" COVID tests, although these versions still required a smartphone and navigation of the Ellume app (not created for blind people) to hear audio instructions and results.

Figure 1.5. "Deaf NYC: Apart + Connected Panel." On May 12, 2020, Deaf residents of New York City—Roxanna Aguila, Carlos Aponte-Salcedo Jr., Patrice Creamer, Marina Fanshteyn, and Alexandria Pucciarelli-Miller—shared perspectives, challenges, and hopes during a virtual panel discussion on the pandemic, hosted by Brianna Di-Giovanni, intern at the Drs. John S. & Betty J. Schuchman Deaf Documentary Center at Gallaudet University. They discussed a range of questions emerging for Deaf New Yorkers in the early months of the pandemic: How has life changed during this pandemic for New York City's Deaf community? When everyone wears face masks, how does that affect interactions? When is information fully accessible, and how can communication be better? Are there signs that are new or signs that have taken on new meaning? Are there ways that Deaf cultural life is uniquely helpful during this time? (Schuchman Center 2020)

As with any dialectic, experiences of disability during the pandemic were hardly defined strictly by either vulnerability or creativity; instead, disabled communities often directly wrestled with this sort of binary thinking, challenging each other to embrace complexity. The pandemic also raised numerous instances of what disability scholars describe as "access friction" (Hamraie 2017; Hamraie and Fritsch 2019), in which actions that increase access for some may limit or hinder access for others.

For example, while masking in public spaces has been a key mitigation strategy, particularly important for immunocompromised people, most masks are opaque and muffle sound, which can pose a barrier for deaf and hard-of-hearing people, especially when reading lips (Rogozen 2020; Stine 2020). Similarly, while options for remote work, schooling, and socializing provided welcome enhancements for those who had long been advocating for such access strategies, for many disabled students—among other groups—remote participation both exacerbated existing inequities and instigated new ones (Beery 2020; Scott and Aquino 2020; Freidus, Fish, and Turner, chapter 6 in this volume).

Solidarity and "Crip Doulaing"

While the disability dialectic suggests resistance and creative response by those who are immediately experiencing conditions of inequality and abandonment, many of our chapters foreground instead cross-disability aid and illness coalitions, what the late disability rights activist Stacey Park Milbern has named "crip doulaing." In conversation with Leah Lakshmi Piepzna-Samarasinha shortly before the start of the pandemic, Milbern underscored the urgency of "disability doulaship":

> I see a lot of disabled people of color doing a ton of work in supporting people rebirthing themselves as disabled (or more disabled). This looks like a lot of things—maybe learning how to get medicine, drive a wheelchair, hire attendants, change a diet, date, have sex, make requests, code switch, live with an intellectual disability, go off meds, etc. etc. . . . I feel like society not having language to describe this transition or the support it requires speaks to the ableism and isolation people with disabilities face in our lives. . . . Without crip intervention, we are frequently left alone to figure out how to be in our bodyminds and in this ableist world. (Piepzna-Samarasinha 2018)

In parallel, the What Would an HIV Doula Do? collective members invoked the history and importance of illness doulas in their zine *What Does a COVID-19 Doula Do?* (WWHIVDD Collective 2020b). Although they point out that "AIDS and COVID have little in common," AIDS activism has had an enduring influence on other illness communities.

In the zine, Jih-Fei Cheng argues that AIDS activists "taught us to research and educate authorities" as well as serve as illness doulas for one another (2020b, 35), while Alexandra Juhasz describes illness doulas as "hold[ing] space for people made vulnerable due to one or many viruses. Doulas make space for fear and love, help and incapacity" (2020b, 22).

The pandemic has not only impacted those who already identified as disabled but also catalyzed new experiences of disability and countless examples of illness coalitions. Perhaps most obviously, COVID-19 has rendered millions of people newly chronically ill, with a range of symptoms affecting vascular, respiratory, immune, digestive, neurological, and reproductive systems, summed up under the term "Long COVID" (Davis et al. 2023). As the journalist and science writer Ed Yong (2021) has described it, patients with Long COVID are now living in a "hinterland of disability," a neglected liminal space between full health and hospitalization or death, "where millions of people are already stuck, and where many more may end up" (see also Yong's foreword to this volume). Like other chronically ill communities whose sicknesses are not easily treated by current biomedical knowledge, people with Long COVID are engaged in activism to gain both recognition and resources, an ongoing fight in which they have often worked in solidarity with existing disability activist movements (Kornstein and Rogers, chapter 8 in this volume).

We also call attention to depression and other mental health experiences and the self-help and mutual-aid networks that were activated in the absence of adequate therapy for most New Yorkers. According to studies by the Pew Research Center and Kaiser Family Foundation, approximately 40 percent of US adults experienced mental health challenges during the pandemic, including new symptoms of anxiety or depression, with increased rates among communities of color, women, teens and young adults, low-wage and other frontline essential workers, and disabled people (Panchal et al. 2021; Pasquini and Keeter 2022; Mbonde, chapter 12 in this volume). Such experiences will continue to have profound impacts, particularly given the disproportionate rates of mental disability (including burnout) among health-care and home-care workers (Sexton et al. 2022; Murthy 2022).

Additionally, the emergence of the pandemic coincided with increased public attention to anti-Black police violence and vigilante attacks targeting Asian American and Pacific Islander communities (spurred by xenophobic attitudes focusing on the virus's origins in China). In response to these multiple traumas, the New York–based Asian American Feminist Collective and Bluestockings Bookstore published *Asian American Feminist Antibodies: {care in the time of coronavirus}* (see figure I.6), a digital zine that encourages solidarity across diverse experiences of illness, labor, and age. The zine collects "practices of care that come out of Asian American histories and politics," in refutation of racialized stereotypes about the virus. (Two contributors to this volume, Rachel Kuo and Salonee Bhaman, are among the zine's authors.)

Networks like Sick in Quarters (SiQ), launched in 2020, hosted smaller community-building workshops online, including virtual "right to mourn" spaces and listening session "hideaways" (Sick in Quarters 2023). SiQ describes its online meet-ups as a "container for collective mourning, the kind of pain and alienation that was already familiar to disabled and immunocompromised lives."[12] These projects thus highlight the importance of grief not only as an individual affect but also as a collective and political process in responding to the pandemic and forging intersectional solidarities.

Many of these same disability networks responded forcefully and with direct action to the "double pandemic" of racism and racialized police violence in the US (Mohapatra et al., chapter 11 in this volume; Mbonde, chapter 12 in this volume). Such activism multiplied exponentially in May and June 2020, following the police murder of George Floyd, when uprisings against anti-Black violence and police brutality took over the recently empty streets of many US cities including New York. Sick in Quarters published the *Stay Safe—COVID-19 Protest Resources* brochure (figure I.7), with advice for decreasing the chance of viral spread during and after direct-action events, as well as information about protest rights and how to stay safe while interacting with police. As discussed in this volume, police and prisons contribute profoundly to experiences of disability through both inflicted injuries and the often-intentional denial of care (Bardelli, Thomas, and Brown, chapter 1 in this volume). In this context, the intersections between prison abolitionist work and disability justice have been some of the most urgent forms of activism throughout (and preceding) the pandemic. Sick of It! A Disability Inside/Outside Project—"a group of abolitionists and disabled activists working to build connections between the free world disabled community and

Figure 1.6. *Asian American Feminist Antibodies: {care in the time of coronavirus}*, by Salonee Bhaman, Rachel Kuo, Matilda Sabal, Vivian Shaw, and Tiffany Diane Tso. (Cover illustration by Amira Lin)

those behind bars"—released the first of several zines in October 2020. These featured "writings about disability justice, strategies of care and work submitted by our incarcerated community, ... [and] a penpal project to connect disabled folks inside to outside disabled penpals" (Sick of It!, n.d.).

Brief Overview of the Book

How to Be Disabled in a Pandemic documents pandemic cultural production alongside pandemic disablement, cross-disability organizing alongside government hierarchies of disability "vulnerability." Part 1, "Living with 'Disproportionate Risk': Policies, Institutions, and Congregate Settings," addresses the specific experiences of disabled people who find themselves inscribed into "risk" and its discourses for diverse reasons. We open with a chapter on incarcerated disabled people and illness as reason for punishment in state prisons (Bardelli, Thomas, and Brown), followed by a chapter on disability and COVID in migrant detention centers, raising the question of who counts as a New Yorker (Salyer). Daily experiences of the coronavirus in New York City have been profoundly shaped by the prior emergence of AIDS in this city, with many policies related to homelessness, long-term care, and quarantine during epidemics having been established in response to that earlier crisis. Thus, the next chapter in our volume examines the legacy of laws governing shelter for unhoused people during the early AIDS epidemic and the ways enforced shelter often exacerbates risk (Bhaman). Other chapters trace the rapidly changing MTA policies for mobility-impaired New Yorkers (Grenier); ableism and racial bias in state and hospital ventilator-allocation protocols (Mills); the loss of services, sociality, and attention experienced by "special ed" students in the schools (Freidus, Fish, and Turner); and adults with intellectual/developmental disabilities living at home, often with aging family members who resumed caregiving as long-standing paid caregivers or personal assistants became unavailable (Ginsburg and Rapp). All chapters here chronicle experiences of living at "disproportionate risk" during the first three years of the pandemic.

Part 2, "Disability Communities: Expertise, Activism, and Solidarity," focuses on crip pandemic doulaship and cultural production. This part opens with an account of people with myalgic encephalomyelitis (ME)

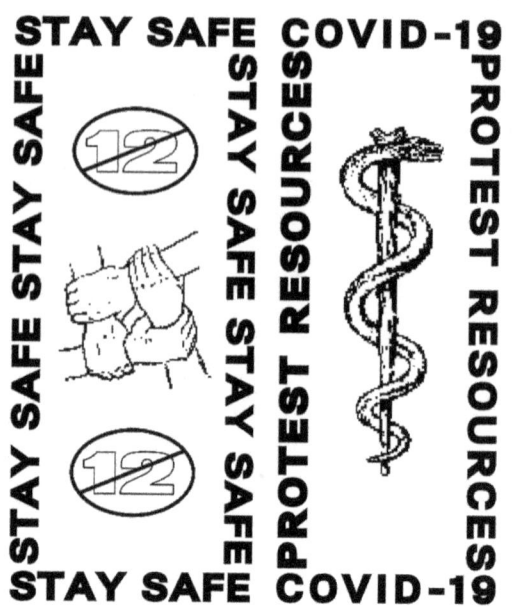

PREPARING FOR DIRECT ACTION

ASSESS RISK LEVELS, BOTH PERSONALLY AND WITHIN YOUR COMMUNITY. DO YOU LIVE WITH, OR OTHERWISE INTERFACE WITH INDIVIDUALS WHO MAY BE AT RISK FOR MORTALITY FROM COVID? IF YOU ARE EXHIBITING ANY SYMPTOMS ASSOCIATED WITH COVID-19, STAY HOME.

TREAT YOURSELF AS THOUGH YOU COULD POTENTIALLY BE AN ASYMPTOMATIC CARRIER; SUIT UP WITH PPE FOR THE PROTECTION OF THOSE AROUND YOU. IT IS IMPOSSIBLE TO COMPLETELY ELIMINATE THE RISK OF THE SPREAD OF THE VIRUS, BUT TAKING PROTECTIVE ACTION CAN DRASTICALLY DECREASE THE POSSIBILITY OF CONTAGION.

SANITIZE HANDS BEFORE, DURING, AND AFTER DIRECT ACTION.

TRY TO ALSO BRING EXTRA MASKS, GLOVES, AND HAND SANITIZER TO SHARE WITH THOSE WHO MAY NOT HAVE BROUGHT THEIR OWN.

KEEP MASKS ON AT ALL TIMES WHEN SPEAKING AND/OR CHANTING: ANY FORM OF SPEECH WILL PROPEL VIRAL DROPLETS FORWARD INTO OTHERS' EYES, MOUTHS, AND NOSES.

REMEMBER THAT COVID-19 AFFECTS AND KILLS BLACK PEOPLE DISPROPORTIONATELY IN THIS COUNTRY. RECOGNIZE THAT STANDING UP IN SUPPORT OF BLACK LIVES SHOULD EXTEND BEYOND THE ACT OF PROTESTING ITSELF. COVID-19 MORTALITY RATES ARE 2.4 TIMES HIGHER FOR BLACK AMERICANS THAN THEY ARE FOR WHITE AMERICANS. SOCIAL DISTANCING IS AN ACT OF SOCIAL SOLIDARITY; PREPARE TO SELF-QUARANTINE FOR 14 DAYS FOLLOWING BEING PRESENT IN A CROWD.

FOLLOWING DIRECT ACTION

IMMEDIATELY AFTER AN ACTION EVENT, TAKE THE CLOTHES YOU WORE IN PUBLIC OFF AND TOSS THEM IN A PLASTIC BAG. TIE IT AND STORE IT AWAY FOR A MIN OF THREE DAYS, AND THEN THOROUGHLY WASH THE CLOTHING.

DON'T FORGET YOUR SHOES: HEAVY VIRAL DROPLETS TEND TO SETTLE ON THEM, SO BE SURE TO TAKE OFF AND SANITIZE SHOES IMMEDIATELY BEFORE ENTERING YOUR HOME. ADDITIONALLY, CELLPHONES CAN BE HOTSPOTS FOR VIRAL ACTIVITY; BE SURE TO THOROUGHLY WIPE YOUR PHONE DOWN IF YOU DID BRING IT WITH YOU.

AFTER YOU HAVE TAKEN OFF AND STORED YOUR CLOTHING, SHOWER; DON'T FORGET TO WASH YOUR HAIR.

SELF-QUARANTINE AFTER PARTICIPATING IN DIRECT ACTION: ISOLATE AS MUCH AS POSSIBLE FOR A PERIOD OF 14 DAYS. DURING THIS TIME, KEEP AWAY FROM LOVED ONES AND COMMUNITY MEMBERS WHO ARE ELDERLY OR IMMUNOCOMPROMISED.

IF YOU MUST GO OUT IN THE TWO WEEKS FOLLOWING THIS ACTION, DO NOT LEAVE YOUR HOUSE WITHOUT A MASK AND/OR GLOVES. WASH YOUR HANDS CONSTANTLY.

LEARN PATIENT ADVOCACY: IF A LOVED ONE OR FRIEND HAS TESTED POSITIVE OR IS UNABLE TO RECEIVE A TEST FOR ANY REASON, UNDERSTAND THAT KNOWING HOW TO PROTECT THEM FROM THE MEDICAL-INDUSTRIAL COMPLEX CAN HELP ENSURE THAT THEY RECEIVE PROPER CARE AND POTENTIALLY SAVE A LIFE.

YOUR RIGHTS

STAY CALM. MAKE SURE TO KEEP YOUR HANDS VISIBLE. DON'T ARGUE, RESIST, OR OBSTRUCT THE POLICE, EVEN IF YOU BELIEVE THEY ARE VIOLATING YOUR RIGHTS. POINT OUT THAT YOU ARE NOT DISRUPTING ANYONE ELSE'S ACTIVITY AND THAT THE FIRST AMENDMENT PROTECTS YOUR ACTIONS.

ASK IF YOU ARE FREE TO LEAVE. IF THE OFFICER SAYS YES, CALMLY WALK AWAY.

IF YOU ARE UNDER ARREST, YOU HAVE A RIGHT TO ASK WHY. OTHERWISE, SAY YOU WISH TO REMAIN SILENT AND ASK FOR A LAWYER IMMEDIATELY. DON'T SAY ANYTHING OR SIGN ANYTHING WITHOUT A LAWYER.

YOU HAVE THE RIGHT TO MAKE A LOCAL PHONE CALL, AND IF YOU'RE CALLING YOUR LAWYER, POLICE ARE NOT ALLOWED TO LISTEN.

YOU **NEVER** HAVE TO CONSENT TO A SEARCH OF YOURSELF OR YOUR BELONGINGS. IF YOU DO EXPLICITLY CONSENT, IT CAN AFFECT YOU LATER IN COURT.

POLICE MAY "PAT DOWN" YOUR CLOTHING IF THEY SUSPECT YOU HAVE A WEAPON AND MAY SEARCH YOU AFTER AN ARREST.

POLICE OFFICERS MAY **NOT** CONFISCATE OR DEMAND TO VIEW YOUR PHOTOGRAPHS OR VIDEO WITHOUT A WARRANT, NOR MAY THEY DELETE DATA **UNDER ANY CIRCUMSTANCES**. HOWEVER, THEY MAY ORDER CITIZENS TO CEASE ACTIVITIES THAT ARE TRULY INTERFERING WITH LEGITIMATE LAW ENFORCEMENT OPERATIONS.

WHAT TO DO IF YOU BELIEVE YOUR RIGHTS HAVE BEEN VIOLATED

WHEN YOU CAN, WRITE DOWN EVERYTHING YOU REMEMBER, INCLUDING THE OFFICERS' BADGE AND PATROL CAR NUMBERS AND THE AGENCY THEY WORK FOR.

GET CONTACT INFORMATION FOR WITNESSES.

TAKE PHOTOGRAPHS OF ANY INJURIES.

ONCE YOU HAVE ALL OF THIS INFORMATION, YOU CAN FILE A WRITTEN COMPLAINT WITH THE AGENCY'S INTERNAL AFFAIRS DIVISION OR CIVILIAN COMPLAINT BOARD.

(SOURCE: ACLU - PROTEST RIGHTS)

RESOURCES

NATIONAL LAWYERS GUILD
212-679-6018

BAIL PROJECT
1-833-425-6TBP

CREATURE FRIEND FINDER
CREATUREFRIEND.ORG

COVID-19 TEST SITE FINDER
HTTPS://MY.CASTLIGHTHEALTH.COM/CORONA-VIRUS-TESTING-SITES/

STAY SAFE
STAY INFORMED
STAY SECURE

Figure 1.7. Sick in Quarters (SiQ), a collective of disabled and chronically ill artists and activists, published this black-and-white brochure online in 2020 with advice for decreasing the chance of viral spread during and after direct-action events. The brochure also contains information about protest rights and how to stay safe while interacting with police.

and other chronic illness activists responding to the emergent disabilities of Long COVID (Kornstein and Rogers). The following chapter, a conversation between Chancey Fleet and Bojana Coklyat, shares the complex experiences of blind New Yorkers, including the patchwork accessibility of remote access, the global organizing efforts of librarians at the New York Public Library, and the "post-pandemic" rollbacks of accessibility gains (Coklyat and Fleet). We also include chapters on immigrants in New York's Chinatown who find community and creativity in a local senior center, while facing increasing vulnerability not only

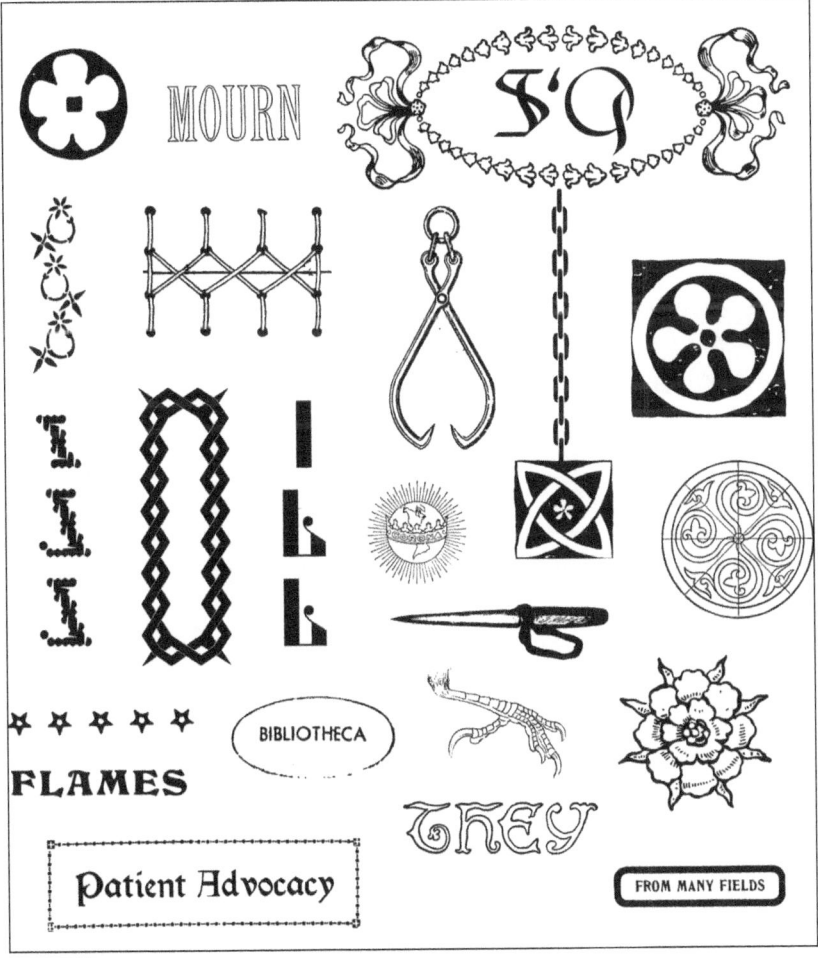

Figure I.8. SiQ T-shirt design. (Courtesy thai lu)

from the pandemic but also from anti-Asian threats and violence (Li); a roundtable of Asian American disability activists discussing tensions as well as coalitions among groups drawn from varied regional, national, caste, and class backgrounds (Mohapatra et al.); and an analysis of the "iron cage" of medical bureaucracy and health-care disparities that challenge Black people's mental health (Mbonde) in the context of the dual pandemics of COVID and anti-Black racism. The following chapter discusses the pandemic sociality and mutual aid of autistic adults, including low-wage essential workers who were temporarily freed by the CARES Act for social and creative pursuits (Ryan). The penultimate chapter considers how New York City's disabled artists found ways to "make art in bed" while studios and other art spaces were closed, embracing the need for rest and creativity in the midst of COVID (Watlington). The second part concludes with a reflection by Amanda Morris, the first disability reporter at the *New York Times*, on what it was like to cover the pandemic in New York City, the stories she was not able to tell, and the ongoing deaths of immunocompromised New Yorkers from COVID in the present.

We are also pleased that this collection is bookended by the words of the celebrated journalist Ed Yong and the late disability activist Judith Heumann. Yong reflects in his foreword to the volume on the limits of legal definitions of disability and the need to center the voices of disabled people in research and reporting. In the coda, we reprint an excerpt from Judith Heumann's 2022 NYU commencement speech, in which she addresses both the experience of COVID that students sustained and the impact of this experience on the future of disability activism. In order to provide further resources for readers and documentation of some of the otherwise-ephemeral cultural production of the pandemic thus far, we have also included a brief timeline of key public health and disability activist events in New York City's experience of the pandemic, a glossary of terms that have been crucial to crip pandemic theorizing, and images of activist media and actions discussed throughout the book.

Ongoing Pandemics, Disabled Futures

As we complete the edits for this volume, we note the recent appearance of many other journals and books filled with academic "postmortems" of the pandemic, mostly focused on its first year alone.[13] Scholars have extrapolated "permanent changes" from 2020 data, ranging from outdoor dining in New York to wealth gains for certain Americans (and higher rents for others) to work-from-home options around the world (already increasingly rolled back). More importantly, far too many "lessons learned" have focused on the experiences of the nondisabled or gains for the well, rather than the essence of a pandemic: infection, illness, mortality, and disability. One thing remains clear: the COVID-19 pandemic and its impacts are certainly not over—for disability communities or anyone—and the curtailment of public health measures has served to exacerbate risk for disabled, elderly, and immunocompromised people once again.

Nevertheless, on September 18, 2022, President Biden declared on *60 Minutes* that "the pandemic is over," adding, "We still have a problem with COVID. We're still doing a lotta work on it, . . . but the pandemic is over" (Pelley 2022). Many other political and corporate leaders not surprisingly followed suit—if they had not already declared a return to normalcy—loosening what few public health measures remained in place. Just days before, New York Governor Kathy Hochul dropped the mask mandate on New York City's public transportation. This was despite protests from disabled activists (Nessen 2022), who quickly criticized such policy changes as a "you do you" approach to COVID-19 mitigation, rooted in individual responsibility rather than collective action. The shift to voluntary masking on public transport put immunocompromised people at risk, as demonstrated by a new set of MTA posters illustrating riders in various states of masking (Lincoln and Sosin 2022; see figure I.9). Moreover, the Biden administration ended the official US public health emergency on May 11, 2023, signaling a new approach to pandemic policy in which the government would no longer fund testing, vaccines, or treatments but would instead offload these and other responsibilities to the private sector (LaFraniere and Weiland 2023; Cubanski et al. 2023).

Still, the SARS-CoV-2 virus continues to mutate and spread globally. As of April 27, 2024, the CDC reports that 1,190,122 people have died from COVID-19 in the US since the start of the pandemic (CDC 2024). The virus itself and factors related to the pandemic (e.g., depression and addiction) have caused a notable reduction in life expectancy for Americans (Ghorayshi 2023). With each revision of our introduction, we have witnessed new variants, patterns of symptoms, and vaccine protocols.

Figure 1.9. MTA "you do you" poster, September 2022. Critics were vocal: "Whoever designed your poster should be fired. It's public endangerment and mask misinformation!!" said Dr. Eric Feigl-Ding, an epidemiologist, in replying to MTA's tweet about the change (Chappell 2022).

In 2022, COVID-19 remained the fourth leading cause of death in the United States, and in the first half of 2023, the elderly accounted for more than 60 percent of all US COVID-19–associated hospitalizations and nearly 90 percent of in-hospital COVID-19 deaths (Rabin 2023; Taylor et al. 2023).

In New York, 46,365 people have died from the coronavirus as of May 9, 2024, about 1 in every 190 residents, a large fraction of those in nursing homes and other congregate settings, many without internet or computer access, and mostly overlooked in popular reporting (NYC Department of Health, n.d.). None of our chapters on congregate settings ends on an optimistic note; none gives any indication that "lessons were learned" from the pandemic to rethink these institutions. In fact, the 2020 New York State budget made it harder to achieve eligibility for home-care services and easier for people to be placed in nursing homes

(New York State Senate, n.d.). By some estimates, 38 percent of early COVID deaths occurred in long-term care and nursing homes alone, and that has been by design (Girvan and Roy 2020).

Strategies for addressing COVID-19 and its lasting impacts must continually evolve. As the microbiologist and essayist Joseph Osmundson writes, "Our work is not to get rid of viruses, or we would, by definition, fail. Our work is to live alongside viruses and to protect as many human lives as we can" (2022, 64). Not surprisingly, disability justice activists remain some of the most vocal critics of a return to so-called normalcy, highlighting preexisting inequities and ongoing threats (especially for immunocompromised people), publishing new survival guides, and reimagining a more just and interdependent future (Piepzna-Samarasinha and Zavitsanos 2023; Mingus 2022).

Activists also continue to demand recognition of Long COVID, noting that each additional infection poses a risk, even for seemingly healthy individuals. The CDC estimates that approximately one in five people

Figure I.10. Photo of the Brooklyn Bridge at night, March 14, 2021, with projections of photographs of some of the thirty thousand New Yorkers who died of the coronavirus during the first year of the pandemic, for the city's first COVID-19 Day of Remembrance. (Photo courtesy of the New York City Mayor's Office; Chung 2021)

Figure I.11. Naming the Lost Memorials (NTL), City Lore, and twenty other New York City community groups created "The Many Losses from Covid-19," a public art memorial along the fence at the entrance to the Green-Wood Cemetery in Brooklyn in May 2020. Since then, volunteer artists and activists have curated NTL memorial sites in New York City, with thousands of nameplates and personalized drawings and photos, created by the families and friends of those who have lost loved ones to the virus. (Photo: Erik McGregor/Sipa USA/Alamy)

with previous infections develops at least one long-term symptom (CDC 2022a; Ledford 2022). Indeed, rates of disablement have risen since 2021 (US Bureau of Labor Statistics 2023). To that end, coalitions like Long COVID Justice have released statements arguing, "We are experiencing a mass disabling event, and disabled people and those with Long COVID must be at the forefront of addressing this unprecedented moment," demanding that political and public health leaders operate from a position of disability justice (Action Network, n.d.).

Our book centers on a lesson provided by Alice Wong (2020) and Leah Lakshmi Piepzna-Samarasinha (2022), that "the future is disabled." Piepzna-Samarasinha elaborates that we must genuinely engage the possibilities of a disabled future, "not just as a cautionary tale or scary story, but as a dream" (2022, 22). Nondisabled people and the "privileged disabled" alike cannot merely learn to live expertly and creatively with viruses to actualize the disabled future (Russell and Malhotra 2002, 218). Rather, the authors in this volume observe the many ways "disabled people are constantly creating an improbable crip future in the face of all that wants to eliminate us" (Piepzna-Samarasinha 2022, 31). At the same time, we caution that the state has gone beyond the usual politics of disposability, mobilizing discourses of disability and care to shore up structural injustice, allocate resources, and institutionalize growing numbers of disabled people who are disproportionately subject to lockdown. In this context, embracing the growing reality that the future is disabled demands that we actualize the dream of disability justice in all corners of New York City and beyond.

May 2024

NOTES

1 James Charlton, in his classic history of the disability rights movement, *Nothing about Us without Us*, writes, "Simply put, this book is about the dialectics of the disability experience: oppression and its opposites, resistance and empowerment" (2000, 5). Since then, the phrase "disability dialectic" has circulated in the work of several other disability studies authors, sometimes in registers distinct from our meaning here.

2 Hart Island is the largest mass grave in the United States, and over a million people have been buried there, from those lost to the flu of 1918 to those lost to AIDS in the 1980s. Hart Island was formerly run by the New York City Department of Correction, which employed incarcerated people at another nearby island, Rikers,

to undertake the labor of reopening or digging new mass graves during each new epidemic. In a cruel echo of history, Rikers inmates were once again brought over to Hart in spring 2020 and paid six dollars an hour to bury the unclaimed bodies of thousands of people who had died in the first months of COVID-19 (Grim 2020). One-third of the burials were Bronx residents (Stabile Center 2021).

3 Michele Friedner to Mara Mills, personal communication, November 12, 2023. See also Friedner (2017) on "disability as 'feel good' diversity."

4 With a similar impulse, in November 2020, the epidemiologists Deborah Wallace and Rodrick Wallace published the brief *COVID-19 in New York City: An Ecology of Race and Class Oppression*. Other collections have looked at racial disparities in infection across the US as a whole or have investigated global inequalities (Thomas, Henderson, and Horton 2022; Wright, Hubbard, and Darity 2022; Manderson, Burke, and Wahlberg 2021).

5 We also connected with other pandemic researchers whose work overlapped with our own—see this book's acknowledgments section—through having remote exchanges focused on ethics, methods, and unexpected findings. (For a more complete list of related projects, please see our website: https://disabilitycovidchronicles.nyu.edu/resources.)

6 For the full ten-point PAUSE plan, as well as "Matilda's Law" for "vulnerable populations," see New York State Governor 2020. Initially admired, Cuomo's leadership collapsed when his political career was torpedoed by a confluence of scandals, including a damning May 2020 report that revealed his strategic undercounting of COVID deaths occurring in nursing homes: long-term care residents who contracted the virus and then were moved to hospitals to die were intentionally left out of tallies.

7 For a powerful chronicle of what transpired in the Coler Nursing Home on Roosevelt Island, see the documentary *Fire through Dry Grass* (Molina and Neophytides 2023).

8 The "lockdown" of nursing homes also had "devastating effects" on residents' physical abilities and mental health, as a result of isolation and short-staffing (National Consumer Voice for Quality Long-Term Care 2021).

9 More recently, homelessness has increased across the United States for reasons that seem to be linked to migration and the government's response to it. See DeParle 2023.

10 We thank Michele Friedner for raising the question of "disability authority" in the Q&A for a "COVID and Cripistemology" panel at the Society for the Social Studies of Science (4S) conference in November 2022, at which several of our contributors presented.

11 For some, the shifts to remote work, education, and other services created new barriers due to limited access to technology, interpretation, or other supports (Weber 2022). Cherokee activist and journalist Jen Deerinwater has detailed the stakes of digital inequality for Indigenous New Yorkers during the pandemic, as well as their technical and economic barriers to "remote access." In New York State, for instance, the Shinnecock lands on Long Island have had only one

internet provider, which charges higher fees than most of the tribal members can afford—60 percent of whom live in poverty. With libraries closed and home internet far from universal, telehealth, remote work, and education became challenges rather than solutions for social distancing. Deerinwater importantly points out that Indigenous people "have the highest rates of disability per capita in the U.S. . . . due in large part to the longstanding impacts of colonialism" (2023, 350).

12 thai lu to Mara Mills, personal communication, November 7, 2023.
13 Works focusing solely on New York City include the self-published memoir *Pandemic NYC: An Insider's Account of a COVID-19 ICU*, by traveling ICU nurse E. G. Whitney (2020); *COVID-19 in NYC: An Ecology of Race and Class Oppression* by epidemiologists Wallace and Wallace (2020); *Covid-19 Response in NYC: Crisis Management in the Epicenter of the Epicenter* (Iavicoli, Madad, and Wei 2023); and *2020: One City, Seven People, and the Year Everything Changed* by NYU sociologist Eric Klinenberg (2024), profiling seven New Yorkers during the first year of the pandemic.

REFERENCES

Action Network. n.d. "Pandemics Are Chronic: A Statement of Commitment to Long COVID Justice." Accessed January 7, 2024. https://actionnetwork.org.

Acton, Kelsie, and Aimi Hamraie. 2022. "Life at a Distance: Archiving Disability Cultures of Remote Participation." *Just Tech*, Social Science Research Council, June 28, 2022. https://just-tech.ssrc.org.

Akobirshoev, Ilhom, Michael Vetter, Lisa I. Iezzoni, Sowmya R. Rao, and Monika Mitra. 2022. "Delayed Medical Care and Unmet Care Needs Due to the COVID-19 Pandemic among Adults with Disabilities in the US." *Health Affairs* 41 (10): 1505–12. https://doi.org/10.1377/hlthaff.2022.00509.

Barbarin, Imani (@crutches_and_spice). 2020. "#stitch with @ramdanielle things will never be the same. Never. You may now become who you thought was disposable. #quarantine #covid19." TikTok, December 13, 2020. www.tiktok.com/@crutches_and_spice/video/6905830183601769733.

———. 2022. "I Started #MyDisabledLifeIsWorthy, Here's Why the Response from Nondisabled People and Medical Professionals Should Alarm You." *Crutches and Spice* (blog), January 26, 2022. https://crutchesandspice.com/2022/01/26/%ef%bf%bci-started-mydisabledlifeisworthy-heres-why-the-response-from-nondisabled-people-and-medical-professionals-should-alarm-you/.

Beery, Zoë. 2020. "When the World Shut Down, They Saw It Open." *New York Times*, August 24, 2020, sec. Style. www.nytimes.com.

Ben-Moshe, Liat. 2016. "Searching for a Rose Garden: Challenging Psychiatry, Fostering Mad Studies." *Mad in America*, September 12, 2016. www.madinamerica.com.

Bergstresser, Sara. 2014. "Adrienne Asch." *Voices in Bioethics* 1 (March 2014). https://doaj.org.

Berne, Patty. 2015. "Disability Justice—a Working Draft." *Sins Invalid* (blog), June 10, 2015. www.sinsinvalid.org.

Bhaman, Salonee, Rachel Kuo, Matilda Sabal, Vivian Shaw, and Tiffany Diane Tso. 2020. "Asian American Feminist Antibodies: Care in the Time of Coronavirus." *Cross-Cutting Analyses* 9. https://digitalcommons.wcl.american.edu.

Campbell, Stephen. 2017. "Racial and Gender Disparities within the Direct Care Workforce: Five Key Findings." Issue brief. Paraprofessional Healthcare Institute, New York, November 2017. www.phinational.org.

Centers for Disease Control and Prevention (CDC). 2020. "COVID-19 Outbreak New York City, February 29–June 1, 2020." www.cdc.gov.

———. 2022a. "Nearly One in Five American Adults Who Have Had COVID-19 Still Have 'Long COVID.'" National Center for Health Statistics, June 22, 2022. https://www.cdc.gov/nchs/pressroom/nchs_press_releases/2022/20220622.htm.

———. 2022b. "Readout of Dr. Walensky's Call with Disability Advocacy Groups and Allies." January 14, 2022. www.cdc.gov.

———. 2024. "COVID Data Tracker." US Department of Health and Human Services. December 30, 2023. Posted January 5, 2024 https://covid.cdc.gov.

Chappell, Bill. 2022. "New York's Subway Now Has a 'You Do You' Mask Policy. It's Getting a Bronx Cheer." KNKX Public Radio, September 8, 2022. www.knkx.org.

Charlton, James. 2000. *Nothing about Us without Us: Disability Oppression and Empowerment.* Berkeley: University of California Press.

Chatzidakis, Andreas, and Jo Littler. 2022. "An Anatomy of Carewashing: Corporate Branding and the Commodification of Care during Covid-19." *International Journal of Cultural Studies* 25:268–86.

Chung, Jen. 2021. "NYC Holds First COVID-19 Day of Remembrance with Touching Brooklyn Bridge Tribute." *Gothamist*, March 15, 2021. https://gothamist.com.

Crimp, Douglas. 1987. "How to Have Promiscuity in an Epidemic." *October* 43 (Winter): 237–71.

Cubanski, Juliette, Jennifer Kates, Jennifer Tolbert, Madeline Guth, Karen Pollitz, and Meredith Freed. 2023. "What Happens When COVID-19 Emergency Declarations End? Implications for Coverage, Costs, and Access." Kaiser Family Foundation, January 31, 2023. www.kff.org.

Davids, J. D. 2020. "COVID-19 (Coronavirus) Preparation for People Living with Chronic Illnesses in the U.S." *The Cranky Queer Guide to Chronic Illness*, March 7, 2020. https://crankyqueer.org.

Davis, Hannah E., Lisa McCorkell, Julia Moore Vogel, and Eric J. Topol. 2023. "Long COVID: Major Findings, Mechanisms and Recommendations." *Nature Reviews Microbiology*, January 2023, 1–14. https://doi.org/10.1038/s41579-022-00846-2.

Deal, Mark. 2010. "Disabled People's Attitudes toward Other Impairment Groups: A Hierarchy of Impairments." *Disability & Society* 18 (7): 897–910.

Deerinwater, Jen. 2023. "Crip Indigenous Storytelling across the Digital Divide." In *Crip Authorship: Disability as Method*, edited by Mara Mills and Rebecca Sanchez, 350–54. New York: New York University Press.

DeParle, Jason. 2023. "Homelessness Rose to Record Level This Year, Government Says." *New York Times*, December 15, 2023.

Ehrlich, Esther. 2006. Neil Marcus, Performance Artist: Interviews Conducted by Esther Ehrlich. Regional Oral History Office. The Bancroft Library. University of California, Berkeley.

Friedner, Michele. 2017. "How the Disabled Body Unites the National Body: Disability as 'Feel Good' Diversity in Urban India." *Contemporary South Asia* 25 (4): 347–63.

Gawthrop, Elisabeth. 2022. "Color of Coronavirus: COVID-19 Deaths Analyzed by Race and Ethnicity." *APM Research Lab* (blog), December 14, 2022. www.apmresearchlab.org.

Ghorayshi, Azeen. 2023. "An 'Unsettling' Drop in Life Expectancy for Men." *New York Times*. November 13, 2023.

Gil, Liliana. 2022. "Beyond Make-Do Innovation: Practices and Politics of Technical Improvisation in Brazil." PhD diss., The New School.

Girvan Gregg, and Avik Roy. 2020. "Nursing Homes and Assisted Living Facilities Account for 38% of COVID-19 Deaths." Foundation for Research on Equal Opportunity, *Medium*, May 7, 2020, https://freopp.org.

Gonzalez-Reiche, Ana S., Matthew M. Hernandez, Mitchell J. Sullivan, Brianne Ciferri, Hala Alshammary, Ajay Obla, Shelcie Fabre, et al. 2020. "Introductions and Early Spread of SARS-CoV-2 in the New York City Area." *Science* 369, no. 6501 (2020): 297–301.

Green, Matthew. 2020. "Coronavirus: How These Disabled Activists Are Taking Matters into Their Own (Sanitized) Hands." KQED, March 17, 2020. www.kqed.org.

Grim, Ryan. 2020. "Rikers Island Prisoners Are Being Offered PPE and $6 an Hour to Dig Mass Graves." *The Intercept*, March 31, 2020. https://theintercept.com.

Hamraie, Aimi. 2017. *Building Access: Universal Design and the Politics of Disability*. 3rd ed. Minneapolis: University of Minnesota Press.

Hamraie, Aimi, and Kelly Fritsch. 2019. "Crip Technoscience Manifesto." *Catalyst: Feminism, Theory, Technoscience* 5 (1): 1–33. https://doi.org/10.28968/cftt.v5i1.29607.

Hartblay, Cassandra. 2020. "Disability Expertise: Claiming Disability Anthropology." *Current Anthropology* 61 (S21): S26–36. https://doi.org/10.1086/705781.

Hill, Charis. 2022. "'Urgency of Normal' Rhetoric Fuels Pandemic Ableism." *Being Charis* (blog), *Medium*, February 9, 2022. https://beingcharis.medium.com.

Hrynyk, Nicholas. 2021. "'No Sorrow, No Pity': Intersections of Disability, HIV/AIDS, and Gay Male Masculinity in the 1980s." *Disability Studies Quarterly* 41 (2). https://doi.org/10.18061/dsq.v41i2.7148.

Hubrig, Ada. 2022. "Disabled Deaths Are Not Your 'Encouraging News.'" *Disability Visibility Project*, January 26, 2022. https://disabilityvisibilityproject.com.

Iavicoli, Laura, Syra S. Madad, and Eric K. Wei, eds. 2024. *Covid-19 Response in NYC: Crisis Management in the Epicenter of the Epicenter*. Cambridge, MA: Academic Press.

Juhasz, Alexandra. 2023. "Pandemic Media." Visual AIDS. https://visualaids.org/gallery/pandemic-media.

Juhasz, Alexandra, and Theodore Kerr. 2023. *We Are Having This Conversation Now: The Times of AIDS Cultural Production*. Durham, NC: Duke University Press.

Kapadia, Melissa. 2020. "Illness Methodology for and beyond the COVID Era." *Perspectives on Urban Education* 18 (1). https://urbanedjournal.gse.upenn.edu.

Khúc, Mimi. 2021. "Making Mental Health through *Open in Emergency*: A Journey in Love Letters." *South Atlantic Quarterly* 120 (2): 369–88.

Klinenberg, Eric. 2024. *2020: One City, Seven People, and the Year Everything Changed*. New York: Knopf.

Kopit, Alison, and Chun-shan (Sandie) Yi. 2022. "A Dialogue and Reflection about the Masks for Crips Project." *Lateral* 11 (2). https://doi.org/10.25158/L11.2.10.

Kukla, Elliot. 2020. "My Life Is More 'Disposable' during This Pandemic." *New York Times*, March 19, 2020, sec. Opinion. www.nytimes.com.

LaFraniere, Sharon, and Noah Weiland. 2023. "U.S. Plans to End Public Health Emergency for Covid in May." *New York Times*, January 30, 2023, sec. U.S. www.nytimes.com.

Landes, Scott D., Julia M. Finan, and Margaret A. Turk. 2022. "COVID-19 Mortality Burden and Comorbidity Patterns among Decedents with and without Intellectual and Developmental Disability in the US." *Disability and Health Journal* 15 (4): 101376. https://doi.org/10.1016/j.dhjo.2022.101376.

Ledford, Heidi. 2022. "How Common Is Long COVID? Why Studies Give Different Answers." *Nature* 606 (7916): 852–53. https://doi.org/10.1038/d41586-022-01702-2.

Lincoln, Martha, and Anne N. Sosin. 2022. "Ending Free Covid Tests, US Policy Is Now 'You Do You.'" *The Nation*, September 9, 2022. www.thenation.com.

Manderson, Lenore, Nancy J. Burke, and Ayo Wahlberg, eds. *Viral Loads: Anthropologies of Urgency in the Time of COVID-19*. London: UCL Press, 2021.

Martens, Bailey. 2020. "I'm 22, Chronically Ill—and Feel Dismissed in the COVID-19 Dialogue." *CBC News*, March 22, 2020. www.cbc.ca.

Mathews, Zoe. 2020. "Art Caplan: Nursing Homes Are the 'Forgotten Institutions' of the Coronavirus Pandemic." *GBH*, April 29, 2020. www.wgbh.org.

Mauldin, Laura. n.d. "About Disability at Home." Disability at Home, accessed December 1, 2022. www.disabilityathome.org.

McRuer, Robert. 2002. "Critical Investments: AIDS, Christopher Reeve, and Queer/Disability Studies." *Journal of Medical Humanities* 23 (3): 221–37. https://doi.org/10.1023/A:1016846402426.

———. 2006. *Crip Theory: Cultural Signs of Queerness and Disability*. New York: New York University Press.

McWilliams, Kate. 2020. "#AccessibilityForAbleds." Twitter, March 7, 2020. https://twitter.com/KateMcWilli/status/1236440655095689216?s=20.

Metcalf, Jerry. 2020. "No, Your Coronavirus Quarantine Is Not Just Like Being in Prison." Marshall Project, March 25, 2020. www.themarshallproject.org.

Miller, Lindsay. 2021. "NYAIL Raises Concerns over COVID Vaccine Eligibility and Process in Letter to Governor Cuomo." New York Association on Independent Living, February 11, 2021. https://ilny.us.

Mingus, Mia. 2011. "Access Intimacy: The Missing Link." *Leaving Evidence* (blog), May 5, 2011. https://leavingevidence.wordpress.com.

———. 2022. "You Are Not Entitled to Our Deaths: COVID, Abled Supremacy & Interdependence." *Leaving Evidence* (blog), January 16, 2022. https://leavingevidence.wordpress.com.

Mizner, Susan. 2020. "COVID-19 Deaths in Nursing Homes Are Not Unavoidable—They Are the Result of Deadly Discrimination." American Civil Liberties Union, June 23, 2020. www.aclu.org.

Molina, Andrés Jay, and Alexis Neophytides. 2023. *Fire through Dry Grass* www.firethroughdrygrass.com.

Moore, Ramey, Rachel S. Purvis, Emily Hallgren, Sharon Reece, Alan Padilla-Ramos, Morgan Gurel-Headley, Spencer Hall, and Pearl A. McElfish. 2022. "'I Am Hesitant to Visit the Doctor Unless Absolutely Necessary': A Qualitative Study of Delayed Care, Avoidance of Care, and Telehealth Experiences during the COVID-19 Pandemic." *Medicine* 101 (32): e29439. https://doi.org/10.1097/MD.0000000000029439.

Morris, Amanda. 2022. "At-Home Coronavirus Tests Are Inaccessible to Blind People." *New York Times*, January 10, 2022, sec. Health. www.nytimes.com.

Murphy, Michelle. 2015. "Unsettling Care: Troubling Transnational Itineraries of Care in Feminist Health Practices." *Social Studies of Science* 45 (5): 717–37. https://doi.org/10.1177/0306312715589136.

Murthy, Vivek H. 2022. "Confronting Health Worker Burnout and Well-Being." *New England Journal of Medicine* 387 (7): 577–79. https://doi.org/10.1056/NEJMp2207252.

National Consumer Voice for Quality Long Term Care. 2021. "The Devastating Effect of Lockdowns on Residents of Long-Term Care Facilities during COVID-19: A Survey of Residents' Families." January 15, 2021. https://theconsumervoice.org.

National Council on Disability. 2021. "2021 Progress Report: The Impact of COVID-19 on People with Disabilities." October 29, 2021. www.ncd.gov.

Nessen, Stephen. 2022. "Hochul's 'You Do You' Guidance Ending Mask Mandate Rankles Some Disabled New Yorkers." *Gothamist* (blog), September 15, 2022. https://gothamist.com.

New York City Department of Health and Mental Hygiene. n.d. "COVID-19 Data: Trends and Totals." Accessed May 22, 2024. www.nyc.gov.

New York State Governor. 2020. "Governor Cuomo Signs the 'New York State on PAUSE' Executive Order." Press Office, March 20, 2020. www.governor.ny.gov.

———. 2021. "Governor Cuomo Announces List of Comorbidities and Underlying Conditions Eligible for COVID-19 Vaccine Starting February 15." Press Office, February 5, 2021. www.governor.ny.gov.

New York State Senate. n.d. "Assembly Bill A5367A." Accessed May 25, 2024. www.nysenate.gov.

Office of the Mayor. 2022. "Mayor Adams Announces Plan to Provide Care for Individuals Suffering from Untreated Severe Mental Illness across NYC." City of New York, November 29, 2022. www.nyc.gov.

Osmundson, Joseph. 2022. *Virology: Essays for the Living, the Dead, and the Small Things in Between*. New York: Norton.

Panchal, Nirmita, Rabah Kamal, Cynthia Cox, and Rachel Garfield. 2021. "The Implications of COVID-19 for Mental Health and Substance Use." Kaiser Family Foundation, February 10, 2021. www.kff.org.

Pasquini, Giancarlo, and Scott Keeter. 2022. "At Least Four-in-Ten U.S. Adults Have Faced High Levels of Psychological Distress during COVID-19 Pandemic." Pew Research Center, December 12, 2022. www.pewresearch.org.

Patsavas, Alyson, and Theodora Danylevich. 2022. "Introduction: Crip Pandemic Life: A Tapestry." *Lateral* 11 (2). https://doi.org/10.25158/L11.2.5.

Pelley, Scott. 2022. "President Joe Biden: The 2022 60 Minutes Interview." *60 Minutes*, CBS News, September 18, 2022. www.cbsnews.com.

Piepzna-Samarasinha, Leah Lakshmi. 2018. *Care Work: Dreaming Disability Justice*. Vancouver: Arsenal Pulp.

———. 2020. "Half Assed Disabled Prepper Survival Tips for Preparing for a Coronavirus Quarantine." Google Docs, March 9, 2020. https://docs.google.com.

———. 2022. *The Future Is Disabled*. Vancouver: Arsenal Pulp.

Piepzna-Samarasinha, Leah Lakshmi, and Tina Zavitsanos. 2023. "A Long Winter Crip Survival Guide for Pandemic Year 4/Forever." Google Docs. Accessed May 23, 2024. www.tinyurl.com.

Plunz, Richard, and Andrés Álvarez-Dávila. 2020. "Density, Equity, and the History of Epidemics in New York City." *State of the Planet: News from the Columbia Climate School*, June 30, 2020. https://news.climate.columbia.edu.

Pulrang, Andrew. 2021. "What Disabled People Are Thinking and Feeling about the Pandemic, One Year Later." *Forbes*, March 21, 2021. www.forbes.com.

Rabin, Roni Caryn. 2023. "Covid Remained a Leading Cause of Death among Americans in 2022." *New York Times*, May 4, 2023.

Riccobono, Mark. 2022. "Letter Regarding the Accessibility of At-Home COVID-19 Tests and Test Requests." National Federation of the Blind, January 3, 2022. https://nfb.org.

Rogers, Emily. 2023. "Virtual Ethnography." In *Crip Authorship: Disability as Method*, edited by Mara Mills and Rebecca Sanchez, 93–98. New York: New York University Press.

Rogozen, Nehama. 2020. "I'm Deaf and I Lip-Read. All Those Masks Are Presenting a Problem." *Slate*, May 12, 2020. https://slate.com.

Ruiz-Grossman, Sarah. 2022. "Disability Advocates Demand Public Apology from CDC Director after 'Hurtful' Comments." *HuffPost*, January 14, 2022. www.huffpost.com.

Russell, Marta. 1998. *Beyond Ramps: Disability at the End of the Social Contract*. Monroe, ME: Common Courage.

Russell, Marta, and Ravi Malhotra. 2002. "Capitalism and Disability." *Socialist Register* 38:211–27.

Schalk, Sami. 2020. "Wounded Warriors of the Future: Disability Hierarchy in *Avatar* and *Source Code*." *Journal of Literary & Culture Disability Studies* 14 (4): 403–19.

———. 2022. *Black Disability Politics*. Durham, NC: Duke University Press.

Schuchman Center. 2020. "Deaf NYC: Apart + Connected Panel." YouTube, May 13, 2020. https://www.youtube.com/watch?v=o2SX9PTfnpw.
Scott, Sally, and Katherine Aquino. 2020. "COVID-19 Transitions: Higher Education Professionals' Perspectives on Access Barriers, Services, and Solutions for Students with Disabilities." Association on Higher Education and Disability, Huntersville, NC. https://ctahead.org.
Sexton, J. Bryan, Kathryn C. Adair, Joshua Proulx, Jochen Profit, Xin Cui, Jon Bae, and Allan Frankel. 2022. "Emotional Exhaustion among US Health Care Workers before and during the COVID-19 Pandemic, 2019–2021." *JAMA Network Open* 5 (9): e2232748. https://doi.org/10.1001/jamanetworkopen.2022.32748.
Sharp, Sonja. 2021. "Californians with Disabilities Are Outraged over Vaccine Deprioritization." *Los Angeles Times*, February 2, 2021, sec. California. www.latimes.com.
Sick in Quarters. 2023. "Hide Away." Instagram, November 25, 2023. www.instagram.com.
Sick of It! n.d. Home page. Accessed May 22, 2024. www.sickofit.space.
Smith, Meghan. 2022. "USPS to Send Free, Accessible at-Home COVID Tests to People Who Are Blind or Low-Vision." WGBH, June 24, 2022. www.wgbh.org.
Stabile Center (Columbia J-School). 2021. "One in Ten Local COVID Victims Destined for Hart Island, NYC's Potter's Field." *The City*, March 24, 2021. www.thecity.nyc.
Stine, Alison. 2020. "I'm Partially Deaf. When Mask-Wearing Came Along, I Had to Rebuild My World." *The Guardian*, August 20, 2020, sec. Society. www.theguardian.com.
Taylor, Christopher A., Kadam Patel, Monica E. Patton, Arthur Reingold, Breanna Kawasaki, James Meek, Kyle Openo, et al. 2023. "COVID-19–Associated Hospitalizations among U.S. Adults Aged ≥65 Years—COVID-NET, 13 States, January–August 2023." *MMWR Morbidity and Mortality Weekly Report* 72:1089–94. http://dx.doi.org/10.15585/mmwr.mm7240a3.
Thomas, Melvin, Loren Henderson, and Hayward Derrick Horton, eds. 2022. *Race, Ethnicity, and the COVID-19 Pandemic*. Chicago: University of Chicago Press.
Thompson, Vilissa. 2021. "Understanding the Policing of Black, Disabled Bodies." Center for American Progress, February 10, 2021. www.americanprogress.org.
Thrasher, Steven. 2022. *The Viral Underclass: The Human Toll When Inequality and Disease Collide*. New York: Macmillan.
Treichler, Paula. 1999. *How to Have Theory in an Epidemic: Cultural Chronicles of AIDS*. Durham, NC: Duke University Press.
Trowe, Nolan. 2022. "On Our Last Legs." *The Nation*, August 26, 2022.
US Bureau of Labor Statistics. 2023. "Civilian Labor Force—With a Disability, 16 Years and Over [LNU01074597]." FRED, Federal Reserve Bank of St. Louis, November 14, 2023. https://fred.stlouisfed.org.
Wallace, Deborah, and Rodrick Wallace. 2020. *COVID-19 in New York City: An Ecology of Race and Class Oppression*. New York: Springer.
Weber, Lauren. 2022. "People with Disabilities Left behind by Telemedicine and Other Pandemic Medical Innovations." *CNN*, March 10, 2022. www.cnn.com.

Whitney, E. G. 2020. *Pandemic NYC: An Insider's Account of a COVID-19 ICU*. New York: Elizabeth Grace Whitney.

Wong, Alice. 2020. "Message from the Future: Disabled Oracle Society." *Disability Visibility Project* (blog), August 14, 2020. https://disabilityvisibilityproject.com.

Wright, Gwendolyn, Lucas Hubbard, and William A. Darity, eds. 2022. *The Pandemic Divide: How COVID Increased Inequality in America*. Durham, NC: Duke University Press.

Wu, Jin, Weiyi Cai, Derek Watkins, and James Glanz. 2020. "How the Virus Got Out." *New York Times*, March 22, 2020, www.nytimes.com.

WWHIVDD Collective. 2020a. "Twenty-Seven Questions for Writers and Journalists to Consider When Writing about Covid-19 and HIV/AIDS." April 2020. https://hivdoula.work.

———. 2020b. *What Does a COVID-19 Doula Do?* https://hivdoula.work.

Yong, Ed. 2021. "Long-Haulers Are Fighting for Their Future." *The Atlantic*, September 1, 2021. www.theatlantic.com.

PART I

Living with "Disproportionate Risk"

Policies, Institutions, and Congregate Settings

1

"We Were Sick, and They Punished Us Even More"

Living through COVID-19 in New York State Prisons

TOMMASO BARDELLI, AIYUBA THOMAS, AND DYLAN BROWN

It was in the early days of February 2020 that news about the novel coronavirus started to spread at Wallkill Correctional Facility, a medium-security prison in New York's Hudson Valley. Marcus—who at the time was serving the last few months of a thirteen-year sentence—first heard about COVID-19, like many of his peers, from one of the TVs in his housing unit's dayroom.[1] Pretty much every day around seven a.m., someone would tune into one of the main news channels, and Marcus remembered hearing stories about infections spreading in China and Italy. A few weeks later, on March 5, 2020, the New York Department of Corrections and Community Supervision (DOCCS) issued the first of a series of memoranda announcing new measures to stop the spread of COVID-19 in New York prison facilities (figures 1.1–3). After minimizing the threat represented by COVID-19, stating that "80% of infected individuals have very mild symptoms," the first memo (figure 1.1), barely a page long, simply recommended that prisoners adopt a few personal hygiene tips, from washing their hands frequently to avoiding touching their eyes. Not even ten days later, on March 14, came a third memorandum (figure 1.3), this time signed by then-commissioner Anthony J. Annucci, announcing the suspension of in-person visits in all New York State prisons for at least a month.[2]

For many incarcerated individuals in New York, the March 14 memo marked a dramatic turn in their awareness of the severity of the crisis at hand. When we interviewed him in early August 2020, Marcus—who had by then been released and was living in a transitional house in the South Bronx—still vividly remembered how the mood in the facility shifted following the announcement by Annucci. By March, he said, both

Figure 1.1. DOCCS memorandum, March 5, 2020.

TVs in his unit's dayroom were constantly broadcasting COVID-related news, and the growing infection rate in the state had become the main topic of conversation for people at Wallkill. Once the death rate started to rise, Marcus recounted, even the more skeptical ones came around: "It was just like every hour the numbers were rising, rising, rising: this is how much people were dying. And once people were seeing that, then it started to get through their minds: 'Oh, this is something that we

> **NEW YORK STATE | Corrections and Community Supervision**
>
> ANDREW M. CUOMO
> Governor
>
> ANTHONY J. ANNUCCI
> Acting Commissioner
>
> **MEMORANDUM**
>
> To: Inmate Population
> From: James A. O'Gorman, Deputy Commissioner for Correctional Facilities
> Date: March 6, 2020
> Subject: COVID-19 – Post in all Housing Units
>
> ---
>
> The health of our staff, visitors and inmate population is of paramount concern and this procedure will be followed in an effort to avoid the introduction of COVID-19 into our Departmental facilities. As a result, during processing, visitors will be questioned regarding recent travel and symptoms related to COVID-19. Based on staff observations and/or answers to the below questions, your visitor may be temporarily denied entrance to the facility.
>
> **Questions for visitors**
>
> Do you currently have a fever or new respiratory symptoms including cough, sore throat or breathing problems?
>
> Have you had a fever or new respiratory symptoms including cough or breathing problems in the last 14 days?
>
> Have you traveled outside the US in the last 4 weeks?
>
> - To China _____ (Date you left that country)
> - To Italy _____ (Date you left that country)
> - To Iran _____ (Date you left that country)
> - To Japan _____ (Date you left that country)
> - To South Korea _____ (Date you left that country)
> - Other _____ (Date you left that country)
>
> Has any member of your immediate family traveled to any of these countries within the last 4 weeks? ___ Which Country _____
>
> Have you been exposed directly to anyone diagnosed with novel Corona virus in the last 4 weeks(Covid-19) ___ Date of last Exposure _____
>
> ---
>
> The Harriman State Campus, 1220 Washington Avenue, Albany, NY 12226-2050 | (518) 457-8126 | www.doccs.ny.gov

Figure 1.2. DOCCS memorandum, March 6, 2020.

should take seriously.' So now you got guys arguing about how everybody should be wearing masks, how everybody should be wearing gloves, how the officers need to be wearing this."

On Sunday, March 22, shortly after the suspension of in-person visits, DOCCS confirmed that the first cases of COVID-19 had been detected in the New York prison system: two people had tested positive at Wende

NEW YORK STATE | Corrections and Community Supervision

ANDREW M. CUOMO
Governor

ANTHONY J. ANNUCCI
Acting Commissioner

MEMORANDUM

To: All Incarcerated Individuals

From: Anthony J. Annucci, Acting Commissioner

Date: March 14, 2020

Subject: Visitation Restrictions in Response to Novel Coronavirus (COVID-19)
Effective March 14, 2020 until April 11, 2020

In December 2019, a new respiratory disease called Coronavirus Disease 2019 (COVID-19) was detected in China. COVID-19 is caused by a virus (SARS-CoV-2) that is part of a large family of viruses called coronaviruses. Recently, community-wide transmission of COVID-19 has occurred in the United States, including New York where the number of both persons under investigation and confirmed cases are rapidly increasing.

The Department of Corrections and Community Supervision (DOCCS) is responsible for the safety, health, rehabilitation, and supervision of nearly 44,000 incarcerated individuals and over 35,000 individuals on community supervision through the tireless efforts of nearly 30,000 employees. The Department's greatest concern is the safety and well-being of our employees and individuals within our care, custody, and supervision, particularly during this developing public health emergency. To that end, the Department must swiftly impose restrictions and precautions to prevent additional spread of infectious viral transmission of COVID-19 in both correctional facilities and the community writ large.

Effective Saturday, March 14, 2020 at 5:00PM, visitation at all correctional facilities is suspended until April 11, 2020.

As this public health emergency rapidly develops, the Department will closely monitor the situation and extend these restrictions as necessary.

Visitation Suspended at All Correctional Facilities. While this suspension of visitation will be temporary, the Department recognizes the immediate impact on incarcerated individuals throughout the correctional system. However, the current situation demands this significant action to safeguard the health and safety of all incarcerated individuals, employees, as well as their families and communities. While in-person visitation will be impossible to replace, the Department will provide the following benefits to encourage individuals to keep in contact with their family and friends during this temporary suspension:

- Five (5) free stamps per week for use in accordance with Directive #4422, "Inmate Correspondence Program,"
- Two (2) free secure messages per week via electronic tablet, and
- One (1) free phone call per week in accordance with Directive #4423 "Inmate Telephone Calls."

This suspended visitation also applies to family reunion programs. However, legal visits will not be impacted by this visitation suspension. Legal visits will be conducted as non-contact (i.e. no physical contact allowed), as requests are submitted, and that option remains available within the facilities.

The Department takes seriously its duty to ensure the safety and wellbeing of those that work, visit and live in our correctional facilities, as well as those who supervise or are supervised in the greater community of New York. During this difficult time, the Department is appreciative of everyone's patience and understanding as we continue to face this virus together.

For further information on COVID-19 and New York's response, please visit:

New York State Department of Health's COVID-19 Webpage
https://www.health.ny.gov/diseases/communicable/coronavirus/

Listing of Local Health Departments:
https://www.health.ny.gov/contact/contact_information/

Centers for Disease Control and Prevention Webpage:
https://www.cdc.gov/coronavirus/2019-ncov/

Figure 1.3. DOCCS memorandum, March 14, 2020.

Correctional Facility, a maximum-security prison a few miles east of Buffalo. The New York City jail system had already reported its first case three days earlier, an infection at the Rikers Island jail complex (Cheney-Rice 2020). Over the next few months, COVID-19 continued to spread rapidly in prisons and jails, a wave of infections only partially captured by official data, due to the lack of systematic testing in the spring and summer of 2020. According to one national study, those in custody died at 3.4 times the rate of nonincarcerated people during that first year (Sugie et al. 2023). And roughly 2.5 times as many incarcerated individuals and pretrial detainees died as staff members in 2020–2021 (UCLA Law COVID Behind Bars Data Project, n.d.).

This chapter focuses on the first period of the COVID-19 pandemic in the New York prison system, spanning just over one year, from the outset of the crisis in March 2020 to the early summer of 2021, which marked the tail end of a second dramatic wave of infections in the state's correctional facilities. During this time, we conducted over twenty in-depth interviews with formerly incarcerated New Yorkers who experienced part of that first pandemic year from behind prison walls. Due to disability, chronic illness, or old age, several of them faced particularly high risk from COVID infection. We also interviewed prisoner rights advocates and several individuals who were supporting an incarcerated family member or loved one in New York during the first pandemic year.

Our participants' accounts document how prisons and jails in New York, as in other states around the country, quickly became major epicenters of COVID-19—with several correctional facilities, such as New York City's Rikers Island (Brown 2020) and San Quentin State Prison in California (Sawyer 2022), recording some of the largest single-site outbreaks nationwide. Inside carceral institutions, crowded living conditions and institutional routines prevented effective social distancing; masks and hand sanitizer, moreover, were not made available until months into the pandemic, and people had little access to information on the risks of COVID and how best to take care of themselves. Prisoners who contracted the virus, including those who were at high risk of complications from COVID-19, were often provided inadequate treatment—when treatment was accessible at all. In monitoring visits to eight New York prisons between 2020 and 2021, the Correctional Association of New

York (CANY), the legally designated independent prison monitor for the state, found that four out of ten incarcerated people reported being unable to access medical care (CANY 2022).

Beyond such organizational features of prison life, our participants recounted, it was the intrinsic logics of carceral governance that made it all but impossible for people inside prisons and jails to receive adequate care in the face of the COVID-19 pandemic. Public health measures to protect the safety of imprisoned people collided with discourses and practices of dehumanization and oppression of prisoners, and of Black prisoners in particular, which are deeply woven into the moral and political fabrics of the US carceral state (Muhammad 2019). As Robert, one of our interviewees, said, "Prison is an oppressive space, by nature. So, when COVID was brought into the picture, prison was still prison. The oppression continued, just in different ways. Imagine being in an environment where you're always oppressed, where you're always treated like less than human, and then imagine being in that same environment during a pandemic." Even before COVID hit, incarcerated people were already exposed to harmful and debilitating conditions, such as unsanitary living conditions, poor health care, and physical brutality by officers. People in state and federal prisons are three times more likely to report having at least one disability compared to the general population, and at least 40 percent of prisoners report having a chronic illness (Oberholtzer 2017). While prisons were already marked by medical neglect and uneven access to care (Friedner 2021), the COVID-19 crisis further amplified the (re)production of disability among the prisoner class. By intersecting with these preexisting harms and vulnerabilities, the pandemic ultimately intensified the "organized abandonment" (Goodman 2020) faced by the incarcerated, as our chapter shows.

Living Shoulder-to-Shoulder in a Pandemic: Lockdowns and Social Distancing in Prisons and Jails

In mid-March 2020, as COVID-19 cases in New York were rapidly climbing, correctional facilities across the state gradually went into full lockdown. After canceling all in-person visits, prisons shut down educational and training programs, suspended congregate religious services, and suspended nonessential labor assignments. In most cases, prisoners' access to the mess hall, recreation yard, and even showers was severely limited. "Basically, everything was put on hold," said Marcus, talking about the first few weeks of the pandemic at Wallkill Correctional Facility: "We were in our cells for most of the day, with no recreation, no [access to] showers. They gave us hot water, and you do all your business with that. You wash up, you do everything. They closed the library, they closed programs. Basically, we were in our housing units all day long."

When COVID-19 first hit, Nicholas was in Eastern Correctional Facility, a maximum-security prison about twenty miles northwest of Wallkill. In his early thirties, Nicholas had already served almost fourteen years and was looking forward to returning home to the South Bronx later that summer. Like Marcus, Nicholas recounted how life came to an almost complete halt at Eastern. For about two weeks, people there were "literally locked in their cells," as if they "were in solitary confinement." Eventually, they were allowed access to the yard again, although on a limited basis. Even more than the physical restrictions—"being in prison, you get used to those," he explained—what stood out in Nicholas's memory of those first few weeks of the pandemic was a growing sense of anxiety among the prison population at Eastern. After Governor Cuomo declared a state of emergency and issued "stay-at-home orders" on March 20, and as people heard from their families on the outside about business shutdowns and shortages in New York City, rumors started to circulate among prisoners that facilities were soon going to run out of basic supplies, including food and medicines. "That was the scariest thing I experienced while I was incarcerated," Nicholas remembered: "Despite all the issues in prison, nothing really scared me so much as the thought that we would be abandoned in our prison cells, to die of either COVID or starvation, dehydration."

While upending the life of prisoners—who found themselves deprived even of the few privileges and activities making prison life bearable—measures such as banning outside visits or limiting recreation time ended up doing little to stop the progressive spread of the virus inside correctional facilities. On March 18, the first person tested positive at Rikers Island jail complex; one month later, the city's jail had become the site of more than 1,200 COVID-19 infections, including 363 incarcerated individuals and 848 Department of Correction or Correctional Health Services staff. At least ninety-one incarcerated people for every one thousand at Rikers tested positive for COVID-19 during the first month of the pandemic, compared with sixteen residents per one thousand citywide. In the same period, five correctional officers working at Rikers and at least two incarcerated individuals had died of COVID-19. If correctional officers had greater initial exposure to the virus because of their mobility, as the pandemic progressed, they also had greater access to mitigation and treatment. While Rikers was hit the hardest, by late April, twenty-three state prisons had recorded at least one positive case, with the biggest outbreaks developing at Fishkill, with seventy-four positive cases out of ninety people tested by May 1, and Sing Sing, with forty-four positives out of fifty-five tested (Marshall Project, n.d.).

In the following weeks, those numbers continued to rise. Yet, due to the almost complete lack of tests available to people locked up, official numbers hardly reflected the magnitude of the contagion inside prisons and jails. At Eastern, which officially was recording only fifteen cases as of May 1, Nicholas said tests were only available for those who were so sick that they had to be hospitalized: "Individuals would request testing, but [staff] would refuse, saying that the only people who are receiving testing are people who are suffering significantly from symptoms that require hospitalization. So, you could literally be going through COVID-like symptoms, and unless you needed to be hospitalized because of those symptoms, you know, you were not going to get tested, because it was only being provided outside of the facility in hospitals, you know. So, there was absolutely no testing going on within the prison."

Similarly, Dan, who, like Marcus, was incarcerated at Wallkill Correctional Facility when the pandemic first hit, reported that it was also virtually impossible for prisoners there to get tested. On May 5, according to DOCCS official reports, only one individual had contracted the virus and tested positive at Wallkill since the beginning of the crisis. From the inside, Dan found that hard to believe:

> Personally, I believe COVID was in there for a while before they actually had positive tests. Because we were—my whole dorm on CD2—was getting sick. We were laid up in our beds for weeks. And we kept going down to sick hall, and they just kept turning us away. And they pretty much just

[told us] to "stay strong" kind of thing. One of my boys, he was laid up in bed for two weeks. He couldn't even—the only time he left his cell was to go to the bathroom. Other than that, I had to make him food and bring him water every night, because he just couldn't move. Like all the statistics and stuff on their website of how many people are testing positive in all of the jails, it just wasn't adding up. Because my family was telling me that there was only a few people here, a few people there, and we were seeing as many people getting shipped out [in ambulances].

There was nothing surprising about jails and prisons in New York, and around the country, turning into major hot spots of infection from COVID-19. With incarcerated people living in close confinement, sharing toilets and showers, and typically sitting shoulder-to-shoulder in mess halls, social distancing was just not an option, despite assurances to the contrary on the part of DOCCS officials. Under such conditions, prison facilities were bound to become epicenters of virus transmission, as public health experts had warned early on in the crisis (Pauly 2020).

That was what Karl, among others, experienced firsthand at Otisville Correctional Facility during the spring of 2020. A medium-security facility located in Orange County, New York, Otisville is known for housing a large population of elderly prisoners, who were likely to have multiple chronic health issues.[3] Karl—who at the time was in his late forties and had only a few more months to go before his release—was friendly with several of the "old-timers" at Otisville. During those months, Karl said, older prisoners were often among the most zealous in trying to protect themselves against contracting COVID: they would try their best to maintain some distance from other prisoners and used the bleach provided by the facility to clean up common areas. Yet, Karl continued, everybody at Otisville remained exposed to infection, no matter what they did:

In Otisville, there are no cells. It's a dorm setting. You have multiple people living right next to each other. Sometimes there are small barriers between the beds, but it's not really a full barrier. It's not like you're closed in a room from each other. I was on the south side, in one of the middle dorms, and we had double bunks. There was no real social distancing. It was kind of hard to do that, and being that we lived in the same dorm together, we were treated like almost we lived in the same house, almost as if you were with your family. Some people stayed in their cubes. There were certain people who tried to socially distance on their own. But then most of the times, we live in the same room, so how can we social distance? Like, okay, we don't sit at the table in the dayroom together, but when I go back to my cube, you're right there. You cough, you sneeze, you fart, I smell it. What real social distancing can you do?

Many of our participants reported similar stories about the futility of social distancing, as well as other measures aimed at minimizing transmission of the disease inside prisons. Several people, for instance, recounted how facilities were rarely able to effectively quarantine those who had been exposed to the virus; rather, what prison administrations called "quarantining" often entailed shuffling asymptomatic people around, thus running the risk of further accelerating the spread of the virus. Both Marcus and Dan told us about an episode that happened at Wallkill at the beginning of April: after an outbreak in one of the housing units, the superintendent ordered moving those who were not sick out of that dorm and into other sections of the prison. "That almost created a commotion among the inmates who were on the other side of the prison," Marcus explained, as individuals were fearful of infection.

In addition to being forced to live in close quarters, incarcerated people were left without basic personal protective equipment throughout most of the first wave of infections. During the early months of the pandemic, not only tests but also face masks and hand sanitizer—which prisoners in New York produced for the general public (Farzan 2020)—were hard to come by in most facilities, when they were not banned altogether. Karl, for instance, recounted how prisoners at Otisville had initially been forbidden to wear face masks, after they had started to tie state-issued handkerchiefs around their faces (Blau 2020). Once that restriction was finally dropped, the facility still would not hand out more than two handkerchiefs per person, while prohibiting families and external organizations from donating masks to the incarcerated population (Mehta 2021). It was not until mid-May, for instance, that people at Green Haven Correctional Facility, the maximum-security facility where Robert was serving the last year of his sentence, finally received surgical masks.

After the numbers of new COVID infections in New York prison facilities reached their apex during the week of April 22, they began to decline steadily, reaching their lowest point in early June 2020. Almost five months after being suspended, in-person visits finally resumed in all state prisons on August 8, 2020. During those summer months, however, little was accomplished to prepare facilities to deal with what was a likely resurgence of the pandemic in the coming months. When new cases started to rapidly climb again in mid-October, neither social distancing nor the prisons' quarantine protocols had gotten any better at stopping the spread of the virus. Karl, for instance, recounted witnessing the same faulty quarantine protocols he experienced at Otisville and Gowanda Correctional Facility, where he had been transferred on September 30, 2020. On December 30, 2020, in-person visits were shut down again in all prison facilities. As in the previous spring, that measure did little to stop the spread of infections, which peaked over a month later, in February 2021.

"Not a Place to Get Sick": Medical Care inside New York Prisons

In the spring of 2020, incarcerated New Yorkers not only were facing a higher risk of infection than the general population but were also more vulnerable to developing severe COVID-19, due to the higher incidence of underlying illnesses, such as diabetes, cardiovascular diseases, and substance use disorders, among the incarcerated (Binswanger, Krueger, and Steiner, 2009). Research has long shown how mass incarceration in the United States functions as yet another negative structural determinant of health, including mental health, in marginalized communities and in communities of color in particular (Bowleg 2020). For those who get caught in the criminal legal system, what are often preexisting poor health conditions deteriorate further, as people lack access to adequate medical care and even to nutritious and healthy food during incarceration (Impact Justice, n.d.).

The chronic stress of carceral life, lack of access to healthy and nourishing food, and neglect from medical staff all contributed to worsen Robert's and Josh's health conditions. Both were released in the winter of 2022, after serving over three decades in New York prisons. Robert, who was in his late sixties at the time of the interview, was suffering from multiple chronic conditions, including diabetes and hypertension. Josh was in his seventies by the time he came home and was dealing with the consequences of glaucoma, which had left him partially blind. In their interviews, the two men described what it was like to seek medical care inside prison, even before the pandemic. In most facilities, Josh explained, a nurse was only available some days during the week, usually just a few hours in the morning; to be seen, one had to sign up the night before for "sick call," which sometimes would take place as early as four or five a.m.

> [To see the nurse] you got to put up a "sick call" slip the night before, and you got to pray that the midnight officer picks it up and brings it to the clinic. Sick call is on Monday, Tuesday, Thursday, and Friday, so if you are dying on Wednesday, Saturday, or Sunday, well, you better be really dying, because if you put in for a medical emergency sick call, and the nurse doesn't think it is an emergency, they are going to write you up. You can even get a five-dollar ticket. One day, I was in Otisville, I don't know what it was, but I started to get spots all over my legs, and they started to actually bleed. So, I go to my officer, and I am like, "Listen, man, I want to go to sick call." So, it was on a Tuesday night, and I am listening to him on the phone talking to the nurse: "Is this really an emergency?" And I am saying, "Yes, I want to be seen." So, I went up there, and she was like, "Oh, this is just a rash. It could have waited until the morning." I got a five-dollar ticket for that and fifteen days loss of commissary.

Similarly, Robert told us about the challenges he faced every time he needed to see an outside specialist for his diabetes, which had become more severe starting in the early 2000s; even when he managed to see a specialist, Robert continued, more often than not, prison health staff would not follow through with whatever the outside doctor had recommended for him: "The biggest problem inside prison is that everything is, 'Here's ibuprofen,' 'Here's the Tylenol pill,' or, you know, "a Benadryl." It's never, 'Let me send you out to see an outside doctor.' And even when they're sending you to a specialist, and then the specialist will recommend them to do something, they are not doing it." Between the substandard care that was provided by the prison medical system and the unhealthy food that Robert was forced to eat, his health deteriorated rapidly: "I was thirty years old when I went in. By the time I got to be forty-five, I was having all kinds of problems: hypertension, prediabetes, arthritis in this joint, that joint. By the time I was fifty-five, I was screwed."

Once the pandemic hit, this same system, which was already failing to address even urgent care needs of the prison population, was suddenly tasked with dealing with an unprecedented medical crisis. In a way, Josh and Robert explained, the system simply continued to operate like it always did: "as a Band-Aid fix," as Robert put it. Several of our participants recounted receiving insufficient care, or being refused medical attention altogether, after developing COVID-like symptoms. Both Robert and Karl, for instance, recounted how no doctor ever visited symptomatic individuals who had been quarantined at Green Haven and Otisville during the early months of the pandemic. While Karl had relatively mild symptoms, he explained, some of those who had been quarantined with him were visibly sick: "They were vomiting, going to the bathroom on themselves, couldn't even get up out of the bed to use the bathroom. That's how sick they were." Still, he continued, "the most that health staff would do was to come and take your temperature, and if you said you had a headache, they would give you some Tylenol. That was the extent of the care you got."

While Josh never contracted COVID, he said the lapse in medical care he experienced during the last year of his incarceration had a severe impact on his health. If the spring of 2020 represented a challenging time for all New Yorkers seeking health-care services—with hospital systems scrambling to keep up with COVID-19 patients—for incarcerated individuals, including those with chronic health conditions like Josh and Robert, medical care became virtually inaccessible. "From 2011 to 2020, I had been going out of the prison for treatment for my eye," said Josh, "then, all of a sudden, it stopped": "I was going every three months to check the visual fields and stuff like that, because I have glaucoma, and every once in a while, he was giving me a shot and special drops for my eye, but it all stopped. When I came home [in February 2022], I was going blind in my right eye. I lost 90 percent of vision. I had to get surgery for both my eyes. And the doctor was like, 'If they had continued the treatment, you could have saved the eye. Now you are lucky if you've got another four or five years.'" Since coming home, both men had been trying to make up for decades of poor medical care, unhealthy living conditions, and low-quality food, all of which had become even worse during the last stretch of their incarceration due to the disruptions caused by COVID. For Josh, that meant spending most of his time at doctors' appointments: "I went to so many doctor's appointments in this last year that I can't go to the doctor until April because my insurance won't pay for it. I'm serious. If I show you the schedule of doctors I went to, it's, like, ridiculous. And it's just, like, you know, more medications. I'm on so much medication now. It's, like, pathetic. It really is. And it's, like, 'Why couldn't I get that care in there when I'm under your care and custody?'" Robert, for his part, was grateful to finally have full control of his own diet: eating healthy and regular physical exercise was how he was trying to keep his diabetes under control.

Contradictions of Carceral Care

Beyond the organizational features of prison life, it was the intrinsic logic of carceral governance that made it all but impossible for incarcerated people to receive authentic care during the COVID-19 pandemic. As many of our interviewees told us, this health crisis did not radically transform but rather reinforced carceral practices of oppression and dehumanization. Sociologists have long documented how dehumanization is central to the functioning of the modern prison. In Erving Goffman's (1961) classic work on the prison as a "total institution," for instance, he shows how prison practices—starting with degrading admission rituals—are designed to corrode an individual's sense of moral worth. In a period of crisis or disaster, Brittany Friedman (2021) has pointed out, such institutional design promotes institutional rather than human survival, with security functions superseding obligations of care. Such foundational investment in a politics of (racialized) disposability sets the prison aside from other congregate settings, such as shelters (Bhaman, chapter 3 in this volume), nursing homes, and housing for disabled adults (Ginsburg and Rapp, chapter 7 in this volume). As a result, during a global pandemic, we see carceral logics supplanting even public health common sense and ultimately informing how prison facilities in New York, and across the US, responded to the COVID-19 crisis.

Several of our interviewees described, for instance, what medical quarantine looked like in New York prisons and jails. When Karl fell sick with COVID-19 in April 2020, during the first wave of infections at Otisville Correctional Facility, he was quarantined under conditions that he described as closely resembling those of solitary confinement:

> I woke up one night with a fever, chills. I was hot one minute, cold the next. So, I went to sick call that morning. They took my temperature. I had 106 temperature. They quarantined me right away, but where they quarantined me was the problem. [They put me] in their box. The room had the old toilet and sink together, but it looked like it hadn't been cleaned or maintained as it should. It was horrible. The windowsill was full of dirt, garbage, and debris. It was unhygienic. It was dirty. . . . I had limited access to shower, because it depended on which officer was working. They treated us like we were in trouble, and we were in the box. We had no access to hot water. We could not make soup, tea, or coffee, because you had to depend on the officer to bring you a bowl or a cup of hot water. And if they felt like it, they brought it, but they usually didn't get it. Most officers treated us like we were in trouble and being punished. We were sick.

The use of Special Housing Units (SHU) cells and protocols in lieu of medical quarantine was not limited to Otisville Correctional Facility: several of our interviewees, for instance, reported that during the early months of the pandemic, prisoners who contracted COVID-19 were being transferred to Fishkill's disciplinary segregation unit, known as S-Block.

Even when COVID health measures were finally put in place, our participants told us, they were often applied in such a way that made clear that their primary purpose was not to promote the safety or well-being of the incarcerated population but rather to further discipline and harass prisoners (Blackwell 2020). Karl recounted how social-distancing rules in the mess hall quickly turned into a "tactic to harass people." At Otisville, he said, nobody was taking the temperatures of people coming into the mess hall, corrections officers often failed to wear their masks, and several "civilians" routinely came to work with flu-like symptoms. Yet, officers were quick to jump on prisoners for not respecting social distance while waiting in line to get their food or for sitting too close to each other at dining tables. Other participants reported how rules around masking were similarly being weaponized against them, with officers threatening to write up prisoners who did not wear their masks correctly.

None of that felt particularly surprising or new to Robert, who had already served over three decades in prison when COVID hit. That is just the "upstate culture," he said: "In all the facilities I have been in, for the most part, that's the culture. Prisoners are treated as less than human. So COVID is just something new that they are now able to hold over the prison population's head. That never fails to happen, you know, that we have something that is out of our control that is used against us. It's leverage."

The health emergency was used as "leverage" not just against imprisoned people but also against their families and loved ones. When visits finally resumed in New York State in the spring of 2021, after facilities shut down again in the midst of the second wave of infections, families faced a new array of requirements to be able to see their incarcerated loved ones. Erika—who at least once a week drove almost three hours from her apartment in Brooklyn to visit her husband at Eastern Correctional Facility—said she saw no problem with rules such as required COVID testing and universal masking, and she was happy to comply with them to keep her husband and his fellow prisoners safe. Other rules, however, seemed to have been put in place just to harass them and to give officers new excuses to control people during visits. Among those, Erika said, was the rule prohibiting any physical contact between incarcerated people and their loved ones during visits, besides a "brief embrace" at the beginning and the end of the encounter. In New York facilities, the rule was still in place in the early spring of 2022, when we met Erika:

> Imagine seeing someone that you love, that you haven't seen in a long time, and you can't even touch them. I haven't kissed my husband in over two years now. To me, that's not fair, because the guards inside, they walk around with no mask, they pat down my husband, so they get to touch him. And me, I can't even touch his finger—and I take a COVID test every time before going in for a visit—because they will end the visit, they will put him in quarantine, and they will give him a tier-three ticket or something.

Conclusion

The New York prison system, as our chapter has shown, was woefully unprepared to face the COVID-19 pandemic. Incarcerated people not only were forced to live in close quarters, with no way of practicing effective social distancing, but were also often denied necessary medical care, as well as access to personal protective equipment such as surgical masks and hand sanitizer. In the prison, moreover, even provisions ostensibly aimed at protecting prisoners' safety and health collided with practices and discourses of punishment and dehumanization. Under such conditions, those who were at higher risks of developing serious symptoms from COVID-19—due to disability, chronic health conditions, or old age—were left defenseless against infection and illness.

While our interviewees denounced the extraordinary conditions they faced during the COVID-19 crisis, most also emphasized how the neglect and abandonment they experienced was nothing new to them. As Robert put it, "Prison was still prison. The oppression continued." Even as COVID has largely receded in prisons and jails throughout New York State, incarcerated people are still forced to endure debilitating conditions with long-term impacts on their health. What is clear is that the COVID-19 pandemic did not transform but rather reinforced logics of carceral control, ultimately intensifying the entanglement of imprisonment, disability, and chronic illness amid the ongoing US carceral crisis.

NOTES

1   All names have been changed to protect the privacy of research participants.
2   Acting Commissioner Annucci officially retired from his role in August 2023 and was succeeded by Acting Commissioner Daniel F. Martuscello III.
3   Otisville has one of the lowest security classifications among medium-security facilities in New York State. Due to this, prisoners serving lengthy sentences are often moved to Otisville as a reward for "good behavior," which has resulted in a large elderly population at the facility.

REFERENCES

Binswanger, I. A., P. M. Krueger, and J. F. Steiner. 2009. "Prevalence of Chronic Medical Conditions among Jail and Prison Inmates in the USA Compared with General Population." *Journal of Epidemiology and Community Health* 63 (11): 912–19.

Blackwell, Christopher. 2020. "In Prison, Even Social Distancing Rules Get Weaponized." Marshall Project, May 28, 2020. www.themarshallproject.org.

Blau, Reuven. 2020. "State Prisoners Punished for Wearing Masks as City Jails OK Them." *The City*, April 3, 2020. www.thecity.nyc.

Bowleg, Lisa. 2020. "Reframing Mass Incarceration as a Social-Structural Driver of Health Inequity" *American Journal of Public Health* 110 (S1): S11–S12. https://doi.org/10.2105/AJPH.2019.305464.

Brown, Alleen. 2020. "Inside Rikers: An Account of the Virus-Stricken Jail from a Man Who Got Out." *The Intercept*, April 21, 2020. https://theintercept.com.

Cheney-Rice, Zak. 2020. "Rikers Reports Its First COVID-Related Prisoner Death." *New York*, April 6, 2020. https://nymag.com.

Correctional Association of New York (CANY). 2022. *"My Greatest Fear Is to Be a Lab Rat for the State": COVID-19 and Vaccine Hesitancy in New York State Prisons.* New York: CANY.

Farzan, Antonia Noori. 2020. "Inmates Are Manufacturing Hand Sanitizer to Help Fight Coronavirus. But Will They Be Allowed to Use It?" *Washington Post*, March 10, 2020. www.washingtonpost.com.

Friedman, Brittany. 2021. "Toward a Critical Race Theory of Prison Order in the Wake of COVID-19 and Its Afterlives: When Disaster Collides with Institutional Death by Design." *Sociological Perspectives* 64 (5): 689–705. https://doi.org/10.1177/07311214211005485.

Friedner, Michele. 2021. "Deaf and Incarcerated in the U.S." Sapiens, June 15, 2021. www.sapiens.org.

Goffman, Erving. 1961. *Asylums: Essays on the Social Situation of Mental Patients and Other Inmates.* New York: Anchor/Doubleday.

Goodman, Amy. 2020. "The Case for Prison Abolition: Ruth Wilson Gilmore on COVID-19, Racial Capitalism & Decarceration." Democracy Now!, May 5, 2020. www.democracynow.org.

Impact Justice. N.d. "Food in Prison." Accessed December 11, 2022. https://impactjustice.org.

Marshall Project. N.d. "A State by State Look at 15 Months of Coronavirus in Prison." Accessed December 11, 2022. www.themarshallproject.org.

Mehta, Akash. 2021. "How New York State Let Covid-19 Run Rampant in Prisons." *The Nation*, May 24, 2021. www.thenation.com.

Muhammad, Khalil Gibran. 2019. *The Condemnation of Blackness: Race, Crime, and the Making of Modern Urban America.* 2nd ed. Cambridge, MA: Harvard University Press.

Oberholtzer, Elliot. 2017. "Police, Courts, Jails, and Prisons All Fail Disabled People." *Briefings* (blog), Prison Policy Initiative, August 23, 2017. www.prisonpolicy.org.

Pauly, Madison. 2020. "To Arrest the Spread of the Coronavirus, Arrest Fewer People." *Mother Jones*, March 12, 2020. www.motherjones.com.

Sawyer, Kevin D. 2022. "Summer of Blood: Voyage Through San Quentin State Prison's COVID-19 Outbreak." *N.Y.U. Review of Law & Social Change* 46. https://socialchangenyu.com.

Sugie, Naomi F., Kristin Turney, Keramet Reiter, Rebecca Tublitz, Daniela Kaiser, Rebecca Goodsell, Erin Secrist, Ankita Patil, and Monik Jiménez. 2023. "Excess Mortality in U.S. Prisons during the COVID-19 Pandemic." *Science Advances* 9 (48), December 1. https://www.science.org/doi/10.1126/sciadv.adj8104

UCLA Law COVID Behind Bars Data Project. n.d. "New York." Accessed December 11, 2022. https://uclacovidbehindbars.org.

2

Second-Class Noncitizens

The Impact of the COVID-19 Pandemic on Immigrants with Disabilities in New York City

J.C. SALYER

The COVID-19 Pandemic in New York City

New York City has long been considered a "global city" (Sassen 2001), defined by an economic and social cosmopolitanism in which residents (human and corporate) consider national citizenship secondary to both local and transnational relationships. New York City is "America's quintessential immigrant city," with over a third of its residents being immigrants from a remarkable array of countries, meaning that cultural diversity is recognized and celebrated in both political and social discourse (Foner 2013, 1). Compared to the rest of the United States, New York City is extraordinarily demographically diverse; for instance, the city has the largest population of people identifying as Black or African American, the largest Chinese population, and the largest LGBTQ population (Legal Services NYC 2016; Moslimani et al. 2023; Rosenbloom and Batalova 2023).

At the same time, the lived experience of New Yorkers is defined by sharp inequality across numerous intersectional axes. Overall, New York City has a higher poverty rate than the nation as a whole (17.9 percent versus 12.8 percent in 2021; NYC Department of City Planning 2022, 9), and the poverty rate for disabled New York City residents is more than double that of nondisabled New Yorkers (Dooha 2015). Moreover, given the high cost of living in New York City, the federal poverty line actually significantly undercounts the number of New Yorkers facing economic precarity (Legal Services NYC 2016, 7). These inequalities are starkly visible along racial lines, with white households having an average income of $98,200 in 2021, compared to Black and Hispanic households that had average household incomes of $52,900 and $48,100, respectively (NYC Department of City Planning 2022, 8). During the COVID-19 pandemic, these preexisting inequalities resulted in significantly greater vulnerability, morbidity, and mortality for marginalized people. For instance, during the first wave of the pandemic, Black and Latino/a New Yorkers died from COVID-19 at twice the rate of white New Yorkers (Barranco, Holtgrave, and Rosenberg 2020, 2). For disabled immigrants in New York City, their intersectional position during the pandemic made them vulnerable to both ableist and xenophobic structures and policies that resulted in unique challenges, risks, and harms.

During the COVID-19 pandemic, the ableism inherent in immigration law and policy caused serious harm to disabled immigrants in two main areas that were already present in pre-pandemic policies and actions but became critical issues when combined with the threats and disruptions of the pandemic. First, disabled immigrants have suffered from an inability to access adequate government benefits and social support because of policies rooted in assumptions about both immigrants and disabled people being burdens on US society and taxpayers. Second, medically vulnerable people in immigration detention faced life-threatening neglect and indifference as they experienced the COVID-19 pandemic in overcrowded and inhuman detention centers. Paradoxically, the harm experienced by disabled people in the first instance comes from overly fixating on the existence of a disability as the essential feature that defines everything about a person's perceived worth, whereas the harm in the detention context stems from utterly ignoring a person's disability and not understanding that in some situations, a person's disability must be accounted for if they are to have an equal opportunity to thrive—or even just survive. Both of these experiences, however, are rooted in an ideology of ableism that sees nondisabled people as the societal norm and fails to afford rights or consideration to individuals seen as deviating from that norm. For disabled immigrants, this situation is compounded by a system that predicates equal legal and social inclusion on citizenship.

Ableism in Immigration Law and Policy

Discrimination against immigrants who are seen as not "able-bodied" goes back to the beginning of federal laws regulating admission to the United States, with the Immigration Act of 1882 denying admission to "any convict, lunatic, idiot, or any person unable to take care of himself or herself without becoming a public charge." These restrictions were enforced, as immigrants traveling through Ellis Island would undergo scrutiny for any sign of physical or mental disability that would result in their deportation, and immigration "inspectors prided themselves on their ability to make a 'snapshot diagnosis' as immigrants streamed past them single file" (Baynton 2005, 37; see also Bateman-House and Fairchild 2008). By the early twentieth century, US immigration law had expanded overt prohibitions on disabled persons to the point where the commissioner general of immigration, in his 1907 report, stated, "the exclusion from this country of the morally, mentally, and physically deficient is the principal object to be accomplished by the immigration laws" (quoted in Baynton 2005, 34). As a result, the number of would-be immigrants deported based on "likely to become a public charge" grounds or because of mental or physical disabilities increased from 1,720 in 1895 to more than 8,000 in 1905 to more than 16,000 by 1910 (Fox and Marini 2018, 6). Immigration law continued to be more restrictionist and embraced eugenical theories, causing Adolf Hitler, in *Mein Kampf*, to praise US immigration laws as a model for German nationality law, because "the American Union categorically refuses the immigration of physically unhealthy elements, and simply excludes the immigration of certain races" (quoted in Whitman 2017, 46). While other de jure discriminatory provisions of immigration law, such as restrictionist racial quotas, have been removed from the Immigration and Nationality Act, overt discrimination against disabled people remains central to questions of whose body is worthy of joining the nation's body politic. As a result, immigration law is explicitly ableist in its valuation and treatment of individuals in ways that defy the progress in gaining rights and changing attitudes that disabled people have achieved in other areas of law and society.

The Public Charge, Welfare Reform, and the Fear of Receiving Assistance

Noncitizens in the United States, even those with a lawful immigration status, are not on an equal footing with US citizens when it comes to accessing health-care benefits and social welfare benefits. The two main limits come from the concept of "public charge" in immigration law, which makes anyone "likely at any time to become a public charge" inadmissible, and from the Personal Responsibility and Work Opportunity Reconciliation Act of 1996 (the so-called Welfare Reform Act), which withdrew nearly all social welfare benefits from undocumented immigrants and severely limited benefits for lawful permanent residents for the first five years they are in the United States.[1] As a result of these policies, many disabled immigrants do not have access to or are afraid to access public benefits, assistance, and health care, which resulted in heightened risks and hardships during the COVID-19 pandemic.

This situation was made worse by drastic changes that the Trump administration made to the public charge rule in 2019. For decades the application of the public charge rule was limited to individuals dependent on cash welfare benefits for subsistence or individuals who experience long-term institutionalization at public expense.[2] In August 2019, this limited application of the public charge rule was overturned by a new rule from the Trump administration that expanded the meaning of public charge to also include receipt of most noncash benefits such as the Supplemental Nutrition Assistance Program (SNAP), Temporary Assistance for Needy Families (TANF), Supplemental Security Income (SSI), housing assistance (including Section 8), and most Medicaid benefits. The new rule "was the most expansive iteration of the public charge rule since its inception in 1882" (Rosales 2021, 1621). In defense of the new rule, the acting director of the United States Citizenship and Immigration Services, Ken Cuccinelli, turned Emma Lazarus's famous poem "The New Colossus" into blatantly ableist doggerel, saying, "give me your tired and your poor who can stand on their own two feet and who will not become a public charge" (quoted in Rosales 2021, 1616).[3]

Many immigrants either have been excluded from accessing health-care benefits by the Welfare Reform Act or are afraid that accepting health-care benefits will result in negative immigration consequences under the public charge rule. Moreover, prior to the pandemic, the Trump administration had broadened the scope of immigration enforcement by instituting a policy that directed Immigration and Customs Enforcement (ICE) officers to "take enforcement action against all removable aliens encountered in the course of their duties" (Albence 2017, 1). This was compounded by the fact that, under the Trump administration, ICE disregarded established policy that generally prohibited making immigration arrests in "sensitive locations" such as hospitals and schools. In one well-publicized case in Texas, immigration officers stopped an ambulance carrying a ten-year-old girl with cerebral palsy on the way to a hospital for an operation, waited outside the girl's room, and took her into custody when she was discharged from the hospital (Burnett 2017). Thus, the environment for many disabled immigrants at the beginning of the COVID-19 pandemic was one of social exclusion and fear of immigration enforcement.

Inadequate and Unequal Support of Disabled New Yorkers during the COVID-19 Pandemic

A study of the experience of immigrant families in New York City who have a disabled child looked at the difficulties they experienced during the COVID-19 pandemic and shows how the challenges of immigration status interacted with the challenges of disability to exacerbate the hardships of the pandemic (Rodriguez and McGrath 2021). The fear of deportation leads to a fear of accessing services and parents tolerating unsafe working conditions, with some parents being hospitalized with COVID-19 as a result (Rodriguez and McGrath 2021, 80).

Families also experienced intersectional discrimination in medical and educational environments in the form of language barriers, medical professionals who were not trained to treat persons with intellectual and developmental disabilities (IDD), and overt anti-immigrant discrimination. The families experienced material hardship with regard to access to food, health insurance, and housing and were unable to access assistance because of a combination of disqualifications under the Welfare Reform Act and not seeking assistance because of a fear of deportation or running afoul of the public charge rule (Rodriguez and

McGrath 2021, 80–81). Additionally, the challenges of online education were exacerbated by lack of access to computers and the internet, language barriers, and the difficulty of online education for children with IDDs. Also, because of fear of immigration consequences, families were afraid to access emergency educational services and programs (Rodriguez and McGrath 2021, 83).

Despite the limits that federal law imposes on immigrants receiving benefits, immigrants in New York City were eligible for some important assistance on the city and state level. For instance, New York State created a $2.1 billion Excluded Workers Fund to provide unemployment benefits to people excluded from other unemployment benefits or other COVID-19 pandemic benefits because of their immigration status. While the Excluded Workers Fund provided much-needed support for immigrant workers impacted by the pandemic who had been excluded under federal law, it required proof of recent previous employment and therefore would not have been available to immigrants who had not been recently employed due to a disability.[4] This is an archetypal case of intersectional discrimination, in which "those who are multiply-burdened" have "claims that cannot be understood as resulting from discrete sources of discrimination" (Crenshaw 1989, 140). While New York's program admirably recognizes the needs and contributions of undocumented immigrant workers, it is completely based on the narrative of immigrants as workers, to the exclusion of other immigrant experiences such as those who have not had wage-labor positions because of disabilities. At the same time, public benefit schemes designed to assist disabled persons are inaccessible to many disabled immigrants because of their immigration status or their fear of immigration consequences due to the public charge rule.

The barriers imposed by the Welfare Reform Act, the chilling effect of the public charge rule, and fear from the increase in immigration enforcement activities resulted in substantial barriers for noncitizens, including disabled noncitizens, to accessing necessary services including medical care during the COVID-19 pandemic (see Ross, Diaz, and Starrels 2020). As noted by doctors working with immigrant communities in the Bronx, "even with substantial symptoms of COVID-19, patients also fear immigration-related consequences of going to the hospital" (Ross, Diaz, and Starrels 2020, 1043).

A Pandemic on Top of a Human Rights Catastrophe: COVID-19 in Immigration Detention

During the first wave of the COVID-19 pandemic in New York City, virtually everyone faced some level of fear and anxiety regarding how to stay safe from the virus's spread. While disruption and some level of risk were universal, it quickly became clear that mortality and morbidity were deeply impacted by preexisting medical vulnerabilities as well as political, social, and economic contexts, such as racism and poverty. For instance, the Black, Brown, and immigrant neighborhoods in the Bronx and central Queens had some of the highest rates of COVID-19 diagnoses and death because of a combination of high rates of COVID-19 comorbidities, disproportionate representation in the public-facing "essential worker" service jobs, and socioeconomic disadvantages in such areas as adequate housing and access to health services (Correal, Jacobs, and Jones 2020; Rodriguez and McGrath 2021; Ross, Diaz, and Starrels 2020). For noncitizen detainees in immigration detention facilities, however, the structural inequalities of the COVID-19 pandemic's impacts were particularly severe, because they were entirely dependent on their warders to take steps to provide a safe environment but, in practice, faced inadequate and indifferent efforts to protect their well-being. For disabled and medically vulnerable detainees, the COVID-19 pandemic made the already overcrowded, unsanitary, and abusive environment of detention facilities potentially life threatening.

Even before the COVID-19 pandemic, immigration detention endangered the health and safety of detainees, and cases of abuse and neglect of detainees with serious medical conditions were well documented (Texas Appleseed 2010; American Civil Liberties Union et al. 2016). A 2017 report be New York Lawyers in the Public Interest (NYLPI 2017), looking at medical and health services at New York City–area immigration detention facilities, found inadequate assessment of detainees' medical needs, a failure to continue predetention medical treatments (such as dialysis and blood transfusions), life-threatening delays in treatment, inadequate management of pain and chronic illness, failure to provide necessary off-site specialized care, and inadequate treatment of mental health issues. The pandemic exacerbated the situation for individuals in detention, particularly for individuals with medical vulnerabilities, who faced a lack of access to personal protective equipment (PPE) such as masks, a lack of regular access to hand sanitizer or soap, a complete inability to socially distance, inadequate testing and quarantine procedures, inadequate provision of vaccinations and boosters, and a lack of appropriate medical care for individuals diagnosed with COVID-19 (NYLPI 2020; Parra 2022). One doctor working with the Medical Providers Network of NYLPI said, "one would be hard-pressed to think of a more effective means for the spread of COVID-19 infection than immigration detention" (NYLPI 2020, 3). One study looking at deaths in immigration detention between 2018 and 2020 concluded that "the death rate among individuals in ICE detention has increased seven-fold between FY2019 and FY2020 amidst the COVID-19 pandemic" and that "COVID-19 has emerged as an important cause of mortality, responsible for nearly three quarters of deaths among individuals in ICE detention since April of 2020" (Terp et al. 2021, 86).

The COVID-19 public health crisis in immigration detention has taken place within the context of a multidecade shift toward more punitive immigration law, policy, and ideology that has included a massive increase in detention as a part of its immigration enforcement strategy. Two statutes passed in 1996, the Antiterrorism and Effective Death Penalty Act (AEDPA) and the Illegal Immigration Reform and Immigrant Responsibility Act (IIRIRA), increased the grounds on which someone could be deported, limited forms of relief from deportation, and expanded the categories of mandatory and discretionary immigration detention. As a result of these changes, immigration detention rates have soared, with an average of 9,011 people being detained on a daily basis in 1996 (before the AEDPA and IIRIRA went into effect), compared to a daily detention rate of 50,165 people in 2019, which is an increase of over 457 percent (US Immigration and Customs Enforcement 2019, 5; Reyes 2018). In September 2019, just months before the COVID-19 pandemic, the daily population was 52,722 (Kassie 2019).[5] In practice, ICE only has direct custody of a small percentage of the tens of thousands of people in immigration detention, with the majority of detainees being held in a labyrinthine "American gulag" system (Dow 2004, 12) of detention centers owned by for-profit corporations and county jail facilities, which contract with ICE as a source of revenue for county coffers. Detainees in immigration proceedings in the New York City area have generally been held in county jails in

New York and New Jersey, as well as a private for-profit detention center in Elizabeth, New Jersey.[6] As the COVID-19 pandemic began to unfold, some of the worst conditions and experiences for medically vulnerable immigrants took place in these county jail facilities. While immigration detention is technically considered civil in nature, as opposed to criminal, and is thus supposed to be nonpunitive, in reality it is operated on a carceral model that reproduces prison-like conditions. Therefore, the conditions and hardships experienced by immigration detainees echo those documented by Tommaso Bardelli, Aiyuba Thomas, and Dylan Brown in New York jails and prisons (see chapter 2 in this volume).

Although there is no systematic tracking of the number of disabled people in the immigration enforcement system, it is clear that a significant segment of the detainee population has one or more disabilities. For instance, a 2010 Human Rights Watch report on mental disability in immigration detention estimated that at least 15 percent of migrants in detention had a mental disability (Mehta 2010, 14). These estimates are supported by the experience of advocates working with detainees in New York City–area detention centers. For instance, doctors working with the Medical Providers Network of NYLPI report schizophrenia, bipolar disorder, posttraumatic stress disorder (PTSD), anxiety, and depression as frequently identified conditions. Additionally, doctors commonly encounter chronic cardiovascular conditions, such as diabetes, hypertension, high blood pressure, and obesity; pulmonary diseases, such as asthma; and other issues such as epilepsy, HIV/AIDS, kidney diseases, and chronic pain issues (NYLPI 2021a, 2021b). For these detainees, the onset of the COVID-19 pandemic brought a number of dire issues. First, medically vulnerable people faced an overwhelming challenge trying to stay safe in overcrowded detention facilities where social distancing was impossible (Meyer et al. 2020). Second, people experienced negative consequences from having to endure even greater physical and social isolation than they had during pre-pandemic imprisonment. Finally, detainees were met with abuse and neglect when they asked for basic assistance or resources to protect themselves during the COVID-19 pandemic (Physicians for Human Rights 2021, 31).

From the beginning of the COVID-19 pandemic, it was clear that the sheer number of people having to live in the communal space of immigration detention made abiding by COVID-19 safety protocols impossible. In response, detainees, medical professionals, activists, and politicians called for ICE to exercise its discretion to release some or all immigration detainees as the best way to prevent detention centers from being major points of COVID-19 transmission and to protect medically vulnerable detainees. Nevertheless, on April 17, 2020, in the midst of the first wave of the COVID-19 pandemic, the acting director of ICE, Matthew T. Albence, stated that ICE's review of its "existing population has been completed" and that ICE had released fewer than seven hundred medically vulnerable individuals out of the thirty-two thousand detainees in custody. In defense of the decision, Albence claimed that releasing more detainees would send the message that the United States was "not enforcing our immigration laws," which would be a "huge pull factor" creating a "rush at the borders" (US House of Representatives Committee on Oversight and Reform 2020). Thus, the decision to continue mass detention during the COVID-19 pandemic was not made based on an evaluation of medical needs or public health risk but based on a political decision to continue to use detention to deter would-be migrants from attempting to come to the United States.

Immigration lawyers providing legal representation to immigrants in detention were among the first to see problems in immigration detention facilities and were among the first to raise concerns about conditions of detention as the COVID-19 pandemic began. Immigration detainees in the New York City area benefit from the New York Immigrant Family Unity Project (NYIFUP), which provides legal representation to virtually every individual who is being held in detention while facing deportation. Unlike the criminal justice system, where indigent defendants receive court-appointed legal counsel, in immigration court, there is no right to legal representation if one cannot afford to hire a lawyer or find pro bono representation. NYIFUP was created and funded by the New York City Council in 2013 as the first public-defender-style system that provides lawyers to detained low-income immigrants facing deportation (see Salyer 2020, chap. 5). NYIFUP services are provided through three of New York City's largest public defender organizations, the Legal Aid Society, the Bronx Defenders, and Brooklyn Defender Services, and it was lawyers from these organizations who did much of the advocacy to try to win the release of medically vulnerable detainees during the pandemic. While a full discussion of the legal theories and all of the court decisions regarding the need to release medically vulnerable immigration detainees due to the COVID-19 pandemic is beyond the scope of this chapter, it is important to recognize that in lawsuit after lawsuit, ICE was found to have failed to take safety precautions to control the spread of COVID-19 in detention and to have failed to identify medically vulnerable individuals who were at the highest risk from COVID-19.

For instance, *Cristian A.R. v. Decker* was a habeas corpus case brought at the beginning of April 2020 on behalf of five individuals being detained by ICE in two New Jersey county jails.[7] The detainees each had preexisting conditions that placed them at high risk for severe illness or death from COVID-19, such as diabetes, hypertension, asthma, high blood pressure, chronic hepatitis B, kidney disease, and conditions that required immune-system-suppressing medications. That case showed that ICE's responses to the threat created by COVID-19 were both inadequate and created their own hazards and hardships for detainees. In these county jails, detainees did not have adequate access to soap, hand sanitizer, and cleaning supplies, meaning that it was not possible for people to follow recommendations on hand washing or to sanitize shared spaces or items, such as toilets and telephones. Similarly, due to the inherently limited space in the jails, social distancing was not possible. Moreover, the consequences of preexisting inadequacies in the medical services available in detention were amplified and exacerbated by the COVID-19 pandemic, with requests for medical attention going unanswered for hours or days or sometimes being ignored entirely.[8]

Additionally, the protocols implemented in response to the COVID-19 pandemic also created hardships and difficulties. Many detainees endured lengthy isolation during lockdowns in which they were confined to their cells for twenty-three and a half hours a day and were unable to communicate with their families and legal representatives. Detention facilities also used solitary confinement in lieu of medical quarantining of positive or suspected cases. Such isolation was harmful to physical and mental well-being but also resulted in potentially ill detainees being cut off from medical care and observation. Because detainees were forced to eat in their cells in an attempt to social distance, overall food quality worsened, and special medically prescribed meals were not provided.

Overall, ICE's reaction to the pandemic was dictated by its ableist perspective and did not adequately consider the heightened risk that

COVID-19 posed to medically vulnerable detainees, nor did it consider the harm that lengthy lockdowns and isolation were causing mentally and emotionally disabled detainees. As a result, one study found that "in 2020, the suicide rate increased 11.0 times the prior 10-year average to 3.4 suicides per 100,000 admissions" and that "there was a substantial increase in suicides inside ICE detention" in 2020 (Parra 2021, 419). Given ICE's lack of attention to the needs of medically vulnerable immigration detainees, scores of courts intervened and ordered the release of medically vulnerable detainees. For instance, the judge in *Cristian A.R. v. Decker* ordered the five detainees released on bond because they were "vulnerable to severe complications and death if they contract COVID-19 and are incarcerated in Facilities at the epicenter of the outbreak where they cannot practically adhere to social distancing guidelines or the adequate level of personal hygiene to stop the spread of the virus."[9]

Applying a Disability Justice Lens to Immigration Law

While we should certainly celebrate the individual court decisions, such as *Cristian A.R. v. Decker*, that have collectively resulted in the release of hundreds of medically vulnerable detainees, this final section briefly argues that in addition to these sorts of case-by-case interventions on behalf of individuals who are at personal risk, advocacy should also subject immigration law and immigration detention to critique through a disability justice lens. Among other things, the disability justice framework demands that we attend to the intersectional identities of disabled persons and recognize that a purely individual-rights-based advocacy has historically failed to incorporate the needs and perspectives of disabled people with multiple marginalized identities (Berne 2015). Disability justice perspectives also recognize the role of ableism as the "root of disability oppression" (Sins Invalid 2019, 15). Both in the realm of access to social benefits and in the realm of immigration detention, the hardships visited on disabled immigrants come from seeing disabled persons as deviations from the social norm and therefore concluding that their needs and experiences are not relevant or worthy of consideration. The experience of disabled immigrants during the COVID-19 pandemic demonstrates the need for a social model of disability with sufficient acuity to refute the threats and challenges that emanate from immigration law's ideology of ableism. For instance, the experiences of families who have disabled children show how the difficulties of the pandemic were multiplied exponentially by long-standing policies that vilified immigrants who cannot "stand on their own two feet," such that families were denied access to health care, as well as assistance with food, housing, and education, that would have been available to them had they not been afraid of immigration enforcement because of their position at the intersection of two distinct axes of inequality. Understanding that the options and experiences of those families are dictated as much by social and political factors as they are by health or medical factors destabilizes the ableist narrative that disabled immigrants are likely to become a public charge because of some inherent defect, which is the narrative that has motivated discrimination against disabled immigrants since the Immigration Act of 1882.

In the case of the immigration detention system, the existence of disabled detainees is largely ignored, and their needs and accommodations are generally unmet. Since 1996, immigration detention has grown exponentially, has become more carceral in nature, and is seen as requiring conditions harsh enough to deter future would-be immigrants from attempting to enter the United States. With regard to detention conditions, this takes the form of overcrowding, substandard food, deficient medical care, and abusive treatment. For disabled immigrants, this "bare life" (Agamben 1998) indifference to human well-being can mean life-threatening aggravation of conditions like diabetes, high blood pleasure, and hypertension; denial of necessary medicines, treatments, and mobility devices or corrective devices; and triggering of PTSD, mental health crises, and even self-harm. Some disabled detainees in the New York City area, with the aid of NYIFUP lawyers, were able to show that the addition of the dangers and hardships of the COVID-19 pandemic into this already punitive environment was more than members of this vulnerable population could reasonably be expected to endure. However, the fact that these individuals needed the extraordinary remedy of habeas corpus relief to save them is strong evidence that the immigration detention system is not suitable or safe for anyone. For each of these medically vulnerable detainees who won relief, there are thousands of people still in detention who were not seen as sufficiently medically vulnerable or who did not have access to legal assistance or who were not in a physical or psychological state to advocate for themselves.

Aimi Hamraie notes in her book examining and critiquing the concept of "Universal Design" that "disability justice resembles Universal Design's early theory, which stressed broad, anticipatory accessibility for the most marginalized, challenged class hierarchies and recognized the limits of formal rights regimes" (2017, 260). The concept of Universal Design was originally coined by Ronald Mace in the architectural context to mean "design of products and environments to be usable by all people, to the greatest extent possible, without the need for adaptation or specialized design" (Mace 1988, 4). Edward Steinfeld and Jordana Maisel have further explained that it is "a design process that enables and empowers a diverse population by improving human performance, health and wellness, and social participation" and that it is highly contextual, "involving continuous improvements, based on resources available, towards the ultimate goal of full inclusion" (2012, 29). In this way, both disability justice and Universal Design are both focused on systematic and structural change rather than reformism. The current immigration detention system is the antithesis of Universal Design, with outright contempt for the diversity of the humanity it imprisons and the variegated needs that this situation creates. A transformative project might start by momentarily lifting our gaze from the abomination that is the current immigration system and asking what would be a Universal Design response that demonstrates what a flexible and inclusive immigration system that promotes health, wellness, and social participation might look like.

NOTES

1 8 U.S.C. § 1182(a)(4).
2 Field Guidance on Deportability and Inadmissibility on Public Charge Grounds, 64 Fed. Reg. at 28,689 (May 26, 1999).
3 It is important to note that the Biden administration has withdrawn the Trump administration's public charge rule and reinstated the earlier, more limited interpretation of the rule. Nevertheless, the scope and application of the rule remain opaque to many immigrants who forgo benefits they and their families are entitled to and need because they fear negative immigration consequences.
4 Of course, being a disabled immigrant does not necessarily preclude employment, and, in fact, disabled immigrants are employed at higher rates than US-born disabled adults (41.1 percent versus 35.1 percent) (Echave and Gonzalez 2022, 10).
5 While the claim behind the passage of the 1996 laws was that these harsh punitive measures were needed to protect citizens from "criminal aliens," the majority of

individuals being detained and deported are not dangerous criminals. A study that looked at who was in immigration detention on the night of April 30, 2019, found that of the 49,396 people in ICE detention, only 36 percent had a criminal conviction of any kind and, of those with criminal convictions, many were minor offenses or even traffic offenses (Transactional Records Access Clearinghouse 2019).
6 Immigration detainees in New York are currently held in the Orange County Correctional Facility (OCCF), the Clinton County Jail, and the ICE-operated Buffalo (Batavia) Service Processing Center. Up until August 2021, immigration detainees were also held in four detention centers in New Jersey: the Bergen County Jail, the Essex County Jail, the Hudson County Jail, and the Elizabeth Contract Detention Center (a for-profit detention center operated by CoreCivic). In August 20, 2021, New Jersey's governor signed a law prohibiting private and public entities from making new detention contracts with ICE. Because of this law, the three county jails no longer engage in immigration detention, but a federal court enjoined the application of the law as applied to ICE's contract with the Elizabeth facility. See *CoreCivic, Inc. v. Murphy*, No. CV 23-967, 2023 U.S. Dist. LEXIS 152099, 2023 WL 5556025 (D.N.J. Aug. 29, 2023). In reaction to the New Jersey law, ICE transferred many of those New Jersey detainees to the New York detention centers in Buffalo and in Orange County.
7 453 F. Supp. 3d 670 (D.N.J. 2020).
8 One survey done between July and October 2020 found that the average time to see a medical professional was four days (Physicians for Human Rights 2021, 27).
9 453 F. Supp. 3d 670, 689 (D.N.J. 2020).

REFERENCES

Agamben, Giorgio. 1998. *Homo Sacer: Sovereign Power and Bare Life*. Stanford, CA: Stanford University Press.

Albence, Matthew T. 2017. "Implementing the President's Border Security and Interior Immigration Enforcement Policies." Memorandum from ICE executive associate director to all ERO employees. February 21, 2017.

American Civil Liberties Union, Detention Watch, Network, and Heartland Alliance's National Immigrant Justice Center. 2016. *Fatal Neglect: How ICE Ignores Deaths in Detention*. www.aclu.org.

Barranco, Meredith, David Holtgrave, and Eli Rosenberg. 2020. "Understanding and Eliminating Minority Health Disparities in a 21st-Century Pandemic." Issue Brief #1. University at Albany, SUNY, NYS COVID-19 Minority Health Disparities Team, July 2020.

Bateman-House, Alison, and Amy Fairchild. 2008. "Medical Examination of Immigrants at Ellis Island." *AMA Virtual Mentor* 10 (4): 235–41.

Baynton, Douglas C. 2005. "Defectives in the land: Disability and American immigration policy, 1882–1924." *Journal of American Ethnic History* 24 (30): 31–44.

Berne, Patty. 2015. "Disability Justice—a Working Draft." *Sins Invalid Blog*, June 10, 2015. www.sinsinvalid.org.

Burnett, John. 2017. "10-Year-Old Girl Is Detained by Border Patrol after Emergency Surgery." *All Things Considered*, National Public Radio, October 26, 2017. www.npr.org.

Correal, Annie, Andrew Jacobs, and Ryan Christopher Jones. 2020. "'A Tragedy Is Unfolding': Inside New York's Virus Epicenter." *New York Times*, April 9, 2020.

Crenshaw, Kimberlé. 1989. "Demarginalizing the Intersection of Race and Sex: A Black Feminist Critique of Antidiscrimination Doctrine, Feminist Theory and Antiracist Politics." *University of Chicago Legal Forum* 1989:139–67.

Dooha, Susan M. 2015. *ADA at 25: Many Bridges to Cross*. New York: Center for Independence of the Disabled. www.cidny.org.

Dow, Mark. 2004. *American Gulag: Inside U.S. Immigration Prisons*. Berkeley: University of California Press.

Echave, Paola, and Dulce Gonzalez. 2022. *Being an Immigrant with Disabilities: Characteristics of a Population Facing Multiple Structural Challenges*. Washington, DC: Urban Institute. www.urban.org.

Foner, Nancy. 2013. "Introduction: Immigrants in New York City in the New Millennium." In *Out of Three: Immigrant New York in the Twenty-First Century*, edited by Nancy Foner, 1–34. New York: Columbia University Press.

Fox, Danielle D., and Irmo Marini. 2018. "History of Treatment toward Persons with Disabilities in America." In *The Psychological and Social Impact of Illness and Disability*, 7th ed., edited by Irmo Marini and Mark A. Stebnicki, 3–12. New York: Springer.

Hamraie, Aimi. 2017. *Building Access: Universal Design and the Politics of Disability*. Minneapolis: University of Minnesota Press.

Kassie, Emily. 2019. "Detained: How the United States Created the Largest Immigration Detention System in the World." *The Guardian*, September 24, 2019. www.theguardian.com.

Legal Services NYC. 2016. *Poverty Is an LGBT Issue: An Assessment of the Legal Needs of Low-Income LGBT People*. New York: Legal Services NYC. www.legalservicesnyc.org.

Mace, Ronald L. 1988. *Universal Design: Housing for the Lifespan of All People*. Rockville, MD: US Department of Housing and Urban Development.

Mehta, Sarah. 2010. *Deportation by Default: Mental Disability, Unfair Hearings, and Indefinite Detention in the US Immigration System*. New York: Human Rights Watch. www.aclu.org.

Meyer, Jaimie P., Carols Franco-Paredes, Parveen Parmar, Faiza Yasin, and Matthew Gartland. 2020. "COVID-19 and the Coming Epidemic in US Immigration Detention Centres." *The Lancet: Infectious Diseases* 20:646–48.

Moslimani, Mohamad, Christine Tamir, Abby Budiman, Luis Noe-Bustamante, and Lauren Mora. 2023. "Facts about the U.S. Black Population." Pew Research Center, March 2, 2023. www.pewresearch.org.

New York Lawyers in the Public Interest. 2017. *Detained and Denied: Healthcare Access in Immigration Detention*. New York: New York Lawyers in the Public Interest. https://nylpi.org.

———. 2020. *Still Detained and Denied: Healthcare Access in Immigration Detention*. New York: New York Lawyers in the Public Interest. https://nylpi.org.

———. 2021a. *Medical Providers Network: Fall 2021 Update Report*. New York: New York Lawyers in the Public Interest. www.nylpi.org.

———. 2021b. *Spring 2021 Report of the NYLPI Medical Providers Network*. New York: New York Lawyers in the Public Interest. www.nylpi.org.

NYC Department of City Planning. 2022. "Highlights for New York City from the 2021 American Community Survey." PowerPoint presentation. New York City Department of City Planning, Population Division, December 2022. https://smedia.nyc.gov.

Parra, Daniel. 2022. "City Council Hearing Probes Conditions for ICE Detainees in New York." City Limits, February 29, 2022. https://citylimits.org.

Physicians for Human Rights. 2021. *Praying for Hand Soap and Masks: Health and Human Rights Violations in U.S. immigration Detention during the COVID-19 Pandemic*. New York: Physicians for Human Rights, January 2021. https://phr.org.

Reyes, J. Rachel. 2018. "Immigration Detention: Recent Trends and Scholarship." Virtual Brief. Center for Migration Studies, New York. http://cmsny.org.

Rodriguez, Diana, and Kathleen McGrath. 2021. "Perspectives of Immigrant Families and Persons with Disabilities during COVID-19." *Developmental Disabilities Network Journal* 1 (2): 72–90.

Rosales, Alessandra N. 2021. "Excluding 'Undesirable' Immigrants: Public Charge as Disability Discrimination." *Michigan Law Review* 119 (7): 1613–38.

Rosenbloom, Raquel, and Jeanne Batalova. 2023. "Chinese Immigrants in the United States." *Migration Information Source*, Migration Policy Institute, January 12, 2023. www.migrationpolicy.org.

Ross, Jonathan, Chanelle M. Diaz, and Joanna L. Starrels. 2020. "The Disproportionate Burden of COVID-19 for Immigrants in the Bronx, New York." *JAMA Internal Medicine* 180 (8): 1043–44.

Salyer, J. C. 2020. *Court of Injustice: Law without Recognition in U.S. Immigration*. Stanford, CA: Stanford University Press.

Sassen, Saskia. 2001. *The Global City: New York, London, Tokyo*. 2nd ed. Princeton, NJ: Princeton University Press.

Sins Invalid. 2019. *Skin Tooth and Bone: The Basis of Movement Is Our People: A Disability Justice Primer*. 2nd ed. Berkeley, CA: Sins Invalid.

Steinfeld, Edward, and Jordana Maisel. 2012. *Universal Design: Creating Inclusive Environments*. Hoboken, NJ: Wiley.

Terp, Sophie, Sameer Ahmed, Elizabeth Burner, Madeline Ross, Molly Grassini, Briah Fischer, and Parveen Parmar. 2021. "Deaths in Immigration and Customs Enforcement (ICE) Detention: FY2018–2020." *AIMS Public Health* 8 (1): 81–89.

Texas Appleseed. 2010. *Justice for Immigration's Hidden Population: Protecting the Rights of Persons with Mental Disabilities in Immigration Court and Detention System*. Austin. Texas Appleseed. www.texasappleseed.org.

Transactional Records Access Clearinghouse. 2019. "Growth in ICE Detention Fueled by Immigrants with No Criminal Conviction." Syracuse University, November 26, 2019. https://trac.syr.edu.

US House of Representatives Committee on Oversight and Reform. 2020. "DHS Officials Refuse to Release Asylum Seekers and Other Non-Violent Detainees Despite Spread of Coronavirus." Press release. April 17, 2020. https://oversight.house.gov.

US Immigration and Customs Enforcement. 2019. *U.S. Immigration and Customs Enforcement Fiscal Year 2019 Enforcement and Removal Operations Report*. www.ice.gov.

Whitman, James Q. 2017. *Hitler's American Model: The United States and the Making of Nazi Race Law*. Princeton, NJ: Princeton University Press.

3

Housing as Health Care

Shelter and Safety across Decades

SALONEE BHAMAN

On May 13, 2020, the New York City Department of Homeless Services (DHS) confirmed that there were 770 cases of COVID-19 across the agency's shelter system. The previous month, the agency also reported that 58 unhoused people had died from COVID-19; 54 had been residents of congregate shelters. As Shelly Nortz (2020), the deputy executive director for policy working for the advocacy organization Coalition for the Homeless, later testified, these statistics meant that the average death rate for sheltered homeless people, when adjusted for age, was 56 percent higher than the New York City average. In March, a few months prior, the city's commissioner of health and mental hygiene had ordered the city agencies to "locate, secure, operate, and make available" noncongregate (in other words, individual) shelter to any unhoused person who needed to be isolated or quarantined in order to stop the spread of COVID-19 among the general shelter population. Congregate settings, the commissioner had decreed, would surely "further the spread" of the illness and endanger vulnerable populations (Nortz 2020). Much like incarcerated people at institutions like Otisville (see Bardelli, Thomas, Brown, chapter 1 in this volume), residents of congregant shelters were unable to take any measures to protect themselves from infection. The realities of a dorm-style congregant setting meant that close quarters were the norm. Moving individuals from congregate facilities was no small task, however. As of March 2020, there were over nineteen thousand single adults housed in DHS shelters, fourteen thousand of whom lived in "congregate dorms."[1] By 2021, some advocates would argue that adjusting for age and other factors, the COVID-19 mortality rate for sheltered single adults was 80 percent higher than for other New Yorkers.[2]

In an attempt to comply with the commissioner's order, DHS transferred several thousand single adults into single-occupancy hotel rooms. These transfers were enabled by large emergency grants from the Federal Emergency Management Agency (FEMA), made to various states in light of the COVID-19 emergency (Dugan 2021; Mehta 2020). However, the vast majority of the agency's clients continued to reside in large congregate shelters. While DHS insisted that it had adequately "de-densified" congregate shelters, the number of people seeking shelter placement increased (Dugan 2021; Mehta 2020). Nortz (2020) testified to the New York State Legislature that many individuals who were unstably housed or paying weekly rent had become homeless as a result of widespread pandemic closures. Moreover, newly issued state policies shutting down the municipal subway system overnight (see Grenier, chapter 4 in this volume) had driven more individuals into the streets and crowded intake centers. In October of the same year, the Legal Aid Society and the Coalition for the Homeless filed a lawsuit, *Fisher v. The City of New York*, on behalf of single adults within the shelter system, imploring DHS to move everyone out of congregate shelter settings and arguing that DHS's refusal to place some adults in single rooms had violated a core tenet of the New York State Constitution.[3] Unlike in most other states, New York continues to be required to provide all adults and families with "adequate" shelter as a part of a consent decree established in 1981. The consent decree is the result of the first case that the Coalition for the Homeless fought, *Callahan v. Carey* (Holtzman 2021; Howard 2013). In January 2021, a judge dismissed these complaints and found that the DHS had taken adequate steps to address and stop the spread of COVID-19 within its facilities.[4] The ruling was a defeat for the unhoused and their advocates, who were attempting to show just one of the ways that the shelter system was unsafe.

Advocates have long rallied against New York City's congregate shelter system, citing crowded and often unsafe conditions even without the additional stressor of a poorly understood and highly contagious respiratory virus. The *Fisher* lawsuit's claims in fact echoed others brought by the Coalition for the Homeless during its four decades of advocacy on behalf of New York City's unhoused populations. One lawsuit, *Mixon v. Grinker*, argued that the city's shelters posed a serious risk to the health of people who were HIV positive.[5] As in the *Fisher* lawsuit, the plaintiffs' claims did more than make a legal argument: they showed the often fatal impact of systems of bureaucratic means-testing and disability verification on the lives of disabled people. This chapter revisits the organizing of people with AIDS that culminated in the *Mixon* case for safe housing for people living with AIDS to show the ways that unhoused activists brought claims about disability and health to bear on the broader housing justice movement. It places these efforts in conversation with the activism around similar issues during the first months of the COVID-19 pandemic, exploring both the ways that New York City's housing bureaucracy responded to the civil rights claims of HIV/AIDS activists and the reproduction of hierarchies of inclusion and exclusion within the category of "disabled." By centering the voices of the individuals caught in the center of these battles, this chapter aims to show how systems of shelter have at once come to embody what disability justice scholar Marta Russell (1998) terms the "money model of disability": at once extracting financial value from disabled bodies while actively working against processes of recovery and health for disabled people. The chapter also addresses the ways that addiction and mental illness have become marginalized within welfare bureaucracies.

Though the *Mixon* and *Fisher* cases were argued decades apart and in response to vastly different pandemics, both show that navigating the city's social service bureaucracies is mediated by experiences of disability, stigma, and means-tested scarcity. The work of both historical and contemporary activists demonstrates not only how the process of disability determination is and was not based on evidence of illness or need but also the ways that state designations of disability exclude those who are perceived as being improperly or insufficiently ill. The lived experiences of unhoused activists then and now offer a different vision of living with disability, wherein poverty, bureaucracy, and multiple forms of illness conspire to limit an individual's chances of becoming healthy. The ways that being disabled compounded the challenges inherent in coping with rapid change of location, loss of caregivers, and proximity to contagion are echoed throughout this volume (Bardelli, Thomas, and Brown, chapter 1 in this volume; Ginsburg and Rapp, chapter 7 in this volume; Coklyat and Fleet, chapter 9 in this volume). Perhaps most saliently, both cases speak to the fact that safe and adequate housing is at once closely linked to health, dignity, and continued flourishing while being nearly impossible to find in institutionalized shelter settings.

Shelter and Accommodation: Establishing Disproportionate Risk

As Nortz (2020) testified, COVID had simply made the need to provide "all people with the basic dignity and safety of permanent housing" clearer and more urgent. She continued, "housing is healthcare, and the absence of it can be deadly." Nortz's statement that "housing is healthcare" was more than a metaphor for DHS clients like Tamara Williams, a *Fisher* plaintiff, who was placed in a congregate shelter where she shared a sleeping area with eleven unrelated individuals. Williams, who has diabetes and chronic obstructive pulmonary disease (COPD), along with a history of heart failure, feared the consequences of catching COVID-19 from one of her shelter-mates.[6] The realities of living with disability had placed her in a shelter where she now risked getting sick or dying due to contagion.

As of 2019, the DHS estimated that 68 percent of single adults, 53 percent of families with children, and 77 percent of adult families who lived in shelters had at least one disability (Coalition for the Homeless 2021). A recent study by the New York City Comptroller also found that the agency's intake procedures inadequately addressed these issues; the study noted that the system often fails to place individuals in shelters that are able to provide them with mental health and substance abuse resources (Office of the Comptroller 2022). Another study found that adults with psychotic disorders like schizophrenia were five times more likely to die from COVID-19; other cofactors included being older, male, belonging to an ethnic minority, and having certain metabolic and respiratory conditions (Hassan et al. 2022). While these statistics alone do not paint a conclusive causal picture of the dangers presented by COVID-19 to people in shelter, they do suggest a context wherein people living in shelters were more likely to be disabled before entering and less likely to receive adequate health care within the shelters themselves.

Access to safe housing was in fact a critical part of Williams's ability to remain healthy. And, as her attorneys would argue, the city was failing its mandate to provide adequate housing by forcing her to live in a crowded congregate shelter during a viral pandemic.[7] While the particularities of transmission and infection of COVID-19 had made the connection between an individual's health and access to housing nearly undeniable, it was not the first time that unhoused individuals and their advocates would make claims to these protections. In 1987, a group of unhoused men with HIV had also brought suit against the city's homeless services agency for placing them in congregate shelters and denying them the right to reasonable accommodations for their illness. Their suit, *Mixon v. Grinker*, and the organized movement of unhoused people living with HIV/AIDS (PLWHA) that it shed light on, succeeded in winning injunctions for several named plaintiffs without fundamentally changing the structures it critiqued—namely, the opaque bureaucracy governing which individuals were "sick enough" to qualify for noncongregate housing.

Historicizing a Right to Shelter

New York City's congregate shelter system has long been a site of fierce protest and contestation between advocates for the unhoused and city officials. Much like in other parts of the United States, "skid rows"—or areas with long-standing populations of unhoused, often disabled, single men—proliferated throughout the 1950s and '60s. While a variety of private charities sought to address the needs of these individuals at least in part, rates of homelessness grew sharply in the 1970s due to a variety of factors, including changing social welfare policies, the rapid deinstitutionalization of state-run facilities housing mentally and physically disabled people, and the hollowing out of traditional sources of low-cost housing in urban areas (Moody 2007; Howard 2013; Holtzman 2019, 2021). In New York City, budget cuts, policies incentivizing the remodeling of low-income housing, and a growing population of intravenous drug users increased the number of people who found themselves on the streets. By the 1980s, New York City had the largest unhoused population anywhere in the United States, with indications that new demographics, like families, were increasingly being displaced due to social service cutbacks and increased housing costs.

A growing number of advocates began to speak out about the city's obligation to address the problem of homelessness. Groups like the Coalition for the Homeless, which was founded in 1979, played an important role in winning the rights to shelter for the unhoused in New York through a consent decree in 1981. However, politicians like then-Mayor Ed Koch had few plans for developing an effective strategy to create safe and affordable housing at scale and instead relied on limited warehouse-style "emergency" shelters (Holtzman 2021; Soffer 2010).

While these shelters were unpleasant and unsafe for all of their residents, they posed a particularly dangerous health risk for a growing subsection of the unhoused population: people living with HIV or AIDS (PLWHA). The syndrome we now call AIDS was first observed by medical professionals in 1981 but would not be linked conclusively to a single virus (HIV) until 1984. While an individual could test positive for HIV, their ability to become legally disabled and access government benefits depended on being diagnosed with one of a number of qualifying "opportunistic infections" that the virus made them susceptible to. A diagnosis sometimes allowed PLWHA to access special types of housing, including single-room occupancy (SRO) units, that were often subsidized by their Social Security benefits and state funds. Becoming "disabled" in the eyes of the state, however, was by design an increasingly challenging task. Beginning with the administration of Jimmy Carter, presidents had instructed the Social Security Administration to cut the number of individuals qualifying for public disability benefits (Russell 1998). For many unhoused people with HIV, diagnosis became impossible for a variety of reasons. Some lacked access to regular medical care from a physician who held their records. Others might have struggled with drug or alcohol use in ways that kept them from being able to seek regular care. Almost all had trouble keeping track of the extensive paperwork required to manage such an illness. Many found that the city's dedicated agency for AIDS services—the Division of AIDS Services (DASIS)—denied them access to expanded services based on arbitrary criteria.

By 1985, an unhoused individual who had been formally diagnosed with AIDS would have had access to some forms of supportive housing paid for through their Social Security disability benefits. Those who did not have such a diagnosis, however, were left in a gray area. Many described the city's congregate shelters, which sometimes housed up to a thousand individuals, as hotbeds of contagion for opportunistic infections like tuberculosis, which could be lethal for someone with HIV.

Residents living with HIV also described experiences of violence, discrimination, and hostility from other residents and shelter staff who learned of their status. Some argued that the shelter system ignored their needs by claiming that no PLWHA resided within the shelter system. These activists argued that as a baseline, adequate shelter should include the privacy, autonomy, and safety of an individual bathroom and kitchen with a refrigerator in order to store specialized foods and medications. Though groups like the AIDS Resource Center had proposed building or renovating individual apartments throughout the city (also known as "scatter site" housing), city officials dragged their feet on funding and supporting these proposals.

Facing down harsh conditions, HIV-positive people began to organize. One group of unhoused HIV-positive activists met regularly through the Coalition for the Homeless. They called themselves Anger into Direct Action (AIDA) and utilized creative and confrontational direct-action protest as a means to draw attention to their cause. Often working closely with the ACT UP New York Housing Committee, members of AIDA—predominantly women, drug users, and the formerly incarcerated—marched, protested, and participated in street theater to demand expanded rights to housing. In one notable circumstance, the group occupied Human Resources Administration (HRA) head William Grinker's office until the agency agreed to adequately house one of its members, Wayne Philips. In another, it placed furniture in the HRA's revolving doors until the agency agreed to offer individuals small stipends to furnish their rooms (Schulman 2021).

In 1988, Philips joined a group of HIV-positive men working with members of ACT UP's Housing Committee and lawyers from the Coalition for the Homeless to file a lawsuit drawing attention to the fact that PLWHA were forced to reside in a shelter system that was toxic to their health. Within the suit, Philips and the other plaintiffs—Kenneth Mixon, Raphael Hernandez Pagan, and Michael Snyder—argued that the city's barrack shelters were "notoriously dangerous and unhealthy," pointing out that many within the shelter population had severe health problems.[8] In addition to issues of eligibility or diagnosis, the suit laid bare that the city's municipal welfare system was not equipped to deal with the needs of those who could not submit to mandatory drug tests or participate in workfare programs. The plaintiffs also prompted city officials to approach the issues raised by homeless AIDS activists with renewed urgency.

The actual litigation of the *Mixon v. Grinker* case would span a time period within which both the definition of "AIDS" and the possibilities for treatment and management fundamentally transformed. In the years between the filing of the lawsuit in 1988 and its final appeals in 1996, several new "opportunistic infections" and diagnostic criteria would be added to the definition of AIDS. Additionally, the Ryan White CARE Act would make available millions of dollars in federal funding for AIDS-specific programs, and the Americans with Disabilities Act (ADA) would offer up a concrete, limited, legal framework for PLWHA to harness in order to defend their civil rights. By the end of the year, the widespread licensing of Highly Active Anti-Retroviral Therapy (HAART) also meant that those who could afford it had access to lifesaving medication. This groundswell of change in a relatively short period of time was due in no small part to the advocacy of PLWHA who shared their stories with government officials, courtrooms, and attorneys.

In the case of the *Mixon* plaintiffs and other unhoused people with HIV who organized around the right to shelter, these stories brought into focus the ways that access to a stable home was intimately connected to an individual's ability to receive care. Moreover, they also shed light on the overlapping disabilities that many PLWHA lived with—most prominently, mental illness and drug dependence. Often stigmatized even within the disability rights movement, the individuals at the center of the movement for medically appropriate shelter were candid about the ways that their experiences with drug use, madness, and HIV were often intertwined in ways that had limited their ability to access medical care, shelter, and other resources.

When local and federal bodies began to convene hearings to assess the scope and depth of this crisis, members of AIDA offered testimony that spoke to the ways that housing access affected every facet of their lives and underscored the ways that the very structure of welfare bureaucracies kept them from getting healthy. Testifying to the National Commission on AIDS in 1989, Ralph Hernandez recalled that he had first begun to notice symptoms of his illness when he came back from serving in the Vietnam War, addicted to heroin. He soon lost his apartment and his job but had trouble accessing care. He testified, "I tried to get into the VA hospital but they wouldn't see me because I was homeless. They wouldn't even let me into the detox program" ("AIDS and Homelessness" 1991).

Struggling to find a place to sleep, Hernandez went to the Washington Heights Shelter, where he recalled, "Other homeless people kicked the shit out of me. Then they called the guards, and the guards threw me out." He then tried to access care at Bellevue, which turned him away because he did not have Medicaid. When he returned to seek treatment at Mount Sinai a month later, he lied, saying that he had lost his Medicaid card and giving a false address. When he was kicked out after his secret was revealed, he went to Grand Central Terminal, where an outreach worker with the Coalition for the Homeless found him. He noted, "The VA had lost all my papers. I have been tested for AIDS three times, but because I am homeless they have lost my records each time." It was only when he joined in the *Mixon* lawsuit that he finally got access to private shelter, which he noted was "a room in a hotel that is really a shooting gallery" ("AIDS and Homelessness" 1991).

Describing a relapse into heroin use, Hernandez continued, "People like me, who are fighting drugs and AIDS, need special help. One Friday, I missed my program. I was too sick to stand up. My knees didn't have strength enough. So I missed my weekend pickup. By Sunday I was detoxing. I called all over, but no emergency room would help me. I even called an 800 number drug hotline, but I couldn't get anything." The only programs he was eligible for were methadone maintenance programs, which he felt left him dependent. "Methadone deteriorates your body. AIDS makes you tired. Methadone makes you wasted so you can't do anything. To fight AIDS you should be drug free. I want to be drug free, but there is nothing out there for me" ("AIDS and Homelessness" 1991).

Wayne Philips, one of the *Mixon* plaintiffs, began his remarks at one AIDS conference by noting that the attendees were unlikely to hear anyone else talk about the "day to day humiliation" experienced by people "living with AIDS who are dependent on the social service system for survival." He went on to describe the anger he felt when he had initially been denied benefits for failing to comply with the work requirements of New York City's public welfare program despite being recently hospitalized for "pneumonia, weight loss, fevers, and fatigue." After living on the street and sleeping on the train for three and a half months after his initial diagnosis, Philips finally applied for public assistance once again when he was hospitalized following a suicide attempt. Despite being sick with a low T-4 cell count, extreme weight loss, and chronic fatigue, he was deemed well enough to be placed into a "public shelter that sleeps 1,000 men in a single room and turns folks out at six in the morning so they don't become too lazy." Frustrated, he turned to the Coalition for the Homeless and joined the *Mixon* lawsuit, through which he produced an injunction that placed him in a single room. In the months that followed, Philips described months-long wait times for benefits that he had already qualified for, including access to the DASIS, Medicaid, and food stamps. Addressing the professional-class conference directly, he continued, "In closing, I don't know much about how policies and guidelines and criteria are made up, but I do know about dehumanization, something that burns within you to break your soul, mind, and spirit. Yet there are those of us who refuse to lay down and die" ("AIDS and Homelessness" 1991).

The *Mixon* plaintiffs were not the only PLWHA who testified about the conditions in the city's shelters. Speaking to the New York City Council's Committee on Homelessness in November 1989, Tommy Cummings noted, "The life of a PWA is a life of confusion, bureaucracy and anxiety," where the "battle to survive and exist from day to day is complicated by a system built on deception and ambiguity." This system, he noted, was full of "backlogged paperwork and red tape" to access "unsafe and unclean" hotels and shelters. Recalling his history of intravenous drug use, Cummings noted that in the throes of addiction, he initially did not mind losing his apartment and his friends, caring only about his fix. But he soon realized that "to be a homeless PWA in New York is no joke.... PWAs who are homeless generally have no medical care, no shelter from the elements except a cardboard box. The shelters are full and more dangerous than the PWA hotels." He continued,

> The City of New York has set up shelters to house the homeless, which in my opinion is the equivalent of putting a bandaid on a shotgun wound. The shelters are large and extremely overcrowded, and there are anywhere from two hundred to seven hundred men on a floor with no privacy allowed the individual, a communal sleeping area, communal toilets and showers, and communal recreation.... The strong will steal from the weak, those not able or too scared to fight back. It is very easy to get sick

in a shelter or SRO because management dumps everyone into the same dorm; the young with the old, the healthy with the sickly.... There is very little opportunity to get your life together in such an environment because one doesn't live in a shelter or SRO. Rather, one struggles to survive from day to day. ("AIDS and Homelessness" 1991)

Cummings's testimony reflected his own experience: he had lived on the streets for over a year when he was diagnosed with HIV but was turned away from DASIS for not being "sick enough" to qualify for an AIDS diagnosis. The stringent guidelines established by the Social Security Administration for being "properly disabled" were here reproduced by a city agency. With the help of the Coalition for the Homeless, Cummings challenged the ruling, receiving a fair hearing that required the agency to recommend that he be placed in housing. He was eventually placed in an SRO on Twenty-Sixth Street and Park Avenue South; he had to get to City Hall from there in order to be seen in court. Unable to afford train fare due to delays receiving his benefits, he recalled explaining his situation to several police officers who refused to let him onto the train without paying a fare. Speaking of the experience, he noted, "You often ask why is it that we miss appointments that are important to us? Why we look so tired? The truth of the matter is that we look tired and miss appointments because we are too sick. We must deal not only with our sick bodies but we must also deal with an establishment that doesn't give a damn about us" ("AIDS and Homelessness" 1991).

By the time *Mixon* was finally appealed, many PLWHA in the shelter system were beneficiaries of limited improvements enabled by federal funding for AIDS services. Decades after establishing an office of AIDS services, New York City had implemented a "Comprehensive Care Plan" that offered enhanced nutritional assistance and social services to unhoused PLWHA. Additionally, the program employed a number of nurses, nurse practitioners, physician's assistants, and doctors to conduct daily tuberculosis screenings, provide on-site medical coverage, and generally "control" the potential for infection. The program also limited the dormitory size to twelve PLWHA, who would continue to share eating and bathroom facilities with shelter residents. These compromises were still a far cry from the permanent and safe housing that would enable PLWHA to focus on their health. They were, however, enough to convince the majority of the New York State Supreme Court's Appellate Division to conclude that the congregate shelter plan remained viable (*Mixon v. Grinker*). Those who could prove that their condition entitled them to better conditions might have been able to access limited improvements, but the structural problems inherent within the congregate shelter system remained intact.

The Crisis of COVID-19

The testimony of the *Mixon* plaintiffs and other PLWHA might have been resonant to Morleen Fisher, the named plaintiff of the Coalition for the Homeless's most recent lawsuit against DHS. Fisher, who is fifty-five years old, has been diagnosed with diabetes, PTSD, and bipolar disorder. At the time of the *Fisher* lawsuit, she had been placed in a sleeping area with ten unrelated individuals and shared a bathroom with twenty. During the day, she worked as a home health aide to an elderly couple and feared contracting the virus both for her own safety and for theirs. When she requested a single room in order to social distance, she alleges that shelter staff told her that "DHS does not put crazy people in hotels."[9]

While it is true that congregate shelters sometimes offer enhanced supportive services—like mental health support, access to social workers, and other forms of "case management" for clients—these services were not universally available at the hotel sites that many others had been relocated to. However, given recent findings that single adults, the category of unhoused person most likely to be placed in congregate shelters, are also more likely to have higher rates of addiction disorder, mental illness, and other severe health problems (Coalition for the Homeless 2022; Burt and Cohen 1989) and less likely to receive treatment for them from the shelter system (Coalition for the Homeless 2022), the disconnect between services and need almost certainly extended beyond the temporary relocations. It is more likely the case that the shelter worker's statement reflected the fact that either Fisher's disabilities were not perceived to be physical or there was an unspoken protocol that only certain types of adults would be relocated to single-room hotels. It is also true that the city's policy of relocating individuals to hotels had been met by some New York residents with hostility and protest.

DHS had placed individuals in hotels before, relying periodically on the practice to alleviate overcrowding since the 1980s. However, recent pandemic-induced emergency measures and federal FEMA funds had enabled city officials to move people in the most crowded shelters to high-end hotels. While relocation was a miracle for some residents who had been living in notoriously overcrowded shelters, their new neighbors found their presence objectionable. The outcry over the large-scale transfers of unhoused clients into hotels in Midtown and the Upper West Side was nearly immediate: internet message boards complained about the visible imprint of the new population, while articles in local newspapers drummed up fears of increased crime and visible drug use (Slotnik 2020).

One site in particular—the Lucerne Hotel on the Upper West Side—became a flash-point issue for many neighborhood residents. The upscale hotel, which was located on Seventy-Ninth Street and Amsterdam Avenue, was made a temporary shelter for 238 men who also received services from Project Renewal, a nonprofit service provider that worked with unhoused residents to provide rehabilitation, therapeutic, and job-training services of various kinds. In the face of the Lucerne's repurposing, complaints from some people in the neighborhood threatened to become litigious (Evershed 2021). In September 2020, mere months after the men were moved into the Lucerne, Mayor Bill de Blasio announced a plan to move them to another shelter in the Financial District. The plans were temporarily halted as legal advocates threatened to bring a lawsuit on behalf of the men. One previously unhoused resident of the Lucerne named Shams DaBaron, who also identified himself as "Da Homeless Hero," also noted that small changes—like bringing the outpatient group that residents had attended uptown—had made all the difference in diffusing conflicts and improving the overall quality of life (*Brian Lehrer Show* 2021a). In October, residents of the Financial District sued the Mayor's Office to keep the unhoused men from being located downtown, further ensnaring the program in controversy (Pereira 2020).

In the months to come, city officials would encounter even more vocal opposition to relocations, like one caller to *The Brian Lehrer Show*'s "Ask the Mayor" segment, who felt that the repurposed hotels in her Midtown West neighborhood had so seriously impacted her quality of life that her life and her neighbors' "lives in the area are ruined from this." In response, the mayor pledged an expanded police presence and assured the caller that use of the hotels is "becoming less and less necessary" and that the administration would soon "start the process of moving people back to the shelters where we can provide the most support for them" (*Brian Lehrer Show* 2021a).

The sentiment reflected policy that was already under way: the approximately ten thousand unhoused New Yorkers sheltered in commercial hotels around the city had received a letter announcing the agency's plans to move them to residential shelters imminently. The letter was slipped under many doors on May 24, 2021, just over a year after New York City and State officials declared a state of emergency (Styville 2021). Offering no specifics on when the move would be implemented, the DHS—the agency in charge of these contracts—informed residents that they might still have a right to individual shelter if they were able to prove that they had special reason to request a private room, with documentation from a doctor or health-care provider (Styville 2021). For many, such documentation would be difficult, if not impossible, to find. After all, so many with seemingly legitimate claims to individual shelter had already been denied.

For Shams DaBaron, the process of eviction and relocation had revealed bigger problems within the shelter system as a whole—problems that spoke to the double standards that plagued many of the drug users who sought help from the agencies tasked with serving them. Calling into WNYC once again in June, after moving out of the Lucerne, DaBaron argued that COVID had revealed existing problems, many of which he thought had "existed forever." In his opinion, the "inhumane" and "flawed" policies toward the homeless that came to light during the emergency spoke to the long-standing fact that people "who were dealing with mental illness and substance use disorder are not afforded the same protection that others with disabilities are" and could therefore not "question what the mayor does" to them: "even if it has a negative effect on our mental health or our ability to combat substance abuse" (*Brian Lehrer Show* 2021b). The issues his fellow residents faced, he argued, were "co-related," but the shelter system refused to deal with it, instead simply profiting off the misery of the unhoused. The experience of being evicted from the Lucerne, DaBaron reflected in various remarks, had traumatized him and many of his fellow residents, triggering some to relapse and others toward self-destructive behavior (helpNYC 2021). Of course, while the shelter hotels significantly reduced the chance of contagion when compared to a congregant setting, the movement and disruption associated with transitioning into a new space had a range of unanticipated consequences for residents with a range of disabilities. While some, as DaBaron describes, found their substance abuse disorders more difficult to manage, others had to modify or adapt to a new set of tools, technologies, and systems when confronted with physical infrastructure that was not designed for accessibility (Coklyat and Fleet, chapter 9 in this volume). As Marta Russell has argued, the disabled bodies of these residents had been rendered profitable within a labyrinthine shelter system enriched by government contracts and emergency funds (Russell 1998; Russell and Rosenthal 2019).

Hierarchies of Harm: Disability Legibility

The medical anthropologist Merrill Singer first coined the term "syndemic" to describe the way that a constellation of interrelated conditions and factors (substance abuse, violence, and AIDS, or SAVA) frequently occurred in tandem and produced particular outcomes for individuals affected by all three. Each condition was influenced not only by medical factors but also by social, economic, and political considerations, including homelessness, poverty, and disenfranchisement (Singer et al. 2017). As new drug therapies and interventions made HIV a manageable condition for many individuals, some remained more likely to die due to infection because of other factors. As a result, the COVID-19 pandemic and the HIV/AIDS syndemic are both ongoing and distinct crises unfolding within the social fabric of New York City (and across the world). They each are of a scale and specificity to merit considered analysis of their respective particularities. Analyzing them in tandem, however, reveals troubling continuity rather than rupture with regard to the politics of social provision. The unhoused people who struggled against the unsafe conditions created by the DHS in 2020 come up against many of the same obstacles first articulated by PLWHA in the 1980s and '90s: a social service infrastructure largely indifferent to, if not productive of, the lived experiences of disability and stigma. Despite nominal legislative protections in the form of the

Americans with Disabilities Act, the task of rendering particular forms of disability legible to state actors invested in either the management of cost or continuity of the shelter-industrial complex emerges as a consistent challenge.

In the two years since Shams DaBaron and his fellow residents were first moved into the Lucerne and the publication of this volume, a new, much-reported crisis has seized New York City's housing and shelter politics: an influx of upward of seventy thousand migrants seeking asylum in the United States. In New York City, unlike many parts of the United States, these migrants were guaranteed a right to shelter thanks to the *Callahan* decision and its subsequent modifications—a state of affairs that New York City officials like newly elected Mayor Eric Adams quickly began to work to dismantle. In the spring of 2023, Adams issued an executive order allowing city agencies to begin to disregard some portions of the consent decree's modifications—including barriers on what kinds of residents were able to be sent to congregate settings. He cited the DHS's inability to accommodate the large volume of migrants coming into the city as a forcing function for the policy modification (Kim 2023). In July, once again citing the high volume of migrants seeking asylum in New York City, the Mayor's Office issued another rule requiring all single, adult men living in shelters to leave and reapply for access every sixty days (Hernandez and Mena 2023). In early October, the Mayor's Office formally petitioned the court to temporarily suspend the *Callahan* consent decree, arguing that the terms imposed by the court had become "outmoded and cumbersome in the face of the present migrant crisis."[10] Three days later, the Adams administration extended the sixty-day limit to apply to migrant families living with children. Of course, people within the shelter system who were undocumented or otherwise classified as noncitizens had already faced increasingly steep barriers to accessing appropriate care or contesting the conditions of their shelter long before the crisis (Salyer, chapter 2 in this volume). And while high numbers of migrants are routinely cited as the cause of the emergency that required the revision of New York City's right to shelter, the new restrictions apply to all residents of New York City's shelters. For four decades, housing and disability justice advocates have been making arguments about the basic rights of unhoused people through the framework created by the *Callahan v. Carey* decision. Within the span of a few months, the

Adams administration has undone decades of the painstaking protections that these activists carved out.

Placing the linked but separate movements for safe and healthy shelter during the first years of the HIV/AIDS and COVID-19 pandemics in conversation allows us to see the ways that civil rights protections alone do not account for the enduring inequalities that disabled people experience within systems like shelters. It reveals how substance use disorders and mental illness continue to be fault lines around which stigma and discrimination have concentrated, limiting the ability of individuals to access care and safety. There is also another continuity between these moments in disability history: the insistence of disabled people on speaking the truths of their lives and experiences, even when met with indifference. Through organizing for bureaucratic change and accommodation, advocates like Shams DaBaron and the activists of AIDA began to identify and articulate how the very foundations of social welfare systems were disempowering to the people they served. Their work challenges us to look toward not just accommodation but liberation.

NOTES

1 Fisher v. The City of New York, 2021 N.Y. Slip Op. 30210 (N.Y. Sup. Ct. 2021), https://law.justia.com.
2 *Fisher*, 2021 N.Y. Slip Op. 30210.
3 *Fisher*, 2021 N.Y. Slip Op. 30210.
4 *Fisher*, 2021 N.Y. Slip Op. 30210.
5 Mixon v. Grinker, 157 A.D. 2d 423 (1990), 88 N.Y. 2d 907 (1996).
6 *Fisher*, 2021 N.Y. Slip Op. 30210.
7 *Fisher*, 2021 N.Y. Slip Op. 30210.
8 *Mixon*, 157 A.D. 2d 423; Coalition for the Homeless Lawsuit and Case Text, Box 12, "Housing for the Homeless, 1987–1988," 1988, People With AIDS Coalition Records, New York Public Library, New York, NY.
9 *Fisher*, 2021 N.Y. Slip Op. 30210, at 8.
10 The City of New York Law Department to Honorable Erika Edwards, New York Supreme Court Justice, "Re: *Callahan v. Carey*, Index No. 42582/1979," October 3, 2023.

REFERENCES

"AIDS and Homelessness: Personal Accounts." 1991. *Yale Journal of Law and Liberation* 2: article 9.

Brian Lehrer Show, The. 2021a. "Ask the Mayor: School Vaccination Sites, 'Homeless Hotels' & Bike Lanes." WNYC, New York, 93.9 FM, June 4, 2021.

———. 2021b. "NYC's Homeless People Are Moved Back to Shelters." WNYC, New York, 89.3 FM, June 29, 2021.

Burt, Martha R., and Barbara E. Cohen. 1989. "Differences among Homeless Single Women, Women with Children, and Single Men." *Social Problems* 36 (5): 508–24.

Coalition for the Homeless. 2021. "Basic Facts about Homelessness in New York." February 2021. www.coalitionforthehomeless.org.

Dugan, Kevin. 2021. "The Homeless-to-Hotels Program Is Ending, and Nobody's Ready." *Curbed*, June 15, 2021. www.curbed.com.

Evershed, Megan. 2021. "How an Upper West Side Hotel Came to Embody the City's Failure on Homelessness." *New Republic*, March 31, 2021.

Hassan, Lamiece, Niels Peek, Karina Lovell, Andre F. Carvalho, Marco Solmi, Brendon Stubbs, and Joseph Firth. 2022. "Disparities in COVID-19 Infection, Hospitalisation and Death in People with Schizophrenia, Bipolar Disorder, and Major Depressive Disorder: A Cohort Study of the UK Biobank." *Molecular Psychiatry* 27 (2): 1248–55. https://doi.org/10.1038/s41380-021-01344-2.

helpNYC. 2021. "Da Homeless Hero's Trauma on Top of Trauma." Medium, July 5, 2021. https://medium.com/helpnyc.

Hernandez, Estafania, and Kelly Mena. 2023. "Adams Limits Shelter Stays for Adult Migrants to 60 Days." *NY1*, July 19, 2023. https://ny1.com.

Holtzman, Benjamin. 2019. "'Shelter Is Only a First Step': Housing the Homeless in 1980s New York City." *Journal of Social History* 52 (3): 886–910.

———. 2021. *The Long Crisis: New York City and the Path to Neoliberalism*. New York: Oxford University Press.

Howard, Ella. 2013. *Homeless: Poverty and Place in Urban America*. Philadelphia: University of Pennsylvania Press, 2013.

Kim, Elizabeth. 2023. "Mayor Adams Orders Exceptions to Decades-Old Right-to-Shelter Law as NYC Preps for More Migrants." *Gothamist*, May 10, 2023. https://gothamist.com.

Mehta, Akash. 2020. "Mayor, Ignoring FEMA, Says NYC Can't Afford Hotel Rooms for Homeless." *The Intercept*, May 1, 2020. https://theintercept.com.

Moody, Kim. 2007. *From Welfare State to Real Estate: Regime Change in New York City, 1974 to the Present*. New York: New Press.

Nortz, Shelley. 2020. "Testimony on the Disparate Impact of COVID-19 on Homeless People before the New York State Legislature." May 18, 2020. www.nysenate.gov.

Office of the New York State Comptroller. 2022. *Oversight of Shelter Placements*. Report 2021-N-5. December 2022. www.osc.ny.gov.

Pereira, Sydney. 2020. "Lower Manhattan Residents Sue City to Block Transfer of Homeless Residents from One Hotel to Another." *Gothamist*, October 14, 2020. https://gothamist.com.

Russell, Marta. 1998. *Beyond Ramps: Disability at the End of the Social Contract*. Common Monroe, ME: Courage.

Russell, Marta, and Keith Rosenthal. 2019. *Capitalism and Disability*. Chicago: Haymarket.

Schulman, Sarah. 2021. *Let the Record Show: A Political History of ACT UP New York, 1987–1993*. New York: Farrar, Straus and Giroux.
Singer, Merrill, Nicola Bulled, Bayla Ostrach, and Emily Mendenhall. 2017. "Syndemics and the Biosocial Conception of Health." *The Lancet* 389 (10072): 941–50. https://doi.org/10.1016/S0140-6736(17)30003-X.
Slotnik, Daniel E. 2020. "What Happened When Homeless Men Moved into a Liberal Neighborhood." *New York Times*, August 18, 2020, sec. New York. www.nytimes.com.
Soffer, Jonathan M. 2010. *Ed Koch and the Rebuilding of New York City*. New York: Columbia University Press.
Styville, Alphonso. 2021. "Good Morning/ The Notice @NYCDHS slipped under everybody hotel door last night. WHAT YALL THINK ABOUT THIS? SHOULD the UNHOUSED be able to stay in hotels at least until September like @fema paid for? @jennyaction @femnomics @NYhomeless @hardlynormal @informnyc." Twitter, May 25, 2021, 8:19 a.m. https://twitter.com/SyvilleAlphonso/status/1397165385896583169t.

4

From Inaccessibility to Pathologized Mobility on New York City's Public Transit

Finding Affordances in a Pandemic

YAN GRENIER

The public transportation system of New York City (NYC) moves 40 percent of all mass-transit ridership throughout the United States. It defines mobility and is recognized as the economic lifeline of the city, the tristate region, and, in many respects, the entire country (Grenier and Arroyo 2022; MTA 2019). At the beginning of the pandemic in March 2020, it was also identified as a vector of contamination, as buses and subways were recognized as sites of propagation of the COVID-19 virus; physical proximity in enclosed spaces posed a risk for riders, especially chronically ill and disabled people (Borkowski, Jażdżewska-Gutta, and Szmelter-Jarosz 2021; Huang and Li 2022; Musselwhite, Avineri, and Susilo 2020; Harris 2020). Under these conditions, many disabled people chose to limit their use of public transit, given the greater risk they faced if exposed to the virus. Some took advantage of the increasing availability of delivery services instead, demonstrating the limited affordances and creative responses to them. Such activities are central to Arseli Dokumaci's (2023) work on the impact of limited affordances. Yet, inaccessible public transportation infrastructures are now widely recognized to produce disabling situations and impede the basic right to the city (to borrow an expression from Henri Lefebvre [1968]). And for still others who were unhoused, the subway provided essential shelter. During the pandemic, the Metropolitan Transit Authority (MTA) attracted enormous media attention as the organization worked to keep the NYC subways open amid various COVID surges. Many riders abandoned public transportation; services were delayed due to the MTA workforce falling ill and dying or testing positive and taking leave. Train operators and conductors experienced the highest rate of COVID-19 infection among MTA workers. Furthermore, safety concerns were raised following violent incidents, concerns also discussed by Bhaman (chapter 3 in this volume) and Mohapatra et al. (chapter 11 in this volume).

On March 22, 2020, with 7,102 active cases of COVID-19 in New York State and an exponential rate of new cases, Governor Cuomo signed two documents: (1) "New York State on PAUSE," which contained a set of rules

Figure 4.1. In January 2021, the MTA inaugurated a memorial that was presented three times daily for two weeks, honoring the 112 MTA employees who died from COVID-19. Large-scale photos of these workers were displayed on screens at Grand Central Terminal, Moynihan Train Hall, 107 subway stations (out of 472) across the five boroughs, NYCT buses system wide, and online. This project was a collaboration between MTA Arts & Design, MTA New York City Transit, and the families of the employees lost to COVID-19, who shared photos and selected the background colors for the display. Titled Travels Far, the memorial took its name from an original poem by former US poet laureate Tracy K. Smith. The online memorial features an original score by composer Christopher Thompson. The poem and composition, both named Travels Far, were commissioned by MTA Arts & Design. The words to the poem and the video tribute can be found at https://new.mta.info/covid-memorial (for further discussion of the Travels Far memorial, see Klinenberg 2024). (Photo: MTA/Marc Hermann, taken during January 25–February 7, 2021, display of Travels Far at MTA NYC Transit Bowling Green Station)

for the general population, closing all nonessential business and banning the gatherings of individuals for any reason, and (2) "Matilda's law," which added measures for "vulnerable populations," which included people over seventy years old and people with compromised immune systems, requiring them to remain indoors (Office of the New York State Governor 2020; Grenier 2023). Extensive measures were taken by authorities to contain the spread of the virus and its impact on health systems, from school closures to lockdowns to travel restrictions (Engle, Stromme, and Zhou 2020; Warren and Skillman 2020).

Transit systems connecting work, schools, businesses, and homes were envisioned as sites of heightened contagion. Mobility and proximity were pathologized by authorities as a vector of COVID-19 transmission (Cresswell 2021), becoming an object of pandemic governance and politics.

By April 7, 2020, human mobility (including public transport, walks, micromobility, and taxis) was down to 7 percent of its usual level in New York City compared to the levels prior to the pandemic (Statista 2022). Under lockdowns and stay-at-home orders, but also out of individual voluntary initiatives to stay safe, immobility became the norm in the city. New forms of relations emerged, and existing modes of remote access expanded, as disabled city dwellers tried to maintain their lives from home and connect with one another while being physically distanced. Early pandemic changes to relationality, small and large, transformed the habits of everyday life, sometimes permanently (Ruder 2021).

This chapter is based on two years of ethnographic fieldwork with a focus on the (im)mobility of disabled people during the pandemic and their relationships to transit infrastructure in NYC prior to and as a result of COVID-19. I adopt a processual and relational view of disability, focusing on "affordances" (Dokumaci 2017, 2023; Gibson 1979; Ingold 1992) as "ways to carry on your life, or alternatively, what gets in the way: opportunities and hindrances" in the production of lived worlds between people and environments, perception and imagination (Ingold 2018, 39). This chapter explores (1) the consequences of historical mobility restrictions on disabled lives in NYC and the formation of individual and collective habits; (2) the cumulative effects of mass immobilization during the pandemic on the lives of disabled people; and (3) the material and digital strategies used by disabled people to (re)form habits within this new context.

During fall 2020, I conducted multiple interviews with people with mobility impairments living in NYC who were frequent users of city transport modalities before the pandemic. I also interviewed disability advocates as well as MTA staff members. These interviews were supplemented with a daily review of digital newspapers, social media feeds of disabled people and organizations, and the gray literature related to mobility infrastructure in the city. Throughout the pandemic, I attended multiple Zoom conferences, workshops, and meetings held by disability organizations such as National Alliance on Mental Illness—NYC (NAMI-NYC), ADAPT New York, Disabled in Action (DIA), Brooklyn Center for Independence of the Disabled (BCID), and the United Spinal Association, on the topics of transportation, housing, disability rights and access, and so on, and public ones such as the MTA and the Office of the New York City Public Advocate and the Mayor's Office for People with Disabilities, to name a few. Finally, I attended both online and in situ protests and events organized by disabled people and their organizations.

(In)accessibility: A New York Story

In New York City, data from the US Census Bureau shows that in 2017, about 930,100 people, or one in nine New Yorkers, reported having an impairment that affects at least one activity of daily life (US Census Bureau 2020). Within that number, 550,000 residents have difficulty walking, and two-thirds of them live far from an accessible subway station. Currently, New York's subway system is composed of 472 stations connecting 122 of the city's 189 neighborhoods; only a quarter, or 114 stations, are designated as wheelchair accessible (Spivak 2019). A report from Manhattan Borough President Gale Brewer's office challenged that number, showing that on a day-to-day basis, elevators are not always cleaned or are not functioning, information is missing, or routes can only be traveled in one direction (Brewer 2019), further limiting the number of accessible stations on a given day. Similarly, Sarah

Kaufman and colleagues (2017) have shown that in 2015, 14,092 outages occurred on subway elevators of New York City, estimating that on average, each elevator had 53 outages per year.

The inaccessibility of NYC transit has a long history of protest and legal action. The first national measures passed by the US Congress to ensure access to the built environment were the Architecture Barriers Act of 1968 and the Federal Rehabilitation Act of 1973 (Section 504), both prohibiting discrimination based on ability in federally assisted programs, which transportation falls under. The MTA disputed the application of the content of Section 504, requiring that facilities designed, built, or renovated with federal dollars should be entirely accessible (US Access Board 1968), which would have meant retrofitting the entire subway system. Litigation around subway accessibility started in 1979 with several lawsuits from disability advocacy groups, leading to a first settlement in 1984 between the Eastern Paralyzed Veterans Association (now United Spinal) and Disabled in Action of Metropolitan New York (DIA) and the MTA (*New York Times* 1984; Elegudin 2022). The settlement resulted in an amendment to the transportation law and the administrative code of NYC to make fifty-four "key stations" of the subway network and all buses in the city accessible and to put in place a paratransit service. Since then, the MTA has been required to spend $5 million a year on accessibility.

Throughout the years, disability groups have filed a series of additional lawsuits against the MTA (Rosenberg 2017; Disability Rights Advocates, n.d.) for failing to install elevators during renovations and for poor maintenance of existing elevators. In 1990, the Americans with Disabilities Act (ADA) was passed, mandating equality of access to public transportation. But the complexity of transit infrastructure and its history, regulations, and financial constraints posed challenges to the implementation of the law. In 1994, as part of a settlement that exempted the agency from full compliance with the ADA and the state's Public Buildings and Transportation Laws, the MTA agreed to make one hundred "key stations" accessible in high-traffic areas by 2020 (Plaut et al. 2017; Evelly 2018).

In 2019, when the MTA's 2020–2024 Capital Program mobilized $54 billion in capital investment at the level of New York State to repair subway infrastructure and improve transit in the city, the MTA agreed to commit $5.2 billion to make seventy stations accessible based on ADA guidelines. The plan proposes that 50 percent of stations will be accessible by 2029, with the year of 2034 scheduled, in vague terms, for the "maximum possible system-wide accessibility" (MTA 2019, 14).

Most recently, in June 2022, two class-action lawsuits were settled between Disability Rights Advocates and the MTA, in which the MTA was legally required to add ramps and elevators to 95 percent of subway stations by the year 2055 regardless of current budget losses (Gold 2022; Kaske 2022).[1] Another lawsuit, filed in October 2022, asks the MTA to fix the gaps between subways trains and platforms, which pose a danger for people with visual and mobility impairments (Martinez 2022).[2]

Figure 4.2. On December 15, 2021, disability activists from Rise and Resist, Brooklyn Center for Independence of the Disabled (BCID), Center for Independence of the Disabled New York (CIDNY), and Disabled in Action (DIA), protest in front of the MTA headquarters on Broadway to demand the signature of a legally binding agreement and the settlement of multiple ADA lawsuits regarding accessibility. (Photo: Erik McGregor)

World-Making in Limited Fields of Affordances: Misfits, Cripping, and Habitual Environments

The historical and structural consequence of the general inaccessibility of the subway system in particular is that many disabled people cannot use the subway and must rely on buses or on the paratransit system, Access-A-Ride (Patel 2019), for everyday transportation. Even if the bus is now considered 100 percent accessible, it has its own history of (in)accessibility (Legal Services NYC 2010). Moreover, bus usage results in longer, slower, and more complicated commutes. Paratransit trips are even lengthier and are indirect, as other riders need to be picked up and dropped off along the routes. Access-A-Ride does not allow for spontaneity, as trips must be reserved at least twenty-four hours in advance. Riders end up being late for appointments, meetings, or work (Evelly 2020). Kaufman and colleagues (2017) report that the dependency on the paratransit service is higher in neighborhoods lacking accessible public transit. According to Sandy Wong and colleagues (2020), "transport options are less accessible and slower for disabled workers than they are for non-disabled workers." Because of these factors, a large portion of disabled riders reduce their transportation usage even in nonpandemic times (Brumbaugh 2018, 9).

Accessibility also comes at a cost. On average, the median monthly rent in neighborhoods with at least one accessible subway station is more than $100 higher than the ones with only inaccessible stations (Stringer 2018, 3). One interviewee explains the negotiations people face regarding their choice of residence: "Some people have no choice. You know, they might have to settle for a place that they like that's accessible, but there are not too many options when it comes to accessibility for traveling. When I moved here, that's the situation I was in. I needed a place immediately. And, you know, at the time, transportation would have had to wait, you know? When you have a place that's accessible and you have a neighborhood that's accessible when it comes to transportation, you tend to pay more."

Access to jobs in the city is also impacted by transit. Before the pandemic, only 41 percent of disabled people had jobs, compared to 71 percent of nondisabled people (DiNapoli 2019, 2). For employment seekers who live in inaccessible areas, it is difficult to access the 2.7 million jobs in accessible areas, and the 608,000 "jobs in neighborhoods without subway accessibility are even more challenging to access" (Stringer 2018, 3). These limitations and disadvantages have profound impacts on people's lives.

Disabled people in NYC must compose their daily lives with these limited affordances and with complicated commutes in a complex and unstable transit system. Rosemarie Garland-Thomson (2011, 594) has written of fitting and misfitting between bodies and the environment. But these singular encounters must also be understood in their processual and developmental contexts: How do changes in the relational environment modify the possibility of action as well as the development of the body-mind over the life course? Disability scholar Arseli Dokumaci uses this approach, embracing "becoming" over the idea of static beings within a field of limited affordances. She argues that disruptions might serve as vectors for productive new entanglements: "it is with this very rupturing that a space opens up for the organism and the environment to re-relate in combinations other than what has so far been thought possible" (Dokumaci 2017, 400). Following her logic, limited affordances in transit have tangible effects on the daily activities of disabled people, rendering the world less habitable and creating recurrent disabling situations and cumulative disadvantages. Such ruptures can also be "world-making" (Dokumaci 2023, 104), as they open up spacetime for ephemeral performative acts that compensate the failures of affordance materialization in their immediate environment, catalyzing unexpected strategies for disabled people to "crip" their worlds (Hamraie and Fritsch 2019, 7) and create openings for alternative becomings.

Inhabiting the World Prior to and During the Pandemic: From Physical to Digital Access

In this section, I use selections from several interviews with disabled interlocutors to exemplify their mobility experiences prior to and during the pandemic, showing how their habits were affected. Many chose to limit their use of public transit, given the greater risk they faced if exposed to the virus; some took advantage of the increasing availability of delivery services instead, demonstrating the kind of limited affordances and creative responses to them that are central to Dokumaci's work on the impact of limited affordances. In an interview with me, Jessica Murray, a white disability mobility activist and associate producer of the documentary *The Biggest Obstacle*, summed up the new dwelling conditions of many people: "A lot of people are staying at home, and they're kind of self-quarantining just because they're at high risk. A lot of people have preexisting conditions that make them high risk, and they don't want to travel on public transit. And they're probably limiting their other trips. And, as a result, it's easier and easier to get stuff delivered these days" (interview, 2020).

Quemuel Arroyo, the newly appointed first chief accessibility officer for the MTA and a wheelchair user, reminds us of the unmet needs of people prior to the pandemic and how the pandemic exacerbated these situations: "Many people with disabilities . . . do not have the opportunity to leave their homes to get bread or milk, like so many of us do. . . . It questions us on how they engage with the community. Not only how do they get the basic needs that they require, but how do they interact with people when they are home ridden, for a lot of cases" (Grenier and Arroyo 2022).

Jonathan works for a disability advocacy group in NYC. As a Black man in his thirties and a manual wheelchair user and as someone who travels frequently for work during a given day, he described some of his pre-pandemic daily commutes in a conversation with me:

> Let's say, if I want to go back to my office, the 6 train goes there. I'm a block and a half away from the 6 [subway train]. My office is a block and a half away from the 6, but there's no accessibility over there either. So, if you leave my house, go to my office in Union Square, you can get there in about thirty-four minutes. That same trip will take me an hour and forty minutes or more. Because I have to leave my house, and I have to go down the block and around the corner and wait for the bus to go up north about a mile away to Hunt's Point, then get to the nearest elevator station. And if that station is open, as far as access goes, then I have to come back down south past my area to get to where I'm going, but then again, I have to get off the train early because I have to transfer to the bus and then take a walk to the office. (interview, 2020)

On a daily basis, he contends with the shifting presence and absence of infrastructural affordances, as components of the subway system are unstable and often fail. Through repeated use, he has gained the expertise to navigate through the limited physical and informational affordances to reach destinations in an otherwise largely inaccessible system. Self-described as an "outside guy," he loves to be out and about between meetings and commuting to them, even with the degree of complexity they pose. By contrast, he described his difficult experience of staying at home during the lockdown—in an apartment he barely inhabited prior to the pandemic—and not being able to go to work, the gym, or to meet friends: "There was no work at one point because we're still trying to figure things out. This is the slowest my life has ever been. And I felt so useless. I was like, 'Why am I getting up?' You know? There is nothing to look forward to. I found myself literally doing the same routine. . . . That's not a life. And it got so boring" (interview, 2020). Jonathan found it difficult to adapt to the affordances of a digital life. He regrets losing professional opportunities, including traveling internationally because of the pandemic. Waiting around his apartment for his Zoom meetings and resorting to delivery for food or Amazon for purchases, he stayed in except for the occasional groceries or visits to his mother's place in Far Rockaway to keep her company and support her after her husband passed away from COVID a few months prior to our interview.

Diane, a Black woman in her forties who resides in Queens and uses a motorized wheelchair, was using Access-A-Ride prior to the pandemic to commute between her apartment and her office in Brooklyn, where she works as a disability advocate:

> I have to go take a bus four blocks from my home. That brings me to the train station, which is, like I said, about twenty minutes away. Then I get on that train, go to the nearest stop to my job. And since I'm in a motorized wheelchair, I either can do one of two things: I can take another bus, or I can wheel. . . . Even though they're accessible [subway stations], my wheels have gotten stuck between the train and the platform. . . . I've had an instance where the elevator wasn't working at the train station that I needed to go out of, and it was right near my job, right around the corner. And because I was going back to work—they had a power outage in the train station. I had to be carried out of the train station by six firefighters carrying my chair and two carrying me. That, to me, is unacceptable. (interview, 2020)

Diane told me that she could not use the train because she has vertigo and the narrowness of the platform makes her dizzy. She tried taking the bus to get to work: "And it's not one bus. It's five buses. It would take me hours to get to work, and I've tried it. And it took me three and a half hours." Her only option remains paratransit, which she took multiple times a week even during the pandemic to get to physical therapy. Apart from these commutes, Diane described her pandemic activities: "I am working remotely. I am on Zoom twenty-four hours a day. It seems like whether it's business or whether it's even pleasure at the time, because people are staying in place, you know." She also stressed the importance of media technologies that allowed transferring her social and professional activities to a digital platform: "Being home is boring, boring to me, but you have to make your life what it is."

These two participants previously benefited from the "On-Demand E-Hail" pilot program, launched initially in 2017 by the MTA, which allowed disabled commuters to book solo taxi rides for the fare of $2.75 (the same as a subway ride), without having to book in advance (Martinez 2021). During the pandemic, the MTA maintained Access-A-Ride services, but the shared rides were replaced with "solo" rides, extending the pilot to every disabled rider with the fees lifted (McDonough 2021).

> It's a unique situation. . . . Instead of using Access-A-Ride, if you choose to, you can use an app on your phone called Curb, and you can have a taxi pick you up literally on demand when you want and travel anywhere you want to go in the five boroughs. . . . It's life-saving, because I've been on Access-A-Ride . . . I want to say since 2012, and it's horrible. . . . This is the first time I've been able to travel spontaneously since before my accident. When you get your confidence back, you want to be able to go out and have fun and not be restricted like you have a babysitter, you know? (Jonathan, interview, 2020)

As a side effect, these changes in affordances of the service drastically enhanced the quality of life of riders, allowing them to take on responsibilities and gain a sense of freedom. Disentangled from the previous service limitations imposed by the MTA and gaining in spontaneity, Jonathan told me that he now could go to his mother's within forty minutes in case of an emergency or to play a support role. But in the summer of 2021, the MTA reinstated shared rides. Consequently, activists from the New York Lawyers for the Public Interest and AARRG! (Access-A-Ride Reform Group) organized protests to maintain solo rides and the safety and efficiency advantages they offered (Grenier 2022). Disability scholars Kelsie Acton and Aimi Hamraie (2022) have shown the importance of "remote access" during the pandemic, but these occasional improvements to mobility services are also part of the genealogy of access and can serve as blueprints for future services.

Access to Work and Digital Affordances: "Thank God for Zoom, as Much as We Hate It"

During the pandemic, as disabled workers worked from home, they did not have to deal with the time-consuming commuting activities or getting prepared before going to the office. Work seekers also had a different experience, as questions of accessibility were blurred with the productivity imperatives of a work market adapting to the mass immobilization of the workforce (Holland 2021; Lander 2021; Lent and Dvorkin 2022). In the early months of the pandemic, the unemployment rate of disabled people more than doubled in NYC. But the new remote options gradually allowed the number of people in the workforce to reach new highs, as "the biggest obstacle" to accessing and maintaining employment—commuting in the inaccessible transit system of NYC—had less of a determining effect (Smith 2022).

Paolo, a Brazilian academic living in NYC, has a rare genetic disease called Larsen's syndrome, which makes it difficult for him to travel long distances; he requires accommodations. In his previous job experiences as a professor of anthropology and disability studies, he was able to walk the short distance to the university without facing obstacles. But in January 2020, he got a new job in another university, and his back got "stuck." As he explained to me, "Starting to teach a new class is a stressful situation, and having that aggravation trying to get around, no elevators working, no escalators working. . . . Somehow, the sociology department came to me asking if I could teach two classes, and I said, 'OK, but I have a disability. Will you help me? Can we work on a schedule?' They said, 'No, we cannot change anything. We need you here in person.' So, I had

Figure 4.3. During the week of March 14, 2022, disability activists from Downstate New York ADAPT planned a multiday sit-in in front of the offices of New York State Assembly member Carl Heastie to include a bill in the final state budget to remove certain restrictions on eligibility for personal and home-care services under Medicaid, which put them at risk of nursing home placement. (Photo: Erik McGregor)

to refuse that job" (interview, 2020). Within three weeks, the department was reoffering him the job as classes went online: "So imagine how much frustration I was feeling at that time. So, it just felt like COVID-19 explicitly showed how people with disabilities do it" (interview, 2020). Since the beginning of the pandemic, Paolo has taught four classes remotely that would have been refused to him previously. This accessibility afforded by COVID-19 to accommodate the nondisabled was long demanded by disabled people and gave rise to the hashtag campaign #AccessibilityForAbleds, created by disability activist Kate Williams to shed light on the ableism, everyday discrimination, and refusal of access (Mills 2022).

Alicia, a young Black woman with chronic musculoskeletal pain, explained that employers did not trust her to work remotely prior to the pandemic because of the triple stigma of race, gender, and disability. She feared that she would not find a suitable job with the accommodations she needed after finishing her master's degree: "When

I was approaching graduation, I was terrified. I didn't think I would be able to find a job that would allow me to have accommodations like that, and then I wouldn't be able to make money. I wouldn't be able to support myself because I already had experienced what it was like to be told, 'No' and 'If you don't'—or, even at one point, you know— 'you could risk just being kicked out.' I'm fine when I'm able to do things from my home, and it doesn't affect the quality of work" (interview, 2020). During the pandemic, she found a job in a start-up as an executive assistant, which is flexible, respects her body rhythms, and allows her to thrive and manage her energy throughout the day but also avoids the impossible and energy-draining commutes. Working remotely, she feels that she has more energy; she is able to work while taking care of herself, having a routine and lifestyle around her body's needs and rhythms: "Yeah, it's not as jobless as it has felt before because this has now become the norm, which is ridiculous. Before graduating, I didn't really think about looking into remote jobs, even though they were probably out there. Even though they probably existed within my field, I didn't even know where to look, and so everything seemed like a dead end at the time. But now almost everyone is offering remote work. I wonder how long it's going to stay like that" (interview, 2020).

Remote work became the norm during the pandemic, and accommodations historically requested by the disabled community ended up being widely offered to a large portion of people who could work from home, to the point of becoming the norm (Lent and Dvorkin 2022; Acton and Hamraie 2022). Many opportunities opened up for disabled people not only because of technological advances but also due to an acceptance of working remotely as a legitimate practice. But as Jessica Murray reminds us, "There's still a digital divide where some people don't have access to it or they don't have access to high-speed internet, and it's hard for them to still be connecting. So, I think it's like a different kind of 'mobility' that it's kind of exposing inequalities on that front" (interview, 2020).

A turn to remote work without a democratization of internet access and affordable electronics will only reproduce the preexisting disparities and further prevent people from participating. Remote access can get us only so far; some of the participants had to move back in with relatives outside the city as the pandemic unfolded since they could not find the necessary affordances to maintain their social and physical needs in NYC.

Disability Politics and New Solidarities

Political participation depends on access to political spaces. Going to meetings or protests is not an easy task when a city's transportation system lacks positive affordances. During the pandemic, many disabled people started to use digital technologies to get involved in meetings and conferences; some joined or formed new alliances. Diane recalls, "I have been in a committee meeting every month with the Mayor's Office for People with Disabilities. There are almost three hundred people on that call, either listening and or participating, because some people have questions and information is being disseminated. But if we didn't have Zoom, where would we be on a phone for an hour and holding to our ear? . . . So, this world has changed" (interview, 2020).

Roger, who is a wheelchair user and a council board member for a disability group, explained how the productivity of the group's meetings was enhanced during the pandemic, as people could join through Zoom and not have to depend on Access-A-Ride or the buses to participate: "It's funny that we've gotten board things done more than when we were physical. So we might end up keeping it like that. We might end up keeping it up, having Zoom meetings for the board" (interview, 2020).

Peter, a white, history PhD student with cerebral palsy with a preference for ethnographic inquiry, told me that he gained more insight and empathy for his own work on disability as he acquired two chronic conditions at the beginning of the pandemic. Immobilized in NYC in his apartment and experiencing the deterioration of his physical state, he felt the urge to get involved politically. He joined with his friend Paolo and other academics from the US, Canada, and Brazil to form a digital collective project on disability in Brazil. The group met online monthly to share their experiences, teach one another how to solve questions around disability during the pandemic, and ensure support: "It's become this big community in which a lot of people are involved. And so I think in a lot of ways, we're still working out sort of what best practices are and what the most healthy leadership rhythms are" (interview, 2020). As a collective, they published papers and gave talks; they also learned about leadership and cohesion in a mutual setting.

Discussion and Conclusion

As we consider the pandemic transit experiences of disabled people in New York City, we should recognize that they are continuous with prepandemic realities. If the mass immobilization revealed one thing, it is the inherent ableism of the "mobilized society." Mobility was not the precondition of social participation during COVID-19; in a time when long-denied accommodations became the norm, people found new ways to connect using digital technology, find jobs, work remotely, get involved in local politics, confront the state, and create alliances internationally. For a time, paratransit solo rides provided more spontaneous commutes, and users could play support roles for others for the first time.

The pandemic produced important ruptures; it also revealed continuities in the city's ableist infrastructure and policy for public transit. In the postcrisis period, the inaccessibility of the transportation system in NYC will remain "the biggest obstacle" and the main disabling vector in the city for years to come. This chapter shows how changes in the relational environment offered opportunities to disabled people to develop new affordances and differentiated subjectivities; reducing these affordances would lead to disabling situations, while enhancing them could lead to greater participation on the part of the city's disabled citizens. Alicia, recognizing how much she and her situation changed during the pandemic because of the new affordances, expressed it succinctly: "Distance, different spaces, and whether and how much our subjectivities can shift because of, yeah, just the space that we're in, if that makes sense" (interview, 2020).

Under the extraordinary pressure of a universally perceived crisis, many forces lined up for alternative accessible worlds to be actualized, changing the lived and experienced conditions of people and their possibilities of adopting freely chosen habits and social roles, when there is intense demand, sufficient political will, and material openings. The emerging affordances mentioned in the interviews, matters of everyday praxis and imagination, comprise the individual and collective pandemic expertise and knowledge of disabled people. They should be considered in both post-pandemic policies and future decision-making processes. Even if the finances of the MTA remain uncertain, the organization is now legally bound to install accessible infrastructures. This is a historic victory on the part of disability advocates. In the remobilization of NYC, these crucial, if underappreciated, pandemic experiences can guide us toward an increasingly accessible future.

NOTES

1 Center for Independence of the Disabled, New York, et al. v. Metropolitan Transportation Authority, et al., No. 153765/2017 (N.Y. Sup. Ct. N.Y. Co.); De La Rosa et al. v. Metropolitan Transportation Authority et al., No. 19-cv-04406 (ER) (S.D.N.Y.).
2 Goldenberg et al. v. Metropolitan Transportation Authority et al., No. 159096/2022 (N.Y. Sup. Ct. N.Y. Co. 2022).

REFERENCES

Acton, Kelsie, and Aimi Hamraie. 2022. "Life at a Distance: Archiving Disability Cultures of Remote Participation." *Just Tech*, Social Science Research Council, June 28, 2022. https://doi.org/10.35650/JT.3036.d.2022.

Borkowski, Przemysław, Magdalena Jażdżewska-Gutta, and Agnieszka Szmelter-Jarosz. 2021. "Lockdowned: Everyday Mobility Changes in Response to COVID-19." *Journal of Transport Geography* 90:102906. https://doi.org/10.1016/j.jtrangeo.2020.102906.

Brewer, Gale. 2019. "Subway Elevators." Office of Manhattan Borough President, New York.

Brumbaugh, Stephen. 2018. "Travel Patterns of American Adults with Disabilities." Issue brief. US Department of Transportation, Office of the Secretary of Transportation, Bureau of Transportation Statistics.

Cresswell, Tim. 2021. "Valuing Mobility in a Post COVID-19 World." *Mobilities* 16 (1): 51–65.

DiNapoli, Thomas P. 2019. "Employment Trends for People with Disabilities in New York City." Office of the New York State Comptroller, New York.

Disability Rights Advocates. n.d. "The History of DRA's Lawsuits against the NYC Metropolitan Transportation Authority." Accessed June 2022. https://dralegal.org.

Dokumaci, Arseli. 2017. "Vital Affordances, Occupying Niches: An Ecological Approach to Disability and Performance." *Research in Drama Education: The Journal of Applied Theatre and Performance* 22 (3): 393–412. https://doi.org/10.1080/13569783.2017.1326808.

———. 2023. *Activist Affordances: How Disabled People Improvise More Habitable Worlds* Durham, NC: Duke University Press.

Elegudin, Alex. 2022. "The Slow Train to NYC Subway Accessibility." *New York Daily News*, June 24, 2022. www.nydailynews.com.

Engle, Samuel, John Stromme, and Anson Zhou. 2020. "Staying at Home: Mobility Effects of Covid-19." SSRN 3565703. https://papers.ssrn.com.
Evelly, Jeanmarie. 2018. "28 Years after ADA's Passage, Subway Accessibility Still 'Disgraceful,' Experts Say." *City Limits*, July 30, 2018. https://citylimits.org.
———. 2020. "MTA Moves Forward with Changes to Access-a-Ride Pilot, Despite Protests from Users." *City Limits*, February 27, 2020. https://citylimits.org.
Garland-Thomson, Rosemarie. 2011. "Misfits: A Feminist Materialist Disability Concept." *Hypatia* 26 (3): 591–609.
Gibson, James. 1979. *The Ecological Approach to Visual Perception*. Boston: Houghton Mifflin.
Gold, Michael. 2022. "M.T.A. Vows to Make Subways 95% Accessible. It Will Take 33 Years." *New York Times*, June 22, 2022. www.nytimes.com.
Grenier, Yan. 2022. "A Protest to End Shared Access-A-Ride Trips and Resume Solo Rides." *Disability Covid Chronicles*, NYU Center for Disability Studies, July 20, 2022. https://disabilitycovidchronicles.nyu.edu.
———. 2023. "New York State Pause Executive Order and Matilda's Law." *Disability Covid Chronicles*, NYU Center for Disability Studies, August 1, 2023. https://disabilitycovidchronicles.nyu.edu.
Grenier, Yan, and Quemuel Arroyo. 2022. "Mobility, the MTA, and COVID in New York City: An interview with Quemuel Arroyo." *Disability COVID Chronicles*, NYU Center for Disability Studies, January 15, 2022. https://disabilitycovidchronicles.nyu.edu.
Hamraie, Aimi, and Kelly Fritsch. 2019. "Crip Technoscience Manifesto." *Catalyst: Feminism, Theory, Technoscience* 5 (1): 1–33.
Harris, Jeffrey E. 2020. "The Subways Seeded the Massive Coronavirus Epidemic in New York City." Working Paper 27021. National Bureau of Economic Research, Cambridge, MA.
Holland, Paula. 2021. "Will Disabled Workers Be Winners or Losers in the Post-COVID-19 Labour Market?" *Disabilities* 1 (3): 161–73.
Huang, Youqin, and Rui Li. 2022. "The Lockdown, Mobility, and Spatial Health Disparities in COVID-19 Pandemic: A Case Study of New York City." *Cities* 122:103549. https://doi.org/10.1016/j.cities.2021.103549.
Ingold, Tim. 1992. "Culture and the Perception of the Environment." In *Bush Base: Forest Farm. Culture, Environment and Development*, edited by Elisabeth Croll and David Parkin, 39–56. New York: Routledge.
———. 2018. "Back to the Future with the Theory of Affordances." *HAU: Journal of Ethnographic Theory* 8 (1–2): 39–44.
Kaske, Michelle. 2022. "MTA to Make 95% of New York Subway Stations Accessible by 2055." *Bloomberg*, June 22, 2022. www.bloomberg.com.
Kaufman, Sarah M., Joanna Simon, and Calloway Hope Aboaf. 2017. *Bringing Innovation to Paratransit*. New York: Rudin Center for Transportation.
Klinenberg, Eric. 2024. "Travels Far (Thankachan Mathai)." In *2020: One City, Seven People, and the Year Everything Changed*, 278–91. New York: Knopf.

Lander, Brad. 2021. *The Impact of Hybrid Work on Commuters and NYC Sales Tax*. New York: Office of the New York City Comptroller. https://comptroller.nyc.gov.

Lefebvre, Henri. 1968. *Le droit à la ville*. Paris: Anthropos.

Legal Services NYC. 2010. "MTA Transit Cuts Challenged by Disabled New Yorkers." August 17, 2010. www.prnewswire.com.

Lent, Melissa, and Eli Dvorkin. 2022. *Access Opportunity: Expanding Economic Opportunity for New Yorkers with Disabilities in the Post-Pandemic City*. New York: Center for an Urban Future. https://nycfuture.org.

Martinez, Jose. 2021. "Taxi Driver Shortage Stalls Passengers with Limited Mobility as MTA Ride Service Sags." *The City*, June 23, 2021. www.thecity.nyc.

———. 2022. "Riders with Disabilities Sue MTA to Close the Gap Between Subway Train and Platform." *The City*, October 26, 2022. www.thecity.nyc.

McDonough, Annie. 2021. "The MTA Isn't Budging on Ending Shared Access-A-Ride Trips." *City & State*, August 2021. www.cityandstateny.com.

Metropolitan Transit Authority (MTA). 2019. "MTA 2020–2024 Capital Program." https://new.mta.info.

Mills, Mara. 2022. "#AccessibilityForAbleds." *Disability Covid Chronicles*, NYU Center for Disability Studies, March 14, 2022. https://disabilitycovidchronicles.nyu.edu.

Musselwhite, Charles, Erel Avineri, and Yusak Susilo. 2020. "Editorial JTH 16–The Coronavirus Disease COVID-19 and Implications for Transport and Health." *Journal of Transport & Health* 16:100853. https://doi.org/10.1016/j.jth.2020.100853.

New York Times. 1984. "Koch Blocks Accord on Subway Access for Disabled People." June 22, 1984. www.nytimes.com.

Office of the New York State Governor. 2020. "Governor Cuomo Signs the 'New York State on PAUSE' Executive Order." March 20, 2020. www.governor.ny.gov.

Patel, Jugal K. 2019. "Where the Subway Limits New Yorkers With Disabilities." *New York Times*, February 11, 2019. www.nytimes.com.

Plaut, Mel, Chris Pangilinan, Hayley Richardson, and Jon Orcutt. 2017. *Access Denied: Making the MTA Subway System Accessible to All New Yorkers*. New York: TransitCenter.

Rosenberg, Eli. 2017. "New York City's Subway System Violates Local and Federal Laws, Disability Groups Say." *New York Times*, April 25, 2017. www.nytimes.com.

Ruder, Ian. 2021. "Pandemic Habits." *New Mobility*, April 1, 2021. https://newmobility.com.

Smith, Molly. 2022. "Disabled Americans Reap Remote-Work Reward in Record Employment." *Bloomberg*, October 3, 2022. www.bloomberg.com.

Spivak, Caroline. 2019. "Accessible Subway Station Numbers in Manhattan Are Inflated, Report Says." *Curbed*, February 6, 2019. https://ny.curbed.com.

Statista. 2022. "Mobility in Selected Cities between March 3, 2020 and June 1, 2021, Compared with Movement Prior to the Coronavirus Outbreak." www.statista.com.

Stringer, Scott M. 2018. *Service Denied: Accessibility and the New York City Subway System*. New York: Office of the New York City Comptroller.

US Access Board. 1968. "Architectural Barriers Act (ABA) of 1968." www.access-board.gov.

US Census Bureau. 2020. "American Community Survey 2015–2019 5-Year Data Release." December 10, 2020. www.census.gov.

Warren, Michael S., and Samuel W. Skillman. 2020. "Mobility Changes in Response to COVID-19." *arXiv*, 2003.14228. https://arxiv.org.

Wong, Sandy, Sara L. McLafferty, Arrianna M. Planey, and Valerie A. Preston. 2020. "Disability, Wages, and Commuting in New York." *Journal of Transport Geography* 87:102818. https://doi.org/10.1016/j.jtrangeo.2020.102818.

5

Vent

Making and Debating the New York State Ventilator Allocation Guidelines

MARA MILLS

At a press conference on May 6, 2020, disability activist Stacey Park Milbern spoke about her fears as a ventilator user facing the COVID-19 pandemic. Lying on her side in bed, with a handwritten sign reading "Equitable Healthcare for All" propped among the sheets in the foreground, she responded to popular reports about ventilator rationing and reallocation:

> It's been pretty scary to navigate COVID-19 as a ventilator user. I was quite frightened early on when my doctor shared that I would likely not survive an exposure. My caregivers, who were not able to fully shelter in place, have had to step back from working with me. As a disabled person, it felt really critical not to get sick. I saw a Public Safety Alert from Santa Clara County, asking people to identify if they use a ventilator for county inventory. I need my ventilator to breathe. My friends and I made emergency plans about what to do if someone shows up at my door asking for my backup ventilator. I was getting advice from friends in medical fields: if disabled people get sick, we may not get care, we may be turned away, we may be discriminated against. (Fat Rose 2020)

In the first months of the pandemic, as hospitals and politicians around the United States began making plans to ration various aspects of health care—from beds in intensive care units (ICUs) to medicines and equipment—activists and advocacy groups for disabled people and seniors demanded that those who were impacted play a role in shaping these policies (Wong 2020). Milbern was cofounder of the Disability Justice Culture Club, a crip of color organizing hub in Oakland, and she also

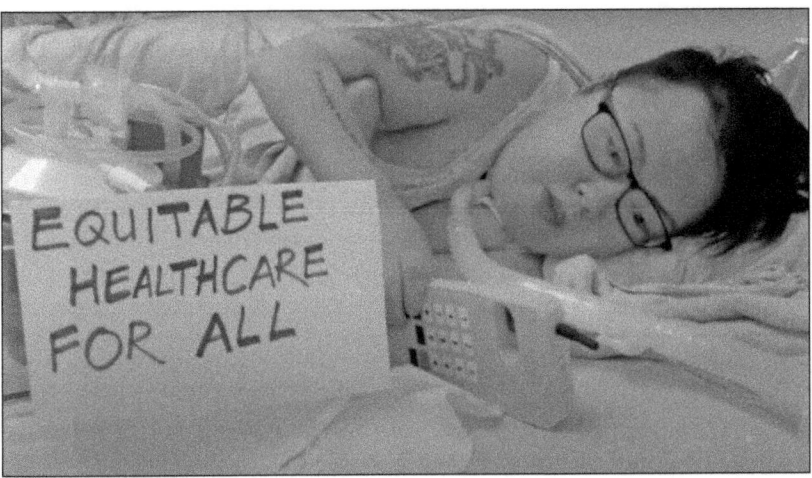

Figure 5.1. Stacey Park Milbern at the California Care Rationing Coalition May 6 press conference. (Fat Rose 2020)

served as a disability adviser to President Barack Obama's administration. Less than two weeks after the press conference, on her thirty-third birthday, she died as a result of complications from a cancer surgery that had been postponed during the first wave of pandemic "lockdowns."

Stories and predictions about the rationing of ventilators flooded the news and social media in 2020. COVID-19 is a respiratory virus, and when patients began overwhelming hospitals in northern Italy in February and March, the world watched in shock as Italian medical societies issued protocols for rationing ventilators by age and disability. Part of a triage process, typically associated with wartime medicine, these protocols recommended assessing patients for the number of remaining "life years" and "presence of comorbidities," with ventilators and other scarce resources allocated to those who were likely to live longer and require shorter treatment times (Mounk 2020; Han and Koch 2020).

The pandemic crested across the US shortly thereafter. Some states already had "crisis standards of care" guidelines (CSCs) incorporated into their emergency plans; others began drafting them (Ne'eman 2020b; Bagenstos 2020; Manchanda, Sanky, and Appel 2021; Ne'eman et al. 2021). The New York State Department of Health (DOH) had circulated a draft ventilator allocation proposal for public comment in 2007, after which other states began to include similar protocols in their CSCs. At the outset of COVID-19, in states where guidelines were nonexistent or not activated by a declaration of emergency, hospitals and sometimes individual physicians created their own ad hoc policies for ventilator triage (Antommaria et al. 2020).

Examples quickly circulated of disabled people being denied treatment for COVID in the US as a result of rationing, sparking massive protest among disability activists. In Austin, Texas, Michael Hickson, a Black man who had sustained a brain injury a few years before, died in hospice in June 2020 after being refused care by a hospital, on "quality of life" premises (Shapiro 2020a). In towns across Oregon—even before any shortages of ICU beds or equipment—several cases surfaced of group homes being pressured to complete "do not resuscitate" (DNR) orders for their residents at the start of the pandemic and of doctors requesting the same from patients with intellectual disabilities. Advocates were quick to note that similar practices long preceded COVID: "There has always been a bias against people with disabilities in the health care system.... It was largely hidden" (Shapiro 2020b).

Samuel Bagenstos, now general counsel for the US Department of Health and Human Services, argued in a May 2020 *Yale Law Review* forum that "the crisis standards of care adopted by hospitals and state agencies often employ explicit disability-based distinctions" (1). Building on a March 2020 opinion essay in the *New York Times* by disability activist Ari Ne'eman, Bagenstos pointed to the 2016 Tennessee government's *Guidance for the Ethical Allocation of Scarce Resources*, which excluded people with "spinal muscular atrophy," among others "requiring assistance with activities of daily living," from hospital admission during state health emergencies (Tennessee Altered Standards of Care Workgroup 2016). In Alabama, the 2010 state triage guidelines—*Criteria for Mechanical Ventilator Triage Following Proclamation of Mass-Casualty Respiratory Emergency*—deprioritized people with intellectual disabilities as well as older people (US Department of Health and Human Services 2020). Even newer ventilator allocation guidelines, such as those published by the University of Washington Medical Center at the start of the pandemic, emphasized "healthy, long-term survival, recognizing that this represents weighting the survival of young otherwise healthy patients more heavily than that of older, chronically debilitated patients"

(Bagenstos 2020, 3). Disability bioethicist Joseph Stramondo also examined these state triage protocols and concluded that many were based on explicit or implicit "quality of life" (QoL) metrics, which have long been the subject of forceful critique in disability studies. Stramondo has contested what is known as "the disability paradox" in mainstream bioethics, insisting that it is not paradoxical for disabled people to rate the "quality" of their own lives highly (2021, 202).

Ventilators are powerful symbols in triage situations, invoked by the "pulling the plug" metaphor and often caught up in hospital management debates about medical futility and health-care costs. Yet, after a state-by-state survey of crisis standards of care for rationing and other aspects of disaster medicine, a team of scholars led by Ne'eman found that disability activists had largely ignored CSCs before the pandemic (Ne'eman et al. 2021). Moreover, prior to COVID-19, only twenty-six states had published guidelines for allocating ventilators during emergencies (Piscitello, Kapania, and Miller 2020). In an example of what the editors of this volume call "the disability dialectic," COVID-19 brought CSCs to mainstream attention, prompting an outcry by disability activists, lawyers, and bioethicists in the press and on social media—as well several complaints filed with the US Department of Health and Human Services by disability advocacy organizations. As a result, many state ventilator triage plans were revised, and additional states created their own guidelines. Ne'eman's team concluded that those CSCs updated "later in the pandemic were more aligned with advocate priorities"—even if ableist and racial biases remained—suggesting that the "disability rights movement's successes in influencing state triage policy should inform future CSCs and set the stage for further work on how stakeholders influence bioethics policy debates" (Ne'eman et al. 2021, 831; see also Tsaplina and Stramondo 2020).

New York was one of the first states to come up with a plan for allotting ventilators during pandemics, and its guidelines have been broadly influential—however, they were never formally activated during COVID-19. When the New York State Task Force on Life and the Law, a bioethics advisory group established by Mario Cuomo when he was governor in 1985, completed an initial draft of the guidelines for the state DOH in 2007, it recommended the outright exclusion of certain patients from ventilator rationing—such as those with severe burns, those with

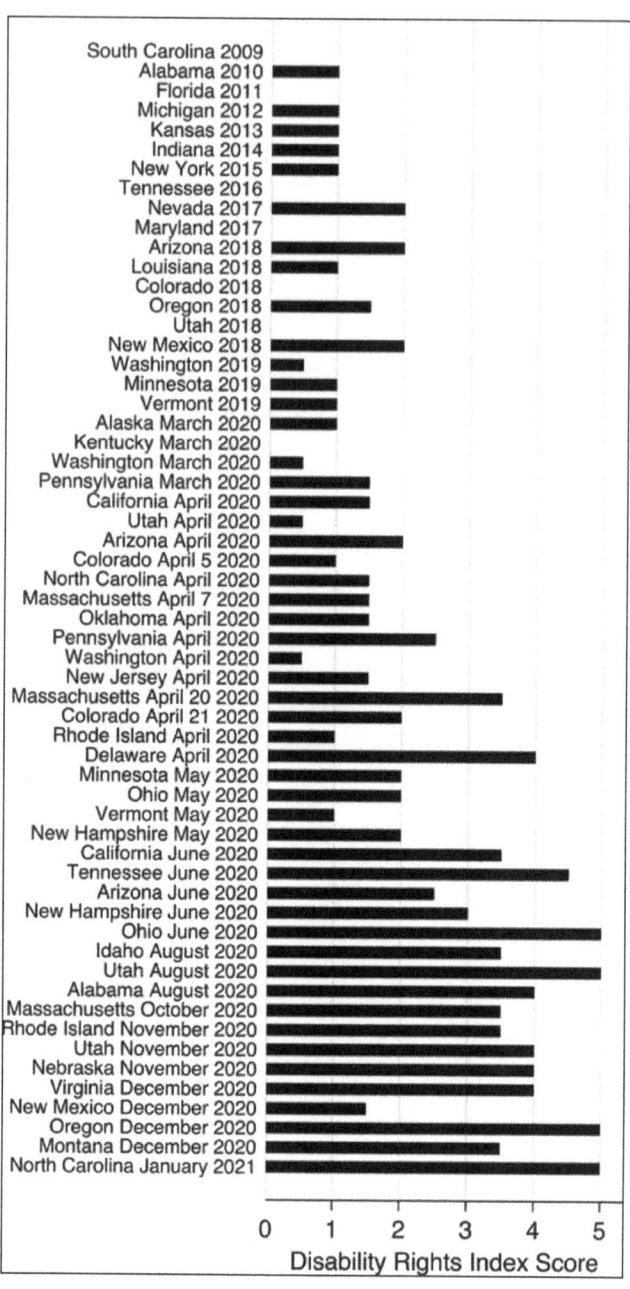

Figure 5.2. Disability rights scores for state CSCs. Multiple versions are shown by date for some states; other states have not produced CSCs and are not represented. "The absence of exclusion criteria, the prohibition of long-term survival, the prohibition of resource intensity, the inclusion of reasonable modifications to clinical instruments, and the inclusion of chronic ventilator protections each constitute one point of five." (Ne'eman et al. 2021, 844)

metastatic cancer, and dialysis users—as well as the use of SOFA scoring (Sequential Organ Failure Assessment) to deprioritize those with a higher likelihood of short-term mortality (NYS Workgroup 2007; NYS DOH 2009). (Short-term mortality was seen as a less ageist or ableist measure than overall "life years.") A group of roughly two dozen volunteers with expertise in medicine, law, and ethics, joined by religious leaders and a small paid staff, the Task Force makes recommendations to the governor and state agencies on health-care policies ranging from surrogacy to genetic testing, often in collaboration with expert workgroups it convenes on those topics. After a long period of public engagement and internal debate about the 2007 draft, the Task Force released the updated Ventilator Allocation Guidelines in 2015, removing dialysis and cancer from the exclusion criteria and including new pediatric protocols (among other changes; see Han and Koch 2020; NYS Task Force 2015). At the time that this chapter was drafted, these guidelines were still published on the New York Department of Health website. Not revised after the advent of COVID-19, they were given a low score of 1 on the Disability Rights Index.

Even if the New York guidelines were never officially "triggered," they have had far-reaching impact: they shaped ventilator protocols at hundreds of hospitals and Veterans Administration health-care centers within New York State, as well as the subsequent development of CSCs in a number of other states (Fink 2009a). During the COVID-19 pandemic, the 2015 guidelines received enormous attention from the press, bioethicists, and disability activist groups like Not Dead Yet (Ne'eman 2020a; Fins 2020a; Pierson 2022; Walsh et al. 2023). Despite the national discussion now surrounding these guidelines—and the enormous amount of state-sponsored labor that went into finalizing them—not only were they never implemented, but Governor Andrew Cuomo went so far as to remark in a 2020 press conference that the state had "no protocol" for ventilator allocation (Kaste and Hersher 2020). Susie A. Han, who directed the review and revisions for the 2015 version, recalls how resource-intensive the process was: "New York's Ventilator Allocation Guidelines represent the culmination of more than nine years of analysis, research, and consensus-building. In total (and not including staff), 69 task force members and adult clinical workgroup members effectively reached consensus on the clinical protocol and the ethical principles upon which the guidelines are based" (Koch and Han 2020, 153). Regarding Cuomo's disavowal, she suspects that he was concerned about "political and public blowback" along the lines of earlier "death panel" controversies (Koch and Han 2020, 154).

Some physicians and hospital directors claimed that the need to ration ventilators was never reached in New York State during COVID-19 and, hence, that the guidelines were irrelevant. In fall 2020, an announcement was posted to the website for NYU's Langone Health, declaring that "prudent planning" and the transfer of fifty-five new ventilators from a state stockpile had allowed the hospital system to avoid rationing (NYU Langone News Hub 2020). Yet, in March, at the outset of the crisis, the *Wall Street Journal* published excerpts of an email written by Robert Fermia, the chair of Langone's Emergency Medicine Department, telling emergency-room (ER) doctors to "think more critically about who we intubate." As the *Wall Street Journal* explained, ER doctors were told that "they had 'sole discretion' to place patients on ventilators and institutional backing to 'withhold futile intubations'" (Ramachandran and Palazzolo 2020).[1] Immediately after this news broke, several outlets reported that NYU had "threatened to fire faculty doctors if they talked to the press without preapproval from the medical center's Office of Communications and Marketing" (Piper 2020). Han argues that Cuomo's abandonment of the state guidelines led to widespread misinformation, mistrust, and disarray in New York hospitals that first spring (Koch and Han 2020). Some hospitals attempted to implement the New York State guidelines on their own, while others worked out ad hoc or institution-based protocols.

To probe the broader questions such guidelines raise for disability ethics and activism, the remainder of this chapter examines the making of the guidelines themselves—namely, the intensive debates among clinicians, lawyers, and ethicists that yielded a fragile consensus on the 2007 draft (and, in turn, the final 2015 recommendation). As it turns out, this consensus was never unanimous, and much of the skepticism of Task Force members and expert consultants regarding the fairness and enforceability of the ventilator allocation protocols presaged the state of affairs at New York hospitals at the outset of COVID-19. In reviewing Task Force minutes, correspondence, tabletop exercises, and other records formerly held in the New York State Department of Health records, it becomes clear that "ventilator allocation" is commonly misunderstood to refer to discrete devices and the rights of individual users. Ventilator allocation is, in fact, an elaborate sociotechnical system (a foundational concept in science and technology studies) involving the distribution of supplies and labor among states, towns, health-care providers, and patients. Wealth disparities, often linked to zip code and race, mean that individual hospitals have unequal resources in the absence of state or national protocols for distributing equipment, oxygen, and workers at the institutional level. Only an expanded definition of both "ventilator" and "allocation" could meet the stated goal of this distributive justice project—which was to "save the most lives" (Han and Koch 2020, e35).

Most disability activists do not contest the need for state CSCs— without them, hospitals and individual doctors will (and did) enact their own, often biased, protocols. Rather, as Ne'eman and colleagues have insisted, disabled people need to be included on CSC decision-making teams. The DOH records show that there was very little input from disabled members of the public in the making of the New York guidelines, perhaps as much from lack of concern among disability activists at the time, or other priorities, as from unsuccessful outreach. Adrienne Asch, a blind bioethicist, became a member of the Task Force in 2007, but her dissent from the consensus on the SOFA protocol was only registered in a footnote to the 2015 edition, noting that she preferred a random lottery for ventilators "for its objectivity" (or circumvention of obvious ableism and other forms of bias), even if it did not maximize the number of lives saved (NYS Task Force 2015, 43).

This chapter concludes with further discussion of activist responses to ventilator allocation during COVID-19 and argues the need for new disability imaginaries of what allocation might mean, especially as more disabled people—hopefully—engage in crisis standards of care planning. Other chapters in this volume detail the many different forms that disability activism has taken during the pandemic: protest, social media campaigns, mutual aid, solidarity, "crip doulaing." What is missing is a disability theory of distributive justice, one that takes into consideration not only eliminating ableism at the level of individual diagnosis in the ICU setting but ensuring access to ventilators and other health resources for broad and diverse groups of people in a given city and beyond. Countless theories of distributive justice have been proposed by philosophers concerned with the sharing of risks, resources, and opportunities across the members of a society (Lamont and Favor 2017). Just as the disability justice movement aims beyond the model of individual disability rights, crip distributive justice would require an expansive definition of disability, including illness and injury; attention to class, race, and region; and a commitment to foundational social change rather than inclusion in an inequitable system (Sins Invalid 2019).

Methods

"Transparency" and "public engagement" were two of the core ethical principles guiding the creation of the New York Ventilator Allocation Guidelines (NYS Workgroup 2007; Antommaria et al. 2020). After publishing the 2007 draft, the Task Force solicited feedback through a variety of channels: thirteen focus groups convened in Albany, Westchester, Buffalo, and New York City; audio- and videoconferences; an email address advertised on the DOH website and in various periodicals; tabletop exercises with New York City hospital staff; and meetings with a group of clinical experts. The focus groups were organized to engage a variety of New Yorkers from diverse education, employment, and income backgrounds: "the elderly (defined as people aged 60+), parents of children under 18, individuals with serious or chronic illnesses, rural residents (defined as people residing in towns with less than 5,000 people), minorities, and young adults aged 22–29" (Han 2023a). Criticisms and comments from these groups led to further rounds of discussion at Task Force meetings (with some changeover of members and directors), eventually culminating in the "final" 2015 guidelines.

Less than a decade later, however, very little is archived or publicly available regarding the committee's internal research and debates, the comments submitted by the public, or the revision and consensus process. I submitted a FOIL (Freedom of Information Law) request with the DOH to obtain copies of the Task Force archives related to the ventilator guidelines—hoping to see what kinds of disability participation and commentary took place—only to learn that the records office apparently never received any materials from the 2015 revision group (directed by Han as well as attorneys Stuart Sherman and Valerie Koch). Moreover the DOH had already purged the materials related to the 2007 draft, when the Task Force was directed by Powell. Fortunately, journalist Sheri Fink had previously FOILed the ventilator records in 2009, obtaining a ninety-five-page transcript of a 2006 meeting between Task Force members and an expert workgroup, ninety pages of emailed public commentary, the situation manual and tabletop exercises presented to staff at New York Presbyterian Hospital, slides and text from public presentations, and the 2009 summary of focus-group discussions created by The Research Associates. Fink published two articles about the 2007 draft guidelines for ProPublica and had saved the records, generously passing them along to me (Fink 2009a, 2009b).

I also wrote to several of the Task Force members involved in the 2007 and 2015 proceedings. Among those who replied, few had detailed memories or extensive involvement with the write-up or any connection at all to the public engagement process. As a volunteer organization, the Task Force meets occasionally throughout the year to discuss a number of different bioethical issues. The clinical working group on ventilator allocation met more intensively to generate ideas to be passed to the full Task Force, with the write-up itself handled by directors or staff—who, like Han, were themselves not present throughout the entire nine-year process. I spoke to Han and Sherman, who did not know what happened to their hard drives or email archives after they left their positions, and to Powell, who was not aware that the 2007 records had been archived at all. In fact, Powell (2022) commented to me that Task Force meetings were designed "to create a safe and private space in which people with sometimes strongly different views could speak freely and in confidence to see if they could arrive at common ground. Having those conversations made public was viewed as a way to kill any opportunity for creative solutions." The DOH policies around archiving clearly need to be articulated to the Task Force as well as the public, and this archiving and transparency gap needs to be addressed at the records level for DOH initiatives with dramatic public impacts—not only as a matter of public trust but as a way to educate citizens about the different scales and perspectives (scientific, government, religious, community) through which complex bioethical policies are considered.

The packet of comments on the 2007 ventilator allocation proposal shows that many health professionals weighed in during the public feedback period, but few other New Yorkers did. The minutes of the March

2006 meeting of Task Force members with outside experts are unusual in that the meeting itself was tape-recorded and thus fully transcribed. Other Task Force meetings on the same topic are not documented. (Han told me that later meetings, leading to the 2015 revised guidelines, were not recorded, nor were minutes or notes archived.) Powell, who introduced and moderated the 2006 meeting, explained to the group the purpose of the recording: to "keep us honest about where we did find consensus, and where we did not" and to "singl[e] out comments that actually might have been extremely useful but didn't find their full range of play during the day's conversations" (NYS Workgroup 2006, 1). Because participants were told the recording was for "internal purposes only" and because the separate records of public commentary consist of individual emails sent to Task Force members or the DOH, I maintain participants' anonymity by summarizing the themes that emerged as points of debate relevant to disability and the subsequent COVID-19 pandemic. Some of these materials were formerly posted on the ProPublica website, linked to one of Fink's articles, but now they are held privately on my and Fink's computers (Fink 2009b). When I offered to return the materials to the DOH, the records officer declined.

Contestation Surrounds Consensus

At the request of the New York DOH, the Task Force on Life and the Law convened a workgroup on "Ethical Issues in Ventilator Allocation in an Influenza Pandemic" in March 2006, cochaired by Gus Birkhead of the New York State Department of Health and Tia Powell, a psychiatrist and bioethicist who directed the Task Force at the time. Concerned about avian flu and responding to the US Department of Homeland Security's claim that "pandemic influenza [was] both the most likely and most lethal of all threats facing the United States," the DOH had drafted a pandemic preparedness plan in 2004 and circulated a revised three-hundred-page draft the week before the workgroup meeting (NYS Workgroup 2007). Based on the federal pandemic plan of 2004, the state plan laid out a range of responses such as social distancing and school closures. The goal of the workgroup was to clarify the ventilator component, thought to be critical for a future pandemic event in the period before a vaccine became available.

The workgroup consisted of roughly three dozen people with clinical and ethics expertise, including several representatives of the New York State DOH; health commissioners from across the state; bioethicists, physicians, and medical directors at Bellevue, Cornell, Columbia, NYU Langone, and Montefiore hospital systems; respiratory therapists and law professors; and representatives of the New York Academy of Medicine and Hastings Center. Several Task Force members also participated.[2] The conversation at the March 2006 workgroup meeting, like the draft guidelines issued the following year, ranged from pre-triage planning for hospitals to palliative care for dying patients and legal aid for doctors who complied with the rationing guidelines. Powell commented at this planning session, "To my knowledge, I'm not sure anyone else is . . . as brave or as foolhardy in actually trying to map out a strategy for this specific problem" (NYS Workgroup 2006).

The state pandemic plan already contained various examples of rationing, for instance, prioritizing health workers and at-risk New Yorkers for vaccines. As part of the ventilator workgroup's more focused rationing topic, it reviewed an article published in February 2006 by John Hick and Daniel O'Laughlin, physicians working with the Minnesota Department of Health and Terrorism Task Force, who recommended Sequential Organ Failure Assessment (SOFA scoring) as "the most useful" tool for predicting mortality in an ICU environment (Hick and O'Laughlin 2006). Later, Powell and the other authors of the 2007 draft guidelines would additionally cite the Ontario Health Plan for an Influenza Pandemic, published in April 2006, which also recommended SOFA scoring. Patients with high scores (high mortality probability) either would not be allocated ventilators or would have ventilators removed and reallocated if their scores worsened over time in the ICU. Prior to SOFA scoring, some patients would be denied ventilators on the basis of a set of exclusion criteria, such as "severe chronic lung disease" or "severe burn." The New York ventilator workgroup essentially adapted these rationing plans, with a particular concern to eliminate any subjective quality-of-life biases by using only "objective" mortality metrics. It termed the New York protocols "guidelines" because they were meant to be "flexible": the 2007 draft explains that the DOH could activate the guidelines for state hospitals in either a "binding" or "nonbinding" manner.

Criticisms of US ventilator allocation protocols during the COVID-19 pandemic have focused heavily on the exclusion criteria and SOFA scoring, finding them to encode a range of ableist and racist biases, as well as subjective presumptions about mortality and even implicit quality-of-life assumptions. But the New York State Ventilator Allocation Guidelines of 2007 and 2015 reached far beyond the emergency-room and intensive-care settings. The "distributive justice" statement in the 2007 draft also discussed the need for fair allocation, or reallocation, of ventilators among different hospitals throughout the state: "A just or equitable healthcare system cannot allow for more expansive access at a prestigious private facility and more restrictive access at a community or public hospital" (NYS Workgroup 2007, 16). Because SOFA scoring seems to be concrete, impacting individuals in a way that is easy to envision, it has dominated the disability activist and ethics understanding of what ventilator allocation means—even though allocation occurs at numerous distinct scales.

Triage plans also take many forms, underpinned by distinct philosophies. A 2020 survey of policies at US hospitals found that more than half did not have a ventilator allocation plan in place at all. Among those hospitals that responded and did have plans (and were not among the 10.4 percent prohibited from sharing their policies), the authors found that "the most frequently cited triage criteria were benefit (25 policies [96.2%]), need (14 [53.8%]), age (13 [50.0%]), conservation of resources (10 [38.5%]), and lottery (9 [34.6%]). Twenty-one (80.8%) policies use scoring systems, and 20 of these (95.2%) use a version of the Sequential Organ Failure Assessment score" (Antommaria et al. 2020, 188). The New York State guidelines of 2007 and 2015, an early adopter of SOFA scoring, were based on the principle of "saving the most lives," rather than the typical hospital procedure of "first come, first served" for providing ventilators to patients. During the workgroup meeting in 2006, this founding principle was debated along with several subthemes related to "ventilators" and "allocation." Much but not all of the deliberation addressed disability explicitly or implicitly, although none of the participants openly identified as disabled. The members of the working group did discuss other potential sources of bias resulting from the makeup of the group, such as the fact that only one person of color was present.

During the COVID-19 pandemic, the presence of Adrienne Asch on the Task Force has occasionally been invoked—in a version of tokenization or even cripwashing (the use of disabled people or disability rhetoric to justify problematic policies)—to demonstrate the inclusion of disability perspectives in the making of the New York ventilator guidelines (Fins 2020a, 2020b). It is rarely, if ever, pointed out that she only joined the Task Force in 2007, and she preferred the random lottery approach, which would give everyone in a particular emergency setting an equal chance, even if it did not optimize the number of lives saved. But even patient lotteries do not solve the problem of allocation between hospital departments, hospitals, cities, and states—that is, between populations rather than individuals—a task for future disability theory.

What Is a Ventilator?

At the start of the 2006 workgroup meeting, Birkhead noted that New York State was already planning to increase the state stockpile of ventilators in preparation for a pandemic. In the open discussion period, it quickly became clear that ventilator use requires much more than devices alone. One participant mentioned oxygen supplies as a limiting factor, as well as federal patterns of oxygen distribution. Others brought up the issue of disposable materials like oxygen meters, cannulas, and other tubing, some of which could not be stockpiled without compromising their integrity over time. Far and away, there was consensus that labor, and not technology, would be the limiting factor in a crisis. Health-care workers would become sick themselves, and some would quit their jobs or flee cities. And already, far too few people were trained in intubating patients, monitoring them while on ventilators, and maintaining the equipment to meet the needs of a pandemic. Even if the state stockpiled an enormous number of ventilators, rationing would be required to address labor, oxygen, and disposables.

At the start of any pandemic, as part of the state emergency plan, hospitals trigger "surge capacity" protocols to convert as many spaces as possible into ICUs. Joseph Fins, a bioethicist, internal medicine physician at New York Presbyterian, and Task Force member, described what this looked like in practice during the onset of COVID-19 in New York City:

An inadequate number of ventilators was met with remarkable innovation. Anesthesia machines were repurposed to ventilate patients, and ventilators were modified to accommodate two patients at a time. Pop-up ICUs were built in converted operating rooms, hospital lobbies, and on regular medical floors never designed for such a purpose. Field hospitals were built on Baker Field in Central Park and the U.S. Navy ship Comfort came to our assistance, docked on the Hudson. . . . Physicians who were not intensivists and hadn't been in an ICU since medical school or residency were given charge of patients who were critically ill, often working beyond the limits of their training. In his Executive Order of March 23, 2020 Governor Andrew Cuomo . . . allow[ed] practitioners to practice outside their usual scope of practice and permitt[ed] practitioners licensed in other states to come to New York in mutual aid during the public health emergency. This also allowed medical students to graduate early (as they did during World Wars I and II) to add to the workforce. (2020c, 142)[3]

Different types of ventilator were called into ICU service, but without activation of the allocation guidelines by the state, hospital systems made their own plans for distributing ventilators as well as ECMO (extracorporeal membrane oxygenation) machines.[4]

Tia Powell and Elizabeth Chuang have similarly described the surge capacity preparations at Montefiore Health System in the Bronx, with the conversion of administrative spaces and gyms into hospital rooms and the onboarding of many trainees. Despite this expansion of capacity, they surmise that "ad hoc rationing" probably took place at the hospitals "hit earliest and hardest" (Powell and Chuang 2020, 63). One Manhattan surgeon I spoke to told me their "hospital looked like a war zone," with operating rooms used as overflow ICUs, plastic shields cordoning larger areas into smaller ones, a rush to install new heating, ventilation, and air-conditioning (HVAC) systems and high-efficiency particulate air (HEPA) filters, and the creation of temporary morgues using refrigerated trucks parked outside hospital buildings. Shortages of oxygen concentrators and oxygen itself also began to be reported, in New York and around the world, not only in hospital settings but for home use by those who were newly disabled by Long COVID and post-COVID symptoms (Sampson 2020; Devereaux et al. 2021; Rivera 2021; Ross and Wendell 2023).

A related aspect of the state emergency plan, enacted during the early months of COVID-19, was the cancellation or postponement of elective surgeries to prioritize the treatment of those who fell ill from the virus. In regular times, the workgroup underscored that 85 percent of ventilators in New York are "encumbered" by those who are undergoing or recovering from surgical procedures, in addition to disabled people in nursing homes, other long-term care facilities, hospices, or private settings (i.e., acute as well as chronic use). One outcome of ventilator rationing—understood in an extended sense—was thus a larger number of deaths than usual from heart attacks and other cardiac issues; more people arrived at hospitals "dead on arrival," and the refrigerator trucks handled those deaths as well as those from COVID. Not only were "elective" cardiac surgeries canceled, but many people experiencing heart problems stayed home as a result of fear or confusion about when to go to the hospital. While activists have protested the possibility of certain disabled people losing their backup ventilators to rationing, there has hardly been any comment about the loss of life from ventilators being shifted away from those who required heart and lung surgeries to those who were newly ill from COVID. As the workgroup participants asked in 2006, who is considered disabled? Is everyone who requires a ventilator (at least temporarily) disabled?

The question was also raised among members of the workgroup of whether ventilators were being overemphasized as a technical fix to the complex problems of public health during a pandemic. How dominant was ventilator allocation in the overall state plan? How much money and time would be spent on ventilator allocation as opposed to, say, vaccines—which would certainly save more lives? Powell and Chuang point out that ventilators turned out not always to be appropriate for the specific impacts of COVID-19, and the use of ventilators and cardiopulmonary resuscitation (CPR) was sometimes medically futile. "By focusing on cure, and specifically on ventilators, we lacked appropriate planning for the predictable and large numbers of fatalities" (Powell and Chuang 2020, 64). Although ventilators help save some lives, they do not provide an automatic "cure" for COVID. In fact, certain types of ventilators as well as prolonged mechanical ventilation are linked to high mortality rates—and ventilators can also leave people with additional lung injuries (Tsaplina and

Stramondo 2020). Elsewhere, Powell has noted that futile mechanical ventilation can lead to a painful or "bad death" (Foggatt 2020).

What Is Allocation?

Allocation was often used synonymously with rationing and triage in the documents I reviewed, partly because allocation requires (or becomes) rationing when resources are scarce. The 2007 draft guidelines narrate certain ethical premises related to rationing about which the workgroup had disagreed in 2006. But even the exclusion chart and scoring criteria in the 2007 draft, which appear to be objective and neutral, had been the subject of much debate.

Regarding who might be favored or excluded in the first step of an allocation protocol, the 2006 workgroup discussed whether health-care workers, especially those risking their lives to help others during a pandemic, should be prioritized for ventilators if they themselves fell ill. Ultimately the committee felt that too many essential workers were involved in health care—nurses, cleaners, food servers, administrators—to make this kind of determination. In the transcript of the taped discussion, there did not seem to be unanimous consensus on the criteria for excluding a person from access to a ventilator either, even though the draft guidelines released the following year proposed a list that included cardiac arrest, cancer, severe chronic lung disease, dialysis dependence, and evidence of a "severe, irreversible neurologic event." In the workgroup, one presenter noted that basing triage "on pre-existing conditions inherently puts an uneven burden on the groups of patients that it's dealing with": "since many of those pre-existing conditions unevenly affect different social groups—disabled, AIDS patients, cirrhotics—I think then that it's internally inconsistent to say we can't value life and social worth, but then making criteria which inherently sort of do value life and social worth" (NYS Workgroup 2006). In the public commentary on the 2007 draft guidelines that resulted from the workgroup meeting, dialysis as a criterion for exclusion generated the most pushback. From nephrologists to advocates at the National Kidney Foundation, people wrote to the Task Force, the DOH, or the email hotline (panflu@health.state.ny.us) to explain the internal diversity of dialysis patients, treatments, and outcomes and to protest "dialysis dependence" as a potential reason for ventilator denial during a pandemic. At a meeting to discuss the draft guidelines in Erie County, health-care workers in attendance pointed out that "hospital staff would find exclusion of patients they treat routinely, such as dialysis patients, to be difficult" (NYS DOH 2006-8). In response, the 2015 guidelines were amended to remove this criterion.

For the second step of the protocol, the workgroup debated using SOFA scoring as a way to assess the short-term mortality of patients in emergency settings, denying ventilators to those with worse (i.e., higher) scores even if they had passed the initial exclusion criteria. Meeting participants queried whether the SOFA measures would even be suitable for the unknown pandemic to come. In the context of privatized health care, others pointed out that SOFA was pragmatic because it was not proprietary, unlike so many other commercial testing systems that would be too expensive to apply widely during a pandemic. Some noted that SOFA scoring might simply be irrelevant during a pandemic: if a hundred people were waiting in an ICU for a ventilator to become available, the system would essentially revert to first come, first served. Furthermore, emergency medical services (EMS) frequently intubated patients in ambulances or in their homes. Would EMS have time to comply with the scoring protocols or to coordinate with hospital ERs and ICUs regarding the patients waiting in line?

SOFA scoring was also to be applied at fixed intervals *after* a ventilator was in use, with patients who showed worsening scores having their ventilators reallocated to newly arriving patients with better scores. The timing and cutoffs for this repeat scoring, and the idea of extubation itself, became a major topic of debate among the workgroup. The 2007 draft guidelines reflect this uncertainty, noting that the workgroup "struggled with the notion of removing less-ill patients from ventilators, particularly those who might recover with continued mechanical ventilation" (NYS Workgroup 2007, 17). However, the guidelines clarified that chronic-care facilities should "not be subjected to acute care triage guidelines" (NYS Workgroup 2007, 29). In other words, disabled people using ventilators in their homes or in a chronic-care facility would not be triaged under this proposal (as has commonly been misunderstood); however, any ventilator user entering a hospital or other acute facility would be subject at that point to the same protocols as everyone else. One participant in the 2006 meeting pointed out the potential ableism of employing any fixed pattern of repeat SOFA scoring: "If people could argue that because their disability differently affects their recovery, the medical criteria should be applied to them differently." Another suggested that it would be "reverse discrimination against the critically ill" *not* to apply the protocols to everyone requiring ventilation (NYS Workgroup 2006). Some workgroup members speculated about exclusion and extubation protocols leading to riots and violence against doctors and nurses, as well as mental health issues for at-risk people, family members, and health-care workers.

Although the use of exclusion criteria and SOFA scoring to withhold or withdraw ventilators from individuals has dominated disability activism during COVID-19, the working group also spent a great deal of time discussing regional allocation. For instance, if New York City was "hit first," would rural hospitals have to transfer ventilators to the city? How would those hospitals get their ventilators back if they needed them? If rural or smaller hospitals typically send patients requiring specialist care to major health centers in the city, would they have to deny their patients access to urban resources during pandemic "lockdowns"? The workgroup was also concerned about poverty and other forms of inequality creating a vastly unfair pattern of allocation between different hospitals, even in a single city, with wealthier people able to "hospital shop." This inequality pertained to disability in unexpected ways, with wealthy and "well-organized" disability rights and disease advocacy groups likely to obtain *more* resources and better care than disabled and nondisabled New Yorkers and migrants in low-income neighborhoods. To convey a sense of the debate, since the meeting transcripts are no longer archived, I offer a few outtakes from the 2006 workgroup meeting:

> Not all hospitals are created equal.

> Hospitals with more limited resources might not be able to buy or rent supplemental ventilators either before or during the crisis. State pandemic plans should assess how to balance the differences among facilities in their ability to pay for and provide surge capacity.

> Are all these assets automatically going to arrive at the places that need it, or are hospitals going to need to go into the market to make up the

gap, and if that's true, then your cash-starved hospitals aren't going to find vendors who want to deal with them.

Hospitals in less affluent neighborhoods typically serve a far larger population base. Thus, a system of rationing that permits wide variation between hospitals in different areas will likely result in excess mortality for the poor.

Ventilators are a symbol, they don't treat the patients, they're a piece of equipment and I really hope that we're thinking about doctors and nurses who know how to take care of these important assets to help patients survive.

To what extent do you think there is a potential for people buying themselves out of the system, in other words setting up private ventilator clinics or some other deal? It's going to happen, it's New York, it's the US, it's a capital, it's a market-driven system.

If there is pandemic flu, it's not going to stop at New York's borders, and the crisis of demand and the crush of demand especially if Connecticut and New Jersey haven't yet begun to meet the challenge of what might happen, is that people will simply cross the bridges and tunnels and come to New York for treatment. I can't imagine if they have a New Jersey address, a sick person will be turned away.

People who have been not well served by the healthcare system until now are likely to have chronic conditions which are going to weigh against them in whatever triage system we set up, so it's not really possible to create just plans and programs in an unjust system.

Community participation doesn't always increase justice because some people are much more organized, specific disease group advocates are, in fact, extremely well organized, much more so than the vulnerable poor so that's just to flag the fairness of that.

The revised 2015 guidelines, which became so influential and controversial, built on the 2007 draft that derived from these conversations, as well as from public commentary emailed to the DOH or collected during focus-group sessions organized by members of the Task Force (NYS Task Force 2015; Han and Koch 2020). Relatively few people emailed their reactions to the publicly posted 2007 draft, which Powell partly attributed to "fatigue for the public in hearing of the pandemic flu" (Powell 2022). The Research Associates, a "market intelligence strategy" company, summarized the results of a December 2008 focus-group meeting in Albany, in which participants were asked to debate scenarios for allocating ventilators to incarcerated people versus police officers, citizens versus undocumented immigrants, and medical versus nonmedical professionals, as well as the potential exclusion of those with "self-inflicted illnesses." Participants varied widely in their opinions, underscoring the need for guidelines with a "clinical algorithm" and greater public education (Research Associates 2009, 2–3, 5). The 2015 revision, chaired by Susie Han of the NYS Task Force (Powell having by then stepped down from the role), maintained the overarching goal of "saving the most lives." SOFA scoring was also maintained, albeit with more specificity regarding timing and metrics and an attempt to restrict exclusion criteria to measures of "short-term mortality," as opposed to more descriptive phenomena such as dialysis use or metastatic malignancy. Mainly, the 2015 revisions entailed new pediatric and neonatal plans and an expanded analysis of legal issues.

In 2020, although New York State did not invoke the guidelines, unequal access to ventilators derived jointly from the absence of statewide protocols and from disparate hospital arrangements, with hospitals either implementing ad hoc plans or voluntarily following the guidelines (despite their biases). Prior and current members of the Task Force have written about the "disarray" in New York hospitals before vaccines became available, resulting from a void in state guidance, with the planning burden placed on departments and already-overwhelmed medical staff (Powell and Chuang 2020; Fins 2020c; Han and Koch 2020). Examples abounded in 2020 of inefficient or unequal allocation between institutions—a topic of much conversation at the workgroup meeting that was not reflected or easily condensed into the guidelines. For instance, it was widely reported that Elmhurst Hospital in Queens—an early "epicenter within an epicenter" of the COVID-19 pandemic—quickly exceeded double capacity in early March 2020, while hospitals just twenty minutes away still had open beds (Dwyer 2020).⁵ Powell and Chuang also note that allocation of protective equipment was not well thought out; thus, hospices, which had ventilators and staffing and could have admitted patients with COVID, were not able to until workers received personal protective equipment (PPE) (2020, 4).

The 2006 workgroup had also warned that the different divisions within a given hospital would probably diverge in their interpretation of triage protocols; for instance, it would always be "the job of the physician to advocate for their patient and so the ICU physician is going to have to advocate for their patient. The ER physician is going to be advocating for their patients" (NYS Workgroup 2006). One physician told me that their New York hospital system created its own ECMO allocation guidelines early in the COVID-19 pandemic, which potentially involved withholding treatment from those who would have received it in nonpandemic times. They had not been aware of the 2015 state guidelines until they read an article about them in the newspaper. At the weekly meetings of the ECMO programs in their system, it soon became clear that some sites were following the internal guidelines more stringently than others. With disposables running out, moreover, the larger hospitals were not reallocating materials throughout the system as they were supposed to. The ECMO physicians were under conflicting pressures from other departments within their hospitals—with managers demanding that the guidelines be adhered to for labor, cost, or legal reasons and ER doctors and intensivists calling "over and over," day and night, to beg for the rules to be waived on behalf of particular patients. In fact, this physician recalled one of the hospital bioethicists—a member of the Task Force—advocating on behalf of a patient who did not meet the hospital's own criteria for ECMO, a sign of just how difficult it is to shift from the model of autonomy (patient and physician) to a population-based or distributive-justice approach. At the same time, all of the hospitals participated in the online COVID database and dashboard hosted by the Extracorporeal Life Support Organization (ELSO), so they could keep track of patient outcomes under different treatment conditions around the world—a kind of tool not considered during the making of the 2007 and 2015 guidelines, which ideally would allow allocation plans to be revised in real time.

Other Task Force members have now documented occasions when ventilator rationing following the 2015 guidelines did occur in New York at the outset of the pandemic. Fins, for one, argues, "Although the official line from the state was that there were enough ventilators to go around, the reality was that the system buckled.... At the peak of the surge, multiple patients were potentially in need of intubation. Not all could be helped" (2020c, 141, 143). He quotes an April 2020 listserv post from an ethicist at Lincoln Hospital, who wrote, "I work at a city hospital in the South Bronx in one of the parts of town most impacted by covid. We came up to the brink 3 weeks ago with no available ventilators of any kind at which time we implemented step 1 exclusion criteria triage (NY State Ventilator Allocation Guideline, 57). Fortunately, the only patients withdrawn from ventilators that day (without advance directive or family permission) were those with true physiologic futility" (Fins 2020c, 144). Many similar stories of rationing in spring 2020 are no doubt forthcoming, from the perspectives of patients as well as health-care workers—despite hospital efforts to silence staff on this issue.[6]

Conclusion: Toward Disability Distributive Justice

Disability activists and scholars have responded to 2020 by demanding new state protocols, revised with input from disabled people. For instance, Ari Ne'eman and colleagues have now called for a reinterpretation of "short-term mortality risk" as the supposedly objective basis of exclusion and withdrawal criteria. While they support the principle of optimizing the number of lives saved—in distinction from Asch's random lottery approach—they argue that "short-term mortality risk should be interpreted narrowly to avoid unnecessarily screening out of individuals with disabilities and to reduce the risk of bias from more subjective longer-term judgments. Our preferred standard would be survival to hospital discharge" (Ne'eman et al. 2021, 834). The 2015 New York State guidelines have yet to be updated, however, and activists have experienced significant setbacks regarding their hopes for revision. For instance, Not Dead Yet, Disability Rights New York, and Neuromuscular Disability Support United recently lost a lawsuit they filed in 2020, demanding that the New York State Ventilator Allocation Guidelines be amended to prevent chronic ventilator users from having their devices reallocated in acute-care settings (Pierson 2022).

Other activists have protested specific elements of SOFA scoring, such as the Glasgow Coma Scale, which measures "consciousness" through eye, motor, and verbal responses and can inappropriately lower the scores of people with speech and motor impairments (DREDF 2020). Along similar lines, Harald Schmidt, Dorothy Roberts, and Nwamaka Eneanya have highlighted the racial bias in the creatinine measure that is also part of SOFA scoring, explaining that "creatinine is higher in Black communities because of higher rates of chronic kidney disease, due to higher rates of diabetes and high blood pressure that are best understood as the consequences of health inequities and structural racism" (2021, 127). Ne'eman and colleagues point out that the state of Massachusetts recently modified its CSC guidelines by reducing the weight given to creatinine within SOFA scoring; they suggest that "this represents a precedent-setting extension of the disability rights framework of reasonable modifications to other systemic inequities" (2021, 841).

These scoring protocols take on even greater significance with the rise of automated/AI (artificial intelligence) systems in health care, which employ decision trees using numeric data like SOFA scores—offering another layer of technological solutionism to the existing misconception that ventilators alone "save lives" (Whittaker et al. 2019). I attended several online hospital-management seminars during the first two years of the pandemic and note the increase of proposals for automating everything from decisions about extubation to distributing patients among hospitals—on the basis of minimal data entry by doctors and nurses.[7] At the same time, the New York guidelines and their reliance on SOFA scoring have come under intense scrutiny from other corners of the scientific community. A team of biostatisticians and pulmonary doctors at NYU recently published a study simulating triage with the 2015 guidelines, using medical records from March–July 2020. They found that most "rationing" occurred not at the first step (exclusion criteria) or the second step (SOFA scoring to decide whether to assign or withhold a ventilator) but at the third step—where ventilators were extubated and reallocated after repeat SOFA scoring. The authors expressed concern "that NYVAG [New York Ventilator Allocation Guidelines] might ration ventilators away from patients with a high chance of survival (44.4%) toward newly intubated patients with a lower chance of survival (34.8%)"—the problem being that SOFA scores miss "prognostic nuances" that health-care providers or triage committees could better assess with a wider range of information (Walsh et al. 2023).

Much of the critical analysis and disability activism surrounding ventilator allocation remains focused on withholding/withdrawing devices from individuals. As many chapters in this volume show, disabled people are experts on rationing, especially in a privatized context that generates artificial scarcity around health care, not to mention an ableist context where implicit triage is the norm (Trowe 2022). Disabled people brought this expertise to the COVID-19 pandemic—and emergency conditions of genuine scarcity—in advocacy and mutual-aid projects such as #ICUgenics and #NoBodyIsDisposable. Patty Berne of Sins Invalid coined the latter phrase before the pandemic, uniting fat and disability activists, to protest the logic of "disposability" that inflects US economic, health, and housing policies for disabled people. #NoBodyIsDisposable became an intersectional and multipronged campaign against "triage discrimination" from the first year of COVID-19. The campaign includes the vital open-access publication "Know Your Rights Guide to Surviving COVID-19 Triage Protocols," a toolkit that offers detailed and clear instructions about necessary legal documents, the cities that have favorable laws, how to find an advocate and engage with triage committees, items to bring to the hospital, and how to request and interpret the contract for one's personal medical equipment (#NoBodyIsDisposable 2020).

Contemplating queer/crip mutual aid strategies as another type of response to health-care shortages and rationing, Emily Watlington describes a work by disability artist Alex Dolores Salerno in chapter 14 of this volume, consisting of a coded phrase embroidered onto a pillowcase (translated as, "Please be discreet, carefully disguising any medication words"; see figure 14.2, also in color in figure P.15). Regarding the Facebook mutual-aid group where this phrase was initially posted, Watlington writes, "The group hoped to enable resource sharing for medication and hormones at a time when these became especially difficult to access, with mass layoffs resulting in lost insurance and with the new risks involved in going to doctors' appointments or pharmacies. But, in an effort to evade surveillance—since sharing prescriptions, no matter how necessary, is illegal—participants were asked to write in code, replacing letters with special characters to evade search or algorithmic detection" (Watlington, chapter 14 in this volume). Might future crip mutual-aid

Figure 5.3. *Pareidolia (Vaccinate Now)*, 2021, Brothers Sick (Ezra Benus and Noah Benus). A black-and-white poster of silhouettes holding syringes. Written above the figures in varying font sizes from top to bottom are "Stop Rationing Care," "Stop Medical Apartheid," "Vaccinate Now," "Global Inoculation Against Viral Fascism," "End Eugenics," and, at the bottom of the image, "End Vaccine Hoarding."

projects emerge around "oxygen inequity" and the limited, unequal availability of ventilators, oxygen concentrators, disposables, and oxygen itself (Ross and Wendel 2023)?

The question remains as to how disability expertise might be extended to regional or population-based allocation. Medicine and disability rights are often at odds with each other, yet both have been dominated by an "autonomy model," focused on the individual, which creates friction for distributive justice projects with a social or societal orientation. Some of this friction is a necessary and urgent check on biased or profiteering state and managerial protocols for distributing labor and resources. Building on the disability justice movement and the cosmos of mutual aid, what remains to be imagined—and will be required of the disability ethicists and activists who contribute to the next set of ventilator allocation guidelines—is a theory of *disability distributive justice*. As the collective project of *How to Be Disabled in a Pandemic* insists, cripping distributive justice requires thinking across disability identification, disability activism, and those groups of people who are marked by class, race, and citizenship status for debilitation—and then written off for their "comorbidities" in pandemic times.

NOTES

1 In April 2020, *Politico* reported on a similar allocation plan in a memo sent by Northwell Health management to its clinical staff (Eisenberg and Goldenberg 2020).

2 The Task Force is a smaller group of roughly twenty people. Current members, some of whom have served decades-long terms, are listed at the New York DOH website (NYS DOH, n.d.). The full list of 2006 ventilator clinical workgroup participants can be found in an appendix to the 2007 draft guidelines (NYS Workgroup 2007).

3 To address the legal liability issues of out-of-state practitioners and those working outside their fields of training, Fins explains, "With intense lobbying from medical groups and the health bar, the governor inserted the Emergency or Disaster Treatment Protection Act (EDTPA) of 2020 into the state budget, which was signed into law on April 3, 2020. The EDTPA extended limited civil and criminal liability in the context of the public health emergency retroactive to March 7, 2020" (2020c, 143).

4 For a personal reflection on post-COVID home oxygen-concentrator use in New York City in 2021, see Pow 2023.

5 In this *New York Times* article, Dwyer quotes Governor Andrew Cuomo as saying, "We don't really have a public health care 'system,' we have a system of hospitals."

6   Ethicists' predictions about age- and disability-based rationing at their hospitals in spring 2020 are also instructive. See, for instance, an interview with Arthur Caplan of NYU Langone in which he tells a reporter for *The Atlantic*, "So you're probably putting kids first and then you're probably putting younger people over much older people just because age is a predictor of resilience.... Then you move to tiebreakers like, are you a health-care worker, broadly defined.... Some people are going to be worried about, if you're psychotic or mentally ill, how could we manage you, even if we tried to put you on a ventilator, would you disrupt the unit, imperil other people, do you need more resources, that kind of thing. So you'd be watching that, too" (Hamblin 2020).
7   See, for instance, the Rotman School of Management (2022) seminar on "Data Analytics in Healthcare."

REFERENCES

Antommaria, Armand H. Matheny, Tyler S. Gibb, Amy L. McGuire, Paul Root Wolpe, Matthew K. Wynia, Megan K. Applewhite, Arthur Caplan, et al. 2020. "Ventilator Triage Policies during the COVID-19 Pandemic at U.S. Hospitals Associated with Members of the Association of Bioethics Program Directors." *Annals of Internal Medicine* 173 (3): 188–94.

Bagenstos, Samuel R. 2020. "Who Gets the Ventilator? Disability Discrimination in COVID-19 Medical-Rationing Protocols." *Yale Law Journal* 130 (2020): 1–25.

Devereaux, Asha, Howard Backer, Arzoo Salami, Chuck Wright, Kate Christensen, Kathleen Rice, Cindy Jakel-Smith, et al. 2021. "Oxygen and Ventilator Logistics during California's COVID-19 Surge: When Oxygen Becomes a Scarce Resource." *Disaster Medicine and Public Health Preparedness* 17 (2023): e33.

Disability Rights Education & Defense Fund (DREDF). 2020. "Letter from DREDF and Additional Organizations Opposing California's Health Care Rationing Guidelines." April 22, 2020. https://dredf.org.

Dwyer, Jim. 2020. "One Hospital Was Besieged by the Virus. Nearby Was 'Plenty of Space.'" *New York Times*, May 14, 2020. www.nytimes.com.

Eisenberg, Amanda, and Sally Goldenberg. 2020. "Northwell Memo Calls for Rationing Ventilators to 'Patients Most Likely to Benefit.'" *Politico*, April 3, 2020. www.politico.com.

Fat Rose. 2020. "Stacey Milbern: California Care Rationing Coalition May 6 Press Conference." YouTube, May 12, 2020. www.youtube.com/watch?v=Oy3WgvCZEjg.

Fink, Sheri. 2009a. "Flu Nightmare: In Severe Pandemic, Officials Ponder Disconnecting Ventilators from Some Patients." ProPublica, September 23, 2009. www.propublica.org.

———. 2009b. "Preparing for a Pandemic, State Health Departments Struggle with Rationing Decisions." ProPublica, October 24, 2009, www.propublica.org.

Fins, Joseph. 2020a. "Disabusing the Disability Critique of the New York State Task Force Report on Ventilator Allocation." Bioethics Forum Essay, Hastings Center, April 1, 2020. www.thehastingscenter.org.

———. 2020b. "New York State Task Force on Life and the Law Ventilator Allocation Guidelines: How Our Views on Disability Evolved." Bioethics Forum Essay, Hastings Center, April 7, 2020. www.thehastingscenter.org.

———. 2020c. "Sunshine Is the Best Disinfectant, Especially during a Pandemic." *Health Law Journal* 25 (2): 141–46.

Foggatt, Tyler. 2020. "Who Gets a Ventilator?" *New Yorker*, April 11, 2020. www.newyorker.com.

Hamblin, James. 2020. "An Ethicist on How to Make Impossible Decisions." *The Atlantic*, April 1, 2020. www.theatlantic.com.

Han, Susie A. 2023a. Email to Mara Mills, February 14, 2023.

———. 2023b. Zoom conversation with Mara Mills, January 31, 2023.

Han, Susie A., and Valerie Gutmann Koch. 2020. "Clinical and Ethical Considerations in Allocation of Ventilators in an Influenza Pandemic or Other Public Health Disaster: A Comparison of the 2007 and 2015 New York State Ventilator Allocation Guidelines. *Disaster Medicine and Public Health Preparedness* 14 (6): e35–e44.

Hick, John, and Daniel T. O'Laughlin. 2006. "Concept of Operations for Triage of Mechanical Ventilation in an Epidemic." *Academic Emergency Medicine* 13:223–29.

Kaste, Martin, and Rebecca Hersher. 2020. "Ventilator Shortages Loom as States Ponder Rules for Rationing." NPR, April 3, 2020, https://news.wgcu.org.

Koch, Valerie Gutmann, and Susie A. Han. 2020. "COVID in NYC: What New York Did, and Should Have Done." *American Journal of Bioethics* 20 (7): 153–55.

Lamont, Julian, and Christi Favor. "Distributive Justice." *The Stanford Encyclopedia of Philosophy*, Winter 2017 ed., edited by Edward N. Zalta. https://plato.stanford.edu.

Manchanda, Emily C. Cleveland, Charles Sanky, and Jacob M. Appel. 2021. "Crisis Standards of Care in the USA: A Systematic Review and Implications for Equity amidst COVID-19." *Journal of Racial and Ethnic Health Disparities* 8 (4): 824–36.

Mounk, Yascha. 2020. "The Extraordinary Decisions Facing Italian Doctors." *The Atlantic*, March 11, 2020. www.theatlantic.com.

Ne'eman, Ari. 2020a. "Do New York State's Ventilator Allocation Guidelines Place Chronic Ventilator Users at Risk? Clarification Needed." Bioethics Forum Essay, Hastings Center, April 3, 2020. www.thehastingscenter.org.

———. 2020b. "I Will Not Apologize for My Needs." *New York Times*, March 23, 2020. www.nytimes.com.

Ne'eman, Ari, Michael Ashley Stein, Zackary D. Berger, and Doron Dorfman. 2021. "The Treatment of Disability under Crisis Standards of Care: An Empirical and Normative Analysis of Change over Time during COVID-19." *Journal of Health Politics, Policy, and Law* 46 (5): 831–60.

New York State Department of Health (NYS DOH). 2006–8. Comments on draft ventilator guidelines emailed to DOH staff. In the author's possession. Previously held in DOH records but now deaccessioned.

———. 2009. "Ventilator Allocation Tabletop Exercises: Situation Manual for New York-Presbyterian Hospital." July 31, 2009. In the author's possession. Previously held in DOH records but now deaccessioned.

———. n.d. "Members and Staff: Members of the Task Force on Life and the Law." Accessed January 4, 2024. www.health.ny.gov.

New York State Task Force on Life and the Law (NYS Task Force). 2015. "Ventilator Allocation Guidelines." New York State Department of Health, November 2015. www.health.ny.gov.

New York State Workgroup on Ventilator Allocation in an Influenza Pandemic (NYS Workgroup). 2006. "New York State Task Force on Life and the Law: Ethical Issues in Ventilator Allocation in an Influenza Pandemic." Transcript of taped meeting (presentations and conversation), March 2006. In the author's possession. Previously held in DOH records but now deaccessioned.

———. 2007. "Allocation of Ventilators in an Influenza Pandemic: Planning Document." New York State Department of Health / New York State Task Force on Life and the Law, March 15, 2007. www.cidrap.umn.edu.

#NoBodyIsDisposable. 2020. "Know Your Rights Guide to Surviving COVID-19 Triage Protocols." July 28, 2020. https://nobodyisdisposable.org.

NYU Langone News Hub. 2020. "A Prudent Plan Helps Some COVID-19 Patients Avoid Ventilators & Ensures Others Have What They Need." *NYU Langone Health Magazine*, Fall 2020. https://nyulangone.org.

Pierson, Brendan. 2022. "Long-Term Ventilator Users Lose Bid to Revive Suit over N.Y. Emergency Guidelines." *Reuters*, November 23, 2022. www.reuters.com.

Piper, Greg. 2020. "NYU Threatens to Fire Its Doctors If They Talk to the Media about COVID-19 Ventilator Rationing." *College Fix*, April 1, 2020. www.thecollegefix.com.

Piscitello, Gina M., Esha Kapania, and William D. Miller. 2021. "Variation in Ventilator Allocation Guidelines by U.S. State during the Coronavirus Disease 2019 Pandemic: A Systematic Review." *JAMA Network Open* 3 (6): e2012606.

Pow, Whit. 2023. "Glitch, Body, Antibody." *Outland*, December 12, 2023. https://outland.art.

Powell, Tia. 2008. "Ventilator Allocation in a Pandemic: Ethical Issues and Clinical Guidelines." Presentation, December 8, 2008. In the author's possession. Previously held in DOH records but now deaccessioned.

———. 2022. Email to Mara Mills, December 19, 2022.

Powell, Tia, and Elizabeth Chuang. 2020. "COVID in NYC: What We Could Do Better." *American Journal of Bioethics* 20 (7): 62–66.

Ramachandran, Shalini, and Joe Palazzolo. 2020. "NYU Langone Tells ER Doctors to 'Think More Critically' about Who Gets Ventilators." *Wall Street Journal*, March 31, 2020. www.wsj.com.

Research Associates. 2009. "Ventilator Allocation Guidelines: State of New York. Focus Group Discussion Summary." January 2009. In the author's possession. Previously held in DOH records but now deaccessioned.

Rivera, Daniella. 2021. "COVID 'Long-Haulers' Spur Unprecedented Demand for Oxygen amidst Shortages." KSL TV, November 4, 2021. https://ksltv.com.

Ross, Madeline, and Sarah K. Wendel. 2023. "Oxygen Inequity in the COVID-19 Pandemic and Beyond." *Global Health: Science and Practice* 11 (1): e2200360. https://doi.org/10.9745/GHSP-D-22-00360.

Rotman School of Management. 2022. "Fifth Annual Research Roundtable: Data Analytics in Healthcare." YouTube, March 22, 2022. www.youtube.com/watch?v=u2n6G3P3xpU.

Sampson, Joanna. 2020. "WHO Warns of Global Oxygen Concentrator Shortage." *Gasworld*, June 25, 2020. www.gasworld.com.

Schmidt, Harald, Dorothy E. Roberts, and Nwamaka D. Eneanya. 2022. "Rationing, Racism, and Justice: Advancing the Debate around 'Colourblind' COVID-19 Ventilator Allocation." *Journal of Medical Ethics* 48:126–30.

Shapiro, Joseph. 2020a. "One Man's COVID-19 Death Raises the Worst Fears of Many People with Disabilities." NPR, July 31, 2020. www.npr.org.

———. 2020b. "Oregon Hospitals Didn't Have Shortages. So Why Were Disabled People Denied Care?" NPR, December 21, 2020. www.npr.org.

Sins Invalid. 2019. *Skin, Tooth, and Bone: The Basis of Movement is Our People, a Disability Justice Primer*. 2nd ed. San Francisco: Sins Invalid. www.sinsinvalid.org.

Stramondo, Joseph A. 2021. "Tragic Choices: Disability, Triage, and Equity amidst a Global Pandemic." *Journal of Philosophy of Disability* 1:201–10.

Tennessee Altered Standards of Care Workgroup. 2016. *Guidance for the Ethical Allocation of Scarce Resources during a Community-Wide Public Health Emergency as Declared by the Governor of Tennessee*. July 2016. https://midsouthepc.org.

Trowe, Nolan. 2022. "On Our Last Legs." *The Nation*, August 26, 2022. www.thenation.com.

Tsaplina, Marina, and Joseph A. Stramondo. 2020. "#WeAreEssential: Why Disabled People Should Be Appointed to Hospital Triage Committees." Bioethics Forum Essay, Hastings Center, May 15, 2020. www.thehastingscenter.org.

US Department of Health and Human Services. 2020. "OCR Reaches Early Case Resolution with Alabama after It Removes Discriminatory Ventilator Triaging Guidelines." April 8, 2020. www.hhs.gov.

Walsh, B. Corbett, Jianan Zhu, Yang Feng, Kenneth A. Berkowitz, Rebecca A. Betensky, Mark E. Nunnally, and Deepak R. Pradhan. 2023. "Simulation of New York City's Ventilator Allocation Guideline during the Spring 2020 COVID-19 Surge." *JAMA Network Open* 6 (10): e2336736. https://doi.org/10.1001/jamanetworkopen.2023.36736.

Whittaker, Meredith, Meryl Alper, Cynthia L. Bennett, Sara Hendren, Elizabeth Kaziunas, Mara Mills, Meredith Ringel Morris, Joy Lisi Rankin, Emily Rogers, Marcel Salas, and Sarah Myers West. 2019. "Disability, Bias & AI Report." AI Now Institute, November 20, 2019. https://ainowinstitute.org.

Wong, Alice. 2020. "I'm Disabled and Need a Ventilator to Live. Am I Expendable during This Pandemic?" *Vox*, April 4, 2020. www.vox.com.

6

High Stakes Schooling

Risk, Protection, and the Education of Disabled Children in a Pandemic

ALEXANDRA FREIDUS, RACHEL FISH, AND ERICA O. TURNER

"Our kids need to get back into school, it's ridiculous. They're not learning anything," said a Bronx mom of a teen with autism who asked not to be identified to protect her child's privacy. But other parents say the health risks of restarting class this summer are simply too great—and even greater for students who may be more medically vulnerable to start, and less able to speak out about safety concerns. "I'm just super scared," said Grisel Cardona, the mother of a 9-year-old with autism in the Bronx. "Regression is something I'm concerned about. At the same time, health comes before all that."
—"Special Ed Can Restart—but Should It?," *New York Daily News*, June 12, 2020

The New Yorkers quoted in the news article in this chapter's epigraph, from the summer of 2020, were not alone. As the first wave of the COVID-19 pandemic waned, families, politicians, and educational leaders hotly debated the risks involved in reopening school buildings. Policy makers and caregivers grappled with making the "right" decision, one that would fairly address the educational, child-care, and health concerns involved (Freidus and Turner 2023). These deliberations repeatedly identified students with disabilities as one of a few groups of children in acute need of in-person instruction. Many caregivers of and advocates for disabled children pushed the New York City Department of Education (NYCDOE) to return these students to school as soon as possible.[1]

However, this push was met with resistance from other caregivers, whose past experiences convinced them that they, rather than the state, were best equipped to protect their vulnerable children from the risks of COVID-19.

Even under "normal" circumstances, our understanding of how to best educate disabled children is complex and contested (Connor and Ferri 2006), and the social safety net available to support these children and their families is extremely limited (Blum 2015). During the global pandemic, these constraints and tensions became even more apparent. New York was the first major city in the United States to reopen school buildings for in-person instruction in the fall of 2020. However, social-distancing guidelines and limited classroom space meant that very few New York City public school students attended school in person five days each week that year. What is more, most families in the city opted for remote instruction when school buildings first reopened in September. Families, educators, and politicians debated individual and policy decisions (Freidus and Turner 2023). Deliberations over remote schooling, access to special education services, and health risks were covered extensively by local news media and tracked intensively by many families.

This chapter closely examines these conversations. We draw on a data set of three hundred local news and opinion articles focused on the terms and impacts of New York City school reopening policies. We analyzed these public data thematically, using a combination of descriptive labels (such as claims advanced by parents, educators, or policy makers), theoretical categories (such as "vulnerability"), and inductive phrases (such as "risk groups") related to school closures and reopenings (for additional methodological details, see Freidus and Turner 2023). We supplement these data with in-depth interviews of seven mothers of disabled New York City students, recruited through local groups for families of disabled children, about their experiences with schools prior to and during the pandemic.[2] Interview data were analyzed using "flexible coding" (Deterding and Waters 2018) in Dedoose software (for additional methodological details, see Fish et al. 2023).

As we analyzed and combined our data, we regularly reflected on how our own social positions affected our interpretations. Although we are all mothers and former classroom teachers, we differ in how we identify racially, where we live, how we understand our children's needs, and whether our children attended school in person during the fall and spring of 2020. In particular, Alex is white, lives in New York, has a disabled son, and sent both her children in person to New York City schools once they reopened; Rachel is white, moved from New York City to rural Vermont early in the pandemic, and sent her nondisabled children in person to school there starting in September 2020; Erica identifies as Black and Asian American, lives in Madison, Wisconsin, and her nondisabled children's school district operated almost entirely virtually until April 2021. We each had personal and professional stakes in school reopening debates and discussions over how to best educate disabled children. We collaboratively reflected on these varied stakes throughout the writing process, generating a more nuanced analysis than we would have achieved otherwise.

Here, we consider how pandemic discourses have positioned disabled kids as vulnerable and public schools as the protector—despite the many glaring ways in which the state has abdicated this role, in education and other arenas. We argue that mothers of these students responded by advocating for and ensuring their children's well-being, acting as "vigilante mothers" (Blum 2015) who individually and differentially bore the burden of this collective failure. The expectation that caregivers—and, in particular, mothers—must advocate for their disabled kids and navigate complex medical and educational systems is not at all new. However, the pandemic foregrounded the many ways that families' individualized "burdens of care" are rooted in structural constraints and scarce resources (Green 2007; Green, Darling, and Wilbers 2016).

Dependent Child, Disabled Child

It is frequently taken for granted that children need protection. In the words of sociologist Julia O'Connell Davidson, children are imagined as a "unitary category of persons defined by their innocence, vulnerability, and lack of agency" (2005, 147). Because children are, as O'Connell Davidson argues, "cloaked by the mantle of victimhood," they are understood to be "without the capacity to defend their own interests" (2005, 59). As such, they are imagined as needing the support not only of adult caregivers but also of the state. According to the political scientists Anne Schneider and Helen Ingram (1993), because children are viewed positively yet lack social power, they are prime examples of "dependent" policy targets. Disabled people are also perceived as vulnerable and dependent on others yet are subject to pervasive ableism that positions their dependence as pathological and uses it as justification for denying their civil rights (Carey 2009; Lloyd 2001; Mauldin and Brown 2021). Despite important differences, both children and disabled people are perceived as "powerless, helpless, and needy": "their problems are their own, but they are unable to solve them by themselves" (Schneider and Ingram 1993, 342).

During times of crisis—such as a global pandemic—concerns about individuals perceived as vulnerable or dependent become particularly acute. Wartime posters, for example, frequently show defenseless or cowering children (Dubinsky 2012). This depiction of vulnerability is, of course, political: the children in these images are "in need of a strong nation state, or revolution, or political party to protect them" (Dubinsky 2012, 7). Schooling is the first line of defense. Examining child rights and vulnerability in AIDS-affected states, anthropologist Nancy Kendall argues that "current efforts to support vulnerable children through schooling are embedded in a liberal model of equality within which each child has an equal right to the same schooling" (2008, 374). However, as Kendall points out, such a model assumes that children are universally vulnerable and in need of the state's protection, seldom accounting for "equity concerns, such as whether different educational models, opportunities, or resource inputs might better serve different groups of children" (2008, 374).

Disabled kids, in contrast, are accorded a status all their own. They are understood to be both like and unlike "all children," a category from which they are often excluded (Lalvani and Bacon 2019). Indeed, because of their dual dependency, it is frequently assumed that disabled children are particularly pitiful and in need of protection. Disability studies and feminist scholarship urge us to reject myths of independence altogether, instead understanding "dependence as the 'normal' state of being in which all people require support and assistance" (Carey 2009, 18; see also Linton 1998). However, in a society that confers rights based on *in*dependence, disabled children are treated as less than fully human (Carey 2009; Piepmeier, Estreich, and Adams 2021).

Still, the categories of both "children" and "disabled people" are clearly far from uniform. Disabled kids' diversity includes age, race, gender, socioeconomic status, and disability type, among other axes of difference. Their vulnerability is both varied and situated in particular social contexts—as is that of all children. This variation often raises the question of *which* children deserve the protection of the state (Annamma 2017; Meiners 2016). Critical scholars of childhood and disability therefore challenge us to "recognize the very real differences between human beings in their capacity for self-protection and autonomy," while refusing simplistic story lines that flatten complex individuals into dependent policy targets (O'Connell Davidson 2005, 4; see also Simplican 2015).

Assumptions of dependence and protection are fundamental to the schooling of disabled students. Widespread perceptions of disabled kids as needing special protection do not necessarily increase their educational opportunities; special education services may provide crucial supports and legal protections but can also stigmatize and segregate students, lower teacher expectations, and reduce access to high-level coursework (Fish 2019; Schwartz, Hopkins, and Stiefel 2021; Shifrer, Callahan, and Muller 2013). Indeed, the classification of children as disabled is, in and of itself, "both protective and risky" (Artiles, Dorn, and Bal 2016, 807).

These educational inequalities have been amplified by COVID-19. During the first few years of the pandemic, disabled students had less access to in-person or live instruction than their peers did, were disproportionately affected by staffing shortages, and were frequently denied special education services (Jackson and Bowdon 2020; Fish et al. 2023). While individual education plans (IEPs) are unevenly implemented in even the best of circumstances, they were widely ignored during the pandemic (Antonios 2021).[3] Schools are always required to involve families in the creation of IEPs; families frequently play a central role in ensuring that these mandates are followed. Intensive effort and social capital are key to this involvement and advocacy (Blum 2015; Wilson 2015). During the pandemic, these expansive expectations for caregivers' involvement in their children's schooling expanded even further. While many families experienced tremendous stress during this time, caregivers of disabled children were stretched particularly thin (Fish et al. 2023; Greer and Pierce 2021).

The Particular Precarity of Disabled Children

Educational policy has long labeled certain groups of children "at risk" and therefore in need of special attention, programs, or interventions (Stein 2004). This designation became particularly high stakes in 2002, when the No Child Left Behind Act (NCLB) required states to monitor the achievement of students who were "at risk" of failing. As Schneider and Ingram argue, policy tools such as NCLB may offer additional resources to dependent groups, but they also stigmatize them (1993, 339). Such labels construct risk as, in Kysa Nygreen's words, belonging to a specific group that is "problem-prone and distinct from an assumed normal" (2013, 43). The extensive list of "risk groups" targeted by NCLB legislation included low-income children and children who were "racial or ethnic minorities"; children with limited English proficiency; foster children and homeless children; children who were frequently absent from or had dropped out of school; children who had been in contact with the juvenile justice system or were gang members; and children who received special educational services.

Lists of risk categories also played a central role in New York City conversations about schooling during the pandemic. For example, in September 2020, a *New York Times* article reported that "New York has an enormous population of vulnerable public schoolchildren who have been largely failed by remote learning," enumerating three groups of primary concern: disabled children, poor children, and children living in temporary housing (Shapiro, Rubenstein, and Fitzsimmons 2020). Many people argued that the scale of need in New York City was "unmatched anywhere else in the country" (Shapiro 2020). Indeed, the *New York Times* reported that administrators and policy makers had engaged in "a series of conversations over the summer in which they tried to determine if one vulnerable group or another should get priority for classroom instruction, but the exercise stalled when they found that the vast majority of students were at risk" (Shapiro 2020). Such analyses framed nearly all children in New York City as at risk. However, disabled students were considered "precarious children" (Blum 2015, 249), presumed to be particularly vulnerable to damage from the pandemic.

Media coverage frequently leaned on these tropes, regularly reporting on the concerns that many caregivers of disabled children expressed about the dangers of remote instruction—often in contrast to calls by disabled and chronically ill communities for remote access (see the introduction to this volume; and Kornstein and Rogers, chapter 8 in this volume). In November 2020, the *New York Post* reported that "parents of children with special needs fear the school shutdown will have devastating consequences for their kids" (Mongelli 2021). In a June 2020 story about remote learning, the *New York Daily News* quoted the mother of an autistic teen saying, "all of a sudden, the rug was just pulled out from under him" (Elsen-Rooney 2020a); that fall, the *New York Times* reported on a mother of a child with speech and motor disabilities asking, "Can we gain the ground that we lost in the seven months without school?" (Shapiro and Zaveri 2020). Pandemic narratives framed access to education as extremely high stakes for kids whose disabilities were presumed to render them less resilient—a quality understood as an inherent, individual capacity to overcome risk and "cope with additional traumatic events in their lives" (Kendall 2008, 373). Disabled kids were seen as having diminished capacity and, therefore, especially vulnerable.

However, families of disabled kids reported more diverse experiences than media coverage indicated. On the one hand, some mothers we interviewed echoed the media's concerns about the dangers that pandemic schooling posed for disabled kids. A white, middle-class mother of an autistic fifth grader explained that her daughter is "just not cut out for the remote world.... Her needs are so much higher, and things don't come naturally to her. She really needs the in-person interaction." This parent's concerns were shared by other mothers who cited their children's needs for the structured social interaction, academic intervention, and special education services that remote instruction lacked. Such comments echoed media portrayals of disabled children as more vulnerable and less resilient. The white, middle-class mother of a sixth-grade girl with attention deficit hyperactivity disorder (ADHD) and learning disabilities, for example, compared her concerns about her daughter to her older, nondisabled brother: "You know, all the kids have gaps. But you can see that some kids can—like my son, he can quickly close that gap, right? Her gap just seems to have gotten wider.... And it was harder and harder to catch up, so it's just like a spiral." This mother, like many other caregivers of disabled children, "didn't even consider remote" an option when it was time to make decisions about the 2020–21 academic year. Her concerns, like those of many caregivers, reflected the twinned discourses of risk and resilience; while both of her children faced challenges, a "gap" posed considerably more danger to her disabled daughter.

However, not all caregivers of disabled kids preferred in-person instruction. Families' experiences with their children's schooling prior to and during the pandemic, together with perceptions of the health risks of COVID-19, influenced some mothers to choose exclusively remote instruction for their children even after school buildings reopened. In New York City, concerns about COVID-19 may have been particularly intense due to the city's very high death and hospitalization rates during the spring of 2020. Some families also felt that their children benefited from remote, rather than in-person, instruction. For example, the Black mother of an autistic eighth grader told us that her son had been so happy with remote learning during the spring of 2020 that he refused to return to school. His mother explained that her child thrived during remote instruction because "he wasn't a target anymore"; no longer distracted by the bullying that permeated his in-person schooling, he was better able to focus and studied more. When he learned that his school would offer only asynchronous instruction the next fall, the boy emailed school administrators to advocate for a continued version of the Zoom sessions that had benefited him during the initial lockdown.

A Latina middle-class mother of an autistic second grader explained why she chose fully remote instruction: "Although his social skill was a bit of a concern for me, I didn't feel like that was anything that couldn't be made up or picked back up again with time. As opposed to if we had a health scare and his life was potentially at risk or anyone else in the household, then that cannot be made up." This mother, like other caregivers of disabled children, carefully weighed the educational and health risks involved in remote and in-person instruction. On the basis of these experiences, they made pragmatic decisions intended to protect their children (see Carey, Block, and Scotch 2020). Rather than expect the state (or, in many cases, their own spouses) to offer resources and protection, these women understood that they must act as good maternal citizens (Lupton 2014), making "disciplined risk assessments and appropriate health choices" for their families (Blum 2015, 29). Their decisions were also informed by the degree to which schools had been responsive to their concerns in the past. These experiences were, as we show in the next section, racially patterned.

Vigilante Mothers and the Dubious Protection of the State

Few media narratives about disabled children reflected the nuanced analysis of pandemic schooling routinely demonstrated by the mothers with whom we spoke. Instead, discussions of policy often focused exclusively on the specter of regression, positioning state provision of in-person special education services as the primary tool used to protect vulnerable disabled children. In contrast, we found that many mothers understood themselves to be the primary source of protection for their kids. Even in the best of times, mothers of disabled kids saw it as their responsibility to reduce any possible risk to their children, "no matter how remote the threat" (Wolf 2011, 69). During the pandemic, educational and health risks appeared quite likely, and maternal responsibilities felt especially urgent.

Most mothers had experienced multiple struggles to access educational support for their children for years prior to the pandemic. They took on the responsibility of making informed choices, advocating for needed support, and navigating complex bureaucracies in order to access the public good of education. They understood that, as Linda Blum argues, "we persist in assigning mothers primary responsibility for children and the major share of blame when things go wrong" (2015, 3). This responsibility—and the labor that accompanies it—is, of course, highly gendered. It is also situated within a neoliberal political economy that, even before the pandemic, relied on individuals to assess, manage, and take responsibility for their life outcomes (Blum 2015; Wolf 2011; Carey, Block, and Scotch 2020).

While the Individuals with Disabilities Education Act (IDEA) is supposed to offer an additional layer of protection for disabled students (Artiles, Dorn, and Bal 2016), many families had long been intimately familiar with the state's failure to protect their children's educational rights. As one mother told a *Daily News* reporter, "We always take what we're given with a grain of salt" (Elsen-Rooney 2020a). This grain of salt was evident as a Latina middle-class mother of a child who uses a wheelchair told us that previous to the pandemic, her son was unable to access his classroom for weeks at a time, due to broken elevators in the school building. In another example, a mother of an autistic child, also Latina and middle class, described with horror a teacher's "nonchalant" reaction to learning that her kindergartener had left the classroom for an extended period without anyone noticing.

As a Black middle-class mother reminded us, special education service provision frequently depends on the efforts of caregivers. This mother, whose son is autistic and nonspeaking, described ongoing conflict with teachers and administrators due to their failure to modify her son's assignments as required by his IEP. She told us, "I'm talking to everyone in positions of power, and no one is really helping me":

> You know, I don't have a problem with communicating, you know, even as far as emails and every detail in the emails. I make time to go to the school. Like, if you call and tell me something about my son, I'm there in less than five minutes. I take the time. I stop whatever I'm doing. Even if I'm at work, I go up. So, there wasn't a lack of communication. And I even told the school, I said, "If this is what you're doing to him, with a parent that's interested in him or educated, what about the other people that can't speak English or don't know the system or, you know, don't know the difference between special education and all the—you know, what are you doing to them?"

As this mother pointed out, caregivers' efforts on behalf of their children are situated in contexts that are "often rife with unequal racial and economic power relationships that manifest between caregivers/parents and school systems" (Voulgarides 2021, 3; see also Fish 2022; Freidus 2020; Wilson 2015). What is more, in Blum's words, each family was expected to tackle institutional constraints, limited resources, and "multiple bureaucratic obstacles" on their own; mothers thus took on the role of "vigilantes on lone quests for justice when institutions had largely failed their kids" (2015, 20).

Pandemic-related restrictions on disabled children's access to educational services and support only exacerbated the need for family advocacy. Families who opted for in-person instruction grappled with significant structural gaps in New York City's hybrid learning program. Due to the need for social distancing, class sizes were dramatically reduced, leaving many special education classrooms severely understaffed. For example, one mother told us that her child with ADHD and learning disabilities had access to special education teachers for only one of eight periods in the school day. Due to staffing shortages, other children were denied access to the paraprofessionals who were supposed to provide them individualized support, as mandated in their individualized educational plans (Zimmer and Zimmerman 2020). Interviews and media analysis demonstrate that schools failed to provide mandated services such as occupational therapy, speech therapy, and physical therapy for many children enrolled in both remote and hybrid instruction. What is more, special education referrals dropped precipitously during the first year of the pandemic, indicating that many more children who might have qualified for special educational support did not have access to "services they probably should be getting, and in any other year they would be getting" (Elsen-Rooney 2020b).

A mother and advocate told the *New York Times* that, based on a survey she had conducted with over one thousand parents of disabled children, "instruction has been spread so thin to the point where it can't even count as special education instruction" (Shapiro 2020). Mothers of disabled children were used to advocating fiercely for their kids, but many feared that the pandemic might further deprive them of the protection to which they were entitled from the state. The pandemic increased their already urgent concerns. As the *New York Daily News* reported, "years of fighting tooth and nail for their children's educational rights has left many parents of special needs kids deeply distrustful that school decisions are being made with their kids' best interests in mind—a worry that's especially pronounced when the stakes are so high" (Elsen-Rooney 2020a).

It is often taken for granted that the state is the ultimate source of protection for vulnerable children; in Kendall's words, the assumption is that "children have the right to adult protection, by their parents or guardians if at all possible and by the state when their parents or guardians are not able to protect them" (2008, 370). However, mothers of disabled children struggled to hold the state responsible for failures to protect their children's rights, both before and during the pandemic. This dubious protection further depended on race, class, and mothers' relationships with school staff, rendering it unevenly available. The need for such "vigilante" advocacy calls into question the state's status as protector. It deepens the privatization of care responsibilities, placing additional considerable and unequal burdens on caregivers to make up for schools' and society's failure to provide equitably for their disabled children.

* * *

As these mothers of disabled children can testify, special education services frequently fail to reach their "targets." The stigma, however, persists. Narratives of risk and protection in special education both reflect and diverge from how we talk about educating "all kids." First and foremost, that category all too often is used to describe only children without disabilities. Disabled children are, instead, assigned to "risk groups." The call to protect these "risk groups" is a double-edged sword; in the words of Alison Piepmeyer, George Estreich, and Rachel Adams, this framing embeds "cultural stories about disability" that "shape power structures and designate certain people as not fully human" (2021, 7). Perhaps more importantly, such discourses deny that we are all worthy of protection.

This denial reflects broader tensions in our social welfare system, which views vulnerability as a static category, rather than contingent and contextualized. It fails to recognize that we all move in and out of vulnerable states and that disability is inevitable for most of us as we age, if not sooner (Mauldin 2022). Within the current system, mothers of disabled kids have little choice other than to fill the void left by the state's inadequate protection. Instead, we might work toward understanding risk and protection as fundamental to an interdependent community, in which we all need and offer care (Linton 1998).

As part of the call to reimagine schooling in the wake of the COVID-19 pandemic (Ladson-Billings 2021; McKinney de Royston and Vossoughi 2021), we suggest that there is an urgent need to center interdependence and shared protection as guiding values in education and as essential to the flourishing of both disabled and nondisabled students. Practitioners and advocates can sponsor school-level conversations and disseminate media messages that challenge educators and policy makers to recognize the importance of mutual care. At the same time, we can collectively problematize the state's overreliance on categorizations of vulnerability in providing much-needed—but often scant—public resources for children and their families. Educators and policy makers can attend carefully to the varied experiences and perspectives of disabled children and their caregivers, working in partnership with families to develop truly inclusive models that integrate care and protection throughout educational processes and structures. To make this possible, we need designated state and federal funding for school redesign initiatives; high-quality, inclusive education programs; additional teachers and paraprofessionals; and ongoing training and resources. If we proceed from the understanding that disability is not a static state, we can build public support for such initiatives.

Reports of pandemic-era "learning loss" and undelivered services often ignore how education systems have long failed and continue to fail disabled children (Fish et al. 2023). A rush to get "back to normal" and "recover" from the challenges of remote schooling (perhaps intentionally) dismisses these realities. As we write this chapter, this "normal" continues to label disabled children "at risk," while simultaneously denying them access to public education (Zimmerman 2023). All too often, we fail to conduct research and imagine policy responses that conceptualize vulnerability as complex and contextualized. By situating disabled children (and all children and all disabled people) as passive recipients of services, we deny the broader social, cultural, political, and economic systems that contribute to our collective vulnerability (Kendall 2008, 372). We therefore consider the failures of the pandemic an opportunity to imagine new systems, systems that offer collective protection for the dependence and interdependence that mark us all.

NOTES

1. Language conventions vary in using person-first language (i.e., "people with disabilities") or disability-first language (i.e., "disabled people"). In this chapter, we will largely use disability-first language, with some variation when capturing the framing of families and the media. We also use the terms "children" and "kids" interchangeably, in the tradition of critical childhood and youth studies (Thorne 1993).

2. We would have liked to talk with disabled kids directly about their experiences and perceptions, since they are the true experts on their experience. However, obtaining approval to interview disabled children poses many institutional barriers, due to the presumed vulnerability and incompetence of disabled people and children. Because we wanted to collect these data in a timely matter, we decided to speak with parents and caregivers of disabled kids instead.

3   IEPs are legal documents that specify the services and accommodations that public schools must provide to disabled children so that they can access a free and appropriate education, as mandated by federal law.

REFERENCES

Annamma, Subini Ancy. 2017. *The Pedagogy of Pathologization: Dis/abled Girls of Color in the School-Prison Nexus*. New York: Routledge.

Antonios, Caitlin. 2021. "Parents of Special Education Students Say the DOE Isn't Sharing Meaningful Data. So They're Collecting It Themselves." *The City*, April 8 2021. www.thecity.nyc.

Artiles, Alfredo J., Sherman Dorn, and Aydin Bal. 2016. "Objects of Protection, Enduring Nodes of Difference: Disability Intersections with 'Other' Differences, 1916 to 2016." *Review of Research in Education* 40 (1): 777–820.

Blum, Linda. 2015. *Raising Generation Rx: Mothering Kids with Invisible Disabilities in an Age of Inequality*. New York: New York University Press.

Carey, Allison C. 2009. *On the Margins of Citizenship: Intellectual Disability and Civil Rights in Twentieth-Century America*. Philadelphia: Temple University Press.

Carey, Allison C., Pamela Block, and Richard K. Scotch. 2020. *Allies and Obstacles: Disability Activism and Parents of Children with Disabilities*. Philadelphia: Temple University Press.

Connor, David J., and Beth A. Ferri. 2006. "The Conflict Within: Resistance to Inclusion and Other Paradoxes in Special Education." *Disability & Society* 22 (1): 63–77.

Deterding, Nicole M., and Mary C. Waters. 2018. "Flexible Coding of In-Depth Interviews: A Twenty-First-Century Approach." *Sociological Methods and Research* 50 (2): 708–39.

Dubinsky, Karen. 2012. "Children, Ideology, and Iconography: How Babies Rule the World." *Journal of the History of Childhood and Youth* 5 (1): 5–13.

Elsen-Rooney, Michael. 2020a. "Class Divisions: Special-Ed Can Restart—but Should It?" *New York Daily News*, June 12, 2020. www.nydailynews.com.

———. 2020b. "Special Ed. Worries: Bug Blamed as 25% Fewer Students Helped." *New York Daily News*, November 4, 2020. www.nydailynews.com.

Fish, Rachel E. 2019. "Standing Out and Sorting In: Exploring the Role of Racial Composition in Racial Disparities in Special Education." *American Educational Research Journal* 56 (6): 2573–2608.

———. 2022. "Stratified Medicalization of Schooling Difficulties." *Social Science & Medicine* 305:115039.

Fish, Rachel E., David Enrique Rangel, Nelly De Arcos, and Olivia Friend. 2023. "Inequality in the Schooling Experiences of Disabled Children and Their Families during COVID-19." In *Research in Social Sciences and Disability*, vol. 13, *Disability in the Time of Pandemic*, edited by Allison Carey, Sara Green, and Laura Mauldin, 135–53. London: Emerald.

Freidus, Alexandra. 2020. "'Problem Children' and 'Children with Problems': Discipline and Innocence in a Gentrifying Elementary School." *Harvard Educational Review* 90 (4): 550–72.

Freidus, Alexandra, and Erica O. Turner. 2023. "Contested Justice: Rethinking Educational Equity through New York City's COVID-19 School Reopening Debates." *Educational Evaluation and Policy Analysis* 45 (3): 437–63.

Green, Sara E. 2007. "'We're Tired, Not Sad': Benefits and Burdens of Mothering a Child with a Disability." *Social Science & Medicine* 64 (1): 150–63.

Green, Sara E., Rosalyn Benjamin Darling, and Loren Wilbers. 2016. "Struggles and Joys: A Review of Research on the Social Experience of Parenting Disabled Children." In *Research in Social Science and Disability*, vol. 9, edited by Sara E. Green and Sharon N. Barnartt, 261–85. London: Emerald.

Greer, Molly, and Chelsea Pierce. 2021. "Examining the Impact of the COVID-19 Pandemic on Caregivers of Children with Complex and Chronic Conditions." *Research, Advocacy, and Practice for Complex and Chronic Conditions* 40 (1): 42–50.

Jackson, Dia, and Jill Bowdon. 2020. "National Survey of Public Education's Response to Covid-19: Spotlight on Students with Disabilities." Research brief. American Institute for Research. www.air.org.

Kendall, Nancy. 2008. "'Vulnerability' in AIDS-Affected States: Rethinking Child Rights, Educational Institutions, and Development Paradigms." *International Journal of Educational Development* 28 (4): 365–83.

Ladson-Billings, Gloria. 2021. "I'm Here for the Hard Re-set: Post Pandemic Pedagogy to Preserve Our Culture." *Equity & Excellence in Education* 54 (1): 68–78.

Lalvani, Priya, and Jessica K. Bacon. 2019. "Rethinking 'We Are All Special': Anti-ableism Curricula in Early Childhood Classrooms. *Young Exceptional Children* 22 (2): 87–100.

Linton, Simi. 1998. *Claiming Disability: Knowledge and Identity*. New York: New York University Press.

Lloyd, Margaret. 2001. "The Politics of Disability and Feminism: Discord or Synthesis?" *Sociology* 35 (3): 715–28.

Lupton, Deborah. 2014. "'It's a Terrible Thing When Your Children Are Sick': Motherhood and Home Healthcare Work." *Health Sociology Review* 22 (3): 234–42.

Mauldin, Laura. 2022. "The Care Crisis Isn't What You Think: Our Problems Are Deeper than a Lack of Care Infrastructure." *American Prospect*, January 3, 2022. https://prospect.org.

Mauldin, Laura, and Robyn Lewis Brown. 2021. "Missing Pieces: Engaging Sociology of Disability in Medical Sociology." *Journal of Health and Social Behavior* 62 (4): 477–92.

McKinney de Royston, Maxine, and Shirin Vossoughi. 2021. "Fixating on Pandemic 'Learning Loss' Undermines the Need to Transform Education." *Truthout*, January 21, 2012. https://truthout.org.

Meiners, Erica R. 2016. *For the Children? Protecting Innocence in a Carceral State*. Minneapolis: University of Minnesota Press.

Mongelli, Laura. 2020. "Dire Impact on Special Ed." *New York Post*, November 21, 2020. www.nypost.com.

Nygreen, Kysa. 2013. *These Kids: Identity, Agency, and Social Justice at a Last Chance High School*. Chicago: University of Chicago Press.

O'Connell Davidson, Julia. 2005. *Children in the Global Sex Trade*. Cambridge, UK: Polity.

Piepmeier, Alison, George Estreich, and Rachel Adams. 2021. *Unexpected: Parenting, Prenatal Testing, and Down Syndrome*. New York: New York University Press.

Schneider, Anne, and Helen Ingram. 1993. "Social Construction of Target Populations: Implications for Politics and Policy." *American Political Science Review* 87 (2): 334–47.

Schwartz, Amy Ellen, Bryant Gregory Hopkins, and Lenna Stiefel. 2021. "The Effects of Special Education on the Academic Performance of Students with Learning Disabilities." *Journal of Policy Analysis and Management* 40 (2): 480–520.

Shapiro, Eliza. 2020. "12,000 More White Children Return to N.Y.C. Schools than Black Children." *New York Times*, December 9, 2020. www.nytimes.com.

Shapiro, Eliza, Dana Rubinstein, and Emma G. Fitzsimmons. 2020. "New York City Delays Start of School to Ready for In-Person Classes." *New York Times*, September 1, 2020. www.nytimes.com.

Shapiro, Eliza, and Mihir Zaveri. 2020. "New York Becomes the First Big City in the U.S. to Reopen All Its Schools." *New York Times*, September 2, 2020. www.nytimes.com.

Shifrer, Dara, Rebecca M. Callahan, and Chandra Muller. 2013. "Equity or Marginalization? The High School Course-Taking of Students Labeled with a Learning Disability." *American Educational Research Journal* 50:656–82.

Simplican, Stacy Clifford. 2015. "Care, Disability, and Violence: Theorizing Complex Dependency in Eva Kittay and Judith Butler." *Hypatia* 30 (1): 217–33.

Stein, Sandra J. 2004. *The Culture of Education Policy*. New York: Teachers College Press.

Thorne, Barrie. 1993. *Gender Play: Girls and Boys in School*. New Brunswick, NJ: Rutgers University Press.

Voulgarides, Catherine. 2021. "Equity, Parental/Caregiver 'Power,' and Disability Policy in the U.S. Context." *International Journal of Inclusive Education*, June 18, 2021.

Wilson, Natasha M. 2015. "Question-Asking and Advocacy by African American Parents at Individualized Education Program Meetings: A Social and Cultural Capital Perspective." *Multiple Voices for Ethnically Diverse Exceptional Learners* 15 (2): 36–49.

Wolf, Joan. 2011. *Is Breast Best? Taking on the Breastfeeding Experts and the New High Stakes of Motherhood*. New York: New York University Press.

Zimmer, Amy, and Alex Zimmerman. 2020. "NYC's Staffing Crunch Takes a Big Toll on Students with Disabilities, Report Finds." *Chalkbeat*, December 1, 2020. https://ny.chalkbeat.org.

Zimmerman, Alex. 2023. "Only 1 in 3 NYC Schools Are Fully Accessible to Students with Physical Disabilities, Report Says." *Chalkbeat*, August 21, 2023. https://ny.chalkbeat.org.

7

Care Work, Creativity, and Unplanned Survival in the Time of COVID

FAYE GINSBURG AND RAYNA RAPP

When New York City became the United States' COVID-19 epicenter in spring 2020, housing for disabled adults with intellectual/developmental disabilities (I/DD) was already precarious. This is especially the case for people of color, immigrants, prisoners, and those living in poverty, who are more likely to be in nursing homes or other congregate spaces, as discussed in chapters in this volume by Bardelli, Thomas, and Brown (chapter 1), Salyer (chapter 2), and Bhaman (chapter 3). They have been at greatest risk of infection and death from COVID-19. Indeed, approximately one-third of pandemic deaths in the US have taken place in long-term-care congregate settings such as nursing homes. The rate is higher when other group-home settings such as assisted-living and intermediate-care facilities are taken into account. New York is no exception (*New York Times* 2021). Additionally, many adults with developmental disabilities and chronic conditions who were living on their own or with family lost their usual programs and support staff as the metropolitan area initially went "on pause" and as front-line care workers began to be numbered among the early and ongoing casualties given their high-risk occupation. Many care workers also quit, and others refused vaccination, making them ineligible for work.

Our virtual fieldwork with adults with I/DD and their families and supporters chronicles their underrepresented experiences of what Shayda Kafai (2021) calls "crip kinship," a network of reciprocity, care, and support for disabled bodyminds within and beyond the nuclear family. This chapter is shaped by what we learned about their aspirations, risks, and frustrations as well as "silver linings" and unexpected possibilities that emerged under pandemic conditions.

We place our research in the context of long-standing advances in medical technologies and caregiving, along with deinstitutionalization and disability civil rights legislation and social movements. All of these have extended the life spans as well as quality of life for an increasing number of vulnerable people, including those with intellectual/developmental disabilities, chronic illness, and genetic disorders. Over the past three decades, the lives of people with a variety of disabilities have radically changed as they have taken advantage of entitlements to attend school, live in the community, and engage in meaningful pursuits into an unanticipated adulthood. Yet people living with these diagnoses also remain particularly subject to marginalization and slow-moving bureaucratic responses to what anthropologist Pam Block calls "unplanned survival" (2020, S70). They represent the increasing presence of disabled people in our shared social landscape, part of a significant demographic shift, what the medical anthropologists Lenore Manderson and Ayo Wahlberg consider a trend toward "chronic living" (2020, 428). Under these evolving circumstances, there are few clear scripts for how to live a resilient life as a disabled adult who requires continual care and support. As a result, adults with I/DD and their allies now find themselves compelled to reimagine their lives, rethinking questions of home, safety, community, and futurity under pandemic conditions. Ideally, in a disability-friendly world, they would have "access intimacy," disability activist Mia Mingus's (2011) apt term for "that elusive, hard to describe feeling when someone else 'gets' your access needs." For many, this kind of support was profoundly disrupted during the pandemic.

To find out how people with I/DD and their families were managing during COVID, we reanimated our ongoing conversations with people drawn from our long-standing ethnographic research focused on understanding what it means to live with a child with intellectual disabilities (Ginsburg and Rapp 2024). From them, we learned how kinship, caring, and creativity get refigured as everyone ages over the life cycle. Now, as their children have become adults and their "circles of support" are aging along with parents in their sixties and seventies, we returned to these interlocutors, to learn how they were faring under the stresses of COVID. We found that the pandemic provoked both existential dilemmas and unexpected catalysts for creativity.

In addition to interviews, we followed online discussions with families pursuing New York State's Medicaid-funded "self-direction" program, a model of long-term care service that helps disabled people maintain their independence at home, prioritizing participant choice, control, and flexibility in selecting and training their own staff (Applied Self-Direction, n.d.). We also participated in virtual creative-arts programs, what we think of as "third spaces" that offer adults with I/DD opportunities to critique their experiences of ableist exclusion while building a vibrant yet fragile community. The film *Isolation Nation*, discussed later in this chapter, is a lively example of this. Furthermore, we tracked the escalating activity of disabled adults on disability blogs, websites, documentary films, and newsletters, as well as activists and allies who used these media to call attention to the triaging of and discrimination against people with disabilities throughout the pandemic. Consider the following vivid instance of such an initiative.

Congregate Housing during COVID: Fire through Dry Grass

For those who had been living in congregate housing, the chaos and disruption caused by COVID was especially dramatic. In such settings, people experienced an alarming escalation in transmission to those with preexisting health risks, resulting in disproportionate deaths. The congregate home resident and activist Andres "Jay" Molina, a wheelchair user and member of the Reality Poets group at the Coler Rehabilitation and Nursing Care Center on New York's Roosevelt Island, started chronicling the sense of panic that ensued as COVID rapidly spread through the facility as healthy residents were made to share rooms with infected patients transferred from other facilities. The title of the documentary that he codirected with Alexis Neophytides, *Fire through Dry Grass* (2023), aptly captures the fear, intensity, and speed of their experience. The film opened in August 2023 to a standing ovation at the Black Star Film Festival (known as the Black Sundance) in Philadelphia, followed by a festival and theatrical circuit tour with a first national broadcast on the prestigious public television series *POV*.

The filmmaker Jay Molina left the Dominican Republic in his late teens for the Lower East Side. As he explained in a 2020 interview with disability activist Alice Wong for her *Disability Visibility Project* blog, prior to COVID, he and other residents experienced a sense of freedom through artistic expression:

> In 2014, I developed a rare lung condition that attacked my vital organs and left me paralyzed. I'm a former baseball player and truck driver, and today a filmmaker, animator, and advocate for people living with disabilities. . . . I live in Coler Nursing Home, . . . where I met my brothers. . . . We are all members of Open Doors, a network of artists, activists and advocates motivated by community building, gun violence prevention and disability rights. Through OPEN DOORS, we formed the Reality Poets, a collective of truth-telling artists bonded through a shared mission to spread a message of realness, resilience and healing. . . . Living on Roosevelt Island we have a lot of freedom and access to the community that as wheelchair users we probably wouldn't have in other places. (Wong 2020)

The situation radically changed with the arrival of COVID. Molina continues,

> Or, I should say we *had* more access, pre-pandemic. . . . I haven't seen my family or had a hug in all this time. I think working on this film, telling our story and making sure our voices are being heard has really helped though. . . . We want people to know what really went on here at Coler and how the administration is lying about it, covering up how many people died and passing blame to everyone else. . . .
>
> A lot of the patients here are undocumented and have no papers, so they are scared to speak out. They feel that they will have no place to go if they get kicked out. The residents fear retaliation from the staff, and the staff is scared to lose their jobs. . . . I guess the answer is, we aren't advocating for institutions like Coler to be abolished. We just want them to be changed, to be more humane. (Wong 2020)

People like Jay Molina and his fellow Reality Poets, all disabled artist/activists living in group settings, have played an outsize creative role in publicizing the particular hazards of the pandemic to those living in congregate housing, who are often low income, immigrants, and people of color. Residents often had no other place to go, while many nurses and aides—also disproportionately African American and Latinx—succumbed to the virus. Nursing-home workers "described short-staffed, disorganized facilities that sometimes lacked adequate protective gear amid the pandemic. Workers fell ill, alongside their patients" (Ivory et al. 2022).

Under these harrowing circumstances, when possible, many families across class, racial, ethnic, and religious backgrounds mobilized to bring their relatives home, where the risk of exposure could at least be partially controlled. For example, an older white Manhattan mother whose autistic son had been living in congregate housing described to us how she removed him after a number of deaths at the facility where he was living. She also grimly suggested that this would be a good time to find spots in such places, which otherwise have long waiting lists due to the shortage of this kind of accommodation.

The Great Resignation

In all our conversations with family members caring for their disabled adult children at home during the pandemic, the first topic of concern was the dramatic and destabilizing loss of trained and often beloved home caregivers and direct support professionals (DSPs). Additionally, their lives were disrupted by the closure of community "day-hab" programs that provide scheduled activities and training to promote social integration beyond their homes. These had long offered structured social life, important relationships, and opportunities for work and creative activities for people with I/DD; without these resources, many, including our interlocutors, found themselves scrambling to create new forms of support as they tried to build pandemic workarounds. The loss of paid caregivers and the programs they staffed were two of many consequential abrupt transformations of an overall complex shift in labor-force participation—particularly for face to-face health and service workers—a phenomenon that has come to be known as part of "the great resignation" (Bove 2022).

For example, Donna (a pseudonym), an African American semiretired professional and mother of two adult autistic children, described what happened as her daughter's day-hab program in her Brooklyn neighborhood shut down. She explained, "Georgia's day-hab program suspended services for quite a while. . . . And then, when they came back, they couldn't promise that they could social distance properly. Everybody on staff was not vaccinated, and I didn't feel like she should go." This disruption also produced unexpected "silver linings," as Donna elaborated:

> Georgia's absolutely thrilled to be at home. She's not missing her day-hab program. I miss her day-hab program because I really think she needs to be out a lot more. She's less anxious. She's actually speaking a lot more. She's reading more. She's learned how to set up a group text. So she sends out texts to the whole family, like for every holiday. So, you know, she'll send out two hundred texts to my loving family, and you know, it's Martin Luther King Day, it's Labor Day, it's Rosh Hashana. I mean, as she finds pictures for every holiday, she bombards the whole family; fortunately, everybody's very understanding and encourages her actually. So that's been a real interesting development for her. (interview, January 20, 2022)

Julie (pseudonym), a white Queens resident and mother of an adult daughter with a complex rare degenerative genetic disease requiring a ventilator (among other supports), quit her job once her daughter needed full-time medical care, managing with support staff and outside programs. Prior to the pandemic, her daughter, Sally, was attending a theater group for people with disabilities that she loved; it went on pause as COVID spread. Throughout the pandemic, the family has found it difficult to find safe help. Many of Sally's personal support staff quit or did not want to get vaccinated, which was not an option since she uses a breathing tube.

Julie described the impact of these circumstances on her own interdependent life: "It used to be that the staff would take Sally out to movies and to visit with friends, which gave my husband and I some respite and one evening a week out. That went on pause with COVID. New workers are much more distant. We are now very isolated. We are 'people people,' and we have missed out on seeing people and seeing Sally's brother and sister. We are afraid to have new people in the house" (interview, December 21, 2021). Such COVID disruptions rippled through the kin and caring networks of virtually everyone with whom we spoke.

The Disability Cliff and the Death Plan

These disruptions provoked more than scheduling instabilities and isolation. Julie went on to describe the specter of her own possible death by COVID, dramatically heightening already-existing profound underlying anxieties about who would care for her daughter when she and her husband no longer could: "Now, I go to bed every night thinking about the future of care for Sally. We have more [funded] allotted hours than we can fill with [safe] caregivers." Her fears resonated with those of every parent we talked to about their adult child's future, raising concerns about what has come to be known as "the disability cliff." As scholar/author and disability activist Michael Bérubé (2018) has written regarding his worries about his adult son with Down syndrome, the disability cliff "is what ensues when an individual with disabilities turns 21 and ages out of the support systems that have sustained him or her from infancy through adolescence. It's where the law ends and a dark, uncertain wilderness begins." As disabled children age into their twenties, thirties, and beyond, these concerns grow ever more existential and material. Consider the comments of the Manhattan parent, author, and activist Marguerite Elisofon, whose public blog, *The Never Empty Nest*, chronicles what it is like to parent her adult autistic daughter, Samantha:

> As Samantha approaches 30 (gulp!) and I'm cruising along in my 60s, she asks me more and more often: "When will I live on my own? I don't want to live with you forever." The feeling is mutual, though we love each other dearly. Our daughter is long overdue to move on in her adult life, and we, as her parents, would happily welcome a more peaceful and private living situation for ourselves. . . . Achieving that goal seems nearly impossible at the moment. . . . About 75% of adults with disabilities currently live with an aging parent or caregiver [and] more than half of families have no plan for the future. How can we have a plan for the future if there are no appropriate and accessible options? (Elisofon 2020)

In May 2023, Marguerite's post bore the title "An Autism Mom Explains Breast Cancer to Her Daughter," telescoping her concerns about the future (Elisofon 2023a). By July, after Marguerite had undergone successful treatment, her oncologist declared that she was going to be okay. She wrote,

> I'm not used to people wanting to take care of me. In normal times, I'm the one who takes care of everyone—especially Samantha. What would she do without me? I can't think about that either. Fortunately, I don't need to for the moment.
>
> "How does your breast feel?" Samantha asks me frequently. "My breast is okay, thanks." . . . But my heart is a different story. (Elisofon 2023b)

Once New York City became the epicenter and New York State went "on pause," the feared reality of the disability cliff loomed much closer. For every family with an adult member with I/DD or chronic illness, the question of aging and risk was heightened and accelerated by the unavoidable sense of terror that parents or other caregivers might rapidly die from COVID, with no plan in place to ensure appropriate care for their loved ones who might need up to 24/7 support. Indeed, one New York "self-direction" parents' listserv had an active thread addressing these concerns that was called "the death plan"—until a few participants requested a diplomatic name change of the subject line to "gravitas." On this long-standing and intimate virtual platform, more than a few parents expressed a taboo thought that many tacitly shared: the painful wish that their adult child would predecease them, given their despair over the difficulty of finding respectful and appropriate care.

When we spoke with Donna, the Brooklyn mother with two adult children on the spectrum, about how COVID shaped the way she considered the future for them, she explained that this issue rapidly arose when her husband got quite sick early in the pandemic.

> Fortunately, we have a third floor and a bedroom up there, and we put him in isolation. And, you know, things were still coming out in terms of your protocol, you know, wearing the gloves and mask. Nobody knew. So, we knew he was really, really sick. . . . So my [autistic] son, Tim, and I would take turns taking food up. . . . We did everything we could. And then, while he was getting sicker, I started to feel sick, maybe four or five days later. It was really difficult back then to get a test. But the doctors just said, you know, "If you're exposed, you should assume you have it as well." And I had the fatigue and the headaches, and I was just exhausted. Then . . . my husband had to go to the hospital. . . . It was scary because, you know, we called an

ambulance, and the kids had to watch him go. We couldn't go with him. So it was really kind of a very scary experience. [I thought] "Who's gonna take care of my kids?" And it was the most frightening thing. Like, we knew we were isolated. Who was gonna be able to come in? Who was gonna be able to help them? Nobody could, really. My kids, they're pretty competent in terms of getting food together, . . . and we had wonderful neighbors who did grocery shopping for us. Our pharmacy was great about dropping medicine off. So we felt like our village really went into high gear and people were there for us, and I feel really, really lucky about that.

Despite the welcome rallying of neighbors and community members, Donna's escalating worries included her daughter's mental health, an issue discussed by other families as well. "Georgia was very, very anxious at the beginning; I think she knew her dad was sick. She knew I didn't feel well, and she couldn't quite articulate this. But she cried like every day for—for two weeks. In the beginning, she knew her world was different. She knew dad was sick. Mommy didn't feel well. No one was doing anything they normally do. And it was very hard for her." Like other parents, Donna also told us how her COVID experience provoked a reconsideration of future arrangements for both her adult children, accelerating the need for new plans:

And I also started thinking, okay, I'm counting on my sister and my brother to sort of be there in case something were to happen to me, but my sister's gonna likely move, and my brother's much older than me. So I've been trying to craft a place where at least I know people and know agencies that can sort of be the support for Georgia. Ideally what I would like is to find an apartment. And when my husband and I are not there, Tim could be there with Georgia with some extra support coming in for her. I'm not quite sure how to craft it, but that's kind of on my radar.

Many others expressed a similar sense of explicit disruption about future plans for their adult children with I/DD, anticipating a time when they will no longer be able to offer care. During COVID, when their demise felt more imminent, they explained to us how they were reconsidering who in their kin and friend networks might act as potential sources of support for vulnerable adult children. A white professional Manhattan mom with an adult daughter, her only child, on the spectrum, for example, had hoped that her best friend might serve as a guardian. The friend's unexpected recent death has disrupted Millie's (pseudonym) sense of an orderly plan as she searches for a replacement, knowing that her California sister is too far away to step in. Julie, discussed earlier, whose daughter's rare disease requires complex 24/7 care, has started training her two other adult children and their spouses to understand and participate in Sally's care, despite her long-standing reluctance to burden them.

A Bronx-based professional white mother, Kayla, told us that her adult daughter, Lydia, has decided not to have children for a number of reasons, including her expectation that she will take over responsibility for her younger autistic brother, Josh. During the pandemic, Lydia became more involved in learning about funding for Josh's programs and attending his Life Plan meetings; she also joined a sibling support group. With supportive care, Josh had been living independently in his own apartment, working, taking classes, and welcoming an older retired "paid neighbor" who looks in on him regularly. When New York City became the epicenter of the US pandemic and was in lockdown, Josh joined his parents, leaving the city with them for the relative safety of their family's country house, where he was able to retain his job as it transitioned to a virtual workplace.

In the summer of 2023, we checked in with the families we had interviewed about their pandemic experiences to see how they were faring. Kayla reported that when it became safe for Josh to return to the city, the resumption of independent living in his apartment was a difficult readjustment. During that transition period, he called on her more than he had before the pandemic. Among the challenges Josh faced was the shift from online day-hab communities back to in-person meetings, adding travel time that interfered with his work schedule. When we asked Kayla what lessons the family learned from the pandemic, she offered the following:

> The lesson is . . . living independently is really important because it forces him to mature, have experiences, and make daily decisions. . . . He feels

more confident as he grows. He is also more often than not happier to be independent, . . . even though he is lonely sometimes. But he has learned to reach out to friends, schedule social activities ahead of time, and deal with the unexpected, a great challenge for those with autism. Having him live independently again is healthy for us, since the responsibility of his care is no longer 24/7, and now we have some privacy too. All told, it is important to note that we did not experience COVID in a traumatic way. We did not know anyone who died, we all had devices, were able to install internet access, had an income, a home out of the city with room enough to have Josh stay with us, and then some. So our perspective is a privileged one. (interview, August 2023)

Donna also had positive updates that she sent by email in August 2023.

We are doing pretty well. Georgia was finally approved for self-direction and we were able to find a lovely "com hab" [support] person who works with her. She has renewed interest in her academic skills . . . and started a baking class at INVICTUS—a bakery established to train autistic adults . . . ; she absolutely loves it. She is also going to the gym more often. I am encouraged by her desire to improve her health. Tim continues to work with [educational advocates for children with learning issues and their families]. He loves the work. . . . He is having a bit of anxiety still about Covid—he doesn't go out as much as he used to because [of] the virus (he has not had it). He did travel to Italy last year with a group . . . and had a great time. He is also still very interested in photography. . . .

My husband experienced long-Covid and it took him a while to recover. Last year, he had to also contend with [other health challenges] Fortunately, he is much better on all fronts and just began a new consulting practice. I have been consulting with the Simons Foundation in conjunction with an autism study working to understand the role of genetics in autism . . . to encourage more African-American families to participate in the research.

Julia was less upbeat. She explained in an August 2023 email that finding caregivers for her daughter, Sally, has continued to be difficult.

> The fear of all things Covid certainly waxes and wanes as we navigate this ongoing pandemic, enjoying freedoms when we can and then continuing to isolate when we must to keep Sally safe. We have not had luck finding the support staff we need and continue to do almost all the care ourselves. . . . The need is so great out there. . . . Sally has once again dipped her toe into life, attending her theatre program 1 day a week . . . along with a nurse who has been with us for over 12 years. . . . It has given Sally back a sense of community, even if just a bit. My husband and I still try to hire respite staff, even for an occasional date night or to just get out and do some errands. . . . I am still doing all of Sally's personal care such as showering, dressing, and all the ADLs [activities of daily life], and my husband helps tremendously by assisting to get her on her ventilator and any lifting.

Her worries about Sally's future were growing:

> As far as the future? It still not only keeps me up at night but consumes my thoughts daily. There is no good solution. . . . We still know that Sally will need to be with us, whether we stay in our current home and make more modifications, or we move to an over 55 community and of course bring her with us. Either way, she will need 24/7 supports and that certainly terrifies me. If she was not medically and physically challenged, there would most likely be more options out there for her independence and future without us. I have started a Facebook group in search of other like-minded families with dependent adult children in our area for support, information, and to make connections [and] brainstorm together and find the right solutions for our loved ones. In the meantime, I plan to live forever and care for my most precious gift. And I will leave you with a saying my husband thought up regarding lack of help, either from friends, family or even the state and the overwhelming isolation we experience always: "People fly over, drop supplies, but nobody lands the plane." We continue to try our best to give Sally the very best life, stay healthy ourselves, and remain hopeful, none of which is easy!

Likewise, when we corresponded with Millie by email in 2023, it was clear that the pandemic had raised the "gravitas" issues that Julie expressed and that we had encountered on the parents' online email group. Millie was increasingly concerned about making a "death plan" for the care of her daughter, Miranda, should she outlive her parents.

> I sank into deep despair.... None of it seems sustainable.... How can I even afford the financial planning work that I need to do to figure out the care part? I feel daunted about ... how to assess if there is any way I can afford any of this given where I am in relationship to retirement (Will I be able to work until I die? Do I want to? Will I have to?) We already worked with special needs financial planners, and I still don't know if/when I should take my Social Security, what happens to Miranda's SSI when I do that, how it impacts her Medicaid, and so on. Getting this right (or doing the very best we can with what we have) seems imperative.... In reality, the whole scaffolding, the whole social support web, is too loosely woven even now, while we're still alive. Or as one expert on special needs trusts said to me: "You've got a 'who problem.' I work with a lot of people with a lot more money than you've got, and they have the same problem you've got: the 'who problem.'" The well-named "who problem" of social networks of support may be more important to solve than the "what problem," or the life/work and financial resources problem.... They seem intertwined. Retrospectively I see that I was so focused on supporting our family, and all of us were so focused on getting Miranda through K–12 and then through college, that our social world became attenuated; our families of origin are far away. The crip kinship idea that is now circulating ... is one pathway, but I have not yet found my on-ramp to that sort of community for our family or for Miranda (though I think she is forging her way mightily).

Imagining Otherwise

The disability community was not exempt from the well-documented intensification and widespread increase in anxiety, depression, and other mental health challenges for New Yorkers (and others) as noted earlier. Indeed, COVID researchers quickly found that people with I/DD were especially vulnerable to the physical, mental, and social effects of the pandemic, due to their reliance on increasingly unstable schedules, breakdowns in daily activities, and the potential precarity of the health of parents and other caregivers. For many, this created an overwhelming sense of vulnerability and loneliness as the usual community supports crumbled (Courtenay and Perera 2020).

At the same time, virtual platforms such as Zoom and FaceTime were increasingly used for mental health support, expanding like mushrooms in a moist forest in response to the growing pandemic panic and fear of face-to-face contagion. Despite the harsh realities and grim discussions of cliffs and death plans, we were also buoyed to learn of creative responses to the rearranging of daily life that the pandemic provoked for everyone but especially for those with intellectual disabilities and their allies. Many support groups for people with chronic disease quickly organized more frequent online gatherings, providing much-needed opportunities for members to talk about their COVID anxieties, while distracting themselves with shared games, movies, and other virtual activities.

These "COVID silver linings" took many forms, from virtual community building and institutional innovation regarding future-centered planning to the most intimate and individual experiences, such as this unexpectedly joyful story of pandemic life. As COVID intensified in spring 2020, Maria Hodermarska, a dramaturg and clinical professor at NYU in music and performing arts, and her autistic activist adult child, Ethan Jones, then twenty-six years old, left New York City to join friends and relatives in Maine. There, Ethan had time to reflect on and embrace their emergent nonbinary and queer identities. On the last day of Pride Week in June 2020, they invited close neighbors to share Ethan's socially distanced outdoor coming-out celebration that featured a rainbow umbrella. In a retrospective conversation with us, Maria and Ethan reflected on the significance of having what we would call liminal time that COVID provided for Ethan to explore new facets of themselves, surrounded by a supportive community.

Isolation Nation

Supportive community was also central to the COVID responses of Outside Voices (OV), a New York City theater company for/by diverse people with intellectual disabilities (ID) that we followed before and during the pandemic. Outside Voices evolved out of a publicly funded day-habilitation program devoted to writing and occasional performances

Figure P.1. Cover of *Asian American Feminist Antibodies: {care in the time of coronavirus}*, a digital zine published by the Asian American Feminist Collective and Bluestockings NYC in May 2020 that circulated widely via social media and other networks. The zine features contributions from many AAPI activists and writers on topics like xenophobic racism, gender-based violence, abolition, disability justice, mutual aid, and more. The cover, by Amira Lin, depicts four AAPI figures in personal protective equipment with a background comprised of scientific iconography of viruses and information.

Figure p.2. Many activists responded to the "double" or "dual" pandemics of COVID-19 and anti-Black racism during 2020, catalyzed by demonstrations protesting the police murder of George Floyd. Amid these interlocking movements, trans and disabled activists also called for recognition of the lives and deaths of trans and disabled people. This mural, painted on a window by the Deaf, trans, Jewish, and Chinese American artist Chella Man, depicts illustrated hands spelling out the message, "Black Disabled Trans Lives Matter," in American Sign Language. The *a* letters in the words "black," "disabled," and "trans" are all connected, and the hands are colored using the colors of the Progress Pride flag. (Photo: Faye Ginsburg, taken on August 21, 2020, on MacDougal Street in Greenwich Village)

Figure P.3. As part of a COVID-19 Day of Remembrance on March 14, 2021, images of New Yorkers lost to the COVID-19 pandemic were projected on the Brooklyn Bridge. The date marked the first known COVID-19 death as well as the more than thirty thousand New Yorkers who died during the pandemic's first year. (Photo: Michael Appleton/Mayoral Photography Office; Brooklyn Bridge Photo Projection creative direction and video design by Brian Tovar, Jason Sherwood, and Alex Basco Koch of Livesight)

Figure P.4. Naming the Lost Memorials (NTL), City Lore, and twenty other New York City community groups created "The Many Losses from Covid-19," a public art memorial along the fence at the entrance to the Green-Wood Cemetery in Brooklyn in May 2020. Since then, volunteer artists and activists have curated NTL memorial sites in New York City, with thousands of nameplates and personalized drawings and photos, created by the families and friends of those who have lost loved ones to the virus. (Photo: Erik McGregor/Sipa USA/Alamy)

Figure P.5. On December 15, 2021, disability activists from Rise and Resist, Brooklyn Center for Independence of the Disabled (BCID), Center for Independence of the Disabled, NY (CIDNY), and other groups rallied in front the MTA headquarters on Broadway to demand the signature of a legally binding agreement and the settlement of multiple ADA lawsuits regarding accessibility. (Photo: Erik McGregor)

Figure P.6. Downstate New York ADAPT activists held demonstrations from March 14 to 18, 2022, in front of the office of New York State Assembly member Carl E. Heastie in the Bronx to oppose the restrictions imposed on Medicaid-funded home-care eligibility in the final state budget. Calling for the repeal of the law, activists explained that these new stricter rules would make people eligible for nursing homes before being eligible for home-care services, adding another level of risk and deterioration of living conditions in the pandemic. (Photo: Erik McGregor)

Figure P.7. *Pareidolia (Vaccinate Now)* is a poster created by the disabled artist duo Brothers Sick (Ezra Benus and Noah Benus) as a reminder that vaccination is urgent but not always straightforward. The Brothers Sick demand an end to medical apartheid, the rationing of care, and vaccine hoarding on a global scale. Sussanne Pfeffer, director of the Museum für Moderne Kunst (Museum of Modern Art) in Frankfurt, named this poster one of the top ten artworks of 2021 in *Artforum*.

Figure p.8. The 2023 documentary *Fire through Dry Grass*, directed by Andres "Jay" Molina and Alexis Neophytides, chronicles the lives of Black and Brown disabled artists during the pandemic. Their poetry underscores the danger and imprisonment they feel in the face of institutional neglect; however, they refuse to be abused, confined, and erased. The film's poster shows the five Reality Poets posed in front of the Coler Rehabilitation and Nursing Care Center on Roosevelt Island, wearing snapback caps and Air Jordans and sitting in powerchairs. (Poster courtesy of *Fire through Dry Grass*; poster design by Guillermo Mena; original Reality Poets portrait by Elias Williams)

Figure p.9. On September 19, 2022, #MEAction organized a series of direct actions in Washington, DC, as part of its ongoing #MillionsMissing campaign—a name invoking people with ME who are "missing" from public life due to the disease. Though the actions were planned in advance, their timing was fortuitous, in that they took place the day after *60 Minutes* aired an interview with President Biden in which he declared that "the pandemic is over." (Photo: #MEAction)

Figure P.10. Given that many people with ME are bed- or homebound, #MEAction also planned social media strategies to enable members who were unable to travel to post from home. (Photo: #MEAction)

Figure P.11. An ad hoc memorial to Christina Yuna Lee, whose murder in February 2022 was reported as part of both a rising tide of anti-Asian violence in New York City and the gendered violence that Asian women face. While many people responded to the violence with calls for increased policing against unhoused people, Lee's family directed proceeds from a GoFundMe campaign to a variety of organizations that Lee believed in, including SafeWalks, a mutual-aid organization accompanying Asian American seniors to and from their homes and transit. (Photo: Salonee Bhaman)

Figure P.12. A vigil in Washington Square Park commemorates the eight lives lost during a shooting at an Asian massage parlor in Atlanta on March 16, 2021. The vigil was hosted by Red Canary Song (RCS) and the Asian American Feminist Collective. The image displays three different art installations. The large installation is titled 韧 *Curtain Armor* and was conceptualized and art directed by Chong Gu and codirected by Yin Q. The portraits hanging on the curtains are titled *Eyes* and were completed by an anonymous massage worker. Behind the curtain are two massage tables, each laid out with food, incense, and offerings in the style of a traditional mourning altar. The food altar was created by Charlotte, a Korean RCS outreach member and former massage worker, and Lisa, a Chinese massage worker based in Flushing, while the funeral altar was created by Wu, another RCS core member and a New York City–based dominatrix. During the rally, organizers noted the ways that Asian massage workers and sex workers are often dehumanized within political and media discourse and drew attention toward the fact that informal economies like unlicensed massage and transactional sex are often the only ways that some disabled people are able to make a living. (Photo: Salonee Bhaman)

Figure P.13. The photograph *View of Protest Traveling Down Park Row*, by the autistic photographer Christopher Lucka, was taken during the Black Lives Matter protests in New York City in the summer of 2020. Unemployed from food-service jobs during the pandemic, Lucka described how unemployment insurance and stimulus checks allowed him the chance to (temporarily) live the way he wants to: to live life rather than make money in largely unfulfilling jobs just to pay rent, including practicing photography and joining racial justice protests. (Photograph courtesy of Christopher Lucka)

Figure P.14. Emilie L. Gossiaux's drawing *On a Good Day You Can Feel My Love for You* (2021). In an interview for *METAL* magazine with Marcus Civin, Gossiaux discusses drawing her guide dog, London, at home during the pandemic: "When the pandemic and the lockdowns happened, I couldn't go to my studio anymore, and I was at home all the time with London. Our bond became the central focus [of my work] again, and I started thinking about this interspecies relationship with her. I was also thinking about being stuck in a city and longing to be in nature again. London strengthened my connection to nature and the animal world. I thought about London and imagined us becoming one being. When we are together, we become like one superbeing. She becomes my eyes, and I become her hands and voice."

Figure P.15. On a sweat-stained, split-open pillowcase, the artist Alex Dolores Salerno embroidered a phrase they found on a queer mutual-aid Facebook group: "Pl3ase be d.i.s.c.r.e.e.t c@refu11y dis.gui.sing @ny m3dicat!on wordz." The group hoped to enable resource sharing for medication and hormones at a time when these became especially difficult to access, with mass layoffs resulting in lost insurance and with the new risks involved in going to doctors' appointments or pharmacies. But, in an effort to evade surveillance—since sharing prescriptions, no matter now necessary, is illegal—participants were asked to write in code, replacing letters with special characters to evade search or algorithmic detection. Salerno titled the piece *ISO: (2020)*, an acronym that stands for "in search of." They made the piece not only in their bed but out of their bed, using their own pillowcase.

Figure P.16. The artist Francisco echo Eraso described that it felt "impossible to make work" during lockdowns but that he was able to weave from bed when he started making work for his two partners. Eraso's two works are both made from the same yellow warp. *Blue and Yellow Tapestry* (2021, collection of María del Mar Hernández Gil de Lamadrid) has four vertical sections that are connected at the ends by golden frays, as if the whole piece is one large squiggle. *Red and Yellow Tapestry* (2021, collection of Alex Dolores Salerno) comprises three vertical stripes; here, the golden ends are cut but still frayed. For so many people, the pandemic induced many kinds of existential rethinking as we abruptly broke from our routines and were left with lots of time to ask big questions, like, Why make art, and for whom? Eraso's response was, like many, to cultivate a smaller and more intimate world while separated from the larger one.

into a group articulating a remarkable radical critique of discriminatory ableism. The OV website explains its commitment to disability justice: "Outside Voices Theater Company wishes you to know the following: We are about advocacy, empowerment, out-of-the-box-thinking and disability pride. We chose our name because we believe that VOICES from the OUTSIDE deserve to be heard. We believe in access. We will not use our quiet, inside voices to get your attention" (Outside Voices Theater Company, n.d.).

Many of the members of Outside Voices overlap with those in Poets of Course, another weekly writing group we attended, whose members have ID (Juhasz 2018). Both groups quickly turned into online support systems for their members, who were physically separated from one another by the March 2020 COVID lockdown. The regular members of Outside Voices and Poets of Course—about twenty participants—are quite wide ranging with regard to ethnic, racial, religious, and class identity. Some live in congregate housing, others share an apartment with supervision, still others live at home as adult children of aging parents, and a few live independently. When the COVID virus hit, members worried about one another. Some took the initiative to quickly add more friends drawn from other ID programs. We watched as the online group welcomed new peers during COVID exile. Clearly, the group was energized by the challenge, responding to individual expressions of distress and fear, sending texts and poems, reminders of one another's valued membership in this morphing community at a perilous time and an instance of how arts activism can build a community of "crip kinship" (Kafai 2021). As one nonspeaking longtime participant using his word board noted, "my inability to speak, called silence, now leaves me so so lonely." Since this member cannot respond to phone calls, the primary connection that many others were using, a deluge of support arrived as phone texts, a powerful demonstration of Mingus's (2011) "access intimacy." Caregivers who accompany some Outside Voices members also became increasingly active in checking up on one another, sharing apps and supplies, and contributing their poems to group readings, thus melding the cared-for and caregivers, supported by founding/ongoing director Cathy James.

These long-term overlapping workshops for writers and performers with I/DD contributed to the evolution of a film, *Isolation Nation*

(Isolation Nation Collective 2021), created in a production workshop supported by JobPath, an offshoot of the Vera Institute of Justice. Founded in 1978 to help people with developmental disabilities find meaningful work, JobPath was a first in New York State and also one of the initial such groups in the country (JobPath, n.d.). The *Isolation Nation* artists' team was recruited via JobPath networks for a six-week project to represent their experiences—before, during, and in an imagined after of the pandemic—with the goal of publicizing the artistry, creativity, and insight provided by those who are too often stigmatized and ignored. Using the skills that participants had already developed in poetry, drawing, sculpture, music, and mixed media, they created the film, *Isolation Nation*. These artists compellingly brought their concerns—past, present, and future—into the video, expressing a fluid sense of temporality, vividly apparent in one of the participant's poems:

> Time is slippery, I keep painting . . .
> Touch is now infection . . . I wish I could touch a friend
> Touch doesn't last, it's non-archival
> Rain runs upwards while we work to do,
> remembering loved ones, carrying them with us . . .
> Time to start building a new world.

Another *Isolation Nation* artist played piano to accompany a song he wrote, belting out, "Future on my mind / Future all the time." This group's concern to creatively build a path forward despite the pandemic resonated with disability scholar Alison Kafer's (2013) insistence on accessible futures for people whose disabilities make them particularly vulnerable.

When we asked Cathy for an update in 2023, she took the opportunity to reflect in an email on the impact of "going remote" and the return of Poets of Course to in-person gatherings as funding dried up for virtual gatherings. As she explained,

> The pandemic isn't over but we have to adjust to this downgrading of the risk. . . . There was an emergence of creativity that occurred online that would have happened differently if we had been meeting in-person for the last few years. . . . I think the most exciting thing to have witnessed was a growing confidence in . . . their own desires and narratives. . . . I can see

people write themselves into ongoing fantasy scripts that fulfill an unexpressed role, be that a villain, a woman, a lover, an aggressor or a person of power. One person is writing this amazing sci-fi story that speaks to humans as colonizers of space. The aliens are the heroes, protecting themselves against an aggressor. Other people have written themselves into expressions of anger or revenge or acceptance. I think this is easier on a screen than it would be in a room and I am really hoping some of that energy can carry over into our "live" work.

Cathy went on to ponder an important question about the general impact of this work. "Is it helpful or harmful to indulge these free expressions of self when real life often crushes and compacts the self into something very one-dimensional? . . . But it is hard not to feel a little complicit in the act of using a band aid on a gaping wound." She is describing a complicated situation that the science writer Ed Yong (2021) calls the "disability hinterland."

Conclusion

In Yong's 2021 *Atlantic Monthly* essay addressing the intersection of disability and COVID in the context of the escalation of long-hauler diagnoses, he notes that "any discussion of the pandemic still largely revolves around two extremes—good health at one end, and hospitalization or death at the other. This ignores the hinterland of disability that lies in between, where millions of people are already stuck, and where many more may end up." He is surely right. However, in our interviews and observations in one part of Yong's "hinterland," we found that despite an accelerating sense of a fraught future for people with I/DD, other initiatives were also rippling across many domains, from caregiving, kinship, and community to creative arts.

Indeed, this concern for the future had some unanticipated outcomes for imagining otherwise, beyond the pandemic precarity experienced by so many people. We were struck by the efforts of Allison Kleinman, a long-standing advocate for people with I/DD and mental health challenges and their families, who focuses on the need for housing and future planning for these disabled adults. The pandemic provoked her to leave her position at a Manhattan nonprofit serving people with disabilities of all ages to start a new initiative, FutureCenteredCare. Its mission is to address the yawning gap in supportive disability futures that became increasingly evident with the arrival of COVID as disabled people, their families, and allies struggled with the "who question"— who will step in to provide care when a family no longer can. As she explained when we spoke with her about this new venture,

> I didn't set out to start a company. That was never a goal. . . . I was hoping others would do a better job, so that maybe I would never have to do this. I think the pandemic had a lot to do with this. All of a sudden people were like, "This thing that I've been putting off and putting off and putting off is much more real than it ever has been." So, you know, I started a lot of conversations during COVID to try to figure that out. And there was momentum. And I was like, "We've gotta use this momentum . . . to start planning for the future while they're scared." I was trying to create an opportunity to say, "Let's change this model or create an enhanced model. What would that look like?" (interview, March 10, 2022)

Our virtual "hinterland fieldwork" during COVID with a rich range of New York City's disabled adults, their families, and allies offers a glimpse of what that model might look like. Beyond the increasing sense of pandemic precarity, we encountered modest but significant aspirations for expansive "crip kinship" models, documentary chronicles of the perils created by congregate housing, and journeys into disability "sci-fi" futurism. As the pandemic becomes endemic, it is vitally important that these too-often-marginalized voices be further amplified, revealing unexpected and emergent possibilities.

ACKNOWLEDGMENTS

We are grateful to our many respondents, allies, and codenizens of varied disability worlds who have provided ongoing and generous energy that has fueled this project, taking the time to share their thoughts and concerns with us; we thank them all. We have used pseudonyms for everyone except those who are professionally and publicly identified. The research on which this article is based was part of a larger National Science Foundation–funded project, "Disability Expertise and Design Justice for Post-COVID Equity." We appreciate its support. Additionally,

Figure 7.1. Poster for the 2023 movie *Fire through Dry Grass*, directed by Andres Jay Molina and Alexis Neophytides. Wearing snapback caps and Air Jordans and sitting in powerchairs, the five Reality Poets pose in front of the Coler Rehabilitation and Nursing Care Center on Roosevelt Island. In their documentary, *Fire through Dry Grass*, these Black and Brown disabled artists chronicle their lives on lockdown during COVID, using their poetry and art to underscore the danger and imprisonment they feel in the face of institutional neglect; they refuse to be abused, confined, and erased.

we owe special thanks to our coeditors, Harris Kornstein and Mara Mills, for their attentive reading and comments on earlier drafts of this chapter.

REFERENCES

Applied Self-Direction. n.d. "What Is Self-Direction?" Accessed May 21, 2024. www.appliedselfdirection.com.

Bérubé, Michael. 2018. "Don't Let My Son Plunge off the 'Disability Cliff' When I'm Gone." *USA Today*, April 2, 2018. www.usatoday.com.

Bove, Tristan. 2022. "40% of People Still Want to Quit Their Jobs, and the Great Resignation Is Here to Stay." *Fortune*, July 21, 2022. https://fortune.com.

Block, Pamela. 2020. "Activism, Anthropology, and Disability Studies in Times of Austerity: In Collaboration with Sini Diallo." *Current Anthropology* 61 (S21): S68–S75.

Courtenay, Ken, and Bathika Perera. 2020. "COVID-19 and People with Intellectual Disability: Impacts of a Pandemic." *Irish Journal of Psychological Medicine*, May 2020, 1–6.

Elisofon, Marguerite. 2020. "Where Will My Autistic Daughter Live When I'm Gone?" *Marguerite Elisofon* (blog), February 14, 2020. http://margueriteelisofon.com.

———. 2023a. "An Autism Mom Explains Breast Cancer to Her Daughter." *Marguerite Elisofon* (blog), May 31, 2023. http://margueriteelisofon.com.

———. 2023b. "An Autism Mom's Cancer Journey Continues." *Marguerite Elisofon* (blog), July 13, 2023. http://margueriteelisofon.com.

Ginsburg, Faye, and Rayna Rapp. 2024. *Disability Worlds*. Durham, NC: Duke University Press.

Isolation Nation Collective. 2021. *Isolation Nation*. www.google.com.

Ivory, Danielle, Robert Gebeloff, Brandon Dupré, Cierra S. Queen, Chloe Reynolds, Yves De Jesus, Laney Pope, et al. 2022. "They Left Craters of Grief: Here's a Closer Look at the Impact of One Million U.S. Covid Deaths." *New York Times*, May 20, 2022. www.nytimes.com.

JobPath. n.d. "About Us." Accessed July 22, 2022. www.jobpathnyc.org.

Juhasz, Alexandra. 2018. "Poets of Course." Fake News Poetry Workshops. http://fakenews-poetry.org.

Kafai, Shayda. 2021. *Crip Kinship: The Disability Justice and Art Activism of Sins Invalid*. Vancouver: Arsenal Pulp.

Kafer, Alison. 2013. *Feminist Queer Crip*. Bloomington: Indiana University Press.

Manderson, Lenore, and Ayo Wahlberg. 2020. "Chronic Living in a Communicable World." *Medical Anthropology* 28: 428–39.

Mingus, Mia. 2011. "Access Intimacy: The Missing Link." *Leaving Evidence* (blog), May 5, 2011. https://leavingevidence.wordpress.com.

Molina, Andres "Jay," and Alexis Neophytides. 2023. *Fire through Dry Grass*. 88 minutes. POV. www.firethroughdrygrass.com.

New York Times. 2021. "Nearly One-Third of U.S. Coronavirus Deaths Are Linked to Nursing Homes." June 1, 2021. www.nytimes.com.

Outside Voices Theater Company. n.d. home page. Accessed September 29, 2021. www.outsidevoicestheater.org.

Wong, Alice. 2020. "Q&A with Andres 'Jay' Molina and Alexis Neophytides." *Disability Visibility Project*, December 16, 2020. https://disabilityvisibilityproject.com.

Yong, Ed. 2021. "Long-Haulers Are Fighting for Their Future." *The Atlantic*, September 1, 2021. www.theatlantic.com.

PART II

Disability Communities

Expertise, Activism, and Solidarity

8

When Postviral Goes Viral

Myalgic Encephalomyelitis, Long COVID, and Pandemic Déjà Vu

HARRIS KORNSTEIN AND EMILY LIM ROGERS

At the start of the COVID-19 pandemic, many disabled and chronically ill people were quick to point out both the short-term implications and long-term consequences that a novel virus might yield: namely, that while the scale of the pandemic might be uncommon, its effects on individuals would hardly be new. In particular, people with myalgic encephalomyelitis (ME; formerly known as chronic fatigue syndrome or by the combined acronym ME/CFS) have drawn on personal experience to highlight the reality that viral infections often result not only in acute symptoms but in chronic illness as well.[1] Articulating this "crip expertise" (Hamraie and Fritsch 2019), though often ignored by media outlets and political leaders, people with ME have challenged conventional public discourse about the ongoing risks of infection, demanding a shift in understandings of COVID as a moment of *crisis* to one of *chronicity*. They have also drawn attention to the limited social and biomedical infrastructure to address what many have (correctly) predicted would be a mass-disabling event. In this chapter, we utilize oral history interviews conducted with several people with ME, alongside social media and ethnographic fieldwork, to document their affective and activist responses to the COVID-19 pandemic, ranging from cautious optimism to intense frustration to coalition-building with newly sick individuals. While there are other ME organizations, our research has focused on #MEAction, an international group that is particularly active in New York.[2] We highlight this work to document a concrete set of meaningful examples in which disabled and chronically ill people have mobilized their own expertise to reframe public discourse, advocate for resources, and directly support people experiencing complex chronic illnesses.

We begin with some background on myalgic encephalomyelitis, a debilitating yet often-dismissed disease. People with ME experience "crashes" after any form of physical or cognitive exertion—its cardinal symptom, referred to as "post-exertional malaise" (PEM), that is not alleviated by rest. The array of symptoms varies from person to person and can include cognitive impairment such as brain fog, unrefreshing sleep, orthostatic intolerance (difficulty with postural changes), and many more (Institute of Medicine 2015). Despite how debilitating ME is, it lacks agreed-upon clinical criteria, biomarkers, approved treatments, or consensus on its cause; ME's funding per disease burden is the lowest of any in the US (Mirin, Dimmock, and Jason 2022). This level of neglect is striking. Many people with ME have been living with this disease for decades, and indeed, it has been on the radar of federal agencies like the National Institutes of Health (NIH) and the US Centers for Disease Control and Prevention (CDC) since the 1980s. Moreover, it is not rare. In 2015, it was estimated that two million Americans have ME, one-quarter are bed-bound, and more than half are unemployed (Institute of Medicine 2015). That number has ballooned in the context of the COVID-19 pandemic, as nearly half of people with Long COVID qualify for an ME diagnosis (Yong 2022; Bonilla et al. 2023; Komaroff and Lipkin 2023). While the mechanisms by which ME produces its debilitating effects are not quite certain, researchers agree that it is typically (though not always) post-infectious, due to a virus of any kind (Chu et al. 2019). Unsurprisingly to people with ME, SARS-CoV-2 is triggering chronic symptoms known commonly as "Long COVID," an umbrella term coined by patient activists (Perego et al. 2020). The clinical presentation varies and does not fully overlap with ME, but nonetheless, the two intersect in their symptomatology as well as advocacy movements.

People with ME foreshadowed the pandemic in two ways, in what we call *pandemic déjà vu*. First, in the early months of the pandemic, lockdowns caused the nondisabled public to experience what many people with ME have lived with daily, given the high prevalence of their home-boundedness and the preciousness of their energy: they had already been leaving the house only for necessities, going to the grocery store twice a month (or ordering delivery), picking up prescriptions when they can, and socializing (and organizing) over Zoom. Second, as many people predicted, the emergence of Long COVID is creating alliances between people with ME and Long COVID given the many similarities between the diseases (Vastag 2020). As the ME activist Terri Wilder has noted, "We're familiar with viral stories. . . . So we kind of predicted this in early 2020. . . . We were like, 'We know this is coming. We can see it a mile away.'"[3] As people with Long COVID flood ME social media groups and activist projects, they experience the same frustration that people with ME have lived for decades.

In this way, Long COVID is both new and not new. It is caused by a completely novel virus and emerged in a pandemic that has become a global-scale mass-disabling event. But ME, like other "long hauling" postviral illnesses (Hebert and Juhasz 2022), has been around for quite some time, and organized ME patient activist groups can be traced to the early 1980s. They have been pushing for the societal and medical acceptance of their disease, to mixed results and much frustration. Still, as media coverage of Long COVID has exploded, postviral illness has suddenly gone "viral," highlighting the complex and contagious (but also, at times, contradictory) relationships between actual viruses and the viral spread of ideas and information (Parikka 2007; Blas 2012; Clough and Puar 2012; McKinney and Mulvin 2019; Cifor and McKinney 2020). In this viral moment of postviral illness, societal interest is piqued, millions have been diagnosed or estimated to have Long COVID (Bach 2022), and unprecedented funding is flowing into research on postviral mechanisms. Despite the fact that there is considerable overlap between Long COVID and ME, activists point out that many media stories and activist campaigns do not even mention ME. In this context, people with ME and Long COVID wonder about many possibilities: Will Long COVID help ME become an accepted, funded disease? Will Long COVID be disproportionately legitimized because it is caused by a discrete virus in pandemic scale, experienced by many people to whom ME remains unfamiliar? Or will Long COVID—despite some dedicated clinics opening up—meet the same fate as ME, neglected by medical and political institutions and without specialists or treatments? Even in the fourth year of the pandemic, these questions largely remain uncertain, and we leave such future predictions behind in order to defetishize novelty and emergency. Instead, we foreground the ways people with ME have *already* "been there, done that"—inhabiting the ambivalent affective space of pandemic déjà vu, while also organizing for institutional recognition, funding, and treatment.

Pandemic Déjà Vu

This collection, and the research behind it, has set out to demonstrate the pandemic's impact on disabled communities. When we conducted our research on ME during the early months of the pandemic, at times it felt as if interviews yielded no significant findings at all. Indeed, a few interviewees were puzzled by our questions asking about "how the pandemic changed things" for them. We had known some interlocutors previously to be quite talkative, but with many of our questions, they had less to say than usual: the pandemic had altered little about their daily lives. "The thing is," one interviewee, Noor, said, "my social life is pretty limited to begin with." That interviewees had little to say on this topic became, in fact, a finding. As Kyla Schuller (2020) put it, "COVID-19 is teaching the ableds what the disabled and chronically ill already know: your ability to leave the house is a privilege that can be lost at any time." Conversely, people with ME already knew the ways that isolation and homeboundedness thins personhood itself (Rogers 2020). People with ME have long been "stuck at home," not because of shelter-in-place orders but because of the nature of the disease itself. Noor continued on the topic of shelter in place, which impacted how far and for what reasons people could travel out of their homes: "I'm pretty much homebound for the most part, in the sense that my outdoor activity is limited, even without the COVID situation. So not much has changed."

Life with ME also equipped people to handle the pandemic—in both emotional and practical senses. Noor had always cherished the moments when she could leave her home. One of the most important lessons people with ME learn, according to Noor, is that you "don't take anything for granted, no matter how trivial or minor it may seem, like even seeing your loved ones." This is also an element of what disability scholars and activists have described as "disability expertise" (Hartblay 2020), "disability life hacks" (Mauldin 2022), and "activist affordances" (Dokumaci 2023): people with ME were well prepared to cope with the pandemic given that they already had to carefully manage how and when to leave their homes. "I mean, like, you have to be better at planning your life and organizing things. Like, if I have to go out to get groceries, I better make sure I have everything on the list right. There can be no room for error. I can't afford to forget things because I'm making that one trip outside, so I better make it count. It's just little things like that." It might sound like Noor was referring to risk mitigation during the pandemic, but she was not. She was referring to her *everyday* experience with debility. For the nondisabled public, especially in New York City (a high-density context that thrives on convenience), the pandemic was a novel challenge emerging from a novel virus, not everyday bodily debility.

This is not to say that the pandemic had no impact on people with ME. Far from it. For one, it impacted medical care. Many Americans skipped routine care and forwent medical procedures due to the pandemic—either because the risk of going to the doctor's office was too high or because such offices were not offering care at all (Anderson et al. 2021). For people with ME, in-home care was especially fraught. For example, the ME and HIV activist Terri Wilder received monthly at-home intravenous treatments, delivered by a nurse who comes to her home. However, in March 2020, she developed COVID symptoms that forced her to delay her monthly treatment by one week. Wilder received a negative COVID test, but it brought into relief the precarious state of care in this particularly acute point in the pandemic. The shortage of personal protective equipment (PPE) complicated treatment. Only through her personal connections with health-care workers was Wilder able to secure PPE for her nurse. Other people, Wilder noted, might not be so lucky. The nurse had told her that many of her clients were not getting their treatments. Ironically, the very thing that is supposed to make ME patients better had the potential to make their condition worse. It was a double bind. Similarly, Noor delayed doctors' appointments and diagnostic tests: she canceled MRIs, stopped seeing doctors in person, and postponed bloodwork. Labs were particularly difficult processes to navigate, as COVID-19 cases were getting tested alongside others seeking bloodwork. Noor relayed to me, in a resigned tone, "I mean, since it's not an emergency, I think it can be postponed."

The theme of the acute versus the chronic raises the question of what Vincanne Adams (2020) has termed COVID's "temporal urgency." However, the framework of "emergency"—the one that Noor invoked—too often overshadows existing structural problems as

Adams points out: "The actual arrival of COVID-19 magnifies preexisting vulnerability." The very fact that patients like Noor had to juggle so many doctors' appointments is in and of itself a facet of life with a debilitating yet misunderstood chronic illness, illustrating the limitations of "crisis" narratives (Roitman 2014). Instead, these were existing problems (déjà vu) magnified by the pandemic.

Additionally, because people with ME cherish the few times they can leave their homes, the pandemic compounded existing isolation. An interview conducted before the pandemic brings this déjà vu into relief. Helga, a Brooklynite, emphasized how everyday interactions in New York City created a bulwark to the complete isolation that many people with ME can experience. In a 2019 interview just before the pandemic, she juxtaposed her life in New York City with when she lived in Washington State: "I was less stressed, and I wasn't isolated. [In New York City], there is no way to be isolated. So, I was pushed to do things and be out in the world with my children and everything. And so I got to feel human every day, a little bit, or a lot compared to us [living] in Washington. Freelancing from Washington was not the same thing as freelancing in New York City. You know, you go to the bodega in your pajamas, and you run into people in New York City. I mean, you know, it's gotta perk you up." Helga worked from home, though unlike many white-collar workers, her setup was not specifically because of the pandemic. It was because this form of work fits her access needs as someone with ME. Yet at the same time, it held the potential to create isolation.

These small interactions that New Yorkers cherished during the pandemic had always been held dearly by people with ME. Virtual platforms like Zoom provide an important means of socialization. But perhaps surprisingly, many people with ME experienced greater isolation despite the *increase* in remote-access events. Noor stopped attending support-group meetings because she so valued going in person—one of the few times she left her house. "My own things were so few and far between to begin with. Then to have this shelter in place imposed on you—for good reason, of course—it can be difficult for sure." Similarly, Wilder explained that "human connection is really important to physical and mental health."

Still, for some people with ME, the shift of public life to newly accessible virtual formats did feel like an expansion of opportunities. The opportunity to participate remotely or asynchronously in cultural events, classes, political meetings, and more left some people hoping for a "new normal" in which institutions would pay greater attention to remote participation and access needs. For example, Sally, a historian by training who does not currently work and is homebound, attended music concerts and opera performances online during the pandemic, reconnecting with a set of art forms, experiences, and personal relationships that she had not been able to participate in since moving back home with her parents in 2010.[4] Specifically, she noted that virtually attending a series of Bach concerts in New York City, and especially knowing that friends were also watching remotely, "felt like the pandemic was giving me my old life back." Sally further expressed hope that these remote opportunities would become permanent, describing, "I was hugely optimistic about the potential for an online-only society, generally felt ecstatically happy about the whole situation, and let myself be pushy about saying so to friends, especially if they were complaining. 'I've been in lockdown for fourteen years' and 'make it permanent' definitely became my catchphrases." Remote technologies are access technologies, but people with ME—like their nondisabled counterparts—also value in-person connection, touch, the encountering of other bodies in the streets that, formerly, was a bread-and-butter facet of being a New Yorker. In other words, people with ME also need to "feel human."

Postviral Affects: Optimism, Resentment, Ambivalence

For people with ME, the sense of déjà vu wrought by the COVID-19 pandemic has catalyzed a number of affective responses ranging from optimism to resentment—and, perhaps most importantly, many conflicting and ambivalent feelings in between. At one end of the spectrum, many have expressed cautious optimism that the global scale of the problem and increased media and political attention to Long COVID might indeed lead to new forms of research and treatment for ME. On the other end of the spectrum, many people with ME directed feelings of frustration and resentment toward political, public health, and media actors (and even close friends) who had neglected their illness and community for decades and only now belatedly expressed interest. Additionally, some also expressed anger and envy toward people with

Long COVID, whom they perceived as receiving swift public attention that people with ME had long been demanding. Not surprisingly, many people have wrestled with complicated feelings in between, including guilt and angst that such a catastrophic pandemic might ultimately benefit them, as well as redoubled skepticism that ultimately nothing would change, as they had seen similar unfulfilled promises in the past. In what follows, we unpack some of these complicated affective entanglements in participants' interviews.

To begin, many people with ME expressed hope that, given the scale of the pandemic and public attention to Long COVID, the sense of pandemic déjà vu might actually amount to gains in recognition or advancements in research for their own conditions and communities. However, there was significant disagreement and debate within communities about whether capitalizing on this attention would indeed be an effective strategy. Just prior to the onset of the pandemic, ME communities experienced an uptick in community activism, biomedical research, and public awareness, exemplified by the wide release of Jennifer Brea's documentary *Unrest*, about her ME experience and the formation of the organization #MEAction. As a result, many believed the ME community was already on the precipice of significant political and research breakthroughs and saw the COVID-19 pandemic as a possible tipping point or once-in-a-lifetime opportunity to advocate for significant investment, particularly given the similarity in postviral mechanisms with Long COVID. As the HIV and ME activist JD Davids explained, he saw COVID-19 as a unique opportunity: "I am perhaps naively sort of excited. It's a terrible thing to be sick and to rapidly lose functioning and not to have the life you anticipated. However, I do think this is the best chance that I'll have in getting treatment for ME." Noor agreed: "I'm optimistic about this situation. It will kind of shine the spotlight on ME and other chronic conditions, and it will bring in the money. 'Cause it's such a hot-button issue. It's so topical that there's no ignoring it anymore."

However, like Davids, some of our interviewees expressed a sense of guilt in their hope, given that it emerged during a time of death and suffering. Or they suggested that they felt as though they ought to feel a greater sense of regret. Such ambivalence gestures toward the "cruel optimism" that Lauren Berlant (2011) describes, in which people's hopeful attachments are ultimately tied to forces that harm them—in this case, decades of biomedical and political neglect leading to searches for hope in a global viral pandemic. However, some people were unabashed in their feelings of optimism—as well as resentment—insisting on their right to feel hope and anger in having lived with an ignored illness for so long. For example, Sally described her feelings as approaching schadenfreude and the pandemic as a form of "poetic justice" in which a "world that ignored a terrible disease for decades [became] inundated and defined by it." She elaborated: "I honestly couldn't discover a smidgen of guilt in myself about the world seeming to go my way only because people were dying. If they'd been paying any attention to chronic illnesses, all that online architecture would have been in place long before, and no transition and much less risk would have been necessary for anyone.... I expect to personally benefit eventually, either by new treatment or by better care. I know this may come across as sadistic, but much of the pandemic has been an incredibly joyous time for me." Sally also described a similar mix of enthusiasm and frustration in how friends related to her illness vis-à-vis the pandemic, noting that some seemed to pay more attention to social media posts about chronic illness than before, though many still failed to understand the severity of her condition.

At the same time, many people with ME were quite cautious in their optimism, noting past moments in which people with ME had their hopes raised but with little to show for it. In an interview in October 2021, Terri Wilder described the situation:

> I think there are some people who might be a little concerned that we're going to get lost. You know, there's billions of dollars going into Long COVID research. Is that also going to include comparison groups with people with ME? ... How do we benefit from this moment? ... This might be our time to get funding, awareness, etcetera. But let's not be naïve about it. We still need our own dedicated money, our own dedicated resources, our own dedicated legislation. We're kind of like riding on the tailcoat [sic]. But what happens when, you know, I don't know, three years from now—is it going to go back to what it was, where nobody talks about ME?

This skepticism was echoed across a range of conversations, particularly on social media, as we observed lively debates about whether and how to try to seize the moment to make connections between ME and

Long COVID while still demanding separate resources for ME. Notably, in an email conversation in January 2024, Wilder reflected on her previous comments, adding, "It has been three years. My life hasn't changed because of Long COVID. There is still no biomarker, no FDA approved treatment, etc. I'm basically on the same medicines that I was in 2017."

Many people with ME also responded with outright frustration and anger directed toward public figures and institutions that they viewed as having not done enough to address complex chronic illnesses prior to, or since the start of, the pandemic. Additionally, given the feelings of déjà vu discussed earlier, many expressed resentment that both the acute and chronic aspects of COVID-19 were being given media coverage and research funding at a scale that had never been available to people with ME. In particular, Anthony Fauci, the director of the National Institute of Allergy and Infectious Diseases (NIAID) and one of the most visible public health figures during the pandemic as a White House adviser, emerged as a complicated figure in ME communities. On the one hand, Fauci was celebrated by many in July 2020 when he made public comments noting that "there is evidence that some people develop a long-term fatigue syndrome from coronavirus infections" and directly named that many would meet certain diagnostic criteria for ME (Fox 2020; Solve ME Initiative 2020). Such a statement was seen by many as a milestone of public and institutional recognition. However, several activists also hold long-standing frustrations with Fauci given his failures to devote serious National Institutes of Health (NIH) resources to studying ME.[5] In an interview, Terri Wilder—whose question at a press conference actually prompted Fauci to mention ME (#MEAction 2020)—explained that activists blame him for forty years of neglect. In September 2023, Fauci incited further conversation when in an interview he suggested an interest in studying ME, raising the question of whether his comments suggested a mea culpa or an attempt at revising history (Cohen 2023; Dakota 2023). In more practical terms, many political and public health leaders have continued to ignore the realities of ME, which actively compounds the repercussions of neglect.

Public health institutions were not the only target of annoyed and ambivalent affects: some people in ME communities also expressed frustrations directed toward the care received by Long COVID patients. While none of our interviewees expressed ire toward people experiencing Long

COVID categorically, we witnessed envious and exasperated grumbling at times in private ME Facebook groups, suggesting that they were given special attention that had often been denied to people with ME. Oftentimes, these were met with comments reminding posters not to grow frustrated at other sick people, as well as reassurances of hope like those mentioned earlier. Additionally, many people with ME complained that they were unable to access care through emerging Long COVID clinics, despite overlapping symptoms and mechanisms. This lack of access suggests some of the complications in thinking about viruses and their aftereffects, particularly in the temporality of crisis rather than chronicity (Adams 2020; Osmundson 2022).

Activism and Alliances

While the activism of people with ME has taken many forms, especially during the COVID pandemic, we highlight three primary (and overlapping) areas of organizing and alliance-building: (1) resource sharing between ME and Long COVID patients and organizations; (2) public education geared toward informing diverse audiences about postviral illness generally and ME specifically; and (3) political organizing targeting political leaders and institutions. All of the examples discussed in the following pages are rooted in or in some ways tied to the work of #MEAction, an organization founded in 2015. #MEAction represents a new generation of ME activism that, in explicitly modeling its work on the HIV/AIDS movement ACT UP, has shifted toward a more disability-justice-informed style of mutual aid, grassroots organizing, and direct action. Such activism often impacts activists' own health and reputations, as they allocate limited energy to this work and go against the grain, challenging conventional narratives. At the same time, we are also cautious not to romanticize this work, noting that it is often messy, whether because of conflicts between groups or contradictions in organizing strategies. In this way, we particularly note some uncomfortable tensions that this activism raises, such as the extent to which the involvement of people with ME is rooted in empathy or solidarity versus a sense of self-interest or opportunism to take advantage of a perceived political opening. Ultimately we see such tensions, or "access friction" (Hamraie 2017; Hamraie and Fritsch 2019), as part of the generative space that many people occupy when the postviral goes viral—and which can ultimately lead to stronger activism and care for all.

Some of the first ME activism to emerge at the start of the pandemic included resource sharing within ME and other disabled communities. For example, JD Davids and others organized a virtual workshop titled "COVID-19 (Coronavirus) Preparation for People Living with Chronic Illnesses in the U.S.," on Saturday, March 7, 2020—about two weeks before New York State's shelter-in-place mandates went into effect (Werning 2020). As the pandemic continued and Long COVID emerged as a concern, with many people suspecting upcoming diagnoses of ME, groups like #MEAction also specifically organized events on this intersection, such as an August 7, 2020, event titled "ME and Long COVID: What's the Connection?" This webinar featured a range of speakers, including a medical doctor and ME activists (among them Wilder and Davids, both interviewed for this project), covering a range of practical topics such as symptoms and diagnosis of ME, pacing strategies to avoid overexertion, tactics for advocating with medical providers, and coping with a new chronic illness. It is worth noting that not only was the content indicative of ME expertise, but so was the format: as several activists mentioned in interviews, they were used to organizing via Zoom and hosting virtual events such as these.

Public education constituted a core of ME activism prior to the pandemic as well; however, with the onset of COVID-19 and the expectations that many people would develop postviral symptoms, these techniques were expanded. Prior to the pandemic, much of this work focused on social media campaigns, with the hope that compelling narratives, data, and memes could themselves "go viral" and capture the public's attention in new ways. While groups like #MEAction have continued such tactics throughout the pandemic, they also seized on new opportunities to target mainstream media with the hope of reaching larger audiences by "speaking through the media," as Wilder put it (referencing her previous work with ACT UP). As #MEAction reported on its website, this included directly reaching out to nearly twenty-five hundred journalists to explicitly make connections between Long COVID and people with ME and to ensure that the latter were recognized for their experiences and expertise—work that seemed to pay off with increased mentions, especially in articles about Long COVID (#MEAction n.d.-b; Reyes 2022).

Additionally, members of #MEAction have long targeted doctors and medical providers with education campaigns, given that many are not trained in or familiar with ME or standards of care and, as such, may provide harmful misinformation, such as encouraging exercise that may incite PEM. In 2019, #MEAction launched a "Postcards to Doctors" campaign, in which members sent handwritten postcards to lists of providers in their states with resources for continuing education programs—a campaign that has been promoted throughout the pandemic, with revised language around Long COVID. In addition, activists with #MEAction New York, including Wilder, successfully campaigned to have the New York State Department of Health include information about ME in a monthly letter to providers across the state. In it, Commissioner Howard Zucker (2021) wrote that, given similarities, "learning more about long COVID may lead to important insights into how to treat individuals with ME due to other viral illnesses." Wilder described this effort as taking one year to come to fruition, and though she had successfully worked with that office to release a letter focused on ME in 2017, she explicitly noted that the similarities between Long COVID and ME offered a chance "to raise awareness": "we've never had that opportunity before." As part of #MeAction's ongoing practitioner education offerings, it also partnered with agencies like the New York State Department of Health Clinical Education Initiative and medical schools throughout the pandemic to host continuing medical education (CME) courses in topics like "Post-Viral Syndrome and ME/CFS: What Every Clinicians Needs to Know" and "Post-Viral ME/CFS: Diagnosing and Treating ME/CFS in the Time of COVID" (#MEAction n.d.-a). Such public and medical education is critical in not only raising awareness in general but also ensuring that more patients have access to informed care.

At the intersection of community resource sharing and public education is #MEAction's #StopRestPace campaign, a series of short videos and other resources released in October 2020 targeting both people experiencing Long COVID symptoms and the general population. In its first video (figure 8.1), several people with ME explain in succession, "After I got sick, I went on to develop myalgic encephalomyelitis (ME). Not everyone with Long COVID will go on to develop ME, but some long-haulers will. People with Long COVID may be pushed to go back to work, gradually exercise, and resume their previous levels of exertion. This

Figure 8.1. A composite of frames from #MEAction's "Stop. Rest. Pace." video showing four speakers, each addressing the camera.

has made so many of us sicker and sicker. So we are asking people with ME to join us in encouraging long-haulers who are showing symptoms of ME to #StopRestPace" (ME Action Network 2020). Related resources explain PEM, strategies for pacing one's daily activities, and specific strategies for children. Several of our interviewees noted that they shared this resource in their own networks.

Finally, ME activists also worked to form both ad hoc and ongoing coalitions with Long COVID activists. In many cases, these alliances amounted to inviting each other to critical meetings with researchers, elected leaders, funders, and other institutional actors, as well as working to align both private and public demands. In particular, ME activists were often able to share background information, as Wilder described meetings where she offered Long COVID activists insight about players at institutions like the CDC. However, Wilder also pointed out that such alliances were also often sources of conflict and frustration themselves. As with any social movement, personalities and feelings often obstructed relationship-building, especially when individuals or groups felt excluded from certain meetings or conversations. As Wilder explained, "There's been opportunities that I felt like we should have both been at the table, and we weren't. . . . If you're going to have a meeting with WHO [World Health Organization], you need to have a person with ME at the table, too. We know the story. We've lived it for over forty years. We could be valuable in those conversations and helping to explain things." Still, meaningful alliances have emerged, such as the National Network for Long COVID Justice (for which Davids is a strategist), which launched in March 2022 and includes #MEAction alongside groups like the Patient-Led Research Collaborative. The network released "Pandemics Are Chronic: A Statement of Commitment to Long COVID Justice," which calls for activists to sign onto a pledge to, among other things, "center, platform, and resource those with Long COVID, complex chronic illnesses, and other disabilities at the forefront of policy, advocacy, and action related to these issues" (Network for Long COVID Justice, n.d.).

On September 19, 2022, #MEAction also organized a series of direct actions in Washington, DC, as part of its ongoing #MillionsMissing campaign—a name invoking people with ME who are "missing" from public life due to their conditions. Though the actions were planned in advance, their timing was fortuitous, in that they took place the day after *60 Minutes* aired an interview with President Biden in which he declared that "the pandemic is over" (Pelley 2022). Activists responded forcefully to this message, lying down in front of the White House holding signs with slogans like "Still Sick, Still Fighting," "Include ME/CFS in Long COVID Research," and "You Can't Ignore ME Now" (figures 8.2 and 8.3). Later in the day, they blocked nearby intersections with their bodies, wheelchairs, and scooters. Additionally, organizers planned social media strategies to enable members who were unable to travel to post from bed or home, including livestreaming, posting updates in real time, and encouraging supporters to amplify these messages (figure 8.4); according to #MEAction (2022), its followers generated one and a half million impressions on Twitter as a result of their activities.

Additionally, in activists' attempts to educate through media coverage, they noted the connections between ME and Long COVID, as the #MEAction advocacy director Ben HsuBorger commented in a press release: "We are sick and disabled with ME/CFS and Long COVID but we are here today, putting our bodies on the line, to tell President Biden that the pandemic is not over, that millions of us are being disabled from post-viral disease, and we need urgent action from our government. . . .

We are calling on President Biden to declare ME/CFS and Long COVID a national emergency" (Oshin 2022). Still, as sociologist and opinion columnist Zeynep Tufekci noted in a *New York Times* essay commenting on the action, ultimately protestors were not arrested for civil disobedience as planned: the police largely ignored their actions, and eventually, most had to end their participation due to the physical exertion (Tufekci 2022). While some ME activists criticized the article for portraying the action as a failure, it nonetheless echoes practical limitations along the lines of what disabled writer Johanna Hedva (2022) asks in "Sick Woman Theory": "How do you throw a brick through the window of a bank if you can't get out of bed?" Still, in an email, Wilder (2024) explained the many organizing outcomes of this action, even if it did not meet their ultimate goal: "There were successes—people with ME and Long COVID showed up, we got some press, we did stop traffic, we did raise awareness to people walking by, we bonded as a community." Moreover, disability studies scholar Lisa Diedrich describes these actions as "a spectacle of illness politics," arguing that "in the case of the #MillionsMissing protest, the spectacle is not civil disobedience and arrest, but a less visible, yet no less powerful, form of embodied resistance—the willingness to make oneself sicker to draw attention to one's illness and the politics surrounding it" (Diedrich 2024, 102).

#MEAction has continued iterations of the #MillionsMissing campaign in subsequent years. On May 12, 2023, the organization along with Long COVID groups installed three hundred cots featuring handmade pillowcases with personal and political messages on the US National Mall (#MEAction 2023). And in May 2024, #MEAction launched a #TeachMETreatME campaign to educate "medical providers across our nation's hospital systems and medical schools" at thirteen institutions in partnership with the Mayo Clinic. The organization also launched a toolkit for activists to participate from home, offering suggested activities by energy level, including posting to social media and emailing their own clinicians to encourage them to take the CME courses (#MEAction 2024).

Conclusion

Thus far, conversations surrounding Long COVID show no signs of abating: postviral is going viral in ways it has never before. By looking to ME,

Figure 8.2. #MEAction protestors lie down for an action in front of the White House, holding signs with slogans like "Still Sick, Still Fighting" and "Urgent Action Needed!!" (Photo: #MEAction)

Figure 8.3. #MEAction protestors carry a banner that reads, "ME/CFS and Long Covid are disabling millions. This is a national emergency," and carry signs with slogans like "Count Us, Code Us, Cure Us." (Photo: John Zangas)

Figure 8.4. Image of an activist protesting from bed, posted to social media. She wears an eye mask and T-shirt that reads, "Still Sick, Still Fighting," with protest slogans written on her pillow. (Photo: #MEAction)

we observe two things. The first is that people with ME were uniquely prepared for the pandemic: they were accustomed to an isolated lifestyle and had already dealt with issues of postviral illness, societal and medical dismissal, government neglect, and the activist strategies that might change things. This is what we call pandemic déjà vu. The second is that this very déjà vu creates the conditions for mixed, ambivalent affects: resentment, anger, optimism, hope. Our interviewees raised thorny questions. How much are these coalitions about altruism—because people with ME relate to people with Long COVID? How much of it is "riding the coattails"—a self-interested opportunism? It is probably all of these things at once. These are uncomfortable questions without consistent answers, as our interlocutors vacillate across this affective terrain. There is an impulse here that some of our interviewees felt guilty about: they simultaneously wanted to help people with Long COVID while also reflecting on the decades of neglect that ME has faced.

While some people with ME stated that they saw the advent of Long COVID "from a mile away," our theoretical framework attempts to grapple with these mixed affects. We propose that déjà vu is not a "gotcha" moment: our aim is certainly not to smugly say, "we told you so." Pandemic déjà vu gestures toward a substantive political project. While many people saw "zero COVID" as the answer to the pandemic and solution to the debility it has wrought, this is a long-foreclosed proposition. The broader problem is the dismissal and neglect of chronic illness. Structural changes could have been in place decades ago had governments taken ME seriously and supported the lives of disabled people even when impairment cannot be biocertified (Samuels 2014). As the scientist and essayist Joseph Osmundson writes, "No body is safe from COVID-19. Rather than render visible any individual body's failure to ward off illness, this illness renders visible our entire nation's failure to care for all of those who are ill" (2022, 156). It is not making individual choices in the hopes of avoiding COVID forever (now a fantasy) that will improve the lives of people with Long COVID, or with ME, for that matter. It is systemic change. It is giving all people good health care. It is changing cultures of work. It is unyoking a person's value from their productivity. It is remediating a stunningly gutted social safety net. It is providing care and cultivating interdependence. By looking at pandemic déjà vu, we can think more capaciously about what disability justice looks like in the context of a mass-disabling event—beyond the temporality of crisis.

NOTES

1 There is a politics to naming diagnoses and diseases (Jutel 2014). Many activists view the term "chronic fatigue syndrome," while used prevalently beginning in the 1980s, as belittling of their disease. Here, we choose to use "myalgic encephalomyelitis" (ME), a term preferred by most of our interlocutors; many also use the combination ME/CFS for wider public recognition. Additionally, we generally use the phrase "people with ME" and "people with Long COVID" to refer to people with these diseases, whether or not they have formal diagnoses—this is customary for many of our interlocutors and other activists, who stress their humanity

rather than health status. Several Long COVID groups also refer to themselves as "patients"—especially to distinguish patient-led research and activism as compared to more institutionalized processes—though there is some disagreement within communities, and we have used this terminology carefully.

2. We dedicate this chapter to the memory of Beth Mazur, a cofounder of #MEAction who died by suicide on December 21, 2023. In a social media post, preserved on *Virology Blog*, ME activist Julie Rehmeyer wrote about Mazur's life and death, "Almost everything she did was behind the scenes, but everyone in the ME world has been profoundly touched by her work. She was an 'elixir' for countless advocates, helping to brainstorm, think through problems, come up with visions for the future, and find energy to keep going" (Tuller 2023). We also thank Terri Wilder for this suggestion as well as for her participation in this project as an oral history participant and her thoughtful feedback on this chapter.

3. Some participants are active in activism and wanted their full name to be used; for other participants, we used pseudonyms.

4. A crip methodological note (Mills and Sanchez 2023): because of Sally's limited energy threshold, she conducted her "oral" history interview via text message, over the course of several months, as her energy and symptoms allowed.

5. For a highly polemic take, see Johnson 2021.

REFERENCES

Adams, Vincanne. 2020. "Disasters and Capitalism . . . and COVID-19." *Somatosphere* (blog), March 27, 2020. http://somatosphere.net.

Anderson, Kelly E., Emma E. McGinty, Rachel Presskreischer, and Colleen L. Barry. 2021. "Reports of Forgone Medical Care among US Adults during the Initial Phase of the COVID-19 Pandemic." *JAMA Network Open* 4 (1): e2034882. https://doi.org/10.1001/jamanetworkopen.2020.34882.

Bach, Katie. 2022. "New Data Shows Long COVID Is Keeping as Many as 4 Million People out of Work." Brookings, August 24, 2022. www.brookings.edu/research/new-data-shows-long-covid-is-keeping-as-many-as-4-million-people-out-of-work/.

Berlant, Lauren. 2011. *Cruel Optimism*. Durham, NC: Duke University Press.

Blas, Zach. 2012. "Virus, Viral." *Women's Studies Quarterly* 40 (1–2): 29–39.

Bonilla, Hector, Tom C. Quach, Anushri Tiwari, Andres E. Bonilla, Mitchell Miglis, Phillip C. Yang, Lauren E. Eggert, et al. 2023. "Myalgic Encephalomyelitis/Chronic Fatigue Syndrome Is Common in Post-Acute Sequelae of SARS-CoV-2 Infection (PASC): Results from a Post-COVID-19 Multidisciplinary Clinic." *Frontiers in Neurology* 14. www.frontiersin.org.

Chu, Lily, Ian J. Valencia, Donn W. Garvert, and Jose G. Montoya. 2019. "Onset Patterns and Course of Myalgic Encephalomyelitis/Chronic Fatigue Syndrome." *Frontiers in Pediatrics* 7 (12). https://doi.org/10.3389/fped.2019.00012.

Cifor, Marika, and Cait McKinney. 2020. "Reclaiming HIV/AIDS in Digital Media Studies." *First Monday* 25 (10). https://doi.org/10.5210/fm.v25i10.10517.

Clough, Patricia, and Jasbir Puar. 2012. "Introduction." *Women's Studies Quarterly* 40 (1–2): 13–26.

Cohen, Jon. 2023. "Anthony Fauci on Becoming the 'Devil' and a Warning for His Successor." *Science*, September 25, 2023. www.science.org.

Dakota (@Dakota_150). 2023. "@minadjenkins @richardvallee Thanks for this, @minadjenkins. I wonder if there's any way this community can leverage Fauci clearly very interested in this field. I know he's retired, but would think his net could still cast wide if he's publicly voicing this 'uncharted' area. Just thinking out loud." Twitter, September 26, 2023. https://twitter.com/Dakota_150/status/1706861917870915747.

Diedrich, Lisa. 2024. *Illness Politics and Hashtag Activism*. Minneapolis: University of Minnesota Press.

Dokumaci, Arseli. 2023. *Activist Affordances: How Disabled People Improvise More Habitable Worlds* Durham, NC: Duke University Press.

Fox, Maggie. 2020. "Coronavirus May Cause Fatigue Syndrome, Fauci Says." *CNN*, July 9, 2020. www.cnn.com.

Hamraie, Aimi. 2017. *Building Access: Universal Design and the Politics of Disability*. Minneapolis: University of Minnesota Press.

Hamraie, Aimi, and Kelly Fritsch. 2019. "Crip Technoscience Manifesto." *Catalyst: Feminism, Theory, Technoscience* 5 (1): 1–33. https://doi.org/10.28968/cftt.v5i1.29607.

Hartblay, Cassandra. 2020. "Disability Expertise: Claiming Disability Anthropology." *Current Anthropology* 61 (S21): S26–36. https://doi.org/10.1086/705781.

Hebert, Pato, and Alex Juhasz. 2022. "Long Hauling." ArtsEverywhere, March 2022. www.artseverywhere.ca.

Hedva, Johanna. 2022. "Sick Woman Theory." Topical Cream, March 12, 2022. https://topicalcream.org/features/sick-woman-theory/.

Institute of Medicine, Committee on the Diagnostic Criteria for Myalgic Encephalomyelitis/Chronic Fatigue Syndrome, and Board on the Health of Select Populations. 2015. *Beyond Myalgic Encephalomyelitis/Chronic Fatigue Syndrome: Redefining an Illness*. National Academies Collection: Reports Funded by National Institutes of Health. Washington, DC: National Academies Press. www.ncbi.nlm.nih.gov.

Johnson, Cort. 2021. "Does Anthony Fauci Finally Get It about Chronic Fatigue Syndrome (ME/CFS)?" *Health Rising Blog*, April 28, 2021. www.healthrising.org.

Jutel, Annemarie Goldstein. 2014. *Putting a Name on It: Diagnosis in Contemporary Society*. Baltimore: Johns Hopkins University Press.

Komaroff, Anthony L., and W. Ian Lipkin. 2023. "ME/CFS and Long COVID Share Similar Symptoms and Biological Abnormalities: Road Map to the Literature." *Frontiers in Medicine* 10. www.frontiersin.org.

Mauldin, Laura. 2022. "Disability at Home." www.disabilityathome.org.

McKinney, Cait, and Dylan Mulvin. 2019. "Bugs: Rethinking the History of Computing." *Communication, Culture and Critique* 12 (4): 476–98. https://doi.org/10.1093/ccc/tcz039.

#MEAction. 2020. "Dr. Fauci Says Post-COVID Syndrome 'Is Highly Suggestive of' Myalgic Encephalomyelitis." July 10, 2020. www.meaction.net.

———. 2022. "#MillionsMissing 2022: Activism from Home Was Beyond Impressive." September 30, 2022. www.meaction.net.

———. 2023. "DC Protest." #MillionsMissing 2023. May 12, 2023. https://millionsmissing.org.

———. 2024. "#MillionsMissing Week Is Here: #TeachMETreatME in Action!" May 7, 2024. www.meaction.net.

———. n.d.-a. "Continuing Medical Education Courses on ME." Accessed May 14, 2024. www.meaction.net.

———. n.d.-b. "#MEAction in the News." Accessed May 14, 2024. www.meaction.net.

ME Action Network. 2020. "#Stop. Rest. Pace." YouTube, October 20, 2020. https://www.youtube.com/watch?v=vabB-bTAmCI.

Mills, Mara, and Rebecca Sanchez, eds. 2023. *Crip Authorship: Disability as Method*. New York: New York University Press.

Mirin, Arthur A., Mary E. Dimmock, and Leonard A. Jason. 2022. "Updated ME/CFS Prevalence Estimates Reflecting Post-COVID Increases and Associated Economic Costs and Funding Implications." *Fatigue: Biomedicine, Health & Behavior* 10 (2): 83–93. https://doi.org/10.1080/21641846.2022.2062169.

Network for Long COVID Justice. n.d. "Commit to Long COVID Justice." Accessed August 8, 2022. https://actionnetwork.org.

Oshin, Olafimihan. 2022. "Protesters Rip Biden on COVID: 'Pandemic Is Not Over.'" *The Hill*, September 19, 2022. https://thehill.com.

Osmundson, Joseph. 2022. *Virology: Essays for the Living, the Dead, and the Small Things in Between*. New York: Norton.

Parikka, Jussi. 2007. "Contagion and Repetition: On the Viral Logic of Network Culture." *Ephemera* 7 (2): 287–308.

Pelley, Scott. 2022. "President Joe Biden: The 2022 60 Minutes Interview." *60 Minutes, CBS News*, September 18, 2022. www.cbsnews.com.

Perego, Elisa, Felicity Callard, Laurie Stras, Barbara Melville-Jóhannesson, Rachel Pope, and Nisreen Alwan. 2020. "Why We Need to Keep Using the Patient Made Term 'Long Covid.'" *The BMJ Opinion* (blog), October 1, 2020. https://blogs.bmj.com.

Reyes, Emily Alpert. 2022. "Got COVID? Doctors Warn Powering through It—Even from Home—Can Worsen Health Toll." *Los Angeles Times*, July 7, 2022, sec. California. www.latimes.com.

Rogers, Emily Lim. 2020. "Staying (at Home) with Brain Fog: Un-witting Patient Activism." *Somatosphere*, October 5, 2020. http://somatosphere.net.

Roitman, Janet L. 2014. *Anti-Crisis*. Durham, NC: Duke University Press.

Samuels, Ellen Jean. 2014. *Fantasies of Identification: Disability, Gender, Race*. New York: New York University Press.

Schuller, Kyla (@KikiSchoonz). 2020. "#COVID-19 is teaching the ableds what the disabled and chronically ill already know: your ability to leave the house is a privilege that can be lost at any time." Twitter, March 13, 2020. https://twitter.com/KikiSchoonz/status/1238456960418275329.

Solve ME/CFS Initiative (@PlzSolveCFS). 2020. "Dr. Anthony Fauci said thursday that the symptoms of #Covid19 recovery resemble those seen in patients with myalgic encephalomyelitis, or ME, once known as chronic fatigue syndrome. http://ow.ly/szMz50Avsjd #SolveME #Covid19 https://T.Co/2rLL5UBZEx." Twitter, July 12, 2020. https://twitter.com/PlzSolveCFS/status/1282425769550118918.

Tufekci, Zeynep. 2022. "Protesters So Ill, They Couldn't Get Arrested." *New York Times*, October 27, 2022, sec. Opinion. www.nytimes.com.

Tuller, David. 2023. "Trial by Error: Julie Rehmeyer on the Heartbreaking Loss of Beth Mazur." *Virology Blog*, December 24, 2023. https://virology.ws.

Vastag, Brian. 2020. "Researchers Warn COVID-19 Could Cause Debilitating Long-Term Illness in Some Patients." *Washington Post*, May 30, 2020. www.washingtonpost.com.

Werning, Kate. 2020. "Coronavirus Wisdom from a Social Justice Lens." *Irresistible* (Fka Healing Justice Podcast), March 10, 2020. https://irresistible.org/podcast/corona.

Wilder, Terri. 2024. Email to the author. January 2024.

Yong, Ed. 2022. "Long COVID Has Forced a Reckoning for One of Medicine's Most Neglected Diseases." *The Atlantic*, September 26, 2022. www.theatlantic.com.

Zucker, Howard A. 2021. "July Commissioner Monthly Letter." New York Department of Health, July 2021. www.health.ny.gov.

9

Blind New Yorkers, Online and Offline, during the Pandemic

BOJANA COKLYAT AND CHANCEY FLEET

Blind New Yorkers faced particular and often-outsized challenges during the pandemic: inaccessible COVID tests, vaccination protocols, quarantine hotels, and online platforms; worries about social distancing, mask detection, and tactile signage in public spaces. They also experienced unexpected gains from remote living, many of which began disappearing as pandemic precautions were lifted by the government, schools, and workplaces. Tech educator Chancey Fleet of the New York Public Library (NYPL) and accessibility expert Bojana Coklyat of the Whitney Museum of American Art discuss their personal experiences and their work with other blind New Yorkers from the moment New York City went "on PAUSE" in March 2020 to the declaration of the end of the public health emergency by the federal government in May 2023, when this conversation was held.

Fleet describes the evolution in the programs she coordinated at the NYPL Heiskell Braille and Talking Book Library. After March 2020, attendance at these programs grew by 500 percent, driven by a mix of New Yorkers who could not or would not come to the library in person as well as blind and low-vision people joining in from all over the country and world. The collective deep dive into digital life forced many emerging users to deepen their understanding of technology, from online shopping to running community meetings on Zoom. The network of blind community wisdom was strengthened by the simultaneous effort of so many people gathering in online library programs to learn and share advice.

Another impact of disability activism during the pandemic is noted by Coklyat: cultural institutions finally became more aware of digital access, implementing to greater and lesser degrees alt text, captioning, and audio description across online platforms. Coklyat and Fleet speculate about which of these access gains will be lasting and which will fall by the wayside as organizations return to in-person programming.

> COKLYAT: What was going on in your life when the pandemic first broke out?
>
> FLEET: In early March 2020, I helped to organize a nonvisual soldering workshop as part of an accessible electronics curriculum for blind and low-vision people. We had such a great time doing high-contact, hands-on stuff. I went from that into the lockdown, and it was a really stark contrast.
>
> My immediate reaction to lockdown was to go into problem-solving mode. I started doing things like calling library patrons and seeing who needed help figuring out how to get on Zoom. I activated our phone tree so we could reach patrons and ask if anyone had an urgent need for tech help that we could provide over the phone. I started scaffolding people who couldn't get online toward being able to do a Zoom, sometimes with the help of a friend or family member or neighbor. What I remember from those early days is being very focused on communication: getting the message out that while we were in lockdown and the Heiskell building was closed, and most library programs had stopped, the library workers had not stopped. In fact, we wanted to be a primary point of contact for anybody who needed help making the pivot online.
>
> Where were you at that moment? What was going on for you?
>
> COKLYAT: The totally changed situation in New York tore at the fabric of my reality. I had been in the Czech Republic on a Fulbright for six or seven months, and then I had to abruptly return to New York City. And I couldn't visit anybody. I couldn't see my family. I couldn't see my dad or my friends. It was incredibly hard not being able to reunite with people while dealing with this "new normal" way of living.
>
> I remember going outside with my cane soon after returning, and I thought, "Well, this may actually be good. I'm just gonna swing my cane wide, and that'll keep people at least six feet away from me." As you know, Chancey, or other blind folks may know, people do not respect the cane, and they run into you on the street. But I was surprised how even during this emergency situation, people still did not respect the cane or my space. So I was like, "I'm not even going

outside anymore, not even for a walk, because I can't." I could not see if people were coming close to me. And I was so worried. This was definitely one my strongest memories of the beginning of the pandemic.

FLEET: I had a different set of struggles with travel and, weirdly, some satisfaction, because as a guide-dog user, I think I get a slightly larger space bubble than a cane user does. My least favorite thing about traveling through the world as a blind person among sighted people is the amount of nonconsensual touching that goes on. It startles me. It distracts me. It makes me brace for the next interruption. During the pandemic, the nonconsensual touching dwindled to almost nothing. I think I was touched without consent by one person in the first four months of quarantine, and it was a cop. Everybody else was suddenly willing to give me the space to figure things out, and as awful as a lot of things were about lockdown, I really enjoyed the personal space that I got back.

But I found that when I put on a mask, it distorted the way I perceive my environment. I do a lot of passive echolocation, meaning that I understand the environment through subtle sound cues. The mask felt like it was dulling and interfering with those cues. I spoke to a friend of mine who is an expert in the psychology of sound, who told me masks really change the shape of your head, and then your brain needs to remap. I had such trepidation and discomfort around walking with a mask on, but of course, I did it anyway. I wasn't walking as much, and I sort of resigned myself to this new level of difficulty. But my blind friend gave me hope that if I stuck with it, my brain would learn to interpret the new shape. And it did! I wear a mask in my workplace and in crowded settings to this day. It's fascinating. My brain has learned to accommodate that new shape. As soon as I got that piece of news, I started sharing it with all the blind people I knew, because a lot of us were going through similar feelings. It was good to know that the discomfort was going to end.

COKLYAT: Yeah, it makes me think about any time you're adapting to something different with your body. Losing more vision in my left eye was uncomfortable. It was unnerving. It was like, "Okay, now maybe I won't go out at night." I had to relearn. I thought, "I'm just going to plan better." As far as my navigation goes, will I take a Lyft, or will I make sure that I have somebody meeting me somewhere? You find different ways to adapt and get used to things.

That first year of the pandemic, I was so diligent with wearing a mask, and then we had that summer after vaccinations started, where it was like, "We're gonna be outside, and we aren't going to wear masks." A lot of people, I think, loosened up a little bit, and I did too. And then the reality of the fall came, and it was like, "Okay we have to put our masks back on." I just remember the psychological weight of it.

I'm wearing the mask again now. It's this uncomfortable thing you eventually adapt to, or you just learn to work around somehow.

FLEET: How did you feel during quarantine about exploring things by touch? Was that something that was on your mind?

COKLYAT: I really, really stuck to my apartment. That's a great question because I love to touch things; I think I've always loved to touch things. But I used to touch so much more—to investigate or explore something, to figure out what it is. It was really hard for me when the pandemic first started—going to the grocery store, to not touch everything, to just make sure I knew exactly what I was getting without having somebody help me. I think that was really tough for me and still is. I touch things to know what they are, and I'm also just a very huggy and affectionate person. And I have to be careful about that.

I notice, too, because now I'm not seeing people's faces or their features as much, I tend to want to connect with them by touch—not touching their faces but either their hand or their arm. What about you?

FLEET: I missed the connection of being able to be physically close to people, to good friends, even though I like my personal space when it comes to strangers. When it comes to navigating the world, I do a lot of touching, and I'm usually pretty unabashed about it. I will touch the vegetables in the vegetable aisle to figure out what I'm looking for, and if I feel something that's got raised writing on it, I'll start touching it and trying to figure it out. That's a tool for me and also a source of entertainment.

Early in the pandemic, I found myself watching myself from the outside, thinking about how sighted people would interpret all of that touch and how much touch was really necessary. I didn't want to present myself as a vector, so I really muted the way that I explored the world during those first few months. But then, thankfully, we learned that surface transmission wasn't the vector we all thought it was at first, and I went back to touching all the things.

COKLYAT: Yeah, I remember washing my vegetables, not just with water but some kind of sterilizing spray or soap and water—you know, every single surface. At that time, because I was more conscientious about touch—or of not touching—I realized how much I did use touch. And I use touch more now, with less vision. If I'm passing by someone, I might just have a hand on their shoulder (not somebody I don't know) or a hand on a wall or a door or whatever surface might be there.

I was recently sharing some food with some people—sesame marinated cucumbers, delicious!—and even though I was trying to keep to my side of the dish, I may have forked this other person's side, even though I was trying to be so safe. And the person noticed and was like, "Here, you can take this." It's little things like that.

FLEET: Yeah, it's almost as though the pandemic raised the stakes on something I had already known. People pay hyper attention to us. I know, as a blind person, that I am being watched, both because I'm a rarity in the world and because the way that I do things is so different. Then the pandemic added this concept that while they're watching us, they're maybe going to see us doing something that is not healthy, not safe. That didn't feel great. Let me raise a question about something happier. What memories do you have of the disability community, or the larger community, providing mutual support or solving problems while we were all stuck in the lockdown period together?

COKLYAT: Oh, it's easy for me to answer that one. I always think about the first Zoom party I went to, called Remote Access. It was really early on in March 2020. I think it was organized pretty quickly. Kevin Gotkin was DJing, and Yo-Yo Lin showed some animations, kind of abstract patterns of color. What was so great was that they hacked Zoom in a way where, for audio description, I was able to call in. There was one link or phone number for the Zoom Meeting experience, with music and illustration, and then there was another Zoom link that I clicked onto with somebody doing live audio description.

They were using Zoom to provide this multisensory event, and at the same time, they included live audio description, not anything that took additional technology or any real intense special training. It was just like, "Let's throw this thing together." There was a real sense of community, and I really appreciated it. I like that kind of creativity—just bringing together the resources and skills people have to provide. What about you?

FLEET: Amazing, nice. I really enjoyed what felt like an audio description and interactive accessibility renaissance during the pandemic. It seems as though folks paid more attention to making online meetings accessible once we all knew that's where we were stuck. There was a lot more discourse about transcripts and different ways to get different people into a Zoom meeting and other things like making slide decks accessible. I feel like the bar was raised from what I had experienced before.

We also had a ton of Zoom watch parties where somebody would broadcast their Netflix, and I don't think that I've ever had so many chances to enjoy open audio description (AD) with a room full of blind and sighted people. It was just the norm in our social circle that everything we chose to watch would have AD and the AD would be open, and we all just rolled with it. In the past, in most situations, I would watch shows on my own. It was really fun to get to experience AD in community.

Another thing that I really appreciated was blind people and allies solving access barriers in real time, with whatever resources they had. For example, Tyler Littlefield [a blind software developer] created an accessible COVID statistics website, because all of the other COVID data sets you could find on public-facing websites had really complicated data visualizations. They were generally inaccessible, so Tyler did some coding and made a stats tracker where you could review what was going on in different states and countries in real time, with really clean, uncluttered tables. I went to that site every day.

A little later on, in summer 2020, when Black Lives Matter protests started sweeping the country, the group Protest Access on Twitter made sure that the images and videos coming out of the movement were accessible to all of us. There was a podcast called *Talk Description to Me* that also offered coverage of Black Lives

Matter. I really felt like that social movement was more accessible to me than I remember other movements being, because people were making a concerted effort. Everyone had been stuck online, and people had time to think about *process.*

It was heavy and important, and it almost feels wrong to focus on how accessible the coverage was. But that being said, if we want things to change, the tools we use for that change should be accessible so that everybody can get on board. It meant a lot to me to be able to be as aware as anyone of what was going on.

COKLYAT: I was thinking about the Black Lives Matter protests and how there is this preconceived notion that blind people don't need to see images. Or, why would they want to, right? What does it matter? You can't see. Would you need to know about an image? This is a never-ending conversation some of us have about ocularcentrism. Sight is at the top of the sensory hierarchy. We put so much importance on what we see. We live in a visual culture, and the images that were coming out about the protests or even the video of George Floyd, these are images that changed the world and started movements. We as blind people, we need to know what these things are like. We need to have these things described. Even though we can't see, that doesn't mean we're not a part of or don't have some kind of responsibility toward these social movements.

I do think there was a huge shift of awareness towards social justice issues over that summer. And I agree that people had more time at home, and there weren't as many distractions, and we were all spending so much more time on the internet. In addition to that, disabled activists were doing an amazing job of making sure there was awareness and action around things like captioning and audio description and image description.

When I got back from my Fulbright, I was scrambling to try to find a job because I wasn't expecting to all of a sudden be trying to pay bills in the United States. But I ended up getting hired by the New York City Museum, Arts and Culture Access Consortium. The specific grant was to research New York City cultural institutions and how they were reconfiguring their programming during COVID. How were they going to move their programming online and make it accessible? How were they going to keep and engage the communities of disabled people they had built up? That was a really eye-opening experience. It helped me delve deeper into the ways the pandemic affected museums and cultural institutions.

How did the library shift their programming, especially since it's so hands-on, with people coming in to use the public computers?

FLEET: I can only speak to what happened in the technology department. Our Braille and Talking Book program was put on hold while we couldn't physically get into the building to ship books. I was determined to contact as many of our patrons as I could, so our volunteers and interns and staff went into our spreadsheet of patrons that come in regularly, and we literally called everyone. We got everyone we could onto a mailing list and started coming up with plans for people who weren't yet routinely online to figure out how they could level up to learn how to use Zoom or even email. Sometimes that meant coaching them on the phone and listening to their computer over a couple of sessions, or sometimes working with a friend or family member or social workers.

My favorite story—because it was so emblematic of the moment that we were in, and it had a good outcome—is about a patron who was in a homeless shelter, who was extremely new to being a blind iPhone user. Somebody in the shelter got COVID, and he found himself whisked away to a quarantine hotel, where he was shown to a room and basically left to his own devices. There was a microwave, a phone, and a TV in the room, but he wasn't able to use them. He also had questions about how to operate the unfamiliar controls in the shower. He was extremely upset and frustrated and shaken about the whole situation.

I had been working with him over the phone while he was in the shelter, teaching some iPhone basics. He didn't yet have the skills to download an app, so I couldn't tell him to solve these problems with an app. I did some thinking: "What's already on the phone?" "Oh, FaceTime is already on the phone." "Do you have anybody you can call in your family or your friend group who will take a FaceTime call? Okay, call that person and show them the shower control. Show them the shampoo versus conditioner, and show them the TV remote and the microwave."

And that's what he did, and he called me back. "I got it. I got it. It's working. It worked!" Later we worked on some more classically independent strategies, like using an OCR [optical character recognition] app. But first we had to solve that problem in the moment by improvising. I spent a lot of time, as did my colleagues and our volunteers, taking all kinds of questions like this and helping people with their immediate needs.

Our attendance went up about 500 percent at library workshops. When we went online, it turned out that we had a captive audience, literally, but also a lot of people that never would have come in person because they had child-care obligations or lived in Long Island or hated to take Access-A-Ride and didn't feel comfortable on the subway. Suddenly all those people could show up, and so workshops that would have brought out five or ten or fifteen people in the old days were drawing forty, sixty, one hundred. We prioritized things that people had an urgent need to know about, like how to get around an online shopping interface to get groceries delivered and where to go online to get reliable information about the crisis as it was unfolding. As time went on, we focused on workshops that might give people a sense of ease or peace or adventure. We did things like tactile drawing with materials that you have in your house or accessible gaming or a YouTube watch party where we'd watch some videos about travel and life as a blind person and then just talk about them. Those ended up being really popular.

I only know about the people we *did* reach, our successes, so it's easy for me to celebrate the wins. It was a big win to bring people together who were geographically far-flung. It was a big win to connect with folks who weren't ready to leave their houses yet and, even before the pandemic, weren't ready or able to come to the library. It was an equalizer for local New Yorkers who were adjusting to blindness or vision loss and still figuring things out to be in a room and in conversation on equal terms with folks who are quote-unquote "leaders in the field" and folks who have a high degree of comfort with blindness or low vision. Getting to observe those conversations unfolding, and what each person had to offer everyone else, was really special. And people in our community are generous with their time and wisdom: we gained volunteers during quarantine who I haven't met in person to this day, and those people are still dedicating their time and skills to keeping our digital programs thriving.

On the other hand, for everyone we reached, there are a bunch of folks that we never did find. There are people that didn't have access to cell phones or that hadn't made a connection to the library before lockdown. I know that for a lot of folks, especially those that acquired a disability during or right before lockdown, it was a really lonely, scary time, and they lost a lot of valuable learning time. I also know that people who had specific needs often found that the systems designed to support them failed utterly during lockdown. For example, services for blind students were inadequate across the board and in many cases couldn't be meaningfully delivered on a virtual platform. It's not optimal to teach Braille from a distance to a beginning reader; that needs to be a literally hands-on activity. There are some things we can do to support someone's study goals from a distance. We had a Braille study group where we talked about contractions or talked about reading techniques and motivated each other. But kids that needed direct instruction or adults that needed it weren't getting it.

When lockdown was over, there was a backlog of people needing services, and we're still feeling the effects of that backlog. I'm still hearing that most of the agencies that provide services have serious waiting lists. So we had our successes online but significant losses too.

COKLYAT: Blind people aren't always being served the way they should be by these government-funded organizations, anyway. Or, you know, customer service can be lacking. There were already so many situations where blind people weren't getting what they needed, and then you throw in a pandemic. And people's priorities were just to keep going, to make sure things were moving along to a certain degree. Access, or ensuring that blind people had viable experiences, went to the wayside in some organizations.

I'm thinking about hospitals, how disabled people were devalued when it came to care during the pandemic. At the start of COVID, I was in a wheelchair because I had a very serious surgery on my right leg where a twelve-inch titanium rod was inserted through my heel and fused my ankle. So I was also using a wheelchair. Oftentimes, health-care professionals would speak to my ex-husband rather than speaking to me. It was difficult getting into some of the spaces where there were vaccinations because we couldn't find the door for people using wheelchairs.

Oftentimes, I found the health-care professionals weren't always wearing their masks, which was concerning. I went to a hospital to get an x-ray on my leg, and the receptionist was not wearing her mask but instead had it pulled down.

I was also interviewed for the *New Jersey Star-Ledger* newspaper about people with compromised immune systems and their experiences during COVID. Most interesting to me are the comments people left on the article, which ranged from "poor thing" to "if you don't want to get COVID, then don't go outside"—basically telling me not to leave my house if I was so worried. The raw contempt that people had for somebody who they didn't even know, who's vulnerable, was astonishing.

FLEET: The accessibility of online sign-ups for COVID vaccinations was also so uneven. In some municipalities, the web portal was accessible, if, of course, you had a high comfort level with screen readers. In other cases, the portal was a barrier. Theoretically you could opt to call a phone number, but the wait times were onerous, and you might miss out on an appointment you really needed that way.

It was also a struggle to find a somewhat-accessible COVID test: clearly, we can't read the little lines. Eventually the National Federation of the Blind and other advocates worked with the Biden administration to identify a fairly accessible Bluetooth-based COVID test so we can read the results with our screen readers. But even that solution is just a starting point: it leaves out people who aren't comfortable with smartphones or who have motor impairments that make the physical aspects of taking the test difficult. Our community is thinking seriously about more inclusive design for home medical tests, and I'm cautiously optimistic that our advocacy will change the trajectory of inclusive test design. But inaccessible testing is still a huge barrier for swaths of disabled people, compounded by privacy concerns around sharing one's test results and the safety issues involved in having someone come close enough to help you administer a test if you think you may be sick.

COKLYAT: Another thing that was highlighted for me while I was researching cultural institutions and talking to them about online programming was the suddenness of their interest in image description and audio description. There were moments when I felt like, "Okay, *really?* Did you need a pandemic to realize you needed alt text? Did you really need a pandemic to remember to do captioning?"

What was also interesting to me was how many different people working in access in cultural institutions talked about fear-based accountability. If one institution is doing a certain kind of access and doing it well, then this other institution wants to make sure they're doing it too, because they don't want to look backward compared to other organizations. There was so much more visibility or awareness around basic access elements like alt text and audio description. I could clearly see the effect of the pandemic and people being online more, because I received so many more questions about consulting. "Do you do verbal description consultation or the 'Alt Text as Poetry' workshop or consulting with image description?"

Why was there more awareness around access for some organizations? I think it's not just one thing. There are multiple reasons. It's awareness of social justice. There are disabled activists pushing for this kind of thing. And we're all online a lot more, and we had more time.

What do you think? Will this interest in access continue?

FLEET: I'll start positive. I think the denser interconnections among people in the disability community are here to stay. I've noticed that although the frequency and intensity and cadence of online gatherings has changed, and we've all kind of worn ourselves out, they're still happening. Those new ties are strong and stable. I'm seeing a lot of online gatherings continue, at the library and outside the library, and I think that's something worth celebrating.

At the same time, I'm seeing helpful protocols wither on the vine. It would be really helpful if anything that can be hybrid is hybrid. We do it at the library, even without great production values. Conveniently, we specialize in nonvisual access, so I don't need my video to be perfect. For example, we did an origami program last Saturday. We had a few people in the library in person and then a greater number of people online. I'm not going to say that it's the easiest thing to pull off a hybrid program, but if we don't try, what are we saying to all the people we welcomed during the pandemic who were joining us for the first time because they were immunocompromised or because they had child-care or work responsibilities that made it geographically impossible for them to come in? If it's going to be a talking and not a hands-on event, why not keep that door open?

I'm seeing a lot of the care and attention that was spent in figuring out how to do things online misspent now, as we're returning to in-person gatherings, which I love doing and which we should celebrate. But from a disability justice perspective, frankly, it's our responsibility to keep that door open and not slam it in the faces of the people that we were so happy to welcome during lockdown. I think lots of organizations, including public service organizations and disability support and justice organizations, aren't keeping that increased level of access for people who need it now that it's not a priority for all of us.

And while we're talking about things that were great for accessibility and that deserve to stay, I really feel like outdoor dining was more accessible—for people with processing issues, hearing issues, or just introversion, and for people who are immunocompromised, of course. It hurts my heart to see those spaces torn down.

COKLYAT: Human nature continues to amaze and disappoint me. We as a society put so much effort into adapting to the pandemic, and then as quickly as possible, we tried to return to what was more familiar and comfortable. As I was working for the Access Consortium, surveying the multitude of different cultural institutions in New York City, I saw sweeping changes in the way people approached access. There were significant changes in the ways we work, in options for experiences, and attention to how we interact online. Disabled people have been asking to work from home for decades, but it was only during the pandemic that it became more of a normalized way to work.

Has all of that been tossed to the wayside? No, but so much of the urgency around care, mutual aid, and interdependence has been muffled. Virtual programming and engaging online experiences are extremely beneficial to a wide cross-section of people, not just disabled people or blind people. So much time, energy, and institutional knowledge was put forth to create dynamic programming online, yet now, so much of that has evaporated. The laser-focused attention to moving cultural institution programming online has been redirected to getting people back into these spaces. Yet, virtual options to participate have not completely disappeared. I believe some of these will remain as a way to bolster attendees, although the robust interactive programming we saw between 2020 and 2021 has diminished. It's always two steps forward and one step back when it comes to accessibility and comfort if you are living with chronic illness or disability.

At the same time, I can't help but think some of the new approaches to in-person disability-centered programming were spawned by having to reconfigure how we programmed events at the height of COVID. For instance, MOMA [Museum of Modern Art] recently presented an event where any blind person could come in and touch selected works. I've noticed that cultural institutions have shifted their thinking regarding the blind people who walk through their spaces. Now that the bell has been rung, it cannot be unrung.

The pandemic also changed and increased the ways blind people live on the internet. It has become normalized to be streaming, to be on your phone texting or scrolling or doing a multitude of other things, no matter what age you are. It makes me question, does the internet bring blind people closer together, or does it force us further apart? Perhaps it's both and more, instead of one or the other.

10

The Everyday Lives of *Qilao* during the Pandemic

SHUTING LI

A small door opens at the bottom of this grandiose landmark building, which housed a city governmental department in the early twentieth century. The gray stone surface, symmetric columns on the facade, and highly decorated cornices convey a sense of heaviness and solemnity, while pigeons resting on the triangular pediments make it look different from any other old building in lower Manhattan. Inside the door, several steps down to the bottom of the stairs, a bright, clean, and open space appears on the left side. This is Rui An Senior Center, a community center for *qilao* (elderly Chinese immigrants aged sixty and over) living in Manhattan, operating since the 1970s.[1] Here, elderly Chinese can have balanced and nutritious meals daily, take various classes customized for them, and attend festivals and events held at the center. White-surfaced desks in pairs with red plastic chairs stand in line along the window. Gray-haired elders gather in twos and threes, sit around tables, and chat or play cards together after lunchtime. Through vibrant plants on the windowsill, a lower-angle view of passing pedestrians and the hustle and bustle of traffic unfolds. Letter-size signs stating, "Please Wear Masks" and "Please Social Distance," hang on the wall. With masks on, some elders sit scattered in the common area engaged in a chorus class, usually taught after lunchtime every Tuesday and Thursday. After singing a popular Minnanhua song "Ai pin cai hui ying" (Success comes with your hard work), they start practicing a Mandarin song, "Gan en" (Gratefulness).[2] This is an ordinary day in Rui An Senior Center after the pandemic reopening.

In late June 2021, about fifteen months after the outbreak of COVID-19, as the number of cases dropped, senior centers across New York City gradually resumed their indoor activities. However, the elderly still faced the risk of getting COVID and developing severe illnesses from underlying health conditions, even with vaccinations. At that time, a series of cautious procedures were conducted to protect elders and workers at senior centers.[3] For example, elders were required to use a contactless forehead thermometer to check their temperature when entering the senior center. Masks and social distancing were mandatory, no matter what activities they participated in. COVID was not the only hazard that elderly Chinese immigrants encountered; racism and hate incidents against Asian Americans increased since the beginning of the pandemic in March 2020. Many violent attacks on Asian American women and elders in news headlines raised people's concerns and anxiety across the country. Given these hazards, what did the everyday life of elderly Chinese immigrants look like in New York City during the different phases of the pandemic? How did they maintain their connections within the community while coping with the increased risk to health and safety during the pandemic? As immigrants, how do they understand "aging," given the contrast between Chinese cultural values and the US context? By chronicling the stories of some of the elderly Chinese immigrants at Rui An Senior Center, this chapter provides a glimpse into their everyday lives in New York City during the pandemic.

I worked with some elderly Chinese immigrants at the center from September 2021 to May 2022 to produce an ethnographic documentary. This short film documents their stories of participating in the production of *Tian shi dao zhi qiang* (Written in the walls), a play about the history of Chinese immigrants in the early twentieth century detained in the Angel Island Immigration Station. During the filming process, I spent most of my time with elders who regularly participated in chorus and dance classes. As a native speaker of Mandarin and Minnanhua, I quickly built close relationships with those who could speak either language. At the center, Cantonese and Mandarin work as the lingua franca among elders who speak different dialects such as Taishanese, Teochew, and Minnanhua. Given my very basic proficiency in Cantonese, elders who could speak both Cantonese and Mandarin often translated for me in the field. I conducted interviews with elders in Mandarin, and they responded in either Mandarin or a mix of Cantonese and Mandarin. All quotes in this chapter are my translations. Drawn from ethnographic observations and interviews, this chapter presents how elderly Chinese immigrants managed changes and challenges that the pandemic brought to their everyday lives. Instead of following the popular narrative of "high risk and vulnerable elders," their stories show diverse and resilient ways of adjusting to pandemic life. The popular idea of "successful aging," expressed in the context of Chinese cultural values, plays a vital role in shaping individuals' perceptions and experiences of aging. Racism also casts a shadow over the everyday life of elderly Chinese immigrants. The concern about their health during the pandemic, intensified fears and anxieties about the increased racial incidents and physical violence in New York City, and the implicit impact of the model minority myth on individuals complicate what successful aging means to Chinese elders in the US. Although many elders at the center experience a degree of debility, "disability" is barely mentioned in their daily conversations. The last part of this chapter addresses what the lack of discussion about aging and disability implies for elderly Chinese immigrants and what we can learn from these stories for the future aging population.

"Staying at Home"

After the chorus class ended, these older students dispersed at different paces: some pulled their chairs back to tables and rest, some went to the kitchen area to get water, and some hung around in the center. As I passed the kitchen, the clack of shuffling mahjong tiles, the instrumental music of Guangdong tunes, and the shouting of "cho!" from the Ping-Pong room mixed together. In order to obey the rules of social distancing and capacity restrictions, a table at the end of the hallway was turned into an extra mahjong table after lunchtime for people who could not fit in the mahjong room. Two big fans were installed at each entry of the Ping-Pong room to accelerate the air circulation. In the meantime, elders were waiting for the dance class to begin in the common area. At a table near the window, Grandma Yi was sipping tea from her water bottle, resting, and waiting for the dance class.[4] Her short gray hair was held back by a pink headband embroidered with white lace. She paired a black cotton long-sleeved top with a black-and-white-striped cardigan. Grandma Yi started learning dance when she was young and became a professional dancer in China before moving to the US in the 1980s. She still dances regularly, even though she is now eighty-five years old. When I asked her about the pandemic's impact on her daily life, she smiled and responded,

> It didn't influence my life a lot. I stayed at home and did nothing special. The grocery store near my apartment offered a special hour for seniors in the morning. I used that hour to buy what I needed, then returned home quickly. If I needed anything small, I would run to the convenience store to buy it and then rush back home. During the lockdown, I was busy writing an article celebrating the fortieth anniversary of the China Acrobats' Association. The bad thing was that I did not dance for several months at the height of the pandemic. I did not get a chance to exercise my body. Until the pandemic eased, I came downstairs to exercise my body in the park.

During my visits to the center, she often invited me to join the dance class. When she called other students in the dance class to warm up, she often said to me, "Exercise with us together. Move your body." For Grandma Yi, dancing is not only her lifelong career and passion but also her daily exercise to keep her body healthy and energetic.

Grandpa Ke was sitting at a table on the right side of the stage, watching these older students dance. He pulled his mask down, sipped the instant coffee in a disposable paper cup, then quickly put back his mask. Before retirement, Grandpa Ke was a mail sorter who operated mail-processing machines and postage meters. In his leisure time, he is passionate about taking photographs. As an amateur photographer, he witnessed the transformation from analog to digital cameras. He once taught photography workshops and donated all his earnings to nonprofit organizations for the Chinese immigrant community. When I asked him about the impact of the pandemic on his life, he nodded and said, "It did impact [my life]." He paused for a while, searching his memory of that period in his mind, then slowly said, "I just stayed at home. I used to travel with my friends to take photos every year. Because of the pandemic, I could not travel like before." He raised his voice and emphasized, "I am old. I am concerned with my health most." Like Grandma Yi and Grandpa Ke, most of my older interlocutors admitted that the pandemic had impacted their daily lives and recalled that they stayed at home and did not go anywhere before the center reopened.

Although local senior centers offered the elderly "Grab & Go Lunches" and "Meals on Wheels" throughout the week, elders lost access to their daily social space when senior centers were closed (Appel 2020; M. Kim 2020). The 2020 shelter-in-place order confined elders in their homes and possibly exacerbated existing mistreatment of elders, such as neglect, increased social isolation, caregiver abuse, and financial exploitation (Elman et al. 2020; Han and Mosqueda 2020). Furthermore, the closure of senior centers reduced the social and gathering space for elderly Chinese immigrants in their neighborhoods and impacted communication between seniors who speak different dialects. Many elderly Chinese immigrants from various regions in China speak diverse dialects, do not speak English, or have limited English proficiency (Hum 2014). As the immigrant population of Fujian descent expanded in the 1990s, Mandarin gradually replaced Cantonese and became the lingua franca of the Chinese immigrant community in Flushing, Queens, and Sunset Park, Brooklyn (Hum 2014). In Manhattan's Chinatown, Cantonese is still spoken most, but the population of Mandarin speakers has also increased. In senior centers in local neighborhoods, elders who speak different dialects can find ways to communicate by finding common parts in their dialects, asking others at the center to translate, or learning the lingua franca. Senior centers in Chinese immigrant neighborhoods provide elderly Chinese immigrants with an accessible space to communicate and socialize in their languages.

As elders faced the pandemic's negative impact on their social and public activities, many described their shelter-in-place experiences as "staying at home" instead of quarantine. "Staying at home" sounds less disruptive than "quarantine" or "lockdown" and implies the mundane and ordinary aspects of their pandemic experiences. Sarah Lamb (2020), drawing from pandemic stories of her older interlocutors, discovered that older Americans felt their lives were less disrupted than younger generations did, although they felt shocked and worried at the beginning of the pandemic. From conversations with my older interlocutors, I also find that most of them did not highlight negative moments during the lockdown period in New York City and instead regarded it as a part of everyday life in this lasting and global pandemic. When I asked them whether they felt bored at home, most female interlocutors said that they were busy and needed to do household work, such as grocery shopping, cooking, and cleaning. In comparison, male interlocutors barely mentioned the household work; some said that they had nothing to do and got bored. These male interlocutors live with their wives, and their wives are more likely to take care of the household work. When these elders cope with the pandemic and aging in a resilient way, gender roles also shape their experiences and perceptions of "staying at home."

Without a doubt, the closure of senior centers had an impact on the social life of the elderly Chinese immigrant community. Nevertheless, the communication between members of the community was maintained online during the closure of the senior center. Grandma Qin told me that she used the social media app WeChat to chat with her friends in the US and China; thus, she did not feel isolated or bored. As a member of the center for years, Grandma Qin volunteered to help organize different activities. She was responsible for leading a small group of elders to play Bingo every Wednesday afternoon. Winning participants receive a small prize, such as a small bag of healthy cookies or noodles. Every participant could win three times at most. Therefore, Grandma Qin always checked with the winners to ensure that the lucky one did not take all the prizes. She also gave cookies to those participants who did not win to cheer them up at the end. She said, "Fairness is important." She is also an active user of her mobile phone and WeChat. After we became friends on WeChat, she often greets me or casually chats with me on WeChat. Although elders may not be as digitally savvy as younger generations are, they are able to learn and use digital technology in their own ways to maintain social connections with the community.

Labeled as "vulnerable and high risk groups" by the World Health Organization, the elderly are generally associated with terms like "precarious," "frail," and "vulnerable" during the pandemic. However, the popular description of the elderly as at higher risk obscures what makes people really vulnerable, such as underlying medical conditions and structural inequalities, reinforcing the stereotypes constructed by ageism and ableism (Verbruggen, Howell, and Simmons 2020). As Joan Tronto argues, "Vulnerability belies the myth that we are always autonomous, and potentially equal, citizens. To assume equality among humans leaves out and ignores important dimensions of human existence. Throughout our lives, all of us go through varying degrees of dependence and independence, of autonomy and vulnerability" (1993, 135). Reflecting on vulnerability, resilience, and aging, Lamb writes, "many of my older interlocutors described a vital resilience that comes with increased age and life experience, giving them a resourcefulness to brave the pandemic" (2020, 179). In my fieldwork, many elderly interlocutors also found various ways to make the pandemic less disruptive to their lives. However, the "vulnerability" foregrounded by ageism and ableism neglects the agency of elders and erases their efforts to seek ways of actively aging in the pandemic. Focusing on how the elderly coped with their vulnerability during the pandemic allows us to orient our understanding of vulnerability and aging into a view that centers elders' agency as well as challenges ableism and ageism.

Behind Successful Aging

Teacher Lu always arrived in the last ten minutes of the chorus class. Turning seventy-five years old this year, Teacher Lu stayed slim and fit. His short, salt-and-pepper hair was trimmed well and neatly combed. He wore a navy short-sleeve suit with knot buttons in the front and a pair of gray cotton pants. The round silver eyeglasses on his nose made him look like a gentle literati in China's Republican era, but the small four-wheel and modern-looking suitcase in his right hand brought him back to the present. Before moving to the US, Teacher Lu had been a professional actor in Hong Kong for about seven years. He performed in Four Seas Players, Pan Asian Repertory Theatre, and various films in the US. Teacher Lu started teaching elders to dance at Rui An Senior Center twenty years ago. "The director [at the center] told me that their average age was eighty-two years old. I was wondering whether they can still move." He paused and smiled: "I was still young at that time." Elderly students and workers at the center politely and amiably called him "Teacher Lu," even if some students were older than he was. In addition to teaching, Teacher Lu directed performances for the dance group. They have performed *Hao Rizi (Good Day), New York, New York, Flamenco Dance*, and other plays. Although Teacher Lu often danced in front of the group to guide them, sometimes he needed to sit down to let his knees rest. Owing to his knee problem, he walked slowly and sometimes limped. But he insisted on coming to the center every Tuesday and Thursday to teach his older students.

In our conversations, Teacher Lu always shared his enthusiasm for performance, various anecdotes about his life, and his optimistic attitude. He rarely mentioned his knee problem and other underlying health conditions. One day, our conversation turn to *yusheng* (the rest of life). Teacher Lu said, "One of my friends asked me, 'How do you plan to live the rest of your life?' I responded, 'What do you mean by *yusheng*?' I still have a long time to go. Elders share some pictures of the infinite sunset all day long. I said, 'No, I still want to see the rising sun.' My window faces the east, and I watch the sunrise daily." Although Teacher Lu did not mention "successful aging," his attitude toward aging resonated with this trending discourse in the US context. John W. Rowe and Robert L. Kahn's seminal book *Successful Aging* underscores four cultural themes that underlie various definitions of successful aging in the US context: individual agency, independence, productivity, and "permanent personhood" (Lamb 2014, 45). As a biopolitical and cultural project, the notion of successful aging motivates people to achieve the ideal of late life, which is independent, healthy, productive, and ageless, through their efforts and choices during the process of aging (Lamb 2014). The idea of successful aging is also reflected in how Teacher Lu coped with the pandemic: "There is a website called Instacart, which can deliver groceries across the country. I didn't know it until I saw it online. So I asked it to send things. If I purchase things in a nearby supermarket or Costco, they can deliver them to my place. Later I started ordering from Costco. Door-to-door delivery was very convenient, so I didn't have any problems at all. I never lacked any resources, either food or toilet paper. I was terrified at the beginning. How could I live without these essential things?" Teacher Lu laughed and said in a determined tone, "You should try your best to convert the bad environment into something good, right? That's why I like this way the most."

Teacher Lu is not the only elder who pursues strategies of successful aging at the center. Grandma Yi also volunteers to lead dance groups at other senior centers. When talking about her motivation to volunteer, Grandma Yi said, "I teach elders to dance in my community in East Harlem, where elders of various ethnicities other than Chinese live. I am a volunteer. I want to change people's perception of Chinese immigrants, make others see our contribution to society." During my ethnographic observations, most elderly students took the chorus and dance classes seriously and practiced what they learn in classes in their own time. When the center held a gala for festivals and community events, they made every effort to ensure that the performance was good. Elders at the center not only pursue positive and vibrant ways of aging but also intend to contribute to the senior center, the Chinese immigrant community, and US society.

Motivated by the discourses of successful aging, the elderly in the US context usually avoid identifying themselves as old (Lamb 2014, 2019) and prefer "the ageless self" proposed by Sharon Kaufman (1986). However, Lamb discovered that her older interlocutors claimed that to be old was "an unexpectedly motivating identity" during the pandemic (2020, 182). They embraced the identity of being old and vulnerable in an affirmative way and formed a new understanding of aging and mortality, which motivated them to practice self-care and cherish everyday life (Lamb 2020). Similar to Lamb's findings, most of my older interlocutors also openly identified themselves as old. In addition to being influenced by the successful aging movement in the US, the perceptions of aging among elderly Chinese immigrants at the center were shaped by the ideal practices of aging in Confucianism. They were keenly aware of the declining health condition and the inevitable death inherent in the process of aging. As the leader of volunteers at the center, Grandpa He frankly used the Chinese proverb "lao de lao, si de si" (getting old and dying) to describe the declining population at the center. Aging and death are topics that can be openly discussed at the center. Confucius said, "liu shi er er shun, qi shi er cong xin suo yu, bu yu ju" (From sixty my ear was attuned; from seventy I could give my heart-and-mind free rein without overstepping the boundaries)" (1998, 77). Confucianism proposes an ideal self who will practice, learn, and cultivate wisdom in parallel with the process of aging. However, the processual structure of cultivating the self is divided by the chronological and rigid understanding of aging. Although the Confucian idea of aging does not guarantee people's agency in accumulating wisdom, the linear structure based on age provides people with a framework that reinforces a relatively respectable position of the elderly in the web of social relationships. In Confucian terms, identifying as old acknowledges more experience and practice in cultivating the ideal self.

In *The Chinese Classic of Family Reverence*, Henry Rosemont and Roger Ames define *xiao* (filial piety) as "a necessary condition for developing other human qualities of excellence" (2009, xii), which works as an ideal relationship between parents and adult children in the family. As the social and cultural norm in Chinese culture, filial piety plays a vital role in shaping people's understandings and experiences of aging. To achieve filial piety, people should nurture elderly parents, raise the future generation, and worship ancestors (Ikels 2004). From observing middle-class immigrant households from Taiwan and Hong Kong in California, Pei-Chia Lan (2002) discovered that many adult immigrant children "transfer" or "subcontract" their obligation of filial care to paid home-care workers. On the one hand, the parental authority of elders declines during the process of immigration, owing to language barriers, cultural differences, and the lack of financial resources. On the other hand, adult immigrant children refer to the norm of independence and individualism in the US to account for the residential separation, the role of social welfare systems in elder care, and the commodification of filial piety by paid care workers (Lan 2002). Therefore, senior centers serving elderly Chinese immigrants become critical actors in the chain of transferring filial piety by offering some care to elderly parents during the daytime. As the Population Study of Chinese Elderly Study (PINE Study) indicates, community centers can function as an alternative source of support for elderly Chinese immigrants: they provide accessible and safe zones, offer meaningful cultural activities, enhance social integration, and improve the mental health of immigrants in later life (Dong, Wong, and Simon 2014; Dong 2014; Kim and Silverstein 2020).[5] Moreover, these senior centers supplement the insufficient practices of filial piety that should have been conducted by adult children. For instance, Rui An Senior Center helps seniors find a cemetery that satisfies Chinese *feng shui* and organizes the annual trip to sweep tombs at the Qingming Festival to worship their ancestors.[6] While embracing the idea of successful aging emerging in the US context, many elderly Chinese immigrants reconfigure it in the context of Chinese cultural values shaped by Confucianism.

While exploring how to age actively in the interactions between Chinese and US values, elderly Chinese immigrants also need to cope with the exacerbated racism and hate incidents against Asian Americans. Yaopan Ma, age sixty-one, died eight months after being violently attacked from behind while collecting cans in April 2021. He was a dim sum pastry chef and lost his job when the restaurant closed during the lockdown period (Kelly 2022). Guiying Ma, age sixty-two, was beaten in the head with a rock while sweeping the sidewalk in front of her Queens home in November 2021. She passed away after a three-month battle (Mays, Rubinstein, and Ashford 2022). From March 2020 to December 2021, the Stop AAPI Hate coalition received 10,905 reports of hate incidents against Asian Americans and Pacific Islanders nationwide.[7] Of the total, 7.6 percent were reported by elders (aged sixty and up) or others on their behalf, and 43.1 percent of elderly victims identified themselves as Chinese (Jeung et al. 2022). Owing to technological, linguistic, and cultural barriers, Asian American elders are highly underreported victims. "Anti-Asian hate and violence instilled a sense of fear and anxiety, especially among Asian American older adults in dense, urban areas" (Jeung et al. 2022, 3). The increasing racism and hate crimes targeting Asian American elders with physical violence and the risk of COVID shadowed the everyday lives of elderly Chinese immigrant communities around the country. Therefore, "safety" was a word that was frequently mentioned in the daily conversations of elders at the center as well.

While students and Teacher Lu practiced the dance together, Grandma Qin raised her right hand and said to the class loudly, "Teacher Lu, it is almost three p.m. Class should end." Teacher Lu stopped his movement, then responded with his sense of humor: "Will it rain today?" Grandma Qin has a habit of checking the weather forecast daily and reminding others at the center to go home earlier if it rains. Since the surge in racial and hate incidents targeted at Asian American elders, particularly those of Chinese descent, elders have been concerned with their safety. Whether it rained or not, Grandma Qin insisted on leaving the center at three p.m. Rather than aggravating people's concerns about safety, Teacher Lu often said in a humorous tone, "Qin says it will rain today," to end the class and informed his students to go home. When saying good-bye to me, Grandma Qin talked to me in a serious tone: "I am very safe. I do not take the subway. The bus goes from a stop near my home directly to the center. You need to be cautious when taking the subway." Grandma Qin lives alone in midtown, while her daughter lives in California and her son lives in Flushing. Although Grandma Qin does not live with her son and his family, her son visits her regularly. She told me that she stayed at home and did not go anywhere during the lockdown period. "When I need something, my son will buy it for me and come to visit me. He drives, or

I will not let him visit me if he takes the subway." Although the subway is considered a dangerous site where racist and hate incidents are likely to happen more generally, elderly Chinese immigrants' concerns and anxiety about safety reflect that they live in a world where racism, xenophobia, and violence are exercised systemically on certain individuals.

Although elders at the center worry about the safety issue, most of my older interlocutors barely used the word "racism" in our conversations. When I asked Grandma Yi whether she had encountered any racial and hate incidents on the subway, she responded, "I have not encountered any discrimination. One time, a high school student bumped into my shoulder on the subway. He was naughty. I asked, 'Why?' Then he left." From Grandma Yi's description, it is difficult to grasp the holistic picture and affirm whether or not it is a racial and hate incident. Living in Harlem, Grandpa Yang uses the subway as his primary transportation every day. One day, he got robbed on his way to the senior center in lower Manhattan. After that incident, he was scared to walk on the street and take the subway. When I mentioned that I had not seen Grandpa Yang for a while, Grandma Qin told me, "He has not come to the center because he was robbed and scared of taking the subway. One day he took the subway to see the doctor. Suddenly a group of tall people sat and stood surrounding him. He sent us a voice message in our WeChat group: 'I am so scared.' Then he got off the subway and walked to the doctor's office." After hearing about what Grandpa Yang encountered, I am haunted by whether this is racial harassment or people's unintended and aggressive movement on the subway. However, in elderly Chinese immigrants' minds, the hostile environment casts a sense of fear, anxiety, and stress over every mundane thing or act in everyday life. These feelings caused by racial discrimination against Asian Americans, particularly Chinese immigrants, exacerbate existing chronic health conditions and intensify mental health problems that are already underreported under the influence of the model minority myth (Chen, Zhang, and Liu 2020). The language barrier and the ambiguity of racial incidents make it more difficult for elderly Chinese immigrants to identify and report them. Stop AAPI Hate also points out that "Asian American elders (older than 60 years of age) and Asian American seniors (older than 65 years of age) are underreported victims of hatred and violence" (Jeung et al. 2022, 5). The language barrier, the cultural differences, and the precarious economic and social status may not equip elderly Chinese immigrants with sufficient resources and discourses to articulate how racism systemically exercises violence on specific individuals. Simultaneously, the hostile environment leads to a generalized sense of anxiety and fear permeating the everyday lives of elderly Chinese immigrants. Instead of directly using "racism" in conversations, my older interlocutors use their everyday experiences of "fear" and their concerns about "safety" to express how systemic racism impacts their everyday lives during the pandemic.

Along with biopolitics and cultural values, Lamb (2019) highlights the role of socioeconomic inequality in shaping people's experiences and relationships to successful or healthy aging, when comparing elite and lower-income participants. In my ethnographic observations, I find that racism also plays a vital role in shaping how Chinese American elders position themselves in relation to successful aging. The exacerbated racism during the pandemic makes the environment more hostile and physically dangerous to elderly Chinese immigrants. In addition to fears and anxiety about their safety, racism implicitly impacts how they perceive successful aging and racial incidents targeted at them. When sharing their views of aging, elders at the center consciously or unconsciously underscored how they overcame the disadvantages of aging to make contributions to the community and society. Although elders' agency in embracing successful aging should not be neglected, the context of racism as the backdrop of people's view of successfully aging should be addressed as well. Grandma Yi emphasized that her motivation to volunteer at local senior centers was to make people, particularly elders of other ethnicities, see how Chinese immigrants can contribute to society. When I asked Teacher Lu why they rehearsed popular Broadway musicals, he said, "The director and I want elders at our center to be assimilated into the mainstream society. We decide to perform the dance of Broadway musicals instead of Chinese classical dances like fan or belt dance." For Grandma Yi and Teacher Lu, being assimilated into mainstream society becomes a signifier of successful aging.

To a certain degree, their interpretations and understandings of "successful aging" coincide with the model minority myth. The model minority myth constructs a stereotypic view that Asian Americans can become successful by overcoming disadvantages through working hard, leveraging strong family ties, emphasizing children's education, and maintaining political moderation, while they cannot completely be assimilated into US society because of their cultural distinctiveness (C. Kim 1999; Wu 2014). Although elders at the center find different ways to maintain their independence in their late life, the socioeconomic inequality and precarity they face are neglected in discourses of successful aging and the model minority myth. Older Chinese immigrants are more likely to live in poverty and crowded multigenerational homes, work as frontline essential workers, and fear being perceived as public charges for accepting public assistance for which they are eligible (Ma et al. 2021). Furthermore, the model minority myth works as a narrative for them to understand and interpret why random harassment and attacks happen to them. Some elders think that those who randomly attack people on the subway have mental health issues; some argue that they are angry at Chinese immigrants because the Chinese are diligent and hardworking. This narrative follows Claire Kim's argument that Asian Americans undergo a process of "relative valorization" in tandem with "civic ostracism" by dominant white stereotypes (1999, 107). Racism not only creates a hostile environment for elderly Chinese immigrants but also exercises its systemic violence by shaping people's perception of aging and their experiences in everyday life during the pandemic.

Visible Debility, Invisible Disability

Although elders I met at senior centers are able to live independently, many of them have some underlying health conditions associated with aging, such as hearing impairment, joint pain, arthritis, sleep problems, and other issues. Grandma Mo is a short and sturdy lady, whose short hair has turned completely white. Although she cannot read or write Chinese, Grandma Mo can communicate with others who speak Cantonese in her mother tongue, Taishanese. She is eighty-five years old and still enthusiastic about playing mahjong and volunteering at the center. When we first met, I could not understand Taishanese, so she introduced herself by showing me her volunteer name card. After I had not seen her at the center for two weeks, one day Grandma Mo slowly walked into the center with her cane in her right hand and the support of her friend Grandma Qin. I greeted her and asked what happened to her leg and whether everything was okay. Grandma Mo told Grandma Qin to translate her words to me. She said, "My leg is *buhao* [not good]." Among my older interlocutors, it is common for them to use "I am old" or "a certain part of my body is *buhao* or *buxing* [not good or not working]" to describe their debility caused by aging, implying the transition of their physical bodies without highlighting any loss of certain abilities.

Hearing impairment is another common debility but was barely mentioned among elders at the center. After Grandpa Yang learned that I speak Minnanhua, every time I met him, he was always happy to talk to me. Grandpa Yang can speak Cantonese, Mandarin, Minnanhua, and a little English. He always had one of his in-ear earbud headphones in his right ear. Although Grandpa Yang could communicate with me in either Mandarin or Minnanhua, I was surprised that he seemed not to fully understand my questions. Instead of being interviewed by me, he became the one leading our conversations. When I asked him about his pandemic life, he talked about his proficiency in different languages and how he learned them. When I asked him about the subway safety issue, he showed me his contact information on a small piece of paper in his wallet. We often started our conversation with my question, then jumped from how he came to the US to his favorite TV show. The last time I saw him was the first time that I did not see him wearing his earbud, but rather, he was wearing a hearing aid. He had never mentioned his hearing difficulties in our conversations before. Every time Grandpa Yang led our conversation in a new direction, I thought my wearing a mask made it difficult for him to hear me. Now I understand that the mask was not the only problem. He tried to guess what I was talking about from fragments he heard and the conversational context. Leading the conversation is his way of avoiding admitting that he has a hearing impairment.

Many elders at the center experience limited mobility, hearing impairment, and other kinds of debilities, but few of them mention them at all. Recognizing the debility of the aging body goes against the idea of successful aging that highlights independence, the maintenance of health, the prevention of diseases, and permanent personhood. Debility, impairment, or disability are implicitly categorized as "failure" in the discourse of successful aging (Minkler and Fadem 2002; Lamb 2014; Rudman 2015). The conceptualization of successful aging emerges from and consolidates ageism and ableism by creating the illusion of success and stigmatizing the loss of abilities. On the other hand, elders' identifying themselves as old allows them to account for becoming physically weak in their late life. Therefore, debility or impairment as the inevitable consequence of aging is acceptable by most of my interlocutors, but disability is rarely mentioned by them. Comparing debility with disability, Julie Livingston argues that debility refers to "functional differences or losses in the body," while disability is "a biosocial identity" that is grounded in the biological body and social relationships (2005, 7). Although disability and aging are likely to be conflated in people's late life, the position of disability outside of the standard view of the life course and people's reluctance to cross the boundary of identities together create a paradox of aging and disability, excluding disability from the process of aging (Grenier, Griffin, and McGarth 2020). Without taking disability into account over the life course, elders rarely identify themselves as persons with disabilities or form social relationships based on the identity of being disabled.

In addition to the separation of disabilities from the aging process, elderly Chinese immigrants' perception of aging is also influenced by the stigmatization of disability in Chinese culture and the obfuscation of disability by the US model minority myth. Terms for disability in Chinese include *canfei* (handicapped), *canji* (disabled), or *canzhang* (persons with disabilities). Wanhong Zhang and Ding Peng (2018) argue that the transformation in terms for disability manifests evolving ideas of disability in the human rights discourse of China. From these three official Chinese definitions of disability, we can see how a negative view of disability in the early twentieth century gradually shifted into advocacy for an inclusive and equal environment for persons with disabilities in the 1980s (Zhang and Ding 2018). Although this transformation is manifested in legislative and administrative policies, social attitudes, and media visibility in China, it has been slow to change the entrenched stigmatization of disability in Chinese culture (Campbell and Uren 2011). The elders at the center were born before 1960, and their perceptions and understandings of disability are likely to have been shaped by the concept of *canfei* (handicapped), which views persons with disabilities as the embodiment of bad karma, useless in society. Linda Chiang and Azar Hadadian (2007) discovered that this Chinese tradition of viewing children with disabilities as the embodiment of bad karma plays a significant role in shaping parents' perception of disabled children in Chinese and Chinese American families in the US as well. Therefore, the stigmatization of disability in Chinese traditional culture still influences how elderly Chinese immigrants view and use disability.

When Chinese people immigrate to the US, Chinese traditional culture is no longer the only factor that forms their view of aging and disabilities. Bridging feminist and disability studies, Rosemarie Garland-Thomson unsettles the limits of disability as identity studies in the US context, "defin[ing] disability as a vector of socially constructed identity and a form of embodiment that interacts with both the material and the social environment" (2005, 1559; see also Garland Thomson 2002). Reimagining disability in feminist, queer, and race studies, Sami Schalk and Jina Kim propose disability as "a relationship to power rather than a legible identity to which one can lay claim" (2020, 38). From this perspective, disability not only becomes a powerful analytical tool to interrogate the power system that channels dominance through normalcy and ability but also provides people with an entry point to examine the entanglement of systemic dominance and structural violence through class, gender, and race.

After two ministrokes in September 2015, scholar Yoonmee Chang was left with nerve damage in her left leg and foot, resulting in clumsy walking. When Chang was having a drink at a restaurant, the restaurant manager thought she was drunk and confiscated her drink. "Race might or might not have been a factor in the restaurant manager's misreading of my body, but if it were, it would not have helped her recognize that I was disabled," Chang says (2018, 243). When constructing the US model minority myth, Asian American bodily disability is made invisible. Obfuscating disability in the body of Asian Americans is also the product and progenitor of the model minority myth (Chang 2018), which intervenes in the conceptualization of successful aging by creating narratives of how elderly Chinese immigrants "overcome" aging by preventing disease through exercise and keeping themselves productive for society by volunteering. The obfuscation of disability marginalizes and neglects the fact of the aging body.

People's perception of aging melds the cultural conceptualization of successful aging with individual life experiences, Chinese traditional values of Confucianism, and the overlapping systems of power during the process of immigration and aging. As anthropologist Clifford Geertz writes, "man is an animal suspended in webs of significance he himself has spun" (1973, 5). Individuals exercise their agency in consolidating, propagating, adapting, and even challenging the webs of significance and relationships of power in which they are embedded. As I socialized with elders at the center and heard them recount their stories, it was difficult to ignore their agency and voices in positioning themselves in webs of social relationships.

Teacher Lu always arrived at the senior center with a suitcase (Li 2022). At first, I thought perhaps he would travel after the class. However, he carried his suitcase every time I met him. I started becoming curious about what was in his suitcase and why he always carried it. Carrying a suitcase to navigate in New York City for an elder with a knee issue is not easy. One day, I left the center with Teacher Lu, and I offered assistance in lifting his suitcase up the stairs. "No, no, no, you don't need to help me," Teacher Lu repeated and quickly lifted the suitcase. "It is empty. It is light." I was surprised to see him lifting the suitcase effortlessly. "This is my cane. It is easier for me to walk and stand stably with four wheels." Teacher Lu gave me an amicable smile. This reminds me of the Swany Bag created by Etsuo Miyoshi and introduced on the Japanese market in 1995. Etsuo Miyoshi not only suffers mobility disability caused by polio but also experiences alienation and the lack of visibility of disability in Japanese culture (Guffey 2020). The Swany Bag is designed to offer users support, enabling them to lean on it; it functions as a kind of rolling cane. Its design also implies fears of marginalization and the stigmatized perception of disability in Japanese culture (Guffey 2020). Under the social pressure of hiding people's disabilities in Japan, the Swany Bag offers people with disabilities a comfortable choice. Although I am not sure whether Teacher Lu was inspired by Etsuo Miyoshi's story and the Swany Bag, I could feel that he was comfortable and confident with the support of his small and modern suitcase. Teacher Lu had also worked as a flight attendant before his retirement. I believe that these suitcases were important companions in his work life, and they continued to accompany him. When I explained to Teacher Lu why I wanted to use the concept of disability to describe his limited mobility, he responded, "I am not scared [of being identified as disabled]. I am best at turning negative feelings into positive energy. I can also put what I purchase in this suitcase. I have many canes, but I think the suitcase is better." Later, he sent me a photo of his other suitcase decorated with a Chinese dragon sticker, texting, "Beautify my life. I am a traveler carrying a suitcase in my life journey."

Creating Community

I still remember the first time I attended the dance class at the center. All of a sudden, an abdominal cramp hit me hard, unexpectedly hard. My face turned pale, and the sweat ran down like raindrops. I was sitting there, burying my face in my arms and regretting that I had forgotten to carry the painkiller with me. Grandma Mo noticed that I was not doing well. She gave me her tiger balm and went to find others to help. After learning I had menstrual pain, Grandma Mo gave me sweet cookies. In Chinese home remedies, eating something sweet eases menstrual pain. Grandma Deng took a moxa stick out of her bag and taught me to do moxibustion, a healing practice in Chinese medicine. They also brought me a cup of hot water and patiently waited for me to recover from the cramps. The pain eased, the cramps ebbed, and I felt myself again. Every time I recall my first appearance at the center, I cannot stop thinking that I am the one who was cared for at the center. Facing the pandemic and the exacerbated racism, they were vulnerable, fragile, and weak. However, this is not the holistic picture. They were caring for each other, their family, and others who needed help. They were coping with the pandemic and structural violence worsened by COVID in their diverse, vigorous, and resilient ways under the influence of Chinese cultural values and the US context. The stereotypes of ageism, ableism, and racism behind the conceptualization of successful aging all require critical interrogation. However, orienting to center elders' voices enables us to understand what they experience and what they need, inspiring us to imagine a future that is more inclusive, open, and accessible to aging people.

NOTES

1 *Qilao* generally refers to elders who are sixty years old and older. It also indicates respectable elders.
2 Minnanhua is the main dialect of Southern Fujian and has spread to other areas, such as Taiwan, Eastern Guangdong, Hainan, and Southern Zhejiang. "Ai pin cai hui ying" (Success comes with your hard work) is a well-known song for Chinese, even if Minnanhua is not the mother tongue for most people.

3 The COVID-19 public health emergency declaration ended on May 11, 2023. Wearing a mask is no longer mandatory at senior centers, although it is always welcome. However, many elders still wear a mask at Rui An Senior Center to protect themselves from getting COVID.
4 Grandma (*nai nai*) and grandpa (*ye ye*), followed by the last name, can be used as the honorific with which young people generally address the elderly respectfully.
5 The PINE Study uses the community-based participatory research approach to study the general health and quality of life of Chinese elders in the Greater Chicago area in 2014.
6 The Qingming Festival is a traditional Chinese festival in which people sweep tombs and commemorate their ancestors.
7 "AAPI" stands for "Asian Americans and Pacific Islanders." The Stop AAPI Hate coalition is a nonprofit organization committed to ending racism and discrimination against Asian Americans and Pacific Islanders.

REFERENCES

Appel, Deirdre. 2020. "Keeping New York City Senior Citizens Fed during COVID-19." Hunter College New York City Food Policy Center, March 25, 2020. www.nycfoodpolicy.org.

Campbell, Anne, and Marie Uren. 2011. "The Invisibles . . . Disability in China in the 21st Century." *International Journal of Special Education* 26 (1): 12–24.

Chang, Yoonmee. 2018. "Asian Americans, Disability, and the Model Minority Myth." In *Flashpoints for Asian American Studies*, edited by Cathy J. Schlund-Vials, 241–53. New York: Fordham University Press.

Chen, Justin A., Emily Zhang, and Cindy H. Liu. 2020. "Potential Impact of COVID-19-Related Racial Discrimination on the Health of Asian Americans." *American Journal of Public Health* 10 (11): 1624–27. https://doi.org/10.2105/AJPH.2020.305858.

Chiang, Linda H., and Azar Hadadian. 2007. "Chinese and Chinese-American Families of Children with Disabilities." *International Journal of Special Education* 22 (2): 19–23.

Confucius. 1998. *The Analects of Confucius: A Philosophical Translation*. Translated by Roger T. Ames and Henry Rosemont. New York: Ballantine.

Dong, Xinqi. 2014. "Addressing Health and Well-Being of U.S. Chinese Older Adults through Community-Based Participatory Research: Introduction to the PINE Study." *Journals of Gerontology: Series A* 69 (S2): S1–S6. https://doi.org/10.1093/gerona/glu112.

Dong, XinQi, Esther Wong, Melissa A. Simon. 2014. "Study Design and Implementation of the PINE Study." *Journal of Aging and Health* 26 (7): 1085–99. https://doi.org/10.1177/0898264314526620.

Elman, Alyssa, Risa Breckman, Sunday Clark, Elaine Gottesman, Lisa Rachmuth, Margaret Reiff, Jean Callahan, et al. 2020. "Effects of the COVID-19 Outbreak on Elder Mistreatment and Response in New York City: Initial Lessons." *Journal of Applied Gerontology* 39 (7): 690–99. https://doi.org/10.1177/0733464820924853.

Garland-Thomson, Rosemarie. 2002. "Integrating Disability, Transforming Feminist Theory." *NWSA Journal* 14 (3): 1–32. www.jstor.org/stable/4316922.

———. 2005. "Feminist Disability Studies." *Signs: Journal of Women in Culture and Society*. 30 (2): 1557–87. https://doi.org/10.1086/423352.

Geertz, Clifford. 1973. *The Interpretation of Cultures*. New York: Basic Books.

Grenier, Amanda, Meridith Griffin, and Collen McGrath. 2020. "Aging and Disability: The Paradoxical Positions of the Chronological Life Course." In *The Aging-Disability Nexus*, edited by Katie Aubrecht, Christine Kelly, and Carla Rice, 21–34. Vancouver: UBC Press.

Guffey, Elizabeth. 2020. "Designing the Japanese Walking Bag." In *Making Disability Modern: Design Histories*, edited by Bess Williamson and Elizabeth E. Guffey, 159–76. London: Bloomsbury Visual Arts.

Han, S. Duke, and Laura Mosqueda. 2020. "Elder Abuse in the COVID-19 Era." *Journal of the American Geriatrics Society* 68 (7): 1386–87. https://doi.org/10.1111/jgs.16496.

Hum, Tarry. 2014. "How Eighth Avenue Became Chinese." *The Margins*, Asian American Writers' Workshop, September 19, 2014. https://aaww.org.

Ikels, Charlotte, ed. 2004. *Filial Piety: Practice and Discourses in Contemporary East Asia*. Stanford, CA: Stanford University Press.

Jeung, Russell, Aggie J. Yellow Horse, Theresa Chen, Anne Saw, Boaz Tang, Alison Lo, Mika Ro, et al. 2022. "Anti-Asian Hate, Social Isolation, and Mental Health among Asian American Elders during COVID-19." Stop AAPI Hate, March 31, 2022. https://stopaapihate.org.

Kaufman, Sharon R. 1986. *The Ageless Self: Sources of Meaning in Late Life*. Madison: University of Wisconsin Press.

Kelly, Mary Louise. 2022. "The Life of Yao Pan Ma, Who Died of an Attack, Prosecutors Say was Racially Motivated." *NPR*, January 12, 2022. www.npr.org.

Kim, Claire Jean. 1999. "The Racial Triangulation of Asian Americans." *Politics & Society* 27 (1): 105–38. https://doi.org/10.1177/0032329299027001005.

Kim, Jeung Hyun, and Merril Silverstein. 2020. "Are Filial Piety and Ethnic Community Engagement Associated with Psychological Wellbeing among Older Chinese American Immigrants? A Cultural Resource Perspective." *Research on Aging* 43 (2): 63–73. https://doi.org/10.1177/0164027520937477.

Kim, Michelle Hyun. 2020. "Out on the Frontlines: This Queer Couple Is Feeding NYC's Chinese Elders with a Loving Touch." *Them*, May 8, 2020. www.them.us.

Lamb, Sarah. 2014. "Permanent Personhood or Meaningful Decline? Toward a Critical Anthropology of Successful Aging." *Journal of Aging Studies* 29:41–52. https://doi.org/10.1016/j.jaging.2013.12.006.

———. 2019. "On Being (Not) Old: Agency, Self-Care, and Life-Course Aspirations in the United States." *Medical Anthropology Quarterly* 33 (2): 263–81. https://doi.org/10.1111/maq.12498.

———. 2020. "On Vulnerability, Resilience, and Age: Older Americans Reflect on the Pandemic." *Anthropology & Aging* 41 (2): 177–86. https://doi.org/10.5195/aa.2020.317.

Lan, Pei-Chia. 2002. "Subcontracting Filial Piety: Elder Care in Ethnic Chinese Immigrant Families in California." *Journal of Family* 23 (7): 812–35. https://doi.org/10.1177/019251302236596.

Li, Shuting. 2022. "Traveling with a Suitcase: Creating Community during COVID in a Chinatown Senior Center." *Disability COVID Chronicles*, October 11, 2022. https://disabilitycovidchronicles.nyu.edu.

Livingston, Julie. 2005. *Debility and the Moral Imagination in Botswana*. Bloomington: Indiana University Press.

Ma, Kris Pui Kwan, Adrian Matias Bacong, Simona C. Kwon, Stella S. Yi, and Lan N. Đoàn. 2021. "The Impact of Structural Inequities on Older Asian Americans during COVID-19." *Frontiers in Public Health* 9. https://doi.org/10.3389/fpubh.2021.690014.

Mays, Jeffrey C., Dana Rubinstein, and Grace Ashford. 2022. "Asian Americans Grapple with Tide of Attacks: 'We Need Our Safety Back.'" *New York Times*, March 6, 2022. www.nytimes.com.

Minkler, Meredith, and Pamela Fadem. 2002. "'Successful Aging': A Disability Perspective." *Journal of Disability Policy Studies* 12 (4): 229–35. https://doi.org/10.1177/104420730201200402.

Rosemont, Henry, and Roger T. Ames. 2009. *The Chinese Classic of Family Reverence: A Philosophical Translation of the Xiaojing*. Honolulu: University of Hawai'i Press.

Rudman, Debbie Laliberte. 2015. "Embodying Positive Aging and Neoliberal Rationality: Talking about the Aging Body within Narratives of Retirement." *Journal of Aging Studies*, January 1, 2015. https://doi.org/10.1016/j.jaging.2015.03.005.

Schalk, Sami, and Jina B. Kim. 2020. "Integrating Race, Transforming Feminist Disability Studies." *Signs: Journal of Women in Culture & Society* 46 (1): 31–55. https://doi.org/10.1086/709213.

Tronto, Joan. 1993. *Moral Boundaries: A Political Argument for an Ethic of Care*. New York: Routledge.

Verbruggen, Christine, Britteny M. Howell, and Kaylee Simmons. 2020. "How We Talk about Aging during a Global Pandemic Matters: On Ageist Othering and Aging 'Others' Talking Back." *Anthropology & Aging* 41 (2): 230–45. https://doi.org/10.1177/104420730201200402.

Wu, Ellen D. 2014. *The Color of Success: Asian Americans and the Origins of the Model Minority*. Princeton, NJ: Princeton University Press.

Zhang, Wanhong, and Ding Peng. 2018. "从残废到残障：新时代中国残障事业话语的转变" [From *Canfei* to *Canzhang*: The Transformation in the Discourse of Disability in the China Disability Program in the New Era]. 人权 / *Human Rights* 3. https://doi.org/10.16696/j.cnki.11-4090/d.2018.03.008.

GLOSSARY OF CHINESE WORDS

Ai pin cai hui ying / 爱拼才会: Success comes with your hard work
Buhao / 不好: not good
Buxing / 不行: not good or not working
Canfei / 残废: handicapped

Canji / 残疾: disabled
Canzhang / 残障: persons with disabilities
Gan en / 感恩: gratefulness
Lao de lao, si de si / 老得老，死得死: getting old and dying
Liu shi er er shun, qi shi er cong xin suo yu, bu yu ju / 六十而耳顺,七十而知天命,不逾矩: From sixty, my ear was attuned; from seventy, I could give my heart and mind free rein without overstepping the boundaries
Qilao / 耆老: elders who are sixty years old and older
Xiao / 孝: filial piety

11

"We Want Cop-Free Communities"

Reflections on Anti-Asian Violences and Safety

MON MOHAPATRA, HEENA SHARMA, YVES TONG NGUYEN, AND RACHEL KUO

The start of the COVID-19 pandemic in 2020 marked highly visible incidents of racial violence against Asians and Asian Americans in the US, as well as the escalation of law enforcement responses to "stop Asian hate." The reductive logic of "Asian hate" has facilitated a carceral politics in which getting *tough on hate* is equated to *getting tough on crime* (Asian American Feminist Collective 2020, 2021; Chalermkraivuth and Sharma 2021). In several widely circulated public incidents, the people arrested have been unhoused, mentally unwell, and/or formerly incarcerated community members left without adequate support after release from violent institutions of prisons and asylums, including lack of access to safe housing or health-care resources.

In the wake of the devastating shootings at Asian massage parlors in Atlanta in July 2021, the Counterterrorism unit of the New York Police Department (NYPD), a unit with military-grade weapons that was established after 9/11, deployed "assets" to Asian communities "out of an abundance of caution." The NYPD announced adding Asian plainclothes undercover officers; notably it started disbanding plainclothes units during the summer 2020 uprisings, because these units often resulted in police fatally shooting community members (Hamid and Kuo 2022). By May 2021, the COVID-19 Hate Crimes Act had passed in the US Senate, almost unanimously, emphasizing the expansion of law enforcement through data collection, public reporting, training, and culturally competent public education campaigns. Back in 2009, the Shepard-Byrd Hate Crimes Prevention Act, which expanded hate crimes legislation to include categories of gender, sexuality, and disability, was attached to the further funding of US militarization, including war operations in Iraq and Afghanistan (Sylvia Rivera Law Project 2009; Reddy 2011). This "war against hate" at home builds on existing carceral systems and War on Terror infrastructures—where rooting out hate domestically justifies ongoing militarized policing and transnational warfare.

Cycles of violence continue to be perpetuated by policing and mass incarceration. We need responses that do not rely on systems of policing and punishment but rather on ways to reconceptualize care and expand our understanding of violence. Different vectors of state and racial violences bring to light adjacent and incommensurable experiences of violence. Jasbir Puar's (2017) framework of debility—the slow wearing down of people due to capitalism and state-sanctioned violence—helps us better understand anti-Asian violence beyond singular disabling acts of violence. When Puar formulated the "right to maim" in relation to the "right to kill" in 2017, she wrote of solidarities between Black Lives Matter and Palestine, from Ferguson to Gaza. In fall 2023 and into 2024, we continue to witness the "targeted debilitation" of Palestinians (Puar 2017), as well as targeted death, through the legitimization of state violence that deems some lives as livable and others as not, also furthering "make die and let die" politics (Hong 2015). For us as Asian Americans, how we understand racialized violence is deeply tied to brutal diasporic histories of colonization, military occupation, and war. State violence is disabling. Our reflections here on anti-Asian violence, where "hate" at home is sustained by both "stealthy" and overt violences of US militarism abroad, continue to shape our theories and practices of solidarity. We seek responses that address both exceptional and "slower" violences that expose people to multiple forms of precarity and vulnerability.

Through the pandemic, we have participated in and organized different projects, workshops, events, and conversations to build and grow a collective practice and material analysis of abolition at intersections with disability justice. This analysis includes deadly police responses to mental health crises; ending the criminalization of survival; language interpretation, access, and translation as a disability justice (DJ) issue; the necessity of decarceration and jails moratoriums for shared liberation; alternatives to policing, such as community-based infrastructures for mutual aid and care; and more. One such project that anchors us is the Sick of It! Project, a political education and community-building pen pal and prison zine project, in which Mon and Rachel are co-organizers with Merlin Sabal and in which Heena is a pen pal. Sick of It! builds solidarity across prison walls and political relationships on abolitionist and disability justice analysis by making the theory and vocabulary of DJ accessible to those who are inside.[1] Developed in the early stages of the COVID-19 pandemic, it marks an effort to show that carceral sites are themselves disabling and that what happens inside impacts the outside. Heena and Yves also organize with Survived and Punished New York (S&P NY), a collective working to end the criminalization of survival, particularly in incidents of domestic and sexual violence—projects include a quarterly newsletter, documenting testimonials during COVID-19 from people incarcerated in New York state prisons, and campaigns to grant clemency and commutation to free people from prisons and detention centers. Mon and Yves have also worked together on the campaign "Free Them All 4 Public Health," an effort that brings together decarceration efforts during the ongoing pandemic, organizing to defund and abolish the NYPD, and calls to close Rikers and stop investments in the city's proposed borough-based jails plan.

The following conversation on safety and state violence brings together reflections on organizing in New York City during the ongoing pandemic at the intersection of abolition, disability justice, and Asian American politics. New York City has a long history of displacement and liberal reform and co-optation of progressive demands, as well as a long history of rebellion and organizing to end the police and prison industrial complex. These reflections offer political frameworks and practices to intervene on the myths of state securitization and carceral logics as pathways to justice and safety. Mon, Heena, and Yves are abolitionist organizers currently based in New York City. Mon is a cocreator of 8 to Abolition and one of the original conveners of the National No New Jails Network. Heena has worked on various survivor-led campaigns, letter-writing projects, and mutual-aid collectives. Yves is an organizer with Red Canary Song, a collective of Asian and migrant sex workers that also organizes transnationally. Rachel is a coleader of the Asian American Feminist Collective. This roundtable started coming together in 2021 at a moment when many of us were tired, burned out, and exhausted. All of us have been part of different projects that have started, ended, paused, and transformed through the ongoing pandemic. Through disability

Figure 11.1. The cover of *Sick of It!*'s second issue features a bed in the middle that has flowers and leaves rising from it. (Image courtesy Mon Mohapatra)

justice frameworks of organizing that prioritize slowness and long-haul organizing (Piepzna-Samarasinha 2019), we locate the work of building toward abolition and shared liberation as ongoing slow and iterative work.

> Rachel: We all know each other from so many different spaces, and everyone is so involved in multiple things and wearing various hats.

Mon, we've worked on several projects together, including 8 to Abolition and Sick of It!, and you've contributed a lot of your creative and organizing practice to events and zines with the Asian American Feminist Collective. Can you share more about your abolitionist organizing during the pandemic and how that work intersects with disability justice?

Mon: I currently participate in various abolitionist fights, including jails moratorium and decarceration campaigns, and organize from values focusing on solidarity, Black power, caste annihilation, and internationalism. Prisons, jails, ICE [US Immigration and Customs Enforcement] detention, foster-care homes, psychiatric facilities, black sites, and so many other sites of social control, coercion, entrapment, and enslavement produce disability while maintaining and reifying a standard (often cis, white, thin) bodymind. As Talila A. Lewis (2020) has written, we cannot understand racism without ableism. What this means is that not only do systems of criminalization and militarization target disabled people, but they also traumatize and debilitate people who are forced into the system through physical, emotional, and mental abuse—and this is by design.

As a co-coordinator for the No New Jails Network, an abolitionist network of decarceration and anti-jail campaigns, I've seen several campaigns focus their efforts on challenging ableist and sanist reforms. These reforms push forward carceral expansion by co-opting the language of mental health care, treatment, and restoration. But as many activists have pointed out, a cage is a cage, and people can't get well in a cell. I wrote for *InQuest* (2022) that the construction of mental health jails or "trauma-informed" jails expanding incarceration via mental health justifications is not new, but this facade co-opts the language of modern-day disability justice and progressive movements.[2] Campaigns, collectives, and narratives resisting this have to elevate a Black and Indigenous disabled and mad perspective when they respond to such proposals.

Another example is the campaign to "Free Them All 4 Public Health" that occurred during the pandemic. This specifically highlighted that incarcerating people doesn't change that we exchange the same air and water, and in fact, health inside local jails impacts the health of people outside. Although the demand is fundamentally just "free them all," we organized to get people out on the basis that jails are breeding grounds for a virus and that those inside jails deserve health care (which they should receive out in the world). This was key to reducing the number of people incarcerated during the first years of the COVID-19 pandemic.

Various campaigns across the country and even the world, including at San Quentin State Prison in California, the Rikers Island jails in New York City, and Cook County Jail in Chicago, successfully organized for massive reductions in the numbers of people incarcerated in 2020. This was also helped by the massive uprising for Black liberation which occurred in the same year. Unsurprisingly, the backlash from correctional institutions was aggressive, and the numbers of people inside jails have skyrocketed since. In some cases, even more people are locked up in the local jail than were prior to 2020.

Rachel: You mentioned earlier that systemic abuse is "by design." In the past, in response to proposed borough-based jails expansion in New York City, you've written for *New Inquiry* (Mohapatra 2019) about how aesthetic and technological design approaches to new jails are costly and appealing ways to brand prison reform and make profit off of caging people. For example, you highlight how the Brooklyn jails plan builds on visions of jails as "justice hubs," which you say expands carceral urban geographies under the guise of providing social services. Mock-ups of the plan included community and retail spaces and an art gallery. In these ways, you show how architects and city planners see the problem of mass incarceration as something that can be fixed through better jail design.

The notion of what you call "good design" for carceral expansion builds on the ways existing systems are designed to police, punish, displace, and exclude people considered "undesirable" to society—can you say a little bit more about these histories as they inform your political work?

Mon: In cities, design feeds and maintains the prison-industrial complex through gentrification and correlating displacement and criminalization of poor communities of color. Additionally, among the origins of this design in the US are settler-colonial concepts of knowledge, body, and medicine (seen, for example, in the ways in which wealthy settlers would travel to Hawaii and Indigenous lands in so-called Canada to "escape" COVID-19) and anti-Black eugenicist logics that have continued since chattel slavery (seen, for example, in the ways travel to predominantly Black countries was banned as the pandemic began).

    I interpret the intersection between abolition and disability justice as that they are one and the same. One cannot happen without the other. Disabled and mad folks need to be at the forefront of responding to capitalism and carceral ableism/sanism/humanism, and in turn, healing justice and abolitionist projects must prioritize access to all kinds as well as rest, care, and flexibility. The violent practice of incarceration can't be designed away by natural light and bigger windows.

Rachel: I appreciate how you point us to thinking about a multitude of ways that we can rest and care for each other and build that into organizing practices. I've been thinking about how a lot of our co-organizing has been done virtually over Zoom and a lot of our practices of care and intimacy happen in the midst of isolation and distance. When Merlin invited us both (Mon and me) to collaborate on Sick of It!, it was from their home, from their bed, and similarly, Merlin and I created the *Care in the Time of Coronavirus* zine together during the earlier parts of the pandemic remotely. They've spoken a lot about how disability justice movements have shown us that revolutionary work can be done from anywhere and can look a lot of different ways (e.g., Sabal 2020).

    Yves and Heena, you've been part of different projects at this intersection of care and access, including both mutual-aid efforts through the COVID-19 pandemic, such as the Elmhurst Hospital workers and the Disability Justice Mutual Aid Fund, and the work of preexisting organizations that sprang into action as crisis struck, like Red Canary Song and Survived & Punished New York. Can you share a little bit more about those projects?

Yves: I was already organizing with Survived & Punished New York and Red Canary Song prior to the start of the COVID-19 pandemic. When the pandemic started in March of 2020, both of those formations started shifting and collaborating with other groups in new ways to address the pandemic's impact on our communities, and we changed the way we organized internally to address the ongoing pandemic.

At the beginning of the pandemic, I joined an informal formation called Free Them All 4 Public Health, which was a group made up of PIC [prison-industrial complex] abolitionists across New York and New Jersey with a demand to free all incarcerated people specifically as a necessity to public health. We understood not only that the spread of COVID would be deadly and uncontrollable in the conditions of prisons, care facilities, nursing homes, mental health facilities, and other packed communal spaces, but also that these institutions have always been a public health crisis, places where people are abused, become more disabled, and are killed. Red Canary Song shifted to primarily providing mutual aid and groceries drops because going to massage businesses to do outreach was risky, and massage workers and sex workers needed even more monetary support.[3]

Heena: I'm always in my bed and taking calls from my bed. Back when the pandemic was starting, I was living in Staten Island by myself, and I felt very cut off. It was hard to connect with people in the city, and I was trying to be cognizant of my position—physically, geographically, and socially. Even though I was living in Staten Island, I'm from New York and went to high school and college here and was in many different spaces around the boroughs. I had strong connections to the community in Queens and friends in Elmhurst and Jackson Heights close to Elmhurst Hospital, one of the peak focal points of the pandemic in New York. I had friends in the area doing intense mutual-aid support to keep their neighbors alive. A friend from high school was thinking about what to do for workers at the hospital who were swamped. I shared her ask and connected her with people in the Street Vendors Project to bring food and volunteers with cars to deliver PPE [personal protective equipment]. We were connecting local vendors, people who were getting sick and couldn't work, and supporting hospital workers in the community.

Then, I got COVID for two months. While I was recovering, that's when the uprising was happening. This was the first time I was noticing how disability was showing up for me. I can't show up at physical actions like I used to. I've had Long COVID since the beginning. It was forcing me to reconcile learning about disability justice and healing justice and organizing in ways that doesn't leave people behind with the ingrained feeling in my brain of not being able to show up and organize the ways I used to. I started thinking about other ways to show up, such as jail support and coordinating the back-end work.

Rachel: That back-end work in movement building is so important and often invisibilized. We often just think about social movements through the big rallies and actions but not the internal processes or the material labor that sustains political organizing.

Heena: I was thinking about how much connecting folks is so valuable. It's hard to consider that these different skills and knowledge bases are important and often linked to ableism. With the Elmhurst Hospital project, I was recognizing that not everyone is the right person to do something. Just because I am excited about or care about something, it doesn't mean I'm the right person to do it. As a South Asian person during the uprisings, I've reflected a lot about anti-Blackness in my communities. What does it mean to be visible in that moment? It's pushed me to think about other ways of organizing in the back end and doing coordination. I don't want to be up in the front and couldn't even if I did, so I thought about how people need money. Fundraising and distributing money without strings attached was powerful. I learned about different ways of showing up, and that's all part of organizing. It's messing up and experimenting. It's about things that don't feel cool, but people have to do it.

The Disability Justice Mutual Aid fund began as a vision of K (Toyin) Agbebiyi, a fellow organizer from S&P NY, who wanted to fundraise so that Black disabled organizers could participate in the uprisings, whether that was for supplies or paying for therapy. I saw a request on K's Twitter about needing help with spreadsheets and thought, "Hey I can do that." The fund was intended to be short-term, and so it was helpful to learn when to end a mutual aid project. It was also a lesson for me about following what the need is rather than a preconceived notion of what someone else's need is.

I'm also building my practice of letter writing. It's been grounding in many ways, and there's something important about a one-on-one relationship. It helps me think about the pace and speed of which things move, like how relationships take time and trust. Letter writing is a different entry point to abolition too, believing that people shouldn't be cut off from human contact. It breaks down ideological walls of who is inside prison and how they should be treated.

Rachel: The aspect of political growth and learning through political practice is something that really resonates, and I think also when we do political work and organizing, we are also changing and transforming our relationships not only with each other but how we see our own relationship to both different systems of violence and possibilities for liberation. Can you say a little bit more about what you've learned in these organizing practices?

Heena: While I was learning about community care and slowing down and applying these ideas in practice to my friends, I wasn't thinking of myself as disabled. It was a big internalized ableism thing and a thing around not feeling disabled enough to call it that. I've had chronic mental health traumas for at least fifteen years, but I kept thinking that it wasn't a disability. While I was learning about all these things and it helped me think about how I connect with other people, I wasn't sure about how to embody that for myself. I had to reconcile that. I'm Indian, and there's community stigmas around mental health, sexual violence, and survivorship that are connected to me not being able to see myself as disabled. There's a notion that we can't afford to be disabled.

Rachel: I feel that a lot too as someone who is Taiwanese. I think growing up and still now, there's a lot of shame and silence that's intergenerational that seeps into both your brain and body. It feels like something you have to bear alone, endure, or overcome. The conversation about mental health, disability, and survivorship isn't always readily available in Asian American communities. It wasn't until my early twenties, when I encountered writing by folks like Leah Lakshmi Piepzna-Samarasinha, Mia Mingus, Alice Wong, and Ching-in Chen, that this started to click for me. Can you speak a little bit more to what you were saying about not being able to afford to be disabled in your community context?

Heena: At a very young age, I was aware of domestic violence in my family and knowing about how my mother and other women in my family survived, who experienced sexual violence. I was born in India, and my family is upper caste, and they came to the states shortly after I was born. It's interesting to think about caste and class, because we didn't have that much money. My dad worked multiple jobs. My mom worked. My grandparents came to take care of me and my sister, and my grandma was also a domestic worker for another South Asian family. These were the economic spaces we were inhabiting, but the upper-caste thing was still there. I mention that because Brahmanical patriarchy is not only practiced against people who are lower caste but also within the same community. It's analogous to how white supremacy is upheld by white women who are also oppressed under its patriarchy yet still vested in its survival.

In my own family, I saw these cycles of violence, but retroactively thinking about it, it was so ingrained that this was a normal thing and you're not supposed to talk about it with people outside the family. My dad and grandfather would call the cops on my mom when she had a breakdown. She experienced psych incarceration when I was a child. I wasn't thinking about this history informing my interest in abolition until recently. There was so much shame that was there, that people weren't supposed to know that my mom had these things. If I was experiencing trauma and depression things, when I was experiencing sexual violence myself, people were saying I shouldn't turn into my mother in needing psychological help.

As I got older, I was interested in organizing around sexual violence and its different intersections—it took me longer to link this to disability. To think about its impact on someone's body and mind, that was far from my thoughts. It's all been part of my healing journey to undo hierarchies of stigmatization. Even now, I feel like I'll be in disability justice spaces, and there are hardly any Asians. It's noticeable and palpable to me.

Rachel: Okay, I want to talk more about this relationship between violence and disability justice that you're pointing out, especially around healing, care, and safety in Asian American communities. We're in a moment when our communities have been grieving and surviving trauma and violence in very public and collective ways. This includes mourning loved ones, having depression and anxiety, and all the while having very different relationships to and experiences of violence. There's a visibility and invisibility of different kinds of violence happening in this moment.

The idea of solidarity has been one that has come up a lot throughout the pandemic—particularly solidarities within and across communities of color, given both highly visible incidents of police murder of Black people and also attacks on Asian people in public spaces. After the 2020 uprisings, we've observed the uses of anti-Asian violence to justify the need for more police and carceral punishment, like the NYPD Hate Crimes Task Force and later the COVID-19 Hate Crimes Act, as the ways to take racism against our communities seriously. Within Asian American communities, even among people and organizations who were very vocally in support of Black liberation movements, there seems to be an undercurrent that misunderstands abolition as only about Asians being in solidarity with Black communities. This limits us to frames that we are against police at the cost of what is seen as "our own" issues, rather than, say, seeing that policing is a form of state violence that is also devastating to Asian communities.

The dominant "stop Asian hate" discourse is insidious both because of the carceral implications and also because it's one of the primary entry points in which people understand "solidarity" with Asian American communities. What have you witnessed or experienced about anti-Asian violence during the pandemic, and how does abolition and disability justice as frameworks help us rethink these spectacles of violence beyond the hate frame?

Yves: I don't think that anti-Asian violence is necessarily more or different—maybe just bolder. I've often said this, but I think Asian people who are more marginalized and more criminalized have been experiencing these types of violence, particularly from the state, forever. It's just that other, more privileged Asian people didn't care, because it didn't apply to them, which is why I find the spectacle of it all really detestable. I think the attention is unprecedented, not the violence. I'm not only a sex worker who is criminalized for my labor and for how I survive under capitalism, but I'm also Vietnamese and grew up having a criminalized family who are drug users and did criminalized labor. I grew up with people who went to prison, and I am currently in community with people who are criminalized and stigmatized.

Figure 11.2. An ad hoc memorial to Christina Yuna Lee, whose murder in February 2022 was reported as part of both a rising tide of anti-Asian violence in New York City and the gendered violence that Asian women face. While many people responded to the violence with calls for increased policing against unhoused people, Lee's family directed proceeds from a GoFundMe campaign to a variety of organizations that Lee believed in, including SafeWalks, a mutual-aid organization accompanying Asian American seniors to and from their homes and transit. (Photo: Salonee Bhaman)

The hate frame around anti-Asian violence just doesn't get to the roots of it, which as I've said, abolition and disability justice can never be untangled and is meant to look at violence and oppression at the roots. The hate frame individualizes the violence of racism instead of challenging broader cultures and structures that produce individuals who are racist. So many more privileged Asian people are complicit in those cultures and structures, so they feel at home calling the sea of highly publicized anti-Asian attacks during the pandemic "hate crimes" and asking the police to do something about it. Meanwhile, the police are attacking other Asian people just out of their purview and always have been.

Mon: Being from an Indian caste oppressor background, I didn't have the same experience that many people, especially East Asian folks and Muslim folks, had at the beginning of the pandemic. I saw the ways in which "Coronajihad" spread across the internet, marginalizing South Asian Muslim communities across the world (Soundararajan et al 2020). I also saw, more closely, in New York City and elsewhere in the US, the ways Asian people were targeted due to racist and uninformed assumptions about the origins of COVID-19.

Simultaneously, Asian Americans and Asian American organizations also occasionally exceptionalized anti-Asian violence emerging at that moment and distinguished it from anti-Black and Islamophobic narratives which dominated during other crises. For me, white-supremacist panic which opportunistically blamed Asian people for bringing the virus to the US was tied up with the ways in which Black, Indigenous, queer, trans, and undocumented communities were abandoned by public health agencies and their eugenicist response to the pandemic. The widespread abandonment of disabled, immunocompromised, and poor people has been rooted in the same racist logic that has driven "yellow peril." I don't mean to reduce all of these unique and specific modes of violence into one thing, especially considering that different identities hold greater risk under the current racial capitalist carceral state. But, what I do mean is that these kinds of othering, where one community is considered anathema while another does not receive resources, find shared motivations in white supremacy, which is in turn strengthened by these exclusions.

For a significant part of the ongoing pandemic, "hate" has been the way to talk about anti-Asian violence, but as many others—particularly abolitionists like Kay Whitlock (Whitlock and Bronski 2016)—have noted, "hate" supposes a one-way kind of violence: hate directed at Asians; that doesn't capture the ways in which Asians both participate in hatred nor the ways in which the state has co-opted hate as a concept in order to entrench hate-crimes policing. As recently as August 2022, New York City directed even more funding to the police to fight so-called hate crimes (Sterling 2022). Yet, not only do the police traffic in what we might call "hate" when they engage in arresting, prosecuting, and caging people, but focusing on hate limits our ability to see all the structures empowering people to engage in violent actions against marginalized people.

Yves: Massage workers and sex workers were completely out of work at the beginning of the pandemic, because of both very real risks and stigma. And disability has always intersected with criminalization, incarceration, and sex work. Many people do sex work because they are disabled, including myself, and many people are incarcerated and criminalized for being mentally ill and disabled. I don't think you can separate criminalization and disability at all. Historically, people, especially Black folks, have been pathologized and demonized in a multitude of ways to justify subjugation. There really is no abolition without understanding disability and including disability justice within your framework. Incarceration and disability clearly show two instances when people's rights can be stripped away and infringed upon immediately.

Rules, regulations, laws, and governance are merely justifications for violence, and then the data stemming from the enforcement of those is used as further justification. When we say these systems are designed to police, punish, displace, and exclude undesirable people, I think it's helpful to ground that in examples, even though there are so many, because people take laws and rules as common sense. I already brought up how Black people in particular are not a group of people who are allowed to be mentally ill and disabled without punishment, and frankly, whether or not they actually are or would ever identify as being disabled, there's a long history of Black people being pathologized anyway.

Heena: I was seeing the stigma of how people were talking about CO-VID and it being an "Asian virus." I was working at a youth nonprofit in the city, and the students and staff I worked with would make offhand comments. When the shooting of massage-parlor workers happened, I had to do some internal organizing within my workplace, because I was really appalled. It was a youth nonprofit about social justice, but they hadn't made any kind of statement internally or to the public about the streak of anti-Asian violence that was occurring.

For me and so many people, it's care networks, resources, political education, support for survivors from their intracommunity that will actually bring us what we need. But, for some other people, it's more like we want to be part of a national report of how many people are hurt. There's a desire of visibility for the righteous anger of our communities being harmed, but we don't want the messy parts of our community—people who are detained, who are incarcerated, people just trying to survive—to be seen. There's anti-Blackness inherent in not caring for those people too. It's also frustrating to see how a lot of privileged folks who were not experiencing the brunt of who bears violence—sex workers, undocumented folks, Southeast Asian people, refugees—so many things were missing from the narrative when people are saying, "We're all the same. We're being attacked." It's also a deflection from violence people enact.

Yves: And, I also want to add—I brought up the stigma towards Asian and migrant massage workers and sex workers because both Asian migrants and sex workers have always been viewed as vectors for disease to be surveilled and criminalized. This isn't to say that everything is completely made up. Marginalized people often do break the law, but we have to understand that the law is targeted. We have to understand how people are colonized and oppressed and then further criminalized for daring to survive in whatever way they can. For example, many multiply marginalized people are poor, lack resources, have been dispossessed from their land, their homes, and their family, so they become houseless or do informal labor like sex work or drug selling. All of those are criminalized under the law directly, not even including all of the adjacent laws to those experiences, such as public nudity laws.

In Survived & Punished, we are often pushing back against narratives built against survivors of gender-based violence, especially survivors who are Black and Latine women, both cis and trans. As soon as you're not a perfect survivor, you are punished for surviving, and women of color are not ever going to be considered perfect survivors. In Red Canary Song, an example of these laws that seem broad but are deeply targeted is massage licensure. On its face, massage licensure seems to make sense, but the licensing test is only in English, making it completely inaccessible to people without fluency. Massage schools are also exorbitantly expensive. When someone practices massage without a license, that's a crime with a felony charge.... Who do we think is the target of law enforcement for practicing massage without a license? These histories inform every part of my political work because it's unpacking these false narratives. Once you unpack them, you see that a lot of the methods framed as being helpful, saving, or benefiting the people affected are actually nothing more than punishment.

Mon: The relationship [between the prison-industrial complex and anti-Asian violence] is one that can't be answered by thinking of "Asian" as a monolith. The experience of Southeast Asian folks in California or Indo Caribbean folks in New York in relationship to the PIC and other carceral systems is very different from the relationship of, for example, dominant-caste Indian Americans or Asians with wealthy and upwardly mobile backgrounds. This distinction is key to understanding the ways Asians are both complicit in and impacted by the anti-Black, capitalist, and cisheteropatriarchal systems of incarceration, criminalization, and policing. There are Asian sex workers and street vendors being regularly targeted by the police, as well as Asian police officers murdering people in grotesque acts of violence.

There are Asian communities advocating for more sophisticated, "improved" hate-crimes policing and surveillance, while there are simultaneously Asian-majority gangs and survivor organizations attempting to move away from their reliance on the PIC. There are communities who come from places that embrace the US empire, while others continue to fight for the sovereignty of their nations against the US.

Figure 11.3. A vigil in Washington Square Park commemorates the eight lives lost during a shooting at an Asian massage parlor in Atlanta on March 16, 2021. The vigil was hosted by Red Canary Song (RCS) and the Asian American Feminist Collective. The image displays three different art installations. The large installation is titled 韧 *Curtain Armor* and was conceptualized and art directed by Chong Gu and codirected by Yin Q. The portraits hanging on the curtains are titled *Eyes* and were completed by an anonymous massage worker. Behind the curtain are two massage tables, each laid out with food, incense, and offerings in the style of a traditional mourning altar. The food altar was created by Charlotte, a Korean RCS outreach member and former massage worker, and Lisa, a Chinese massage worker based in Flushing, while the funeral altar was created by Wu, another RCS core member and a New York City–based dominatrix. During the rally, organizers noted the ways that Asian massage workers and sex workers are often dehumanized within political and media discourse and drew attention to the fact that informal economies like unlicensed massage and transactional sex are often the only ways that some disabled people are able to make a living. (Photo: Salonee Bhaman)

For me, when thinking of anti-Asian violence, I think about what violence we mean and who perpetrates it. White supremacists who blame and attack Chinese Americans for COVID-19 are not so different from the white supremacists who patrol the ICE detention centers that detain and torture Pakistani immigrants, and this is just one example I can think of. There are existing legacies of Indigenous antisettler struggles and Black abolitionist liberation struggles, as well as legacies of Asian American solidarity and anti-imperialist resistance, that we can now learn from to better criticize the PIC as a nonsolution for the myriad challenges Asian communities are facing in the US and beyond.

Rachel: Thank you all so much for these reflections and provocations on how we keep our communities safe, how we care for one another, and how we imagine new political possibilities.

NOTES

1 Thank you to Merlin Sabal for guidance and support in this project and for being an incredible organizer of the Sick of It! Project and collaborator in the Asian American Feminist Collective zine *Care in the Time of Coronavirus*.
2 Examples of this include the new 350-bed women's jail in Travis County, Texas, in 2021; plans to build psychiatric units at Rikers in New York by 2027; and the mental health jail-expansion plan in Orange County, California, in 2016.
3 For more on the experiences of disabled sex workers during the pandemic, as part of an oral history conducted with Sinnamon Love of the BIPOC Adult Industry Collective for the NYU *Disability Covid Chronicles*, see Kornstein 2022.

REFERENCES

Asian American Feminist Collective. 2020. "We Want Cop-Free Communities: Against the Creation of an Asian Hate Crime Task Force by the NYPD." *Medium*, September 3, 2020. https://aafcollective.medium.com.
———. 2021. "Cop-Free Communities: An Asian American Feminist Teach-In." YouTube, May 4, 2021. www.youtube.com/watch?v=IYYCzRtygbk.
Chalermkraivuth, Chalay, and Heena Sharma. 2021. "Policing Won't Stop Anti-Asian Violence—Solidarity Will." *The Nation*, July 20, 2021. www.thenation.com.
Hamid, Sarah T., and Rachel Kuo. 2022. "Towards Collective Safety: Transformative Methodologies." September 7, 2022. SSRN. https://papers.ssrn.com.
Hong, Grace Kyungwon. 2015. *Death beyond Disavowal*. Minneapolis: University of Minnesota Press.
Kornstein, Harris. 2022. "Filling in the Gaps: Sinnamon Love on Disability and Sex Worker Organizing in the Covid-19 Pandemic." *Disability Covid Chronicles*, October 11, 2022. https://disabilitycovidchronicles.nyu.edu.

Lewis, Talila A. 2020. "Why I Don't Use "Anti-Black Ableism (& Language Longings)." *Talila A. Lewis Blog*, August 17, 2020. https://medium.com.
Mohapatra, Mon. 2019. "Good Design . . . for Whom?" *The New Inquiry*, March 27, 2019. https://thenewinquiry.com.
———. 2022. "Unwell in a Cell." *InQuest*, April 21, 2022. https://inquest.org.
Piepzna-Samarasinha, Leah Lakshmi. 2019. *Care Work: Dreaming Disability Justice*. Vancouver: Arsenal Pulp.
Puar, Jasbir. 2017. *The Right to Maim: Debility, Capacity, Disability*. Durham, NC: Duke University Press.
Reddy, Chandan. 2011. *Freedom with Violence: Race, Sexuality, and the US State*. Durham, NC: Duke University Press.
Sabal, Merlin (@fierce_invalids). 2020. "The disabled community has a long legacy of building intimacy across distance & isolation. Calling friends & comrades, coworking over zoom, & building space for rest and joy even in dire circumstances, is keeping me going. This zine has kept me going. 1/2 #FeministAntibodies." Twitter, April 10, 2020. https://twitter.com/fierce_invalids/status/1248661850474061827.
Soundararajan, T., A. Kumar, P. Nair, and J. Greely. 2020. *CORONAJIHAD: An Analysis of Islamophobic Covid-19 Haterspeech and Disinformation: The Implications on Content Moderation and Social Media Policy*. Oakland, CA: Equality Labs. www.equalitylabs.org.
Sterling, Anna Lucente. 2022. "City Provides 'Historic' Funding for Manhattan DA Hate Crimes Unit." *New York One*, August 26, 2022. https://ny1.com.
Sylvia Rivera Law Project. 2009. "SRLP on Hate Crime Laws." https://srlp.org.
Whitlock, Kay, and Michael Bronski. 2016. *Considering Hate: Violence, Goodness, and Justice in American Culture and Politics*. Boston: Beacon.

12

Mental Health and Black Futurity

Life, Birth, and Caregiving in Double Pandemics

NADIA MBONDE

When I ask Willow, an Afro–Puerto Rican young woman in her twenties, if quarantine has helped reduce the stigma of mental illness, she responds, "I think it will because now we have something to compare it to. When we're talking about having a hard time or feelings of not being able to escape ourselves, we can say, 'Well, how was your quarantine like during that lockdown where no one could do anything? That's how it feels to me on a constant basis.' And that comparison I think helps people understand better, and hopefully it makes them care more. I don't know if it will, but I hope so."[1]

Willow aspires for the world to be a more accepting and inclusive place to live with mental illness, and she believes the collective experience of isolation during the pandemic may help realize her vision. Willow's words depict one of the many Black visions of futurity that I encountered as I conducted virtual and in-person socially distanced interviews in 2020 with eleven people in the New York metro area living with mental illness. Using material from eight of the qualitative interviews I initially conducted as well as eighteen subsequent interviews conducted from 2021 to 2022, this chapter presents a sample of my interlocutors' experiences that underscore visions of Black futurity amid the devastation of the COVID-19 pandemic and police brutality, what I and many others have called a "double pandemic."

Considering Black futurity at this moment resists preconceived notions of the disposability of Black life by making the seemingly impossible possible, namely, the survival and flourishing of Black life in spite of the forces of imperialist-white-supremacist-capitalist-patriarchy that seek to destroy it (hooks and Guy-Sheftall 2015). In this chapter, I use ethnographic vignettes of devastation and futurity in conversation with Afrofuturism through Octavia Butler's prophetic science-fiction novel *Parable of the Sower* (1993), which envisions how Black people forge their future amid an apocalypse, not unlike the ongoing COVID-19 pandemic and deteriorating effects of late-stage capitalism that we are experiencing now.

My usage of the term "double pandemic" emerged with the zeitgeist concerning multiple pandemics coinciding with COVID-19. After George Floyd was murdered by a Minnesota police officer in the summer of 2020, my interlocutors and cultural commentators, including the comedian Trevor Noah on *The Daily Social Distancing Show*, discussed the effects of COVID-19 pandemic against the backdrop of police brutality. Isaac Addo (2020) uses "double pandemic" to discuss the escalation of racial discrimination against noncitizens and people of color globally, especially those of East and Southeast Asian descent in the US, at the outset of the COVID-19 outbreak. Janine Jones (2021) uses the term "dual pandemic" to describe the interaction between COVID-19 and systemic racism that exacerbated negative outcomes for communities of color within the education system. In the context of Black birth workers supporting expectant and new parents in the first six months of the COVID-19 pandemic, Julia Oparah and colleagues describe the lethal lack of labor support due to hospital restrictions as "a crisis on top of a crisis" (2021, 3). Jallicia Jolly (2021) highlights the triple pandemic of COVID-19, racism, and the Black maternal health crisis. Public health scholars have adopted a "syndemic perspective" in designing services to tackle the confluence of COVID-19 and mental health and chronic illnesses (Saqib, Qureshi, and Butt 2023). This ongoing discourse of multiple disasters has also included the climate crisis.

The double pandemic was evident in each of my interlocutors' stories. During each of the interviews, it was impossible for the participants to divorce their experience of the COVID-19 pandemic from the racial health disparities and the transnational reckoning with police brutality against Black people. Statistics show that Black people have had higher rates of COVID-19 infections, hospitalizations, and deaths than white individuals (Vasquez Reyes 2020). This social fact shaped my interlocutors' anxieties about getting infected. While the catalytic police killings of Ahmaud Arbery, Breonna Taylor, George Floyd, and others occurred in the United States, the impact of their deaths reverberated around the globe on social media, with Black Lives Matter protests in New York and thousands of other cities where, in many instances, police violence against people of color is equally pervasive.

Together constituting a double pandemic, the two global crises contributed to my interlocutors' mental health challenges and experiences of multiple forms of marginalization. The double pandemic affected their mental health in significant ways, producing symptoms of suicidality, panic attacks, depression, anxiety, and psychosomatic symptoms that aggravated other preexisting conditions, such as diabetes and heart disease. This was exacerbated for parents of disabled children with mental health challenges, who had minimal support for themselves, let alone to care for their children, with the absence of the community support and resources they had previously. Given the importance of biological and social reproduction to forging Black futures, the latter part of the chapter highlights how mental-health-related complications were further exacerbated for pregnant people and parents in the early months of the COVID-19 pandemic.

The Impact of COVID-19 on Black Mental Health

Sadie, an industrious manager and grandmother originally from the South, had an unwelcome confrontation with law enforcement during a wellness check. Her experience illustrates the ways in which Black people with mental illness have experienced the double pandemic. Concerned about her worsening suicidal ideation, white members from a support group she attended contacted a mental health support team to check on her. The support-group members did this without regard for the risks this would pose for a Black person since police are first responders at wellness checks.

Unequipped to deescalate mental health emergencies, police presence is likely to result in the injury or death of the person in crisis. Many of the slain Black people whose names have become hashtags, including Sandra Bland, Tanisha Anderson, Deborah Danner, Ezell Ford, Daniel Prude, and Walter Wallace Jr., lived with mental illness and were either shot during a wellness check while they were in psychiatric crisis or died in police custody (Katz and Bradley 2020). Cognizant of this, Sadie states, "I was pleasant with [the police officers], but they remained with their hands on their guns the whole time. And because I had a nephew here who's Black, I didn't want anything to happen to him. Because he started coming out to my aid, I went [with the officers] voluntarily because I didn't want . . ." Sadie's voice then trails off, omitting the possible outcome of her nephew's death at the hands of the police.

As a result of the inhumane treatment of Black people with mental illness by law enforcement, my interlocutors present a central question for conceptualizing Black futurity, namely, *How do we create a world in which mental illness is not stigmatized or a potential death sentence for Black people?* They answer this question from a number of angles. For example, Joshua, who works in public policy and advocacy at an international mental health organization, is working toward implementing local community-based crisis-response programs that do not involve police as first responders; rather, they employ peers with lived experience who can offer compassionate support and critical sensitivity to the nuances of each case. Working at the same organization as Joshua, Cassie, the support group manager, started a Black mental health support group in March 2020, at the outset of the COVID-19 outbreak. Despite initial pushback from her white coworkers, the virtual support group made its debut supported by a celebrity grant, providing an important peer-led mental health resource for Black individuals who were cloistered in their homes. Claiming their diagnoses by attending biweekly Zoom meetings to commune with folk who share similar experiences, Black people with mental illness created social bonds across ages, genders, and state lines. Participants shared tips to manage triggers and symptoms, traded notes about medications and telemedicine providers, and commiserated over the causalities of the double pandemic. Most notably, the group transformed the people who attended. The safe space eased the dehumanizing effects of stigma and discrimination and celebrated the participants' resilience and survival under excruciating circumstances.

Other interlocutors described different experiences of virtual safe space. As Sadie discussed her experience of teletherapy and telepsychiatry, she saw the benefits of virtual mental health care. In addition to the convenience of skipping the commute and time spent in the waiting room and places of potential COVID exposure, for Sadie, remote care reduces the stigma of mental illness. Although the conditions of quarantine may induce mental illness, Sadie recognized that now people have different avenues for addressing their issues, be it through telemedicine, teletherapy, online support groups, and so on. While these new options for mental health care can provide more anonymity since people do not need to be seen in person at an office, Sadie observed that "more people are claiming mental health issues." She emphasized, "The *right* people [celebrities like Taraji P. Henson, Chris Rock, Meghan Markle, and Kanye West] are saying that they have mental health issues," and society is benefitting as a result. This has been an unexpected benefit of an otherwise devastating time.

Olamina, a dancer, teacher, and doula, envisions another model of a future in which Black people are recognized in their full humanity.[2] She conveyed her experience of the double pandemic while grieving the loss of one of her best friends. She felt dehumanized by her experience of white allyship while she mourned her friend. Olamina expressed frustration at the sudden awakening of non-Black people who joined Black Lives Matter protests and began reaching out to Black people in their networks in recognition of their plight. Black people having always endured violence and discrimination, she found these new eager allies patronizing. Their "activism" and sudden interest in how she was coping with the deaths of George Floyd and Breonna Taylor overlooked her personal grief, her "small grief," as she terms it—the loss of a loved one, a grief common to all humans regardless of race. By giving greater weight to her "big grief"—universal Black oppression—white allies disregarded Olamina's humanity and reinforced their own racism. Thus, Olamina envisions a future in which the small grief of Black life can be attended to and not just the big grief that galvanizes the (often temporary) support of white allies.

The widespread pandemic experience of unemployment also had diverse consequences. Olamina remarked, "The CARES Act [which granted stimulus checks and unemployment benefits] didn't make things better, but because I was doing far less for the first few months of quarantine, I was saving way more money, even though I was paying rent for an apartment I wasn't in. I wasn't eating out. I wasn't getting on the subway. It was so weird when I realized it costs me more to live and work than it does to just live."

By contrast, Willow found that the support from unemployment insurance enabled her to fine-tune her self-care practices, therapy, and medication management, and now she feels more confident about returning to work. With greater self-knowledge and an ability to "center [her]self" through exercise, yoga, meditation, and a microdosing practice, Willow feels more self-assured in asking for accommodations to take time off work instead of quitting outright like she usually does when she gets overwhelmed.

Disability and animal rights activist, artist, and scholar Sunaura Taylor aptly conveys the political implications of Willow's and Olamina's sentiments about work. Taylor (2004) declares, "The right not to work is the right not to have your value determined by your productivity as a worker, by your employability or salary." Critiquing capitalism, Taylor argues that people with disabilities have been "indoctrinated to fetishize work, romanticize career, and to see the performance of wage labor as the ultimate freedom." As Olamina and Willow experienced the positive effects of unemployment on their mental health as well as financial security, they became capable of appreciating their intrinsic value by simply existing. Their temporary pandemic-induced circumstances potentially enabled them to practice the more liberatory systems of care that Taylor envisions. These pandemic circumstances took on unanticipated personal resonance for me and other new parents early in the pandemic.

COVID-19 and Heightened Challenges to Maternal Mental Health

The pandemic ensued shortly after I gave birth to my first child in 2020, giving me the opportunity to learn from my own lived experience of mental health challenges during my postpartum period. As a result, my ethnographic research expanded to include pregnant and postpartum people navigating mental health challenges under the threat of COVID-19.[3] I conducted additional virtual interviews with nine participants in the New York area, most of whom identify as postpartum or expectant women and mothers, changing their names and other self-identifying information to protect their anonymity. While some began to claim these diagnoses because of pandemic circumstances, not all of the pregnant and postpartum participants in my study identify with psychiatric disability. Both the formal diagnoses and self-diagnosed labels my participants most commonly identified with were depression and anxiety.

The COVID-19 pandemic revealed structural inequalities shaping the mental health of expectant and new parents in New York and across the United States. In New York State, Black birthing women have been dying at eight to twelve times the rate of white birthing women (NYC Health 2010). In 2023, these numbers persisted throughout the earlier years of the pandemic and still have not declined, given that the Fund for Public Health NYC (2023) reports that Black women and birthing people in New York City are nine times more likely to die from a pregnancy-related cause than their white counterparts are. The 2022 CDC report on pregnancy-related deaths highlights mental health conditions as the leading underlying cause of death. Suicide and overdose are the leading causes of maternal mortality in the US, accounting for 20 percent of deaths in the postpartum period (Policy Center for Maternal Mental Health 2023; Raiff et al. 2022). Though suicide and overdose are not reported as leading causes of death among Black women, Black women are twice as likely as white women to report having suicidal thoughts (Policy Center for Maternal Mental Health 2023). Studies reveal psychiatry's inability to address Black maternal mental health effectively. Almost 40 percent of Black birthing people experience perinatal mood and anxiety disorders (PMADs), twice the rate of their white counterparts, but they are less likely to receive treatment (Keefe, Brownstein-Evans, and Polmanteer 2016).

Mental-health-related complications are an understudied contributor to Black maternal mortality. Recent studies demonstrate the relationship between physical and mental health in the perinatal period beyond suicidality and substance use, which probably impacts Black women and birthing people disproportionately. Christina D. Kang-Yi and colleagues found that "women with psychiatric disorders prior to pregnancy were more likely to have pregnancy complications including pregnancy hemorrhage, preterm labor and preterm birth, after controlling for age, race/ethnicity and chronic illness status pre- and during pregnancy" (2018, 300). Preconception interventions and prenatal monitoring were vital to reducing pregnancy complications for women with psychiatric disorders. Interventions that improved birth outcomes included treatment for posttraumatic stress disorder (PTSD) and nicotine dependence; increase in physical activity; modifying diet, alcohol consumption, and other risky behaviors; and psychiatric treatment, both talk therapy and medication management. And vice versa: birth complications impact postpartum mental health. For instance, a study found that postpartum hemorrhage is a risk for mental ill health (Parry-Smith et al. 2021).

At the outset of the COVID-19 pandemic in March 2020, the context for birthing shifted significantly as several restrictive measures were put into place. These restrictions consisted of New York Governor Andrew Cuomo's mandate for all nonessential workers to stay home (except for necessary exercise or shopping) under new statewide lockdown measures. As such, New York City hospitals temporarily barred pregnant patients from having vital labor support. By cutting off labor support of partners and doulas from birthing people, COVID-19 hospital restrictions caused harm to Black mothers, making them especially at risk for PMADs. Research indicates an increased prevalence of PMADs, as the COVID-19 pandemic created conditions that exacerbated maternal mental health issues, including increased anxiety, depression, stress disorders, and sleep disturbance, especially under the isolating mandates of quarantine and social distancing (Raiff et al. 2022; Mandavilli 2021; Gammon 2020). Luna, a Black doula, expressed that "no Black birthing person should die at the hands of the medical industrialized complex" and that postpartum people should be given more support to recover physically and psychologically.

My interviews with therapists, reproductive psychiatrists, doulas, and mental health advocates shed light on the impact of these restrictions on birthing people. For example, protocols to accommodate the sensitivities of the high percentage of women with a history of sexual trauma were not taken into consideration. Yet, given New York's years-long effort to reduce racial inequities in the maternal mental health system, Cuomo's administration disregarded how restrictions on labor support would impact Black and Hispanic expectant mothers.[4] Despite the common knowledge in public health that the presence of doulas and birth partners improves birth outcomes, doulas, fathers, and other nonbirthing parents were initially prohibited from accompanying birthing people, who were forced to labor alone in stressed, unstaffed hospitals responding to the lethal threat of COVID-19.[5]

The weeklong ban on labor support, irrespective of COVID-19 positivity rates, had unanticipated consequences that were felt long after the ban was lifted. Bureaucratic restrictions that were developed after Cuomo's initial lockdown measures often prevented birthing people from utilizing their own social support and resources for self-care. A study conducted by Gus Mayopoulos and colleagues (2021) reports that approximately 50 percent of women in the sample who tested positive for COVID-19 sustained symptoms of acute trauma in response to childbirth. This was especially true for Black birthing people, who died of COVID-19 at more than twice the rate of their white counterparts (Vasquez Reyes 2020). COVID-19 exposure presented a new risk to low-income pregnant patients, especially among Black and Hispanic people, as they already face a multitude of life-threatening hazards. In addition to reporting increased pain during delivery, the COVID-19-positive group of women birthed newborns with lower weights, many of whom were admitted to neonatal intensive care units. These complications amid social isolation increased the risk of traumatic birth experiences, which has been associated with the risk of psychiatric morbidity.

Birthing people who did not contract the virus were equally impacted by the alleged safety measures, as studies indicate that various forms of birth trauma were endured by American women who gave birth during the first wave of the pandemic. Restrictions on labor support created birth trauma that, in turn, resulted in mental health challenges in the postpartum period. People who gave birth during this time were likely to experience high levels of anxiety while being denied visitors as well as the opportunity to room with their newborns. The remnants of the early restrictions on labor support are felt today, as doulas are more likely to be asked for certifications to attend their clients' births in the hospital and experience resistance from staff when providing support.

The theorist Ivan Illich classically discussed the role of the medical system in inducing ill health; this is evident in long-standing and worsening Black maternal mortality and morbidity. Illich uses the term "social iatrogenesis" ([1974] 2000, 13), defined as a disease, complication, or other adverse effect produced by any form of medical action, including diagnosis, intervention, or error. According to Illich, debility is produced "by increasing stress, multiplying disabling dependence, generating new painful needs, lowering the levels of tolerance for discomfort or pain, reducing the leeway that people are wont to concede to an individual when he suffers, and abolishing even the right to self-care" ([1974] 2000, 13). A consequence of social iatrogenesis, the increase in maternal mortality was in part a result of the negligent public health response to the threat of COVID-19 causing disruptions in access to health care, pharmaceuticals, transportation, housing, and employment (Thoma and Declercq 2022; Metz, Collier, and Hollier 2020).[6] Hospitals and clinics altered their care practices by spacing out appointments and conducting visits exclusively via telehealth. The abrupt transition to virtual visits resulted in missed or delayed diagnoses, as patients did not have adequate medical equipment at home, including blood-pressure monitors to detect hypertension. The overrun medical system could not provide them with continual attention from staff.

Distress, uncertainty, and fear were tangible on the labor and delivery floor during the pandemic. The doula Stephanie Schiavenato illustrates this in her piece "Birthing under Investigation" (2020), in which she describes what it was like for her clients, who are predominantly people of color, to give birth amid the threat of COVID-19. One of Schiavenato's clients, who was denied labor support because of her positive COVID-19 test, "was made to birth alone and treated as a threat to her newborn" (Schiavenato 2020). Feeling like a criminal for becoming infected, Schiavenato's client likened her birth experience to prison, an iron cage in which medical staff isolated her, kept her under surveillance, and separated her from her baby. Some doulas who could not attend their client's birth in person offered virtual support to circumvent restrictions. Under this mode of care, doulas were able to coach their clients on comfort measures, such as breathing, changing positions, and self-massage. The Brooklyn-based doula organization Ancient Song, "a birth justice organization working to eliminate maternal and infant mortality and morbidity among Black and Latinx people" (Ancient Song Doula Services, n.d.), created a virtual platform for its clients, although director Chanel Porchia-Albert explains that not everyone has access to the necessary technology (Meyerson 2020).

On April 20, 2020, pressure from advocates also resulted in Cuomo's launch of a COVID-19 Maternity Task Force with Secretary to the Governor Melissa DeRosa and sixteen others, including medical professionals, midwives, and advocates, united in the goal to "establish better, safer options for childbirth" (Engel 2020). After a week of birthing people laboring in hospitals alone, pressure from a coalition of women's health activists, professional birth attendants, and disability rights activists advocating for the right for pregnant people to receive labor support promptly reversed Cuomo's mandate and eased restrictions on hospital labor support. Despite the revised protocols allowing pregnant people to bring one support person, the initial constraints had already set bureaucratic confusions and contradictions into motion. Many birthing people remained cut off from support to help them humanize their experience amid the overmedicalization and depersonalization of hospital births. Private hospital systems, including Mount Sinai West and New York Presbyterian, decided to adhere to their own guidelines and continued to refuse pregnant patients labor support (Syckle and Caron 2020). Hospitals allowing one guest in the delivery room made patients face the predicament of deciding between their partner or their doula, evidently alienating numerous expectant parents.

Pandemic Parenting and the Effects of Neoliberalism

Though my New York interlocutors gave birth outside the time frame when oppressive hospital restrictions were in place, collectively their experiences reveal both the deleterious effects of the COVID-19 pandemic and public health mandates on maternal mental health and "deep fragmentations, inequalities, and dysfunctions within maternity care that existed before the pandemic began" (Davis-Floyd and Gutschow 2021, 1). The flaws in the mental health and maternity care system can be attributed to the long-standing oppressive structural forces of capitalism and neoliberalism that induce distress and disablement, regardless of whether a person has a re-existing mental health condition or diagnosis. As a political and economic form of governance, neoliberalism promotes personal responsibility for social risks, such as maternal-infant mortality and morbidity. According to neoliberal rationale, problems such as maternal mental illness are not attributed to public social-structural factors but to individuals, families, and associations in the private sphere. Those who are most vulnerable, those with preexisting mental health challenges and traumas, were left to cope as self-regulating individuals, bereft of social resources or support.

Throughout the pandemic, many people struggled with insufficient social support while sustaining the ideological burden of neoliberalism that attributes full responsibility to mothers for their own health and safety and that of their children. They contended with constraints that negatively impacted maternal mental health both before and during the pandemic. These included insufficient postpartum medical attention to ensure that the mother is healing, lack of screening and treatment for PMADs, and insufficient health-insurance coverage in the postpartum period to cover medical and mental health expenses. Many also faced income insecurity, lack of adequate maternity leave, social isolation, inadequate support with child care, and trouble with breastfeeding and formula shortages. While there is evidence that disturbances in maternal mental health are triggered by hormonal changes and physiological stressors imposed on the body throughout pregnancy and childbirth (Barnes 2015; Nau and Peterson 2015; Puryear 2015), disability studies scholars also highlight the social component of psychological distress and disablement. Despite my participants' use of psychiatric language to describe their experiences of anxiety, depression, or psychosis, their circumstances indicate what Arthur Kleinman (2012) calls "social suffering" or what Faye Ginsburg and Rayna Rapp (2013) term "disabling social conditions" that exclude full participation in society.

Shared themes across all my interviews with mothers demonstrate the presence of disabling social conditions in their postpartum experiences. These respondents described the grief and rage associated with being socially isolated while healing from childbirth and caring for a newborn, in some cases, entirely on their own. Numerous parents mourned the loss of their support systems from their extended families and communities as well as child care provided by schools and other institutions for their other children. Additionally, many expressed rage toward the disabling social conditions of working from home while juggling domestic and child-care duties with little help from their partners. Given that the ableist emphasis on wage labor determines a person's value based on their employability, efficiency, and productivity, aspects of the pregnancy and postpartum experience, such as immobility, fatigue, and brain fog, are contained within capitalist constructs of disability. Instead of performing "wage labor as the ultimate freedom" (Taylor

2004), some birthing people who experienced the luxury of repose afforded by the conditions of the pandemic enjoyed a newfound freedom in increased mental well-being that they would not have experienced otherwise.

For example, my daughter's birth in January 2020 was fortuitous, two months before the onset of COVID-19 in New York, allowing me to extend my recovery long after the three-month transition period commonly referred to as the "fourth trimester." The timing was such that stay-at-home orders began as soon as my postpartum doulas completed their service, allowing my partner to support me at home while receiving unemployment (what I half jokingly call the longest paid paternity leave in US history). Further support from stimulus checks, the federal Special Supplemental Nutrition Program for Women, Infants, and Children (WIC), and my academic institution, as well as mutual aid through the mental health peer support group I attended, helped me resist neoliberal compulsions to search for remote work on top of the full-time job of caring for my newborn and recovering from the trauma of mental health crises I experienced during pregnancy.

My own experience demonstrates how pregnant and postpartum people, especially those living with psychiatric disabilities, benefit from divesting from the capitalist labor economy. A post-pandemic future that values the reproductive labor of pregnant and postpartum people requires citizens to challenge capitalist and neoliberal logics. The COVID-19 pandemic demonstrated that life, birth, and caregiving continue when the wheels of capitalism slow or grind to a halt. Yet the question remains: *How can people with psychiatric disabilities continue to thrive if they do not want to participate in the capitalist work economy?*

Lessons Learned: Avenues for Healthier Perinatal Experiences

Although the COVID-19 pandemic presented unprecedented circumstances, there are many lessons that must be carried into our "post-"pandemic future if the US is to ameliorate its abysmal state of maternity and maternal mental health care. The collective trauma of the pandemic has raised awareness about mental health, unlike at any other time in history. My interlocutors demonstrate that the truism that "there is no health without mental health" is particularly accurate in the perinatal period. The effects of the restriction on labor support in the early days of the pandemic show the inhumane nature of solitary birth, violating patient and human rights. In general, isolation during the perinatal period is experienced as an impossible demand, as parents have to keep a newborn alive while trying to keep their own head above water. Public health policies addressing crises must include the perspectives of knowledgeable health-care professionals, essential workers, and activists so that decisions are evidence based.

Although digital technologies are no panacea for the trauma of isolation, the empowering use of the internet nonetheless presents opportunities for community support and access to mental health care services, especially for marginalized pregnant and postpartum people. The number of people without internet access demonstrates the urgency to close the digital divide and presents a strong case for governmental programs to provide underserved birthing people with internet access. Additionally, people with internet access who work remotely must remain vigilant about employers' invasive use of technology that makes telework a continuous presence in the home, interfering with child-care and household responsibilities, rest, and self-care.

The Black disability scholar Sami Schalk (2018) draws on Octavia Butler's *Parable of the Sower* to resist ableist assumptions that technology will usher in a disability-free future. Without a vision in which Black disabled people survive and thrive, we are bound to reproduce technologies that fail to meet our needs in the present moment. As Alison Kafer elucidates, "The futures we imagine reveal the biases of the present; it seems entirely possible that imagining different futures and temporalities might help us see, and do, the present differently" (2013, 23). Butler's 1993 prophetic dystopian novel, set in the 2020s, uncannily parallels our ongoing sociopolitical reality. The societal deterioration witnessed during the coronavirus pandemic seeded the chaos that has persisted several years later. Despite Butler's bleak vision, which mirrors our tumultuous times, her Afrofuturistic work at least provides hope that Black people survive, unlike sci-fi genres that kill off the little Black representation they have. Instead of total annihilation in the midst of adversity, Butler envisions how Black people build their own communities, plant their own Earthseeds or philosophies for how to live through calamity, and forge their own futures.

NOTES

1. Willow and other names of interlocutors are pseudonyms. I also conceal other identifying information to protect their privacy. This interview excerpt was originally published in Mbonde 2021.
2. This pseudonym derives from Lauren Olamina, the protagonist of *Parable of the Sower*.
3. In my study, I define my postpartum interlocutors as parents of infants and toddlers. I use the terms "pregnant and postpartum people," "birthing people," and "parents" instead of or in addition to "mothers" since the aforementioned terms are gender-inclusive, acknowledging that not all people who give birth identify as mothers or women, including nonbinary people and transmen. The term "women" is used in referenced statistics and clinical studies because of the language and limitations of the current research. The extent to which these data are representative of all birthing people, regardless of their gender identities, is unknown.
4. Prior to the COVID-19 pandemic, the Cuomo administration pushed for a Doula Pilot Program to allow Medicaid coverage for doulas to address the high Black maternal mortality rate in New York State (New York State Department of Health 2019).
5. Research from the American College of Obstetrics and Gynecology (2018) indicates that doulas can improve outcomes by shortening labor, decreasing the need for analgesia, decreasing operative deliveries, reducing stress, and increasing satisfaction with the labor experience. People who use doulas often credit them with eliminating unnecessary medical interventions and empowering birthing people with information to advocate for themselves.
6. Between 2019 and 2020, the National Center for Health Statistics (NCHS) reported an 18.4 percent increase in the mortality rates of pregnant women in the US (Thoma and Declercq 2022).

REFERENCES

Addo, Isaac Yeboah. 2020. "Double Pandemic: Racial Discrimination amid Coronavirus Disease 2019." *Social Sciences & Humanities Open* 2 (1): 100074.

American College of Obstetrics and Gynecology (ACOG). 2018. "Screening for Perinatal Depression." www.acog.org.

Ancient Song Doula Services. n.d. "About Ancient Song." Accessed April 24, 2024. www.ancientsongdoulaservices.com.

Barnes, Diana Lynn. 2015. "The Psychological Gestation of Motherhood." In *Women's Reproductive Mental Health across the Lifespan*, edited by Diana Lynn Barnes, 75–90. Cham, Switzerland: Springer.

Butler, Octavia. 1993. *Parable of the Sower*. New York: Four Walls Eight Windows.

Centers for Disease Control. 2022. "Four in 5 Pregnancy-Related Deaths in the U.S. Are Preventable." Press release. September 19, 2022. www.cdc.gov.

Davis-Floyd, Robbie, and Kim Gutschow. 2021. "Editorial: The Global Impacts of COVID-19 on Maternity Care Practices and Childbearing Experiences." *Frontiers in Sociology* 6:721782.

Engel, Currie. 2020. "Childbirth during a Pandemic: New York State Launches a Plan." *NY City Lens*, April 30, 2020. http://nycitylens.com.

Fund for Public Health NYC. 2023. "Black Maternal Health in NYC: A Discussion and Call to Action." July 26, 2023. https://fphnyc.org.

Gammon, Katharine. 2020. "The Psychic Toll of a Pandemic Pregnancy." *New York Times*, December 14, 2020. www.nytimes.com.

Ginsburg, Faye, and Rayna Rapp. 2013. "Disability Worlds." *Annual Review of Anthropology* 42:53–68.

hooks, bell, and Beverly Guy-Sheftall. 2015. "Mapping Desire: Archaeologies of Change." New School, October 11, 2015.

Illich, Ivan. (1974) 2000. *Limits to Medicine: Medical Nemesis, the Expropriation of Health*. London: Marion Boyars.

Jolly, Jallicia A. 2021. "I Survived Childbirth during Three Pandemics—COVID, Racism, Black Maternal Health Crisis." *USA Today*, May 27, 2021.

Jones, Janine M. 2021. "The Dual Pandemics of COVID-19 and Systemic Racism: Navigating Our Path Forward." *School Psychology* 36 (5): 427–31.

Kafer, Alison. 2013. *Feminist, Queer, Crip*. Bloomington: Indiana University Press.

Kang-Yi, Christina D., Sara L. Kornfield, C. Neill Epperson, and David S. Mandell. 2018. "Relationship between Pregnancy Complications and Psychiatric Disorders and Their Treatment: A Population-Based Matched-Controlled Group Comparison." *Psychiatric Services* 69 (3): 300–307.

Katz, Sarah, and Dominic Bradley. 2020. "Sandra Bland, Eric Garner, Freddie Gray: The Toll of Police Violence on Disabled Americans." *The Guardian*, June 9, 2020. www.theguardian.com.

Keefe, Robert H., Carol Brownstein-Evans, and Rebecca S. Rouland Polmanteer. 2016. "Having Our Say: African-American and Latina Mothers Provide Recommendations to Health and Mental Health Providers Working with New Mothers Living with Postpartum Depression." *Social Work in Mental Health* 14 (5): 497–508.

Kleinman, Arthur. 2012. "Medical Anthropology and Mental Health: Five Questions for the Next Fifty Years." In *Medical Anthropology at the Intersections: Histories, Activisms, and Futures*, edited by Marcia C. Inhorn and Emily A. Wentzell, 116–28. Durham, NC: Duke University Press.

Mandavilli, Apoorva. 2021. "More Pregnant Women Died and Stillbirths Increased Steeply during the Pandemic, Studies Show." *New York Times*, March 31, 2021. www.nytimes.com.

Mayopoulos, Gus A., Tsachi Ein-Dor, Kevin G. Li, Sabrina J. Chan, and Sharon Dekel. 2021. "COVID-19 Positivity Associated with Traumatic Stress Response to Childbirth and No Visitors and Infant Separation in the Hospital." *Scientific Reports* 11 (1): 13535.

Mbonde, Nadia. 2021. "Visions of Black Futurity amidst the Double Pandemic of COVID-19 and Police Brutality." *Somatosphere*, May 11, 2021. https://somatosphere.com.

Metz, Torri D., Charlene Collier, and Lisa M. Hollier. 2020. "Maternal Mortality from Coronavirus Disease 2019 (COVID-19) in the United States." *Obstetrics & Gynecology* 136 (2): 313–16.

Meyerson, Collier. 2020. "Doulas Are Going Virtual." *Intelligencer*, April 12, 2020. https://nymag.com.

Nau, Melissa L., and Alissa M. Peterson. 2015. "Chronic Mental Illness in Pregnancy and Postpartum." In *Women's Reproductive Mental Health Across the Lifespan*, edited by Diana Lynn Barnes, 123–58. Cham, Switzerland: Springer.

New York State Department of Health. 2019. "New York State Doula Pilot Program." November 28, 2022. www.health.ny.gov.

Noah, Trevor. 2020. "George Floyd, Minneapolis Protests, Ahmaud Arbery & Amy Cooper." *The Daily Social Distancing Show with Trevor Noah*. YouTube, May 29, 2020. www.youtube.com/watch?v=v4amCfVbA_c.

NYC Health and Mental Hygiene, Bureau of Maternal, Infant Reproductive Health. 2010. "Pregnancy-Associated Mortality: New York City, 2006–2010." New York City website. https://www1.nyc.gov.

Oparah, Julia Chinyere, Jennifer E. James, Destany Barnett, Linda Marie Jones, Daphina Melbourne, Sayida Peprah, and Jessica A. Walker. 2021. "Creativity, Resilience and Resistance: Black Birthworkers' Responses to the COVID-19 Pandemic." *Frontiers in Sociology* 6 (636029): 1–10.

Parry-Smith, William, Kelvin Okoth, Anuradhaa Subramanian, Krishna Margadhamane Gokhale, Joht Singh Chandan, Clara Humpston, Arri Coomarasamy, Krishnarajah Nirantharakumar, and Dana Šumilo. 2021. "Postpartum Haemorrhage and Risk of Mental Ill Health: A Population-Based Longitudinal Study Using Linked Primary and Secondary Care Databases." *Journal of Psychiatric Research* 137:419–25.

Policy Center for Maternal Mental Health. 2023. "Issue Brief: Maternal Suicide in the U.S.: Opportunities for Improved Data Collection and Health Care System Change." September 13, 2023. www.2020mom.org.

Puryear, Lucy J. 2015. "Postpartum Adjustment: What Is Normal and What Is Not." In *Women's Reproductive Mental Health Across the Lifespan*, edited by Diana Lynn Barnes, 109–22. Cham, Switzerland: Springer.

Raiff, Elizabeth M., Kristina M. D'Antonio, Christine Mai, and Catherine Monk. 2022. "Mental Health in Obstetric Patients and Providers During the COVID-19 Pandemic." *Clinical Obstetrics and Gynecology* 65 (1): 203–15.

Saqib, Kiran, Afaf Saqib Qureshi, and Zahid Ahmad Butt. 2023. "COVID-19, Mental Health, and Chronic Illnesses: A Syndemic Perspective." *International Journal of Environmental Research and Public Health* 20 (4): 3262.

Schalk, Sami. 2018. *Bodyminds Reimagined: (Dis)Ability, Race, and Gender in Black Women's Speculative Fiction*. Durham, NC: Duke University Press Books.

Schiavenato, Stephanie. 2020. "Birthing under Investigation." Society for Cultural Anthropology, May 1, 2020. https://culanth.org.

Syckle, Katie Van, and Christina Caron. 2020. "Women Will Not Be Forced to Be Alone When They Are Giving Birth." *New York Times*, March 28, 2020. www.nytimes.com.

Taylor, Sunaura. 2004. "The Right Not to Work: Power and Disability." *Monthly Review*, March 1, 2004.

Thoma, Marie E., and Eugene R. Declercq. 2022. "All-Cause Maternal Mortality in the US before vs during the COVID-19 Pandemic." *JAMA Network Open* 5 (6): 1–4.

Vasquez Reyes, Maritza. 2020. "The Disproportional Impact of COVID-19 on African Americans." *Health and Human Rights* 22 (2): 299–307.

13

Disability Justice, Material Needs, and Mutual Aid

Lessons from Autistic Communities during the Pandemic

CARA RYAN

In March 2020, I was living in New York City finishing up my final year of doctoral course work and beginning to make plans for dissertation fieldwork in France. I had been engaged in research with autistic New Yorkers for two and half years and had developed close relationships with many of my interlocutors. From the moment New York became the epicenter of the pandemic and through the summer of 2020 and beyond, I witnessed the importance of autistic community in times of crisis and, although not autistic myself, benefited from it enormously. Over the summer, when I became a member of our Disability Equity in the Time of COVID-19 research team, I interviewed some of my long-standing research participants, while also speaking to others who responded to my open invitation to autistic adults and their family members to participate in our research; I wrote about some of my initial findings in a short blog post on *Somatosphere* (Ryan 2021a). Three things stood out to me from the data I gathered in the summer of 2020. The first was that the most challenging part of the pandemic and restrictions on movement for many of the autistic people I interviewed was not isolation or fears over becoming ill—although those were certainly present. The most challenging aspect of life during COVID was often related to financial insecurity brought on by the sudden economic shutdown. Four of the eight New York City metropolitan-based residents I interviewed lost employment, and two were furloughed. A second surprise was that some of those I interviewed felt that their lives had improved in certain respects during the pandemic, often related to their economic situation becoming slightly less precarious for a brief period once temporary financial support offered by the federal and state government materialized. Third, many of the autistic people I interviewed were surviving because of the mutual aid they were practicing. Autistic mutual aid did not emerge with the pandemic, but among my interlocutors, it intensified and took on new importance.

In the fall of 2020, I relocated to Toulouse, France, to conduct my dissertation research on the changing categorizations of autism in France and efforts to make the French university system inclusive of autistic students. Unexpectedly, over the course of that research, I observed, documented, and sometimes participated in autistic-run communities of support and care. Like the ones I had documented in New York, these French networks had also been prompted or strengthened by the pandemic. This chapter focuses on my research findings from New York while briefly touching on how some of my findings related to autistic mutual aid resonated with what I witnessed in France. I conclude the chapter by considering why autistic practices of care and mutual support are not more widely recognized and celebrated.

Disability Justice and Material Needs: Reflections from New York City

Amanda, an autistic woman in her thirties, was someone with whom I was in regular contact during the earliest months of the pandemic.[1] We were checking in with each other frequently, and I knew she was going through a challenging time. But it was not until I interviewed her after she agreed to take part in our team's research on disability and the pandemic that I fully understood the depths of despair she had been experiencing or the fact that much of this turmoil was sparked by the threat of experiencing even greater economic precarity than she already lived. Amanda had gone into a deep depression in the first couple of months of the pandemic. Although at the time of our interview, the worst of it had subsided, she was still struggling with an erratic sleep schedule and felt she was relying too heavily on alcohol to manage anxiety. The reasons why she fell into such a deep depression are multifaceted, but listening to her explain the triggers clearly indicates how fear over her changing economic situation was at its core:

> I got pretty bad depression. And I couldn't really do much of anything but cry at the very beginning. I was really depressed by what was going

on. The siren sounds every two minutes were starting to get to me because I live near a hospital. And if I did have to go out, I felt like I was going to die or something. The grocery stores were very scary. The one time I took a walk, I saw somebody take a body bag out and put it in a van, so that was kind of weird. But that was normal, and it was near a funeral home . . . because I live near a funeral home and a hospital. . . . I think that was bad for everyone because that was the most ridiculous amount of sirens I've ever heard in my life. . . . But then I also had no job, and I didn't get unemployment. I waited for seven weeks to get approved for unemployment. So I was worried about money. . . . That was the hardest part, I think, worrying about when I'm going to get this unemployment.

As traumatic as seeing a dead body, hearing endless sirens, and the intense fear of going outside were, the "hardest part" was worrying about money and employment.

Amanda's financial situation was already precarious pre-pandemic. She receives monthly Social Security Disability Insurance (SSDI) payments, but they do not come close to covering rent and other basic expenses, particularly given the high cost of living in New York City.² Prior to the pandemic, she was getting by each month by walking dogs, a grueling job that entailed traveling all over the city and only being able to keep between 40 to 60 percent of what she earned, with the rest going to the businesses that contracted out her labor. As hard as it was, it was better than her previous job delivering Whole Foods groceries: pushing a two-hundred-pound cart around cobblestone streets in downtown Manhattan. When I asked Amanda about what people should know about her experience as a disabled person during the pandemic, she said, "A lot of adults are low income on the spectrum, and . . . a loss of [a] job can be frightening." Indeed, in the US, even before the pandemic, the employment rate among autistic adults has been lower than for any other disability category, and autistic adults who are employed often work in low-wage, part-time jobs (Roux et al. 2015).

Eventually Amanda received unemployment assistance from the New York State, as well as the pandemic relief money that was provided by the federal government to the majority of Americans. This made an enormous difference and was one of the key reasons she was able to lift herself from the depths of her depression. For Aaron, an autistic man in his forties who shares a tiny rent-controlled studio apartment with a roommate and who at the time of our interview was in the process of applying for SSDI, the pandemic relief money allowed him to feel secure for the first time in a very long period. He often has to borrow $100–$200 from his roommate, a senior citizen on a very fixed income, at the end of each month to pay his bills—which he then pays back at the start of the next month. This is a cycle he uses out of necessity but certainly not one he likes: "It's not, you know—he's not my family, and it's not—and he doesn't—he isn't—he's a senior, and he has his own limitations, understandably so. That was not sustainable and not fair. And to anybody, to him or myself or anybody, . . . what . . . what, what the stimulus has done is I haven't had to bother my roommate, my friend, anymore. So, I've been financially actually independent."

Being temporarily unemployed and quickly receiving unemployment insurance from New York and pandemic relief money from the federal government provided a welcome change for Christopher, an autistic man in his early thirties. Between April 2020 and December 2021, the US federal government issued direct payments to 165 million Americans via the CARES Act, the Consolidated Appropriations Act of 2021, and the American Rescue Plan Act of 2021. These payments—widely referred to as "stimulus checks"—provided direct cash assistance to people struggling financially due to the pandemic and its impact on the economy (US Government Accountability Office 2022). Christopher was temporarily unemployed when the coffee shops he worked at were closed from mid-March to late May 2020. Unemployment insurance and the one-time stimulus check allowed him the chance to (temporarily) live the way he wants to—to live life rather than make money in largely unfulfilling jobs just to pay rent. He explained to me that being out of work but still receiving enough money to live (in fact, receiving more money from unemployment than he usually makes in his barista gigs) gave him the ability to truly structure his days the way he wanted: becoming immersed in reading a novel, watching a film, reading about politics, or editing photos, for example. And when in the summer of 2020, the Black Lives Matter protests began after the murders of George Floyd, Breonna Taylor, and others, he was able to participate and to

Figure 13.1. *View of Protest Traveling Down Park Row.* (Photo by Christopher Lucka, 2020)

document them through photography, an art form he has been practicing for several years.

Christopher explained to me how, in his opinion, life as an autistic person can be difficult and challenging and sometimes painful, but thinking about the endless amount there is to learn and discover brings a sense of joy into his life. Although he will never be able to watch every film or read every book he wants to, just knowing that there is so much out there to encounter brings him a sense of fulfillment that low-wage service jobs do not. Service work is exhausting and often leaves scant time to enjoy life. In Christopher's estimation, the particular fatigue he feels from service work is directly related to the extra social vigilance required of him as an autistic person. He is on hyper alert at work since he lives in fear of accidentally hurting a coworker's feelings by misreading a social situation or not recognizing, and therefore offending, regular customers, two possibilities he attributes to the ways his autism-spectrum condition plays out.

For Jack, an autistic man in his thirties living in the suburbs of New York City, receiving the COVID-19 stimulus check was especially beneficial since he was already struggling to make ends meet at a part-time job in a machine shop, a job he then lost during the pandemic. He had previously worked full-time as an environmental engineer but left that job in the fall of 2020. Jack receives SSDI, but it has never been enough to live on. He brought up the criticism that many Republican politicians leveled against the expanded unemployment benefits and COVID stimulus checks: that it resulted in people making more money than they did previously. For Jack, this is a ridiculous argument because it neglects the fact that people were not making enough money to live on prior to the pandemic. At the time of our interview in summer 2020, he had just returned to work after finding a part-time job with the US Census Bureau. He was very pleased with the pay: $23 an hour, $7 more per hour than he ever made in his environmental engineer profession.

Some of my respondents found "silver linings" related to the pandemic that were not necessarily connected to improved material circumstances. I have borrowed the phrase "silver linings" from one of Ginsburg and Rapp's interlocutors, a mother of two autistic adult children (see chapter 7 in this volume) because it so perfectly encapsulates what many of my interlocutors experienced during the pandemic: unexpected yet positive developments during a period of crisis. During the depths of Amanda's despair, she developed a newfound interest in painting and has since become a prolific artist: "I needed to paint for some reason. I've never really painted before that. So, I ordered paint, and then it just felt like I painted a lot after that. . . . I don't really understand it. I just draw how I felt. I was drawing human figures, screaming and crying and falling off of cliffs and stuff, really kind of dark stuff."

Nick, someone in his thirties who has a higher-education degree and a thriving career in the technology industry, worked full-time from home during the pandemic when his office temporarily shut down. He appreciated having more time without his regular long commute. Having more control over his time allowed him to exercise during his lunch break. He explained that he has been on a weight-loss journey for the past several years. He gained a lot of weight in his early twenties

Figure 13.2. *The Machine Consumes the Faceless Workers*, painting on acrylic on Canvas, by Amanda Porche, 2020.

because food became a way for him to cope with the significant bullying he experienced in college as an autistic person. Nick's entire experience with the pandemic has been overall quite positive. "I've been thriving," he told me, explaining that that was the specific reason he volunteered to take part in my research; he wanted to share an experience with me that might not be typical. In addition to having more time to exercise, Nick has had more social opportunities—mostly virtual—than previously because many people he had lost touch with have reached out to him via social media. He has also taken some day trips with two friends he knows through an autism support group. Additionally, his professional field, data science, has been booming during the pandemic, and so several recruiters have been connecting with him on LinkedIn. In fact, although his contract at a major telecommunications company was not renewed during the pandemic, he immediately secured another job at a start-up.

Yan, an autistic man in his thirties living in New York City, was very ill in March 2020 (probably with COVID, but due to the major testing shortage in the beginning of the pandemic, he was never able to confirm this). His grandparents, whom he relies on daily for significant support, were extremely ill with COVID; one of them was hospitalized. This was a harrowing time for him. Yet, he found something positive from the experience: he became a bit more independent:

> I was having a very hard time, you know, getting myself to really cook on my own and to, you know, really . . . become a more independent person. You know, I mean, I'm still doing it, but I was doing it a lot more a few years ago than now, not because I was lazy but just because I kind of fell into a bit of a rut in life and was having a harder time doing it. And so, I think this whole pandemic actually got me to renew that goal, . . . and now I'm having cooking lessons with my grandmother. And in all fairness, I think that in some ways it's good that I'm doing that because it's been really helpful and stuff. . . . The reason why I was having some trouble doing this before was because I had my tasks really spread out before me and a lot of things to do at one time. As you might know, people with Asperger's are not really great at multitasking. Here, because I was staying at home all the time, I really didn't have as much to do, so I could concentrate more on doing certain things. But because I couldn't go out so much to eat because it made no sense to order out, especially during the early part of the pandemic, I actually did have to learn to cook on my own. So that really helped that part as well, because we all have to actually eat meals to survive obviously.

Some people also felt that their autism diagnoses had actually prepared them for the social isolation of the pandemic, with Tom explaining, "For me, I've been, to a certain extent, social distancing my whole life. Avoiding people has never been too much of a problem. But it was certainly a shock to people off the spectrum because they really did." This sentiment is one that has been expressed by many disabled people since the earliest days of the pandemic (Pulrang 2021).

Despite pandemic "silver linings" experienced by many of my interlocutors, I in no way wish to present an overly rosy picture of their experiences. Many people explained how challenging the experience had been. Several people lamented the loss of in-person social interaction and the loneliness of being at home. One person said, "You know, I just want to hug my friends again. I just want to hug all my friends," multiple times over the course of our discussion and commented on how Zoom and online socialization does not replace real face-to-face interaction. Two of my interlocutors commented on the difficulty of communicating online, which they speculated was specifically related to their autism. One man explained how the Zoom platform is particularly challenging for people with attention deficit hyperactivity disorder (ADHD) and with Asperger's (the term he identifies with) because it is difficult to follow nonverbal communication since it can be unclear where to look.[3] Another person explained that she does not like Zoom and that non-face-to-face, that is, text-based online forums, are even worse because they can lead to misunderstandings: "I think for me, it's better to have my tone of voice because I get into a lot of arguments if I'm on that [text-only] format. I just don't like them. And people online can hide behind their computer screen, so people can be assholes."

As noted earlier, Amanda was not the only person who had experienced a deep bout of severe depression during the pandemic. For Henry, who also became extremely depressed, the most distressing part of the pandemic was the fear over the permanent loss of "safe spaces" he has worked so hard to find. He is an avid fan of the arts, and his social network has been tied to the artistic world of New York City. Although he has recently become involved in an arts program inclusive of people with developmental disabilities, one he is extremely passionate about, many of the friends he has made in the city are through various theater and other arts circles that are not specifically geared toward disabled people. The social life he has built for himself, a life surrounded by artists, is one he loves and one that is far more appealing than the social groups in which he was previously involved in his hometown—groups designed for people with developmental disabilities, led by professional, nondisabled staff. He was terrified that because of the way the pandemic has impacted the arts, many of his friends will permanently move away from the city, and he would be forced back into social groups for autistic and other disabled people in Connecticut: "I get scared that I'll be back in my hometown in Connecticut, in these groups again and being mistreated and judged. And I don't want that."

The father of a high-needs autistic teenager explained that life under the shadow of COVID has really not been particularly stressful for their family. At the time of our interview, five months into the pandemic, he, his wife, and his two teenage sons had mostly been at home in their three-bedroom apartment in Manhattan. His son's school closed, and he struggled with attending classes online; but the school gave him permission to do assignments with his parents asynchronously. When he is not doing the assignments, he has mostly been watching TV, something he loves. He has been quite happy. Echoing a finding highlighted by Freidus, Fish, and Turner in chapter 6 in this volume, his father suggested that although the switch to online learning had been hard for him and his wife, it was probably not as stressful as it was for parents of "typical" children, who are caught in a "rat race": "He didn't want to do his homework, but it was not a big deal. And we didn't do that much because the other thing is, you know, unlike parents of typical children, who are worried that their kids are falling behind, we have no particular goals. What is it falling behind, you know? It's great. . . . It's not like there's some rat race." As well as things have been going, he explained that if the pandemic had occurred a few years ago, things would have been much more stressful. His son went through a period of puberty during which he could be extremely aggressive. If the pandemic occurred then, their situation would have been much different:

> We're really fortunate this COVID stuff happened now because if it happened a couple years ago, it would have been desperate and miserable because I couldn't leave. I really couldn't leave him alone with just my wife because she's much smaller than he is. And so at that point, I was really the only one who could handle him on my own. Even then, I needed help from my older son because he—you know, it's really intense. We've had almost no incidents like that in the past four months, and when we have, we know why. Before, it was just—it would come out of nowhere. And now, there were a couple things where we could see what the frustration was about. We could see it coming. . . . It was understandable. It was legible.

Being at home much more than before was not easy for Jack, the former environmental engineer. He described becoming obsessed with politics in ways that had become distressing. He explained that he is a very passionate person; before the pandemic, he could spread his passions to a variety of specialized interests that gave him pleasure, politics being only one of them. Pre-COVID, he participated in various Meetup groups, followed some sports, and so on. During the pandemic, he had fewer opportunities to spread his passions over a variety of interests, which led to him becoming fixated on politics and unable to think about much else. Interestingly, Jack's major concern as an autistic person living during the pandemic was that people have become less accommodating. He worried that the gains made for autistic acceptance and inclusion in the past couple of decades could dissipate since there is now so much desperation for so many:

> I feel like there has been a shift where, before COVID-19, there [was] still a lot of misunderstanding among society about people on the autism spectrum. But there are a lot of people who are like, "Okay, we know people on the spectrum have this. How can we accommodate to these people? We need to make accommodations." So there was that. And then I feel like once COVID-19 hit, there was a shift of, "Okay, so you have problems. So what? Now we all have problems, so I don't really care." I felt like among certain people in society the shift of, "Well, now I have problems, too. So, you know, tough luck." Like, I definitely felt that to be the case.

With Jack's concerns about autistic acceptance in a neurotypical-dominated world in mind, in the next section, I return to the necessity of autistic community.

Developing Networks of Mutual Aid in New York City and France

Amanda, Aaron, Christopher, and Jack had all met previously in a larger social support group for autistic adults, one I had observed during earlier research. The three of them, as well as a couple of other people, became particularly close, so when the pandemic hit, they relied extensively on each other. Aaron was especially worried about Amanda, but everyone was having a hard time. Aaron started organizing weekly, and then twice-weekly, Zoom meetings where people could discuss their worries and ask each other for help. They were also there for each other by text and phone calls, but the regular group meetings seemed essential for navigating the scariest days of the pandemic. I participated in many of the Zoom meetings, often using my NYU Zoom account to be the meeting's host so that our conversations could continue beyond the thirty free minutes the platform provides for those who do not have a paying subscription. Although I am not autistic, the abruptness of the shelter-in-place orders and the stress of living in New York City, one of the earliest epicenters of the pandemic, affected me (like all New Yorkers) deeply. I benefited from my autistic friends' and research participants' support meetings, and I even spent my birthday during the first year of the pandemic with them on Zoom. These meetings organized by Aaron lasted several months. They also started a channel via Discord—a place for Amanda to share the immense amount of artwork she created during the pandemic, Christopher to share his photography, and other friends to post items of interest. The support provided to each other was mostly emotional but at times material as well, including one person gifting another an old computer when theirs broke.

In late fall 2020, I said good-bye to my autistic friends in New York and headed to Toulouse, France, to begin my dissertation research, focused on the changing categorizations of autism in France. My French research has focused primarily on an innovative national initiative to make the public university system inclusive of autistic students. My fieldwork began and ended during the pandemic: fall 2020–spring 2022. In fact, just a couple of weeks after my arrival in France, with case numbers soaring and the hospital system under severe strain, the country began its second period of strict measures, which required most residents to stay indoors except for limited exceptions. This "confinement," as it was widely called in France, was much stricter than the shelter-in-place orders I had experienced in New York. Over the course of my research, I discovered that, like in New York, autistic people were coming together to provide each other solidarity and support, especially during the pandemic. And like in New York, I found these networks not only important social phenomena to document as an anthropologist but a practical source of support for myself, a foreigner living alone, far away from home during a pandemic.

Although I did not set out to explore autistic communities of care in France, they became an important part of both my research and life there. In this section, I discuss two French autistic communities. Before delving into them, an important caveat concerning a key difference between my observations in New York and France: The social safety net is much stronger in France than in the US. Essential basic needs are far more likely to be met for residents in France than in the US. This does not mean that there are no disabled people in France living in precarity, especially if they are unemployed and/or experiencing difficulty being officially recognized as a disabled person by the state through the MDPH (Maison départementale pour les personnes handicapées)—a lengthy and complicated bureaucratic process.[4] And unfortunately, as in the US, disabled people face ableist discrimination. It also must be noted that in France, autism has been a highly stigmatized condition, and autistic people have often not been able to access education and other key services (United Nations 2021). Yet certain basic needs are met in France for all residents, disabled or not, including universal health care. University education is also free and available for any student who has passed an exam at the end of high school. I point out these key differences because, while I am certain there are autistic people living in extremely precarious situations in France, none of my French autistic interlocutors shared with me material-related concerns that were as severe as some of my American autistic interlocutors did. While I documented sentiments of isolation and an overall stress of living during a pandemic among my interlocutors in both places, in New York, enormous challenges among many I interviewed were related to precarious work and housing situations that crumbled under pandemic conditions; I did not document these same challenges among my French interlocutors.

The two autistic-run communities I spent time with during my research in France were affiliated in some way with *l'Université Aspie-Friendly* (The Aspie-Friendly University) project, my major field site.[5] Café Asperger is an online community of people from all over France and beyond who meet on Friday evenings on Zoom; it is organized and led by an autistic university professor. It began as an in-person local initiative at the University of Clermont Auvergne. When COVID hit and life merged online, so did the Café; suddenly digital, it became advertised more widely, and students (and others) from across France began attending. *La Bulle!* (The Bubble) is an association of autistic university students from campuses in Toulouse that are part of the national Aspie-Friendly network. They host weekly meetings on their Discord channel.

These meetings originated during the confinement to facilitate a way to check in with each other during a period of intense isolation. After the confinement ended, the Discord meetings continued. I observed three key elements present in both the Café and *La Bulle!* that have led me to consider these spaces as sites of autistic mutual aid and helped me reflect on the autistic mutual aid I previously observed in New York City. These elements are (1) an overall environment of "bienveillance" (kindness and generosity), (2) a flexible and informal nature, (3) and a form of mutual aid understood as a pleasurable exchange of give and take without an expectation that any giving needs to be met with the same level of receiving, and vice versa.

Bienveillance is a word that came up a lot in Café meetings. The word can be translated into English as "kindness," but that translation falls somewhat short. *Bienveillance* is more of an overall attitude of generosity and kindness to others, leading to a shared well-being. In addition to tangible things like classrooms designed with the sensory needs of autistic people in mind, technological innovations that aid in accessibility, and increased awareness of autism, I was always struck that *bienveillance* was brought up time and again as a key component in making the university system inclusive for autistic students. Advice was regularly given and discussed about finding *personnes de confiance* (trusted people) at the university who could help an autistic student when in need. Whether these people had significant knowledge of autism or not was less important than whether they were a kind and open (*bienveillant*) person. Stories were often shared about such people: a kind professor, a generous secretary in a department, a "neurotypical" friend.

Participants in the Café did not just speak about *bienveillance*; they practiced it. In meetings, when attendees would share an issue they were dealing with—the stress of isolation during the pandemic, a difficult academic situation such as an interpersonal issue with a faculty member, a physical or mental health concern, or the like—people would react to each other not only with practical advice but with kindness and immense amounts of empathy. The same was true in *La Bulle!* meetings. For example, when newcomers expressed anxiety or in one instance disclosed their status as transgender, old-timers rushed in to introduce themselves as nonjudgmental and welcoming. As I had in New York

City, I personally benefited from the *bienveillance* of these communities. Although in the beginning, I was ostensibly attending *La Bulle!* meetings and Café sessions solely for research purposes, having a place to be (even virtually), filled with kind individuals during the most isolating months of pandemic conferment, was a comfort. I also benefited from the practical advice people shared during the Café, taking up online yoga as a way to manage stress, for example.

Another key element in both the Café and the weekly meetings of La Bulle!, and something that was very reminiscent of autistic-run communities I had come to know in New York, like Amanda, Aaron, Christopher, and Jack's pandemic community, was the groups' flexible and informal nature. People came and left as they pleased. There always seemed to be a regular group of people present in both communities, but newcomers arrived and departed as they wished. There was never an obligation to have a camera on, and most people across both Zoom and Discord kept them off. Some people only participated in the chat; others participated only vocally, and some just listened. When cameras were on, it was not uncommon to glimpse a pet cat or see someone crocheting. I have argued elsewhere that although dominant narratives of autism portray autistic people as rigid, I have found that among the autistic groups with which I have done research, a flexible nature is a key element in these communities' sociality (Ryan 2021b). My pandemic research showed that online platforms allow for a greater level of flexibility. And as Aimi Hamraie and Kevin Gotkin (2023) importantly point out, online spaces that allow for remote participation in social events, work, telemedicine, and beyond, which became commonplace for everyone during the pandemic, were often originally created by and for disabled people.

Conclusion: Autistic Mutual Aid

The autistic communities I have described in this chapter—all sparked by or strengthened by the pandemic—can be understood as practicing mutual aid. Mutual aid as an organizing practice is classically associated with the Russian anarchist political philosopher Peter Kropotkin (1842–1921). Anarchist groups have long formed intentional communities of mutual aid, based on an ideal of collective cooperation, as opposed to individual competition, as beneficial for the survival of communities and indeed the entire human species. Although the communities discussed here were not explicitly practicing mutual aid or any political project in an intentional way (although some of my New York interlocutors were familiar with the concept of mutual aid and anarchist practices and were involved in various leftist political movements), I nonetheless argue that the social phenomena I observed and sometimes participated in are all instances of a specific form of autistic mutual aid. While mutual aid is often associated with anarchism, as the American scholar/activist Dean Spade argues, "there is nothing new about mutual aid—people have worked together to survive for all of human history" (2020, 136). The *bienveillance*, the flexible and open nature of these communities, and the fact that there was no barrier to entry, for example, no proof of an autism diagnosis required, are what make me understand them as practicing mutual aid. As the journalist Jia Tolentino (2020) writes, this is a key difference with government-sponsored support and with charity: "A distinctive quality of mutual aid, in general contrast with charity and state services, is the absence of conditions for those who wish to receive help."

In the US, mutual aid and its anarchist associations became popular fodder in the mainstream media when the pandemic led to the creation of numerous networks of support. As Mills and colleagues note in the introduction to this volume, during the pandemic, disabled people in New York City immediately mobilized to provide each other support, including the Crip Fund, which was organized by disabled artists. However, mainstream media rarely focused on disabled mutual-aid networks during the pandemic, despite their long history. The autistic scholar and activist Leah Lakshmi Piepzna-Samarasinha (2018) reminds us that autistic and other disabled people have been practicing mutual aid since long before it became a trendy topic. Disabled people have done this for the simple reason that without it, survival is impossible. Piepzna-Samarasinha's *Care Work: Dreaming Disability Justice* (2018) provides an important history of what they call "care webs or collectives" of disabled people in the US and the critical but too often overlooked role that Black and Brown queer disabled people have forged in the creation of these networks. Piepzna-Samarasinha also reminds us that sometimes these "care webs" have been intentionally created to also have political aims; other times, they simply exist because "care webs are just life, just what you do" (2018, 41).

Indeed, mutual aid is a fundamental element of the human experience. Giving is what makes us human. The anarchist anthropologist and political activist David Graeber, drawing from Marcel Mauss's classical anthropological essay *The Gift* (1925), argued that generosity is a key element in human societies. As Graeber (2008) pointed out, "Mauss emphasized the 'pleasure' and 'joy' of giving: In traditional societies, there was not assumed to be any contradiction between what we would call self-interest (a phrase that he noted could not even be translated into most human languages) and concern for others; the whole point of the traditional gift is that it furthers both at the same time." Within the disability community, the artist and activist Constantina Zavitsanos has evoked a similar sentiment about the necessity and pleasure of giving and receiving that runs counter to a capitalist logic of a "reciprocal give and take" (Mills and Sanchez 2019). Autistic mutual aid highlights a necessary alternative to contemporary economic ideas of humans as inherently selfish and individualistic, who give only because of a rational calculation. Autistic mutual aid reminds us that humans are social creatures, and generosity—the key to sociality—is pleasurable.

Having basic human needs met—food, shelter, access to education, health care—is a necessity for disability justice. Where our current governments fall short, disabled communities such as the autistic networks of care I have documented here often step in. And even for those whose material needs are met, because we are an interdependent species, care communities are still essential. Mutual aid is everywhere and yet is often not widely recognized as an important and viable alternative for creating the "more just world that might emerge" (Ginsburg, Mills, and Rapp 2020) from the pandemic. It is not because mutual-aid groups exist in secret; they are not invisible but "invisibilized." As Spade argues, "Mutual aid work is mostly invisibilized and undervalued in mainstream and left narratives about social movement resistance, despite its significance as a tool for opposing systems of domination" (2020, 147). Mutual aid practiced by disabled people is even more "invisibilized," as scholars/activists like Piepzna-Samarasinha point out. I contend that autistic communities practicing mutual aid may be especially "invisibilized" because of ableist stereotypes that autistic people are socially disinterested. Elsewhere, I have written about what I termed "invisible autistic infrastructure" (Ryan 2021b). By "invisible," I meant that stereotypical ableist understandings of autism impede a wider recognition and appreciation of autistic-run communities. While such networks are everywhere, they often go unnoticed by dominant society, especially because they exist outside of a biomedical, commodified "autism industrial complex" (McGuire 2016). Inspired by Spade (2020) and Piepzna-Samarasinha (2018), I now think "invisibilized" might have been a more apt word.

Specific mutual-aid communities, disabled or not, are typically ephemeral. The Zoom meetings that Aaron organized during the height of the pandemic eventually ended. Some members of the group are still in touch; others have drifted apart. In the later stages of the pandemic, Amanda fell deep into the trenches of an opioid addiction that nearly took her life. At the time of this writing, she is proudly seven months sober, and her recovery community is currently the most important one in her life. She is taking online university courses and is hoping to go into the field of addiction therapy so that she can support others who are struggling. The cycle of mutual aid, fortunately, continues.

NOTES

1. In this chapter, some of my interlocutors are identified by their real names, others by pseudonyms. Here, as in all of my writing, I use pseudonyms unless a research participant has specifically asked me to use their name.
2. SSDI (Social Security Disability Insurance) and SSI (Supplemental Security Income) are programs from the US government that provide financial assistance for eligible disabled people.
3. Terminology around autism is often debated. The term "Asperger's syndrome" is part of these debates, with some people preferring not to use this term, particularly since its removal from the *DSM-5*. Many still identify with the term, and in my research, I follow a common anthropological practice of using the term that one's interlocutors use to describe themselves.
4. French disability communities scored an enormous victory in July 2022: after a lengthy campaign by disability activists, the sum of money that some disabled people are entitled to (called the Allocation aux adultes handicapés or AAH) will no longer be impacted by the income of a spouse or domestic partner. (This is not true in the US, where marriage can sometimes disqualify a disabled person from receiving their supplementary entitlement.)

5 In fall 2023, the project's name changed to *l'Université Atypie-Friendly* (The Atypical-Friendly University).

REFERENCES

Ginsburg, Faye, Mara Mills, and Rayna Rapp. 2020. "From Quality of Life to Disability Justice: Imagining a Post-Covid Future." *Somatosphere*, June 2, 2020. http://somatosphere.net.
Graeber, David. 2008. "Give It Away." The Anarchist Library. https://theanarchistlibrary.org.
Hamraie, Aimi, and Kevin Gotkin. 2023. "Remote Access: A Crip Nightlife." Imagining America, February 27, 2023. https://imaginingamerica.org.
McGuire, Anne. 2016. *War on Autism: On the Cultural Logic of Normative Violence*. Ann Arbor: University of Michigan Press.
Mills, Mara, and Rebecca Sanchez. 2019. "Giving It Away: Constantina Zavitsanos on Disability, Debt, Dependency." *Art Papers*, May 15, 2019. www.artpapers.org.
Piepzna-Samarasinha, Leah Lakshmi. 2018. *Care Work: Dreaming Disability Justice*. Vancouver: Arsenal Pulp.
Pulrang, Andrew. 2021. "What Disabled People Are Thinking and Feeling about the Pandemic, One Year Later." *Forbes*, March 21, 2021. www.forbes.com.
Roux, Anne M., Jessica Rast, Julianna Rava, Kristy Anderson, and Paul Shattuck. 2015. "National Autism Indicators Report: Transition into Young Adulthood." Life Course Outcomes Research Program, A. J. Drexel Autism Institute, Drexel University, Philadelphia.
Ryan, Cara. 2021a. "Disability Justice and Material Needs: Reflections on the Experiences of Autistic New Yorkers Living Under Covid-19." *Somatosphere*, February 19, 2021. http://somatosphere.net.
———. 2021b. "Invisible Autistic Infrastructure: Ethnographic Reflections on an Autistic Community." *Medical Anthropology* 40 (2): 129–40. https://doi.org/10.1080/01459740.2020.1849185.
Spade, Dean. 2020. "Solidarity Not Charity: Mutual Aid for Mobilization and Survival." *Social Text* 38 (1 (142)): 131–51. https://doi.org/10.1215/01642472-7971139.
Tolentino, Jia. 2020. "What Mutual Aid Can Do during a Pandemic." *New Yorker*, May 11, 2020. www.newyorker.com.
United Nations. 2021. "Experts of the Committee on the Rights of Persons with Disabilities Raise Questions about the Medical Approach to Disability Used in France." August 23, 2021. www.ungeneva.org.
US Government Accountability Office. 2022. *Stimulus Checks: Direct Payments to Individuals during the COVID-19 Pandemic*. GAO-22-106044. Washington, DC: GAO. www.gao.gov.

14

Making Art in Bed

EMILY WATLINGTON

Rest is often framed as time to recuperate or recharge, so that one can begin working again. But humans do not actually run on batteries, and a closer look at art history helps us evade neat distinctions between rest and work—distinctions that often have the effect of devaluing time spent doing the latter. A smattering of canonical works have in fact been made in bed or while asleep. Take, for example, the celebration and documentation of dreams by Surrealists like Salvador Dalí and Leonora Carrington or the canvases painted literally in bed by their compatriot Frida Kahlo. Yvonne Rainer made several rest-based dances, such as her 1965 "mattress dance," part of *Parts of Some Sextets*, in which dancers sit, rest, and pile atop mattresses. There's also Rainer's *Hand Movie*, a dance she choreographed from her hospital bed in 1966. And there's Mladen Stilinović's 1978 performance *Artist at Work*, which is typically exhibited as a series of photographs that show the Croatian artist resting in bed. He wanted to argue, as he explained his performance in the 1993 manifesto "In Praise of Laziness," that "there is no art without laziness" ([1993] 2011).

For the Surrealists, the turn to dreams was a deliberate, political turn away from the tyranny of logic and efficiency. These artists watched the "rational mind" build machines that enacted the horrors of World War II, but they could not make sense of the resulting atrocities and so resigned to absurdism or escaped to dreamlands (Merjian 2022). For Rainer, the choice to celebrate rest involved honoring the choreography one finds in everyday movements. At times, her approach was informed by the periods of illness she experienced (Rainer 1965). For Stilinović, laziness was anticapitalist critique. He wrote his manifesto just after the fall of the Iron Curtain, as capitalist ways of life began trickling into his country. In one especially searing line, he states that "artists in the West are not lazy and therefore not artists, but rather producers of something" ([1993] 2011). All of which is to say that many artists throughout history have explored the value of rest as a political act.

The same is true of a generation of disabled artists working from bed today. In 2016, the Berlin-based Korean American artist Johanna Hedva (2016) wrote an essay called "Sick Woman Theory," during the height of Black Lives Matter protests that they were too sick to attend. The event prompted them to challenge the equation of activism with marching in the streets and to reconsider the different forms that protest and refusal can take. Their influential essay helped galvanize a generation to explore the politics of rest, and Hedva built on those earlier ideas in their 2020 book *Minerva: The Miscarriage of the Brain*, which includes essays like "On Lying Still for the Hours of the Afternoon" and "A Decade of Sleeping." In the latter, Hedva states, "I wrote most of this book, maybe all of it . . . in my sleep. . . . I write as soon as I wake, but it is through writing that I fully awaken" (2020, 178).

The COVID-19 pandemic hit amid a growing movement to make art from a place of rest through an explicitly disability-justice-oriented lens. Exemplary pre-pandemic works include Constantina Zavitsanos's *I Think We're Alone Now (Host)*, a foam mattress topper stretched like a canvas but also sagging, bearing imprints and sweat stains that index the bodies of the guests who have slept on it (figure 14.1). Then, during lockdown, countless artists, especially in New York, became unable to safely visit their studio spaces and, as in many other professions, began crafting new rituals for working from home. Many found themselves in cramped apartments, where they turned their beds into makeshift studios; some started working in new materials, formats, and sizes as a result. For several disabled artists, this practice was not new. These conditions brought about a distinctive set of logistical constraints and conceptual prompts, but importantly, it slid right in alongside the values of the works they were already making. These include works that insist on the value of rest and that honor resistance to conventional forms of productivity or that explore how capitalism can conflate a person's ability to work in normative ways with their worth in ways that have damaging impacts on the lives of disabled people. I reached out to three artists whom I suspected worked this way, and to my delight, all three confirmed my suspicions.

Figure 14.1. Constantina Zavitsanos, *I Think We're Alone Now (Host)*, 2008–16, Collection of Museum für Moderne Kunst MMK. An open rectilinear wood frame leans against a wall, encasing a soft foam mattress topper that shows the wear of eight years' sleep of many people. Its slow, entropic geometries form as its contents spill on the back wall to find support. (Photo: Diana Pfammatter, Museum für Moderne Kunst (MMK), Frankfurt, Germany, 2021)

On a sweat-stained, split-open pillowcase, the artist Alex Dolores Salerno embroidered a phrase they found on a queer mutual-aid Facebook group: "Pl3ase be d.i.s.c.r.e.e.t c@refu11y dis.gui.sing @ny m3dicat!on wordz" (figure 14.2). The group hoped to enable resource sharing for medication and hormones at a time when these became especially difficult to access, with mass layoffs resulting in lost insurance and with the new risks involved in going to doctors' appointments or pharmacies. But, in an effort to evade surveillance—since sharing prescriptions, no matter how necessary, is illegal—participants were asked to write in code, replacing letters with special characters to evade search or algorithmic detection. Salerno titled the piece *ISO:*, an acronym that stands for "in search of." They made the piece not only in their bed but out of their bed, using their own pillowcase. To me, the gesture speaks to how such requests for life-sustaining material needs—the result of dire conditions and state failure—are enough to keep one up at night. The slow, all-consuming process of hand embroidering that request gestures toward how difficult it was to think of things other than survival and solidarity during lockdowns.

Salerno's broader practice not only carves space for honoring the importance of rest but draws attention to the politics of who has access to it. Their eleven-minute 2020 video *El Dios Acostado (The Sleeping God)* tells

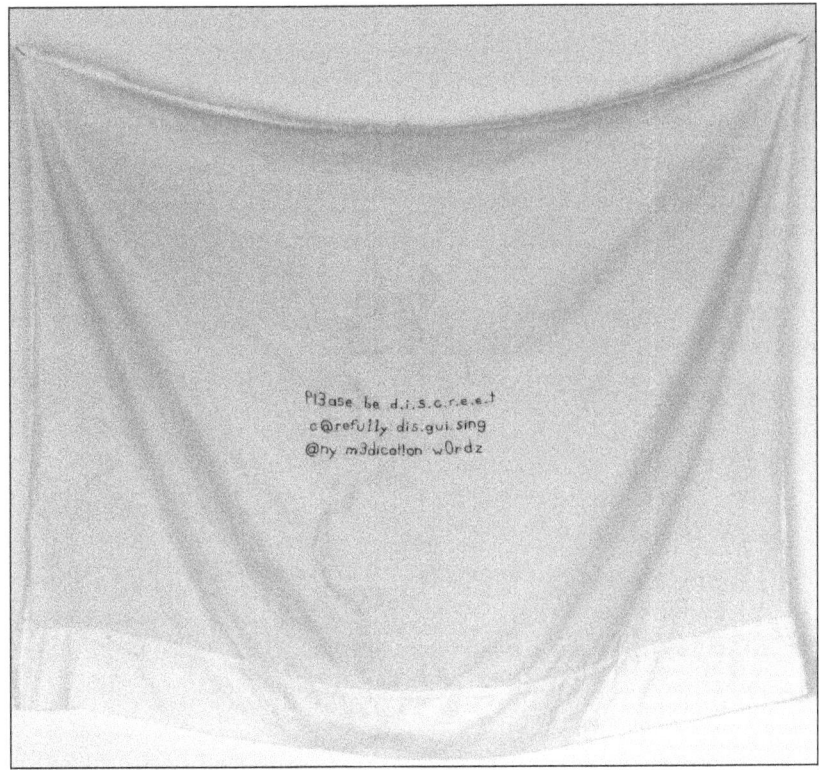

Figure 14.2. Alex Dolores Salerno, *ISO:*, 2020.

the story of Vilcabamba, Ecuador. In the 1970s, some North American gerontologists became fascinated with the town for its supposedly high concentration of centenarians, eventually nicknaming it the "Valley of Longevity." In a voice-over, Salerno's mother, who grew up nearby, reflects on the region's beloved qualities: its healthy air, its hospitable inhabitants. The gerontologists believed that those conditions—plus the mineral-rich water, the largely plant-based diet fostered by fertile soil, and the frequent hikes that accompany life in a valley—all contributed to lasting health. American expatriates have been flocking to the town, attracted to its peaceful pace and in search of long lives. But the resulting gentrification has produced inequities, causing the cost of living to increase and creating barriers to rest for locals. Importantly, the video itself is set to what the artist calls a "pace of rest." Rather than squish audio descriptions between moments of dialogue, Salerno folds them into the narration, then repeats them in English and in Spanish, implicitly asking why accessibility features should be bent around exclusionary standards rather than allowed to transform a work's entire premise. They also refuse to privilege one language over another for the sake of speeding things up.

As Salerno described to me in a 2020 studio visit, their practice explores how capitalism and colonialism are both disabling forces and frames rest as an act of resistance. Their video tells one of the many stories from the long, dark, and ongoing history of "medical colonialism," or the practice of subjecting people from the Global South to medical experimentation. Following the theorist Jasbir Puar, they critique the inequity faced by individuals who are treated as experimental subjects, who cannot afford health care, or who live in polluted environments, yet in a manner that does not equate disability with tragedy. And several of their works take the bed as a subject and a material: *At Work (Grounding Tactics)* (2020) is a platform bed frame topped not with a mattress but with diamond-plate industrial rubber flooring. Typically, one finds this material in spaces where workers stand on their feet all day: it prevents slipping and, being a softer surface, makes this strenuous demand slightly more tolerable. Underneath are cubbies with heating pads, tarot cards, candles, and stim toys. The cubbies also house numerous books, like Leah Lakshmi Piepzna-Samarasinha's *Care Work: Dreaming Disability Justice* (2018) and Jonathan Crary's *24/7: Late*

Capitalism and the Ends of Sleep (2013). In remaking the bed in a material that evokes labor done while standing, Salerno evokes the toll taken on the bodies of manual laborers, many of whom risk their health for minimal wages or have long commutes that cut into much-needed rest time. The work seeks, in Salerno's words, to frame sleep as "a need and a right," rather than "an aid to production."

It is important to honor the kinds of activities that take place in bed and to prioritize rest, but this is not to romanticize the profound negative impacts of isolation, of working in cramped apartments, and of trying to make art while disabled people and essential workers faced and/or feared death. It is also the case that working from bed can have damaging effects by allowing work to encroach further into one's sleep, or by making it more difficult to set rest-inducing boundaries. Another artist, Francisco echo Eraso, told me that it felt "impossible to make work" during lockdowns but that he was able to weave from bed when he started making work for his two partners (one of them being Salerno). "Two [projects] were so easy because they were acts of care," he told me. "Everything else feels so futile" (Eraso 2022). Eraso's two works are both made from the same yellow warp. One has yellow and light-blue wefts, and the resulting form has four vertical sections that are connected at the ends by golden frays, as if the whole piece is one large squiggle (figure 14.3). The other comprises three vertical stripes with crimson and scarlet wefts; here, the golden ends are cut but still frayed (figure 14.3). For so many people, and perhaps to state the obvious, the pandemic induced many kinds of existential rethinking as we abruptly broke from our routines and were left with lots of time to ask big questions, like, Why make art, and for whom? Eraso's response was, like many, to cultivate a smaller and more intimate world while separated from the larger one.

It is perhaps not surprising that the preceding two examples of work made in bed in New York during the pandemic are textile works. Working with fiber is often laborious, methodical, and repetitive and has long been used to pass time in domestic settings. Soft and pliable, textiles are often used to make a home comfortable, cozy, and inviting. We rest on textiles, and many techniques allow makers to fold up or transport their work; they do not require hard, flat surfaces, as drawing or painting do, surfaces rather antithetical to a bed. And they tend not to create huge

Figure 14.3. Francisco echo Eraso, *Blue and Yellow Tapestry*, 2021. (Collection of María del Mar Hernández Gil de Lamadrid)

Figure 14.4. Francisco echo Eraso, *Red and Yellow Tapestry*, 2021. (Collection of Alex Dolores Salerno)

Figure 14.5. Emilie L. Gossiaux, *On a Good Day You Can Feel My Love for You*, 2021. A contour drawing shows two sets of legs extending from the right edge of the page. One ankle is being licked by the long pink tongue of a yellow lab. The dog, tongue, and legs are colored in with crayon.

messes that you would not want in your sleep space, as paint or clay or woodworking might.

But the artist Emilie L. Gossiaux, working from her studio apartment in Manhattan, managed to develop an impressive method for drawing from bed. In fact, Gossiaux has rethought all the conventions of drawing to suit her own access needs. The artist, who is blind, uses ballpoint pen to create tactile indentations on newsprint paper. Typically, she observes her subjects by memory or by touch; often, when memories are fresh and vivid, she will draw them more than once. ("It's kind of like playing your favorite song over and over again," she once told me; Gossiaux 2022). She keeps her crayons in small envelopes with braille labels on them, describing each color in relation to a specific memory: Listeria is the Huffy bicycle she had growing up. Brick Red and Fuzzy Wuzzy combine to make her mother's Estée Lauder lipstick. Tropical Rainforest is her father's '80s Jaguar car.

Figure 14.6. Emilie L. Gossiaux, *True Love*, 2021. An expressive contour drawing shows a human figure with six nipples holding hands with a dog who has two breasts.

Gossiaux started working from bed in 2018. She was completing a residency in Scotland and found herself jet-lagged. Few things make work time and sleep time bleed together quite like trying to adjust to a new time zone. But she increased the habit during the pandemic, when she was working without a studio or even "a proper table to work at." These days, she has a studio downtown, but she still finds "working in bed so freeing": "I can just be comfortable; I can focus more" (Gossiaux 2022).

In an interview for *METAL* magazine, Gossiaux discusses drawing her guide dog, London, at home during the pandemic:

> When the pandemic and the lockdowns happened, I couldn't go to my studio anymore, and I was at home all the time with London. Our bond became the central focus [of my work] again, and I started thinking about this interspecies relationship with her. I was also thinking about being stuck in a city and longing to be in nature again. London strengthened my connection to nature and the animal world. I thought about London and imagined us becoming one being. When we are together, we become like one superbeing. She becomes my eyes, and I become her hands and voice. (Civin, n.d.)

But there is an important distinction between the role the bed serves in many of the art-historical precedents I began with and in works by Eraso, Salerno, and Gossiaux. For these disabled artists working in New York apartments during lockdowns, the bed is no metaphor. It is not a stand-in for a bygone socialist era or an optional choreographic prop. Instead, it reflects a material reality born of constraint. Still, in drawing our attention to that material constraint and asking us to question how rest and work, the bed and the studio, relate, the artists have nonetheless fashioned the bed, to varying degrees, as a meaningful site of resistance to ableist ideas of artistic production.

REFERENCES

Civin, Marcus. n.d. "Emilie Louise Gossiaux—Interdependence." *METAL*. Accessed January 5, 2024. https://metalmagazine.eu.

Eraso, Francisco Echo. 2022. Email to the author. August 3, 2022.

Gossiaux, Emilie L. 2022. Unpublished interview with the author. August 2022.

Hedva, Johanna. 2016. "Sick Woman Theory." *Mask Magazine*, January 2016.
———. 2020. *Minerva: The Miscarriage of the Brain*. San Francisco: Sming Sming.
Merjian, Ara H. 2022. "Surrealism & Politics." *Art in America*, April 2020, 36–43.
Rainer, Yvonne. 1965. "No Manifesto." Artwork.
Stilinović, Mladen. (1993) 2011. "In Praise of Laziness." In *Tekstovi / Texts*, unpaginated. Zagreb.

15

Reflections on Being a Disability Reporter during the Pandemic

AMANDA MORRIS

When the pandemic began, I was a science reporter. As summer vaccine trials started in 2021, the media largely focused on underrepresentation of people of color in the trials. While this is an important topic that should be covered extensively, with each new story, I remember wondering why there was no mention of another large group being underrepresented in the trials: disabled people, especially disabled people of color. In the course of my own reporting, I had found that both vaccine and drug trials often excluded people with immune-system issues or underlying health conditions, who were, ironically, the same people who would need vaccines or drug interventions most. I had the nagging sense that something big was being missed.

Ten months later, a period of time that felt like both an eternity and not so long at all, I got an incredible opportunity: to be the inaugural disability reporting fellow for the *New York Times* and cover disability as a full-time beat for the first time at a major, legacy news outlet. It was a position I feel incredibly blessed to have held, but it was also filled with impossible choices, made more difficult by the pandemic and the huge toll COVID-19 had on virtually every type of disability.

Each week, I received dozens of emails asking me to write on different issues relating to the pandemic, as well as personal accounts from disabled people about the struggles they faced. Choosing which stories to focus on felt like chipping away at a massive stone that weighed heavily on my mind. I had to remind myself that my own health mattered too and that unless outlets devote more time and resources to covering disabled communities, either as its own beat or within already-existing beats, I couldn't expect to capture every story myself. I also knew that I couldn't only focus my coverage on the pandemic's toll on disabled people, because too often, the stories of disabled people have *only* been told through a lens of suffering, and I wanted to reflect a wider range of stories on my beat.

Part of the issue with disability coverage in the media is that disability isn't well represented in newsrooms. In the United Kingdom, we know that roughly 14 percent of working journalists have a disability, thanks to a 2017 "Diversity in Journalism" report from the National Council for the Training of Journalists. In the United States, we don't have any data at all—a worrying sign that news organizations are not being held accountable for representing this aspect of diversity. Instead, I must actively search for every other disabled journalist I know, and I have sometimes felt alone in the newsroom. When disabled people aren't in the newsroom, the overall coverage of stories pertaining to disability often suffers.

In the course of the year, I wrote about battles over mask mandates in schools (Morris 2021c), the benefits of remote learning for some disabled students (Morris and Anthes 2021), the ways in which other students with disabilities fell far behind because of remote learning (Morris 2021b), the challenges people with Long COVID faced getting disability benefits (Morris 2021a), the inaccessibility of COVID-19 at-home tests (Morris 2022a), immunocompromised people seeking additional vaccine doses (Morris 2022b), and the frustration immunocompromised people felt as governments and organizations relaxed COVID-19 precautions without a plan for how to protect them (Morris and Astor 2022). And yet, I still only offered readers a small glimpse into all the profound ways that the pandemic impacted my community. That glimpse was made smaller still by the fact that each story was often limited to around twelve hundred words. But even if I were given pages and pages to write a whole book, like this one, it wouldn't capture everything.

What was hardest, harder than choosing which stories to cover, was picking which voices would be included in my articles. With the word limits I had, I could only fit three, maybe four, different disabled people's perspectives into each story. In order to get a true sense of what was going on in these communities and speak authoritatively on general trends, I needed to interview many more. The experience of reporting on disability during a pandemic is one of holding other people's stories inside me, knowing that the public may never comprehend the full scope of human suffering that occurred—and that I probably won't either.

I wasn't able to write about the immunocompromised children who were stuck at home, watching cartoons and playing video games instead of going to school because their schools had lifted mask mandates without any other safety measures. I never wrote about the ways in which mental health disparities worsened during the pandemic. I haven't yet written about the fight for disability accommodations at work for those who are newly disabled or for immunocompromised people being asked to return to offices or about the economic struggles of people with Long COVID who have been out of work for over two years. And not enough has been written about the ongoing collapse of home and community-based services and reliable, safe care work during the pandemic or about how supply-chain woes and staffing shortages have caused medical equipment and medical treatment to be harder to access.

Some people still stick with me, even if they never made it into an article. I think especially about a mother whose immunocompromised daughter, Elizabeth, was eight years old when I initially reached out to them during the Omicron surge in January 2022. I had been asked to contact families whose children would be at risk if they had to go to school in person without masks or other protection measures. Part of the assignment was to let the children speak for themselves about the situation. Elizabeth told me that her favorite color was a glittery pink, blue, and purple combination that she called "galaxy." She was worried about getting COVID but hoped that eventually everyone would get vaccinated. She said that when she grows up, she wants to help other children with medical issues like her.

My editors decided not to use Elizabeth in the article because I had interviewed other children who were older and, therefore, more articulate. I kept in touch with her mother, though, and reached out to her periodically, because I cared as a person, not just as a journalist. By March 2022, Elizabeth had been life-flighted in critical condition to the hospital because she caught COVID. At the time, much of the world was moving on from mask mandates and social distancing despite imperfect vaccination rates and subpar protections, and many people I knew in my personal life didn't seem to think much about immunocompromised or disabled people. Or, if they did, they weren't talking about it.

Others were dismissing immunocompromised people and their concerns as "over the top" or "overboard." But in the case of Elizabeth, her mother had been right to be afraid. I didn't want to write an article about Elizabeth's situation, because something about doing so—about asking her mother to do an interview with me in some of the worst moments of their lives, when Elizabeth was fighting for her life—didn't feel right. Still, I wanted to show the world that this was happening. With her mother's permission, I decided to tweet about the incident, writing, "This pandemic is still very real & still very, very scary for some."

Indeed, conducting interviews with people who felt incredibly isolated, ignored, or left out, while simultaneously seeing the world do little to help them, was profoundly difficult—and I think has been the biggest challenge of my career so far. To me, every person I interviewed was so obviously real—I heard their voices, I got photos and texts from them long after the interviews ended and the articles were published, and I listened to them cry. I felt a grief that I knew was only a puddle of sadness next to the deep lake of grief my sources felt.

As a journalist, I work not to take sides on any issue and to try to understand different perspectives. But, with each article I published, it didn't feel like I was taking a side. I was not advocating for any particular action or solution. Each article simply focused on the truth, which is that disabled people were suffering disproportionately from the pandemic. Like all good journalists, I was trying to get people to understand what was happening and, perhaps, to care.

I don't know how much of a difference the articles I wrote made. There were times when it felt like my articles were just another shout into a void of news fatigue, pandemic fatigue, or perhaps just general apathy. There were times where the public conversation minimized or ignored the impact of the pandemic on disabled lives. But there were validating moments too: when I got dozens of emails from disabled people who thanked me for making them feel seen, when I noticed people in power acknowledging disabled communities more, and when readers told me that I opened their eyes to something, or someone, they had never considered in the past.

In the end, it feels impossible to tell the stories of every disabled person's experiences during the pandemic. Everything you read in this book, or in the news media, is only a small portion of our lives. By the time my fellowship ended, Elizabeth was still in the intensive care unit. She spent most of the summer of 2022 in the hospital and, at one point, went into respiratory failure. US society had, for the most part, moved on from the pandemic. People went to the beach, traveled, returned to the office, held barbecues and parties and weddings.

I don't write this to demonize people who did these things, because I did them too. I traveled, I went out dancing, I ate at restaurants, and I got together with friends. I caught COVID. I felt better after a week (save for one toe that continues to tingle). I remained isolated until I tested negative. I've had the privilege to move on. But I'm choosing to continue considering COVID and recognizing those who are still at risk.

Elizabeth does not have the same abilities to move on. She almost died from COVID and, for the moment, is still at risk of catching it again. Even once her doctors have determined that the world is safe again for her, she will grow up knowing that there were some people who refused to get vaccinated or stay home when they were sick to protect her—an ugly truth that may take years for her to fully process. For her and many others with disabilities, the COVID era seems unending, and even when it does end, the ramifications will last for years to come. Their stories do not end here.

As awful as this pandemic has been for disabled people, it has also pushed their narratives further into mainstream conversations. The pandemic revealed worrying gaps in the care system that left people vulnerable, showed just how inaccessible the world can be, and gave others a small taste of what it's like to stay at home for fear of getting sick. Furthermore, the sheer number of people thought to have Long COVID—estimated to be in the millions—has caught the attention of governments, the media, and the general public.

For the first time, major legacy news outlets like the *Washington Post* and the *New York Times* have hired staff devoted to covering disabled communities. It's my hope that this is just a start. I hope we start to see extensive coverage of the ways disabled people support each other with mutual-aid efforts, such as distributing masks during wildfire season in California or sharing technology hacks to solve problems or ease challenges. I'd love to read more stories about the evolution of a new tactile language that deafblind people are creating, about the vibrant community of autistic people who identify as trans and nonbinary, or about the athletes who chose to take on the tough sport of wheelchair rugby, otherwise known as murderball. I'm not sure when the pandemic will be behind us or if we will ever be rid of COVID, but someday I really, really hope we will be able to read stories about the joy of immunocompromised people who finally feel safe. Stories about disabled people during the pandemic shouldn't be, and I hope won't be, the only stories we read.

REFERENCES

Morris, Amanda. 2021a. "Another Struggle for Long Covid Patients: Disability Benefits." *New York Times*, October 27, 2021, sec. U.S. www.nytimes.com.

———. 2021b. "Parents of Students with Disabilities Try to Make Up for Lost Year." *New York Times*, September 17, 2021, sec. New York. www.nytimes.com.

———. 2021c. "The U.S. Says Texas' Ban on School Mask Mandates May Violate Disabled Children's Rights." *New York Times*, September 30, 2021, sec. U.S. www.nytimes.com.

———. 2022a. "At-Home Coronavirus Tests Are Inaccessible to Blind People." *New York Times*, January 10, 2022, sec. Health. www.nytimes.com.

———. 2022b. "When Three Shots Are Not Enough." *New York Times*, January 3, 2022, sec. U.S. www.nytimes.com.

Morris, Amanda, and Emily Anthes. 2021. "For Some College Students, Remote Learning Is a Game Changer." *New York Times*, August 23, 2021, sec. Health. www.nytimes.com.

Morris, Amanda, and Maggie Astor. 2022. "Vulnerable to the Virus, High-Risk Americans Feel Pain as the U.S. Moves On." *New York Times*, February 17, 2022, sec. U.S. www.nytimes.com.

Coda

Toward a Disability Future

JUDITH HEUMANN

Judith "Judy" Heumann (1947–2023) was an internationally recognized disability rights activist, widely regarded as one of the leaders of the disability rights movement. She began her career as an activist in the 1960s, when she sued and won her case against the New York City Board of Education to be allowed to work as a teacher in New York City. Heumann was instrumental in the historic Section 504 Sit-In of 1977 and in the development and implementation of other groundbreaking disability rights legislation. She worked in the Clinton and Obama administrations, as an adviser at the World Bank, and as a senior fellow at the Ford Foundation. Her story is featured in the Oscar-nominated documentary *Crip Camp: A Disability Revolution* (2020) and her book *Being Heumann: An Unrepentant Memoir of a Disability Rights Activist* (2020). She continued to be active until her death at age seventy-five on March 5, 2023. See https://judithheumann.com.

On May 18, 2022, Heumann was an NYU Honorary Degree recipient and commencement speaker. She spoke compellingly about the experiences of disabled people during the pandemic. We are honored to be able to use her words as a coda to this book.

* * *

I've led protests that have closed down traffic on Madison Avenue. I've led peaceful sit-ins of federal buildings. I've testified before Congress on more than a few occasions. And I've even been the subject of a Comedy Central "Drunk History" story. I have to confess, though, that nothing made me so apprehensive as the prospect of preparing remarks for your graduating classes. Why? Well, usually graduating classes are filled with people who have just finished their degrees, who are on the precipice of heading out into the world, and in many, but not all, cases, they are individuals who have yet to experience a major challenge or disruption in their lives. You completed your studies one or two years ago. You are already out, working or pursuing further degrees or otherwise moving on with your lives. And as for disruptions, if the last two years don't count as life altering, I'm not sure what does. I've lived through a lot of upheaval in my life, but even for me, the last two years have been singularly remarkable.

Back in 2020, I was so excited at all the opportunities that were coming up. I was promoting my new book, *Being Heumann*, and participating in film festivals to support the documentary *Crip Camp*, which would later be nominated for an Oscar. It never occurred to me that all the events coming up on my calendar wouldn't just go ahead as planned. I still remember appearing on *The Daily Show* with Trevor Noah [on March 4] and just days later at Brooklyn Academy of Music. Then suddenly, by the following week, it was as though someone had slammed on the brakes to the entire world and everything was different. Anyone who knows me will tell you that I am a capital *E* for "extrovert." I love meeting people and being out and about, being part of the hustle and bustle of the world. You can take the girl out of Brooklyn, but you can't take the Brooklyn out of the girl. I do not like to sit still! I cannot presume to know how it was for you to have a global pandemic happen in the middle of your school year. But for me, suddenly the world felt much smaller and a lot quieter.

And then came what we in the disability community feared: disabled people dying because our lives were considered less worthy of treatment; Deaf people being hospitalized with no access to sign-language interpreters to understand what was happening or to meaningfully participate in decision-making about their care; people losing access to personal assistance services they needed to be able to live independently and avoid ending up in institutions. Over two hundred thousand residents and staff in long-term-care facilities died of COVID, which accounts for more than 23 percent of all COVID deaths in the US, and many were unable to see their families even at the end of life. At times like that, it can be easy to feel overwhelmed, to feel powerless to change things, or to just give up and take it for granted that nothing can be done.

But the disability community knew better. We're used to people telling us there are no solutions and then creating our own, so we did what we do best. We reached out to each other and to our allies, and we mobilized across communities to make change to benefit and include everyone in society. We demanded that the civil rights laws that we fought so hard for be enforced in health-care facilities, workplaces, transportation, schools, and elsewhere. We formed networks of support to keep each other connected and nourished in body and mind. And we smiled as society at large suddenly discovered online video-conferencing technologies and workplace flexibilities that disabled people had been at the forefront of developing and advocating for long before the rest of the world realized they could be part of a new normal. And we embrace the ever-widening diversity of our community and the strength that we know comes with that. The disability community is one that anyone can join at any time, so our identities are naturally intertwined with all other groups in societies around the world. And with more people self-identifying as having a disability because of Long COVID and society's increased interest in discussing mental health because of the impacts of the last two years, I am hopeful that yet more people will feel empowered to embrace their disability identity and that everyone will finally realize that disability is different. It is not deficiency.

You probably heard the Dr. Martin Luther King Jr. quote that "injustice anywhere is a threat to justice everywhere." What is less often quoted is what he said next: "We are caught in an inescapable network of mutuality, tied in a single garment of destiny. Whatever affects one directly affects all indirectly." If we haven't learned that after the last two years, I'm not sure what it will take to get people to recognize the truth of those words. We simply can no longer take for granted that what affects others, for better or worse, and wherever they are in the world, won't also impact us all. The last few years have been hard and, at times, heartbreaking. No question about it. But like the finest of swords, or chocolates if you prefer, the tempering you've experienced in the forge of the pandemic has made you stronger, even when you might not always feel that way.

That's why I am so excited about the world you are going to rebuild and are already shaping with your creativity, your power, and your diverse voices. Now and in the coming years, there are myriad issues that will require us to come together across diverse communities if we are to meet those challenges, whether it is global climate change, promoting biodiversity, protecting democracy, preserving our reproductive rights, creating communities that are more resilient, equitable, and inclusive, or simply supporting each other as we muddle through the daily challenges of life. Please know, and I know you believe, that you are up to those challenges. I wish you strength and good fortune as you move forward with your lives. And remember, never take for granted that you too have your part to play in weaving the strands of that single garment of destiny. Thank you.

APPENDIX A

New York City Pandemic and Disability Activism Timeline

This timeline was assembled by the authors, and represents key moments relevant to the chapters in the book.

December 2019	First reports of COVID-19 in Wuhan, China.
February 29, 2020	First confirmed case of COVID-19 diagnosed in New York (Manhattan).
March 2020	Thousands of New Yorkers contract the virus without official diagnosis. Despite widespread news reporting about viral transmission from China, a Mount Sinai study in June 2020 points to Europe as the source of most early NYC infections.
	Activist group #MEAction releases #StopRestPace campaign to share the expertise of people with ME/CFS (myalgic encephalomyelitis/chronic fatigue syndrome) with those who have Long COVID as well as broader publics.
March 7, 2020	A New York City coalition hosts a webinar called "COVID-19 (Coronavirus) Preparation for People Living with Chronic Illnesses in the U.S.," attended by approximately one thousand people.
March 9, 2020	A group of disabled and chronically ill artists in New York City organize Crip Fund to pool money and distribute food, medicine, and other aid to people needing in-home care.
March 12, 2020	Mayor Bill de Blasio issues a state of emergency, and Governor Andrew Cuomo bans attendance at large events.
March 13, 2020	The Centers for Medicare and Medicaid Services issues a guidance for nursing homes, restricting all visitors.
March 15, 2020	Mayor de Blasio closes all New York City Department of Education (NYC DOE) schools.
March 18, 2020	First person in city custody tests positive for COVID-19 at the Rikers Island jail complex.
March 22, 2020	New York State on PAUSE begins. "Nonessential" businesses close statewide, and remote work begins on a massive scale, though many sectors and types of work are deemed "essential" (including manufacturing, restaurants, certain types of retail, news media, financial institutions, construction, logistics, and many others). Social distancing begins in public spaces, with people asked to remain six feet apart. Parties and other gatherings are prohibited, and ill people are asked to quarantine at home. "Matilda's Law" lists separate rules for "vulnerable populations," such as remaining indoors, wearing a mask in the presence of others, and avoiding public transportation unless absolutely necessary.
	First confirmed cases in the state prison population: two people test positive at Wende Correctional Facility.

March 23, 2020	Remote instruction begins for all NYC DOE students.
March 27, 2020	An economic stimulus bill, the Coronavirus Aid, Relief, and Economic Security Act (CARES Act), is signed into law by then-president Donald Trump.
	New Yorkers begin clapping and banging pots and pans every evening at 7 p.m. to express their gratitude to nurses, doctors, and emergency workers on the front lines who are putting their lives at risk.
March 30, 2020	US Naval Ship *Comfort* arrives at Pier 90 in the Hudson River, initially to assist overwhelmed hospitals by treating overflow patients without COVID. On April 6, crew members began treating COVID patients; however, the ship's assistance turns out not to be required, and it departs on April 30.
	First New York prisoner dies from the coronavirus: fifty-eight-year-old Juan Mosquero, who tested positive at Sing Sing Correctional Facility in Ossining, NY.
April 2020	NYC begins burying people who have died from COVID on Hart Island, a potter's field, the largest mass grave in the United States. Burials are overseen by the NYC Department of Corrections, which hires inmates to bury the dead—who are disproportionately elderly, low income, Black and Latinx, and residents of The Bronx and Queens. In the first year of the pandemic, an estimated one-tenth of deaths in NYC are buried there.
April 5, 2020	Michael Tyson, fifty-three, dies at Bellevue Hospital after testing positive for COVID-19 while in custody at Rikers Island. He had been detained over a technical parole violation since February 28.
April 10, 2020	Most Americans receive a stimulus check of $1,200 as part of the CARES Act. There are two subsequent stimulus payments in December 2020 and March 2021. Disabled people who receive SSDI or SSI are eligible to receive stimulus payments without affecting their existing benefits; however, undocumented immigrants are excluded.
April 11, 2020	Mayor de Blasio announces that six thousand unhoused NYC shelter residents will be relocated to area hotels.
April 17, 2020	Governor Andrew Cuomo requires face masks for all New Yorkers in public settings.
May 6, 2020	For the first time since the launch of the New York subway in 1904, it stops running overnight, shutting down between 1 a.m. and 5 a.m. for disinfection.
May 25, 2020	George Floyd is murdered by a white police officer in Minneapolis.
May 28, 2020	Demonstrations begin in New York City protesting the death of George Floyd. Black Lives Matter actions condemning police violence and anti-Black racism continue throughout spring and summer.
June 1–7, 2020	Mayor de Blasio orders an 11 p.m. curfew (shifted to 8 p.m. on June 2) for New York City, the first since 1943.
September 21–October 1, 2020	NYC DOE school buildings open for hybrid learning.
November 3, 2020	Joe Biden wins the US presidential election against Donald Trump. The COVID-19 pandemic plays a large role as a key topic and a practical consideration that shifts norms around campaign tactics, debate and convention venues, and the mechanics of how and when people vote, expanding the use of mail-in ballots. Disabled activists foreground disability as a political issue through campaigns like #CripTheVote, Rev Up, and RespectAbility. Joe Biden and most major Democratic candidates create disability policy platforms.

November 18, 2020	NYC citywide positivity rate exceeds 3 percent. All NYC DOE buildings are temporarily closed the next day.
December 7–10, 2020	Elementary and District 75 schools (which serve students with complex disabilities) reopen for hybrid learning.
December 14, 2020	First person in the US receives the vaccine—an ICU nurse in Queens, NY.
February 25, 2021	Middle schools reopen for hybrid learning for some students.
March 14, 2021	The NYC Mayor's Office holds its first "COVID-19 Day of Remembrance," marking a year since NYC's first known COVID-19 death was confirmed. By now, thirty thousand New Yorkers have been lost to the virus. The faces of many who have died are projected on the Brooklyn Bridge to honor their memory, and all New Yorkers are invited to share their memories of loved ones lost via #COVIDMemorial.
March 22, 2021	High schools reopen for hybrid learning.
May 20, 2021	In response to AAPI (Asian American / Pacific Islander) activism (including social media campaigns such as #StopAsianHate, which went viral in early 2021), President Biden signs the COVID-19 Hate Crimes Act. The act supports measures to raise awareness about COVID-19-related hate crimes, offers grants to states for hate-crime hotlines, and creates a Department of Justice officer position to review such hate crimes. Many AAPI and abolitionist groups critique the framework of hate crimes as a feature of carceral politics.
June 15, 2021	Governor Cuomo officially "reopens" New York State, lifting all remaining state-mandated restrictions. This follows earlier stages of a multiphased plan, with data suggesting that 70 percent of New York adults had received at least one vaccine dose. Vaccinated people are no longer required to wear masks in most public spaces, and capacity limits in certain businesses are no longer in effect. Many disabled and chronically ill people contest this "reopening" as premature.
June 30, 2021	Contracts for NYC area-hotels to provide rooms to unhoused shelter residents expire, with few renewed.
July 26, 2021	Long COVID is included as a disability under the Americans with Disabilities Act (ADA), on the thirty-first anniversary of the act.
August 2021	Mayor de Blasio announces the "Key to NYC" program amid a wave of the Delta variant of COVID, requiring customers to show proof of vaccination to enter restaurants, museums, and other venues. Publicized as the first mandate of its kind in the US, vaccination rates increase across the city after the program starts on September 13.
December 6, 2021	In response to the contagious Omicron variant, Mayor de Blasio issues the "first-in-nation vaccination mandate" for all private-sector workers, starting December 27.
January 7, 2022	On *Good Morning America*, CDC director Rochelle Walensky comments on deaths from the Omicron variant of COVID, and was quoted saying: "These are people who were unwell to begin with. And yes: really encouraging news in the context of Omicron." In response, disability activist Imani Barbarin creates the hashtag #MyDisabledLifeIsWorthy, which goes viral, sparking wide-ranging conversations about neo-eugenics. Within a week, on January 14, Walensky meets with disability advocacy groups to apologize for her comment.
January 15, 2022	Michelle Go is fatally pushed onto a subway track at the Times Square station, part of a wave of anti-Asian violence in NYC during the pandemic.
February 13, 2022	Christina Yuna Lee is followed into her Lower East Side apartment by a stranger and killed. A few days later, a memorial of flowers, candles, and "Stop Asian Hate" signs on the sidewalk outside her building is vandalized.

March 2022	The Network for Long COVID Justice launches "Pandemics Are Chronic: A Statement of Commitment to Long Covid Justice." This coalitional effort demands that "in the third year of the pandemic, we must end practices and policies that ignore, and further marginalize, disabled and chronically-ill people."
March 14–18, 2022	Disabled activists of Downstate New York ADAPT hold a sit-in in front of the office of NYS Assembly member Carl E. Heastie in the Bronx to oppose the restrictions originally imposed on Medicaid-funded home-care eligibility in the state budget of 2020. These new, stricter eligibility for home- and personal-care services would make people eligible for nursing homes before being eligible for home-care services, adding another level of risk of exposure, contributing to the deterioration of living conditions in the pandemic.
May 2022	The US reports that over one million Americans have died of COVID.
September 18, 2022	President Biden declares, "The pandemic is over," on *60 Minutes*.
November 29, 2022	NYC Mayor Eric Adams, a former police captain who took office in 2022, announces an eleven-point plan that would allow unhoused and/or mentally disabled people to be involuntarily hospitalized, with NYPD and DOH teams deployed in subways to remove "those appearing to have serious mental health issues," leading to protests and litigation.
May 5, 2023	The World Health Organization officially declares an end to its designation of COVID-19 as a "public health emergency of international concern." This is just days before the White House's public health emergency officially expires on May 11, which also terminates the CDC's public posting of COVID-19 case counts. In the wake of these shifts, activists continue to pressure governments and institutions for policies to protect disabled, immunocompromised, and other vulnerable communities. For example, #KeepMasksInHealthcare includes a week of action in May 2023 to demand the reinstating of mask mandates in health-care settings.
May 11, 2023	A coalition of twenty NYC-based organizations, including Long COVID Justice NYC, organizes "Naming the Lost: The Many Losses from COVID-19," a political memorial in Green-Wood Cemetery in Brooklyn. The event, which is also livestreamed, includes speeches, poetry, and other examples of art and performance to honor those who have died. This event is one of many organized by the Naming the Lost coalition throughout the pandemic.
November 25, 2023	Sick in Quarters holds a HideAway event online, "a space for SiQ community and comrades / listen to one another / share current pandemic anxieties & tools." (Figure A.1)
May 19, 2024	The Naming the Lost coalition of NYC community groups once again remembers those lost to COVID-19, organizing "A Big, Slow, Majestic Covid Memorial" along Green-Wood Cemetery's fence, encouraging the public to add nameplates. The livestreamed event activated the memorial with a procession, traditional singers, and a remembrance ceremony inspired by disability justice writer Leah Lakshmi Piepzna-Samarasinha's words from her book *The Future Is Disabled*: "Everyone is holding so much grief right now, and it's so hard, but it's kind of created this bigger slower, majestic space to be real with what's going on and organize from that space."
August 14, 2024	Nassau County, east of New York City, institutes a ban on wearing masks in public, citing concerns related to protests against the Gaza war. Despite health and religious exemptions, many disabled activists raise objections to this added layer of political surveillance that once again dismisses their serious concerns. Mayor Adams and Governor Hochul earlier expressed support for mask bans; as of this writing, no legislation has been passed at the city or state level.

Figure A.1. A poster for SiQ's HideAway series, which was presented virtually.

APPENDIX B

Keywords from the Pandemic: A Disability Glossary

Keywords are condensed theories and spurs to action: this glossary is an archive of crip pandemic theorizing. Some of the keywords in our glossary originated as hashtags, others as academic terms; still others are ableist terms that galvanized disability resistance. Most are cited in the chapters of this edited collection, and all have shaped our thinking as we have grappled with diverse disabled experiences of the COVID-19 pandemic. Glossaries also have a role in disability studies, joining plain language and other approaches that help make text accessible and actionable (Acton 2023). Like other public glossaries and syllabi (e.g., Patsavas et al. 2022; Wong 2022), our compilation is a way to share disabled knowledges.

ACCEPTABLE LOSS

A military term for a "tolerable" number of casualties or deaths incurred in pursuit of a combat goal or in medical triage situations. Early in the pandemic, the number and kind of "acceptable losses" from COVID-19 began to be debated in epidemiology and the popular press with regard to the cost of public health measures or the availability of ventilators and vaccines. The deaths of older and immunocompromised people were routinely framed as acceptable losses, prompting dissent from disability activists (Cha and Keating 2022). For instance, in 2022, Roan Boucher of Pollinator Press Art created the linocut "Disabled People Deserve to Live" (figure A.2), posting it to Instagram along with a comment about the ableism of "acceptable loss" as a premise for public health policy.

COVID EXCEPTIONALISM

COVID exceptionalism is a form of "disease exceptionalism," understood in the medical community as an occasion when a particular disease

Ableism has informed the US's pandemic response since the beginning. Last week, CDC Director Rochelle Walensky cited the "encouraging" data that the majority of Covid deaths are in those with 4 or more pre-existing medical conditions. This statement and its phrasing lay bare what disabled people have seen clearly—that their/our lives are disposable to those who are guiding public health policy, that the deaths of disabled people are considered an acceptable loss.

Rather than protecting the most vulnerable, our leaders have asked us to carry the burden of survival alone, so everyone else can act as though things are "normal." Disabled people (and fat people, pregnant people, elders, and other vulnerable folks) are not expendable. People of color and poor people are not expendable. Our public health response is based on eugenicist logics, insisting that we normalize millions of preventable deaths.

A humane and coherent public health strategy would take a fraction of the money and energy our government spends on militarism, incarceration, and policing. The lack of action on Covid is an extension of this violence, an unacceptable—if predictable—response from a society that values white supremacy and profit for the wealthy over the survival and care of its people.

Figure A.2. Roan Boucher, Pollinator Press Art, linocut, January 2022.

galvanizes funding, public attention, publications, and resources—sometimes to the exclusion of research or treatment for other public health concerns. As Sandro Galea put it in "Reckoning with Covid-19 Exceptionalism" (2021), "disease exceptionalism can be both a blessing and a curse." COVID exceptionalism has raised awareness of infectious diseases, while drawing attention away from other escalating causes of mortality, such as drug overdoses. Disease exceptionalism can also sometimes lead to social change. Galea writes, "HIV exceptionalism served to spark movements that elevated justice-based approaches into the collective consciousness, transforming care received by, for example, LGBTQ populations. COVID-19 exceptionalism will be a success only if it can lead similarly to a reckoning with the factors that resulted in the COVID-19 burden among minoritized racial and ethnic groups, for example."

COVID-19 DOULA

What Does a COVID-19 Doula Do? is the name of a zine created in the second week of March 2020, written by the community of long-standing activists identified as What Would an HIV Doula Do? "as people in the US were finally waking up to the emergency" (WWHIVDD Collective 2020). Contributors to the *What Does a COVID-19 Doula Do?* zine brought their knowledge of HIV/AIDS care, responding "in words, actions and images to the unfolding, unprecedented, global crisis of the COVID-19 pandemic" (WWHIVDD Collective 2020). This project grew out of the exhibition *Metanoia: Transformation through AIDS Archives and Activism*, organized by the ONE Archives Foundation and the Lesbian, Gay, Bisexual and Transgender Community Center New York and curated by Katherine Cheairs, Alexandra Juhasz, Theodore (ted) Kerr, and Jawanza Williams for WWHIVDD.

That same month, Kevin Gotkin, Louise Hickman, and Aimi Hamraie of the Critical Design Lab developed "Remote Access: Crip Nightlife Participation Guide" (2020), a "disability-centric . . . guide for remote nightlife" inspired by the expansion of the doula role by the WWHIVDD community: "We understand a doula as someone who holds space during times of transition." By extension, access doulas "help monitor gathering[s], looking for ways to help enhance access, . . . a role for folks who want to help get creative with the resources we have" (Gotkin, Hickman, and Hamraie 2020).

The idea of the access doula that emerged during the pandemic is now used more widely in the disability community, revealing the influence on the present pandemic of prior social movements catalyzed during the HIV/AIDS pandemic.

COVID-19 TRAUMA

By summer 2020, psychologists and other health experts began to recognize the array of traumatic impacts of the pandemic, from individual trauma due to the loss of loved ones and jobs to the "secondary trauma" of health-care workers witnessing unprecedented deaths to the collective trauma experienced by residents of abruptly and radically transformed cities. On July 27, 2020, the New York City Department of Health published an online notice titled "Acknowledging Psychological Trauma and Promoting Resilience during COVID-19." As of May 2024, the New York City Department of Health and Mental Hygiene (2020) maintains the following "Statement on COVID-19 Trauma" on its homepage:

> The Health Department acknowledges how stressful and painful this pandemic has been. The loss of loved ones, jobs, businesses, homes, and livelihoods, combined with feelings of uncertainty, sadness, fear, and worry, have been a huge weight on us all. We acknowledge that Black, Indigenous, and people of color (BIPOC) have been disproportionately impacted by COVID-19 and continue to experience and resist the daily impact and reality of years of disinvestment, racism, biased treatment and oppression.
>
> We acknowledge the historical and contemporary injustices in government and health care that have deepened distrust and contributed to the causes of individual and collective trauma and structural inequities. The Health Department names racism as a public health crisis and commits to becoming an anti-racist institution that acknowledges our history, takes action to eliminate inequities, and protects and promotes the health of all New Yorkers.

CRIP FAMILY RECIPES

In a roundtable on disabled community care during the pandemic, art therapist and professor Sandie Yi discussed collective approaches, using the phrase "crip family recipes." Yi's recipe metaphor counters biomedical approaches to care, offering an alternative rooted in intergenerational familial practices that balance ordered structure with a spirit of improvisation, an openness to interpretation, and an adaptability for multiple flavors. As Yi notes, "I was really thinking about how, you know, 'this is my grandma's recipe.' And I don't have the same ingredients from her generation or the technique. But I'm going to adapt something that I have. . . . And most of us weren't taught that 'this is your crip family.' And so I like to think that we are creating a family together. And there could be our family recipes" (Patsavas et al. 2022). That is, unlike an algorithm or a prescription, a recipe is always already relational and material, subject to change based on whoever is engaging with whatever ingredients, tools, and skills are at hand. It is also meant to provide nutrition and sustenance, rather than solve a discrete problem. Finally, the variability in preparing a recipe gestures toward the unique experiences and "flavors" of different disabilities and disabled individuals, acknowledging that while certain models may be shared in common, there is much to be learned from diversity and divergence as well.

CRIP SPACETIME

Crip Spacetime, the title of a 2024 book by disability scholar Margaret Price, is also a concept that many disabled writers turned to during the pandemic. Building on crip time and critical disability studies, Price argues that during the pandemic, many nondisabled people found themselves experiencing circumstances well-known to those with disabilities who experience a sense of shrinkage of their "spacetime": "housebound, unable to predict what might happen next week, trying to plan in advance for future debilitation, anxious, frightened, and suddenly dependent on strangers for their own health and safety" (2021, 262). Price shows how academia's disabled workers have unique experiences of space, time, and being. Their diminished realities differ from those of nondisabled colleagues, what Price theorizes as "crip spacetime." COVID-19 led to "the compression of more work into increasingly limited time frames," with budget cuts and job loss, "while those still employed are expected to do (even) more with (even) less. . . . The pandemic, while sometimes extolled as a chance to slow down, offers that pleasant kind of slowness only to the most privileged" (Price 2021, 262). Price urges that "collective accountability is the only way forward to equity and justice, especially for disabled academics" (2021, 273). These insights regarding the exacerbation of inequalities produced by the pandemic and the need for "collective accountability" have had an ever-widening impact among disabled academics and their allies. The lessons learned by long-term chronic illness activists, particularly those with ME/CFS who have often felt marginalized and silenced, took on new prominence. Their longstanding disability expertise provided emotional and practical resources for people experiencing similar debility for the first time as a consequence of COVID-19.

CRIPISTEMOLOGIES OF CRISIS

In the introduction to a spring 2022 special issue of *Lateral*, the journal of the Cultural Studies Association, disability studies scholars and issue editors Alyson Patsavas and Theodora Danylevich present the idea of "cripistemologies of crisis: emergent knowledges for the present." They provide a framework for understanding the impact of the pandemic, arguing that "epistemologies of chronicity, illness, and trauma offer indispensable lenses through which to rethink—and care for—our collective present." This special issue encourages the wider disability community to consider how the sense of crisis produced by the pandemic expands bodymind knowledge. Patsavas and Danylevich argue that this experience provides a foundation for an "epistemological toolkit to theorize and survive everyday states of trauma, madness, and illness as the lived impacts of such quotidian and ongoing violence." They ask "what crip futures can be conjured through a centering of experiential, collective, and speculative ways of knowing with/in/through crisis," adding to an already-rich body of writing on crip futurity that preceded the pandemic.

CRIP CRISIS COMPETENCIES

At various stages of the pandemic, and especially in its early days, disabled people were often called on to offer their expertise in managing illness, risk, access, and care to broader publics and institutions. However, as with many moments in which marginalized communities receive increased attention, these interests in crip epistemologies often proved to be a double-edged sword: on the one hand, offering greater recognition but, on the other, relegating disabled knowledges to an exceptional moment of crisis, rather than positioning them as integral in challenging entrenched ableist structures. In elaborating on "cripistemologies of crisis," Patsavas and Danylevich (2022) at first describe this phenomenon as "crip crisis knowledge" but then revise it to "crip crisis competencies," playfully nodding toward the insidious language of neoliberal appropriation and institutionalization of such ways of knowing—without actually learning from people most impacted.

CRISIS METHODS

Researchers working in moments of crisis and trauma often find it difficult to express the emotional tolls of their work. Even when theoretical or methodological conventions encourage scholars to be reflexive about their positionalities or to express certain vulnerabilities, they are rarely trained to address personal emotions, let alone to offer or accept care in the face of collective traumas. As disability sociologist Laura Mauldin writes of pandemic-related research, "I needed to hear that . . . someone else had been gutted by their project. But I also needed explicit guidance for how to have the courage to be vulnerable within my work, while at the same time adequately caring for myself and my participants in the process. That is, in the middle of all these crises, of all the trauma, I needed a *care plan*" (2023, 3). Mauldin offers the phrase "crisis methods" to describe a "trauma-informed frame" that recognizes the deep challenges but also the opportunities of addressing such crises with care for both researchers and their collaborators.

DIGITAL PUBLIC SPACES

In December 2020, NYU researchers Mona Sloane and Jordan Kraemer published the white paper *Terra Incognita NYC: Mapping New York City's New Digital Public Spaces during the COVID-19 Outbreak*. This report surveys the sudden move of work, education, advocacy, social and religious life, health, and exercise online at the start of the pandemic, across the five boroughs of New York City. While not focused on disability experiences, the findings provide context for the hybrid New York City of 2020 and beyond: the frequent anchoring of digital spaces in local communities; the simultaneous transformation of digital and outdoor space in the city; the urgent need for new kinds of home technology to afford remote access to work, education, and social life; and the equally urgent need for public interest technology and infrastructure to ensure more equity and privacy than corporate infrastructure offers.

DISINFORMATION

Rampant "disinformation" about the pandemic on mainstream news platforms and social media encouraged information sharing, crip doulaing, and mutual aid within disability communities. The *Oxford English Dictionary* defines "disinformation" as "the dissemination of deliberately false information" (as opposed to simply incorrect "misinformation"), which might range from propaganda to "fake news" to health scams.

DISPOSABILITY / #NOBODYISDISPOSABLE

"No body is disposable" is a phrase used by Patty Berne of Sins Invalid, long before the pandemic, to protest the logic of "disposability" that inflects US economic, health, and housing policies for disabled people. According to the #NoBodyIsDisposable website (n.d.), "In 2019, Max Airborne re-ignited the phrase as the hashtag #NoBodyIsDisposable, along with Stacey Milbern and Dawn Haney, in an action with Fat Rose and Disability Justice Culture Club to bring Fat and Disability communities together. In 2020, the #NoBodyIsDisposable Campaign came together to resist triage discrimination during the COVID-19 pandemic." The #NoBodyIsDisposable action published "Know Your Rights Guide to Surviving COVID-19 Triage Protocols" on its website in 2020. Throughout 2020–21, the hashtag was often used on social media in combination with #NoICUgenics.

DOUBLE PANDEMIC

The phrase double pandemic (or "twindemic") emerged in 2020 and spread virally, with diverse meanings. One of its first uses appeared in an October 2020 issue of *Social Sciences and Humanities Open Journal*. In the article "Double Pandemic: Racial Discrimination amid Coronavirus Disease 2019," author Isaac Yeboah Addo shows how "the emergence of the COVID-19 pandemic has seen an escalation of racial discrimination against non-citizens and people of colour in many places around the world."

In 2021, author Briana Starks offered a helpful elaboration in the journal *Qualitative Social Work*: "Often called the double pandemic, the interconnectedness of the Covid-19 pandemic and the pandemic of racism (both anti-Black and anti-Asian) in 2020 have exacerbated inequalities and followed predictable historical pathways. However, as most individuals from marginalized backgrounds know, the pandemic of racism is nothing new. It has been superimposed on top of the pre-existing racism, xenophobia, blaming, and 'othering.' The common roots of all this lie in White supremacy" (2021, 222).

The "double pandemic" has also been used to underscore the likely possibility of multiple overlapping pathogenic pandemics (sometimes referred to as a "syndemic"). For example, the science writer Ed Yong authored a July 2020 interrogation of this possibility, asking, "What happens if another pandemic starts before this one is over?"

HINTERLAND OF DISABILITY

Science writer Ed Yong was particularly alert to how disabled and chronically ill people experienced the pandemic. In an influential September 1, 2021 essay in The Atlantic, "Long-Haulers Are Fighting for Their Future," he introduced the phrase "hinterland of disability" to describe the situation of "long-haulers" in particular. As he explains, "Any discussion of the pandemic still largely revolves around two extremes—good health at one end, and hospitalization or death at the other. This ignores the hinterland of disability that lies in between, where millions of people are already stuck, and where many more may end up.... The choice we make about how to study this condition will define the toll that SARS-CoV-2 takes for years to come." His idea of the hinterland of disability gave public recognition to an important and often marginalized dimension of the pandemic experience. This was especially important for the increasing numbers of immunocompromised and/or chronically ill people, as well as long-haulers dwelling in that hinterland, particularly as the COVID-19 emergency was declared "over."

ILLNESS METHODOLOGY

This term is Melissa Kapadia's (2020), coined in 2016 and expanded in 2020 for the COVID era, to refer to "an embodied set of practices that centers the ill researcher" and "illness epistemologies." Illness methodology includes "license to research from the body," trauma- and justice-informed research, going beyond institutional review board (IRB) ethics standards, building access into research design, and recognizing that "research as an industry operates under ableist values" (Kapadia 2020).

MEDICAL GASLIGHTING

In February 2022, Mike Mariana published an article in *The Guardian* titled "The Great Gaslighting: How Covid Longhaulers Are Still Fighting for Recognition." Mariana, who lives with ME/CFS, describes the "misdiagnosing and psychologizing" of COVID long-haulers as a form of "medical gaslighting"—a deceit or manipulation that causes a person to question reality and their own sanity. Mariana argues that medical gaslighting can lead to "medical PTSD" as well as social stigma and lack of treatment.

NECROPOLITICS

The Cameroonian historian and political theorist Achille Mbembe introduced the term "necropolitics" to describe political power as a process for managing life and death, in which states assume the power "to define who matters and who does not, who is *disposable* and who is not" (2003, 27). According to this framework, governments are equally (if not more) concerned with the management of death as they are with the maintenance of life, determining not only who lives and dies but the quality of people's lives, often along racialized lines. As such, Mbembe argues that such administrative power results in "the creation of *death-worlds*, new and unique forms of social existence in which vast populations are subjected to conditions of life conferring upon them the status of *living dead*" (2003, 43, original emphasis). Many other scholars have engaged these theories; for example, Lauren Berlant (2007) has described the state's active neglect of marginalized populations as "slow death," while Jasbir Puar (2017) has theorized how states often stop short of facilitating outright death, instead conveying a "right to maim" by leaving populations *debilitated* by various injuries. While Mbembe's term is meant to be applied to ongoing regimes of power, and not only during crises, the COVID-19 pandemic provides an acute example of how many people in power were quick to let certain populations not only die but also become disabled (often exacerbating existing forms of discriminatory disposability).

ORGANIZED ABANDONMENT

The abolitionist geographer Ruth Wilson Gilmore popularized this phrase (drawing on David Harvey's work) to describe a historic shift in the twentieth century from the state's provision of resources—such as education, health care, housing, and other social welfare programs—to the revocation of such support, leaving individuals to fend for their own well-being through the false choices of capitalist marketplaces. Increasingly, the nonprofit sector has ballooned to fill these gaps in service, though, as Gilmore argues, organizations are often detached from any political analysis or real community ties. Thus, this term, also sometimes referred to as "state abandonment," implies less a specific project than an organizing logic, which, as Gilmore describes, results in a racialized "group-differentiated vulnerability to premature death" (2007, 28). The COVID-19 pandemic exposed and exemplified many instances of organized abandonment: from disabled people who were treated as disposable in health-care settings to "essential workers" whose labor was needed to provide lifesaving services but received inadequate compensation or protections to shifts away from government provided or mandated resources like free testing and treatments once the Biden administration declared the pandemic "over."

PANDEMIC ABLEISM

This straightforward phrase describes the unique forms of ableism instigated or exacerbated by the COVID-19 pandemic, rooted in ideologies of neo-eugenics and policies of neglect. As activist and writer Charis Hill (2022) explains, "Since day one of COVID, people like me have been presumed disposable, complementing longstanding societal messaging that being disabled is intolerable. . . . [The pandemic] response has been the most glaring, acute, widespread ableism many of us have ever experienced. The determination to approach COVID mitigation with as few measures as possible in order to allow the most freedoms possible fails to acknowledge whose freedoms are granted and whose are disregarded." As authors throughout this volume demonstrate, pandemic ableism has been evident across nearly every aspect of life, from official government policies in health care, prisons, and schools to everyday social interactions in which disabled people are positioned as burdensome or expendable.

PANDEMIC FATIGUE

The World Health Organization (WHO) has defined "pandemic fatigue" as "people . . . feeling demotivated about following recommended behaviours to protect themselves and others from the virus." As some people grow tired of precautionary measures and the glut of information about the threat of catching COVID-19, they may begin to disregard public health recommendations. For many others, pandemic fatigue refers more straightforwardly to feelings of weariness or depression as a result of years of pandemic anxiety and restrictions. The related term "zoom fatigue" arose in response to the overuse of this teleconferencing platform.

PANDEMIC NIHILISM

This phrase points to a popular defeatist attitude—embodied by many political and public health leaders and members of the general public—that death and disability from COVID-19 are inescapable, and as such, that there is little value in preventative efforts. Pandemic nihilism may thus be understood as a more extreme and structural corollary to *pandemic fatigue*. Beatrice Adler-Bolton, cohost of *Death Panel Podcast* and coauthor of *Health Communism*, explains that this nihilistic sentiment has been increasingly noticeable among liberal and leftist leaders—noting that early calls for community care and critiques of the Trump administration's pandemic policies quickly vanished once privileged populations gained access to measures like vaccines and the Biden administration took office (Adler-Bolton 2022b). She describes this pessimistic attitude as defined by an individualistic sentiment of "because of what's already happened, how do I convince myself fighting for better pandemic policy is worth it? Why should I care?" (Adler-Bolton 2022a). Relatedly, Adler-Bolton (2022a) invokes the provocatively-rich phrase "deaths pulled from the future," derived from an essay published in the *Milwaukee Journal Sentinel* in 2020, arguing that many leaders have articulated a narrative "framing of deaths from Covid-19 as somehow preordained," thus justifying policies that fail to protect vulnerable people.

PANDEMIC PROFITEERING

This phrase is closely related to the more general term "disaster profiteering," which journalist Naomi Klein explains is "the way private industries spring up to directly profit from large-scale crises" (Solis 2020). In the case of the COVID-19 pandemic, as in many kinds of disasters—war, natural disasters, health crises, and others—not only did new companies emerge to profit from offering specific products and services, but many existing pharmaceutical, health-care, technology, and other corporations also shifted their work to take advantage of the financial opportunities they perceived in offering personal protective equipment (PPE) and essential equipment and services (or simply by raising prices). In other cases, individuals "profiteered" by hoarding and reselling PPE. In 2020, US Senator Cory Booker introduced the Prevent Emergency and Disaster Profiteering Act of 2020, although it did not pass; similarly, the nongovernmental organization Oxfam America advocated for a COVID-19 profits tax to discourage inequitable profiteering and reinvest COVID-19-related profits into relief and recovery efforts (Lusiani 2020). For more information on specific cases of pandemic profiteering, see ProPublica journalist J. David McSwane's book *Pandemic, Inc.* (2023).

PANDEMIC REVISIONISM

Dr. Katelyn Jetelina is an epidemiologist and the author of the popular online newsletter *Your Local Epidemiologist*, inaugurated in March 2020 to update a wide range of readers across the globe on the developments of the pandemic. She translates the "ever-evolving public health science so that people will be well-equipped to make evidence-based decisions" (Jetelina 2023). In July 2023, she argued that we have entered a new phase of the COVID-19 pandemic that she calls "pandemic revisionism," defining it as an "impulse that seduces us into swapping cheap talking points for the thorny, difficult decisions we actually faced—and may face again with the next novel virus" (Jetelina 2023). For example, pandemic revisionism suggests that the wide-ranging and controversial school closures in the US were "wrongheaded" despite evidence to the contrary.

PANDEMIC ROLLBACK

Amid the overall devastation of the pandemic, many disabled activists celebrated victories in policies and new cultural norms that improved their lives—several of which they had been demanding for years. However, as the pandemic was increasingly declared "over" in a rolling series of declarations by various global and local political leaders, public health workers, businesses, and organizations, many of these hard-won resources were taken away. Such actions angered people who pointed out the hypocrisy of providing essential resources only in times of extreme crisis. These rollbacks (also called "post-pandemic rollbacks") included the revocation of many different kinds of benefits: increased and more flexible unemployment payments; SNAP funds; free coverage of pandemic-related health care (such as testing, vaccines, and postexposure treatments); more flexible Medicaid eligibility; eviction protections; masking requirements; and access to telehealth and other remote access options.

PANDEMIC SOLUTIONISM

In a 2023 *Digital Culture and Society* article, the media and technology scholars Felix Maschewski and Anna-Verena Nosthoff address "pandemic solutionism," in which they "investigate how Big Tech companies have used the pandemic to increase their social, political, infrastructural, and epistemic power" (2023, 43). They examine how Alphabet/Google, Apple, Facebook, and Amazon responded to the public health crisis with technological solutions. They call this strategy "pandemic solutionism": "the belief in the potential to solve the complex virological crisis of COVID-19 through the integration of digital tools" (2023, 43). Maschewski and Nosthoff argue that these companies present themselves as saviors "capable of acting more promptly than the state, pushing pandemic solutionism and taking up tasks without being burdened by democratic deliberations. In doing so, they have manifested their infrastructural power, which frequently (such as with contact tracing) establishes the normative framework in which political and social actions take place" (2023, 43).

In addition to the antidemocratic tendencies of pandemic solutionism, some disabled people found themselves excluded due to limited access to technology needed for remote work, education, and telemedicine. As the disabled Cherokee activist Jen Deerinwater (2023) argues, for Indigenous New Yorkers with and without disabilities and with extremely high poverty rates, the digital divide has been even more pronounced, given long-standing technical and economic barriers to "remote access." Thus, technological fixes to the pandemic presented challenges rather than solutions.

PANDEMIC THEORIZING

Influenced by the foundational disability rights slogan "Nothing about us without us" (Charlton 2000), this collection is premised on the understanding that there is no adequate theory of the pandemic that is not a disability theory, yet the diverse voices of disabled people affected by COVID-19 are too often underrepresented and inadequately theorized.

In the spring 2022 special issue of *Lateral: Journal of the Cultural Studies Association* on "cripistemologies of crisis," historian and disability studies scholar Jiya Pandya (2022) poses the question, "What is pandemic theorizing?" The experience of COVID-19, she suggests, brings paranoia and repair into productive tension; a sense of suspicion is necessary for bodymind safety. At the same time, crip reparative approaches such as "mutual aid lists, survival tips, and guidelines on safe protesting and direct action" are essential to localized world-building, which forms part of a long history of practicing intimate and relational modes of care.

Together, these approaches highlight that pandemic theorizing remains open-ended, growing with the inclusion of diverse disability experiences and localized world-building.

PEDAGOGY OF UNWELLNESS

In the 2024 book *Dear Elia: Letters from the Asian American Abyss*, scholar-activist Mimi Khúc traces the experiences shaping the contemporary Asian American mental health crisis from the university to the COVID-19 pandemic. She reframes mental health through what she calls a "pedagogy of unwellness": the recognition that we are all differentially unwell. She argues that we can no longer do Asian American studies without Asian American mental health—and vice versa. Khúc focuses on Asian American unwellness, inviting readers to recognize the sources of their own unwellness, suggesting that there are alternative ways of being that open new possibilities for collective care.

PRIVILEGED DISABLED

Disability activists-writers Marta Russell and Ravi Malhotra coined the term "the privileged disabled" in their chapter "Capitalism and Disability" in the 2002 *Socialist Register*. In considering "the prospects and limitations" of the disability rights movements, they critique "a strategy of disability liberation politics entirely dependent on purchasing power

[that] is so impoverished as to be of assistance to only a tiny fraction of the most privileged disabled people. It also tends to marginalize the concerns of women and minorities" (2002, 218). The radical potential of disability rights, they argue, is undermined by an individualist free market ideology. They write, "The ability to access the marketplace is cold comfort to the huge proportion of disabled people living in poverty or near-poverty conditions" (2002, 218). This important critique recognized the inequalities within and across the disability rights movement, influencing the development of a wider intersectional focus on disability justice. During the pandemic, the increasingly stark contrast between the privileged disabled and those who are impoverished and/or institutionalized was evidence of the capitalist hierarchies that Russell and Malhotra describe. At the same time, the emergence of mutual-aid networks offered a glimpse of the utopian possibilities within disability communities.

RACIAL ABLEISM

Racism and ableism often intersect in profound ways. This term speaks to the unique experiences of disabled Black, Indigenous, and people of color (BIPOC) who not only endure racism and ableism as distinct forms of oppression but, following theories of intersectionality by Kimberlé Crenshaw (1991), also experience these forces as deeply intertwined. Unfortunately, the COVID-19 pandemic was a time of many examples of racial ableism, as discussed throughout this book, from the disproportionate viral exposures and deaths in Black and Brown communities to the stereotypes and violence targeted toward Asian American communities to the police killings of Black disabled people whose Blackness and disabilities were often mutually perceived as "threats" by police (Thompson 2021).

Moreover, disabled BIPOC representation has been limited in popular and social media: an issue that the Black disabled activist Vilissa Thompson brought to the fore in launching the hashtag #DisabilityTooWhite (Dunn 2020). As an academic field, disability studies has also too often failed to take up the intersections of race and disability, especially the specific needs of disabled people of color, as analyzed by Kristen Bowen, Rachel Kuo, and Mara Mills in "#DisabilityStudiesTooWhite" (2023).

We note that the specific term "racial ableism" is attributed to the disabled Indigenous Australian (Koori) sociologist John Gilroy (2022), though variations and other concepts have been used by many disabled BIPOC scholars and activists historically in similar ways.

REMOTE ACCESS

In "Life at a Distance: Archiving Disability Cultures of Remote Participation," disability scholars/activists Kelsie Acton and Aimi Hamraie (2022) argue that the move to "remote access" during the pandemic was well-known to many disabled people for whom "remote participation was a familiar, necessary, and still-contested part of daily life." While access is conventionally used to indicate efforts to make the public sphere inclusive for disabled people, "within disability culture . . . remote access is a significant (though largely undocumented) dimension of social and vocational life." As Acton and Hamraie explain, "Although remote access precedes the pandemic, this phenomenon finds continuity with the forms of exclusion that disabled people face (and respond to) in our contemporary era. Prior to the pandemic, many disabled people requested—and were denied—access to remote learning, work, healthcare visits, conferences, and other opportunities." The need for remote access intensified during the pandemic, revealing inequalities in power relations and resource allocation. Recognizing the lack of documentation of disabled people's remote access creativity, Acton and Hamraie (2022) launched the Remote Access Archive in 2021.

SOCIAL MURDER

This phrase was coined in the nineteenth century by the socialist philosopher Friedrich Engels ([1845] 1975) to describe capitalism as not merely an economic system but one that also produces profound social effects, including war, imperialism, and other forms of violence. Such effects are not always experienced directly as violence, however, but are also normalized through policies and discourses. In the context of the COVID-19 pandemic, social murder thus refers to the ways that capitalist imperatives shaped policies resulting in death, debility, and disability—especially policies that rushed to "reopen" and resume "business as usual" at the expense of vulnerable people's well-being. As historian Nate Holdren described in an episode of *Death Panel Podcast*, "Capitalism is a social system that is lethal. . . . If we think of the public health phrase 'social determinants of health,' . . . the phrase means the health of any individuals or groups is not primarily or only the result of those individuals' and groups' actions. Rather, their health is the result of the social context they live in. . . . Capitalist societies determine people's health in capitalism-specific ways" (Holdren, Vierkant, and Cartus 2023).

SOCIOLOGICAL PRODUCTION OF THE END OF THE PANDEMIC

The Death Panel is an independent podcasting collective that addresses politics, culture, and public policy from the left. When President Biden declared the end of the COVID public health emergency on May 11, 2023, it produced an influential episode titled the "Sociological Production of the End of the Pandemic" (Death Panel 2023). Tracing the narrative of the pandemic under Biden, it analyzes how the US came to "end the pandemic" not by stopping COVID but by renarrating its social and political meaning.

VIRAL UNDERCLASS

In the 2022 book *The Viral Underclass: The Human Toll When Inequality and Disease Collide*, the professor and journalist Steven Thrasher writes that COVID-19 made "millions, if not billions, of humans consider for the first time how living with a common virus can make a person feel like a pariah" (2022, 267). Thrasher helps us understand why viruses can have disparate outcomes in communities of color. This work builds on his long-standing writing about the HIV/AIDS epidemic and the social vectors, including racism, ableism, the law, and austerity, that help create the viral underclass in both pandemics.

VIRTUAL HOME BUILDING

This is Amy Gaeta's phrase for relations of care, mutual aid, expertise, and friendship on social media, especially for disabled and chronically ill people isolating at home during the pandemic. Gaeta writes,

> By engaging with disabled people on Facebook and Twitter, I've made connections strong enough that together we've shared our utmost secrets, offered financial support without ever being asked, wrote and created, planned international disability justice campaigns, cried, laughed, and never let one another forget our worth. These relationships have sustained me when I could not do so myself; this is the utmost sign of

interdependence. I feel at home when I am supported, I am visible, and I am held accountable. Hence, I know I am home with the online disability community because they have made me a better, kinder person and all I want is to support them in their projects, goals, and happiness. (Gaeta 2020)

REFERENCES

Acton, Kelsie. 2023. "Plain Language for Disability Culture." In *Crip Authorship: Disability as Method*, edited by Mara Mills and Rebecca Sanchez, 58–72. New York: New York University Press.

Acton, Kelsie, and Aimi Hamraie. 2022. "Life at a Distance: Archiving Disability Cultures of Remote Participation." *Just Tech*, Social Science Research Council, June 28, 2022. https://just-tech.ssrc.org.

Addo, Isaac Yeboah. 2020. "Double Pandemic: Racial Discrimination amid Coronavirus Disease 2019." *Social Sciences & Humanities Open* 2 (1): 100074. https://pubmed.ncbi.nlm.nih.gov.

Adler-Bolton, Beatrice. 2022a. "Deaths Pulled from the Future." Substack newsletter. *Blind Archive* (blog), January 3, 2022. https://blindarchive.substack.com.

———. 2022b. "Pandemic Nihilism [Is] Not the Solution.'" *Democracy Journal*, May 12, 2022. https://democracyjournal.org.

Berlant, Lauren. 2007. "Slow Death (Sovereignty, Obesity, Lateral Agency)." *Critical Inquiry* 33 (4): 754–80. https://doi.org/10.1086/521568.

Bowen, Kristen, Rachel Kuo, and Mara Mills. 2023. "#DisabilityStudiesTooWhite." In *Crip Authorship: Disability as Method*, edited by Mara Mills and Rebecca Sanchez, 244–58. New York: New York University Press.

Boucher, Roan (Anti-Oppression Resource and Training Alliance). 2022. "Disabled People Deserve to Live." Instagram, January 11, 2022. www.instagram.com/p/CYmYN9KFjkv/.

Cha, Ariana Eunjung, and Dan Keating. 2022. "Covid Becomes Plague of Elderly, Reviving Debate over 'Acceptable Loss.'" *Washington Post*, November 30, 2022. www.washingtonpost.com.

Charlton, James. 2000. *Nothing about Us without Us: Disability Oppression and Empowerment*. Berkeley: University of California Press.

Crenshaw, Kimberlé. 1991. "Mapping the Margins: Intersectionality, Identity Politics, and Violence against Women of Color." *Stanford Law Review* 43 (6): 1241–99. https://doi.org/10.2307/1229039.

Death Panel. 2023. "The Sociological Production of the End of the Pandemic." SoundCloud, May 11, 2023. https://soundcloud.com.

Deerinwater, Jen. 2023. "Crip Indigenous Storytelling across the Digital Divide." In *Crip Authorship: Disability as Method*, edited by Mara Mills and Rebecca Sanchez, 350–54. New York: New York University Press.

Dunn, Lisa. 2020. "Vilissa Thompson, Creator of #DisabilityTooWhite, Brings an Intersectional Lens to Disability Advocacy." InclusionHub, December 29, 2020. www.inclusionhub.com.

Engels, Friedrich. (1845) 1975. "The Condition of the Working Class in England." In *Collected Works of Karl Marx and Frederick Engels*, vol. 4, 295–596. New York: International.

Gaeta, Amy. 2020. "Virtual Home Building and Rebuilding: Disabled Communities in the COVID-19 Pandemic." *Disability Visibility Project*, March 26, 2020. https://disabilityvisibilityproject.com.

Galea, Sandro. 2021. "Reckoning with Covid-19 Exceptionalism." *JAMA Health Forum* 2 (12): e214854. https://jamanetwork.com.

Gilmore, Ruth Wilson. 2007. *Golden Gulag: Prisons, Surplus, Crisis, and Opposition in Globalizing California*. Berkeley: University of California Press.

Gilroy, John. 2022. "Indigenous People with Disabilities Face Racism and Ableism. What's Needed Is Action Not Another Report." *The Conversation*, August 9, 2022. http://theconversation.com.

Gotkin, Kevin, Louise Hickman, and Aimi Hamraie. 2020. "Remote Access: Crip Nightlife Participation Guide." March 2020. bit.ly/RemoteAccessPartyGuide.

Hill, Charis. 2022. "'Urgency of Normal' Rhetoric Fuels Pandemic Ableism." *Being Charis* (blog), *Medium*, February 9, 2022. https://beingcharis.medium.com.

Holdren, Nate, Artie Vierkant, and Abby Cartus. 2023. "DP x S23: How Capitalism Kills: Social Murder and Covid-19 (Session 2)." *Death Panel*, SoundCloud, September 19, 2023. https://soundcloud.com.

Jetelina, Katelyn 2023. "It's Time to Talk about Pandemic Revisionism." *The Ezra Klein Show, New York Times*, August 29, 2023. www.nytimes.com.

Kapadia, Melissa. 2020. "Illness Methodology for and beyond the COVID Era." *Perspectives on Urban Education* 18 (1): 1–3. https://urbanedjournal.gse.upenn.edu.

Khúc, Mimi 2024. *Dear Elia: Letters from the Asian American Abyss*. Durham, NC: Duke University Press.

Lusiani, Nico. 2020. "Pandemic Profiteers Exposed." Oxfam, July 22, 2020. www.oxfam.org.

Mariani, Mike. 2022. "The Great Gaslighting: How COVID Longhaulers Are Still Fighting for Recognition." *The Guardian*, February 3, 2022. www.theguardian.com.

Maschewski, Felix, and Anna-Verena Nosthoff. 2023. "Pandemic Solutionism: The Power of Big Tech during the COVID-19 Crisis." *Digital Culture and Society* 8 (1): 43–66. https://papers.ssrn.com/sol3/papers.cfm?abstract_id=4454582.

Mauldin, Laura. 2023. "Crisis Methods: Centering Care in a Precarious World." *SSM—Qualitative Research in Health* 4:1–8. https://doi.org/10.1016/j.ssmqr.2023.100319.

Mbembe, Achille. 2003. "Necropolitics." Translated by Libby Meintjes. *Public Culture* 15 (1): 11–40. https://doi.org/10.1215/08992363-15-1-11.

McSwane, J. David. 2023. *Pandemic, Inc.* New York: Simon and Schuster.

New York City Department of Health. 2020. "Acknowledging Psychological Trauma and Promoting Resilience during COVID-19." www.nyc.gov.

New York City Department of Health and Mental Hygiene. 2020. "Statement on COVID-19 Trauma." www.nyc.gov.

#NoBodyIsDisposable. 2020. "Know Your Rights Guide to Surviving COVID-19 Triage Protocols." July 28, 2020. https://nobodyisdisposable.org.

———. n.d. Home page. Accessed May 20, 2024. https://nobodyisdisposable.org.

Pandya, Jaya. 2022. "On Navigating Paranoia, Repair, and Ambivalence as Crip Pandemic Affects, or, I'm So Paranoid, I Think Your COVID Test Is about Me." *Lateral* 11 (2). https://csalateral.org.

Patsavas, Alyson, and Theodora Danylevich. 2022. "Introduction: Crip Pandemic Life: A Tapestry." *Lateral* 11 (2). https://doi.org/10.25158/L11.2.5.

Patsavas, Alyson, Theodora Danylevich, Margaret Fink, Aimi Hamraie, Mimi Khúc, Sandie Yi, and Corbin Outlaw. 2022. "Crip Pandemic Conversation: Textures, Tools, and Recipes." *Lateral* 11 (2). https://doi.org/10.25158/L11.2.6.

Price, Margaret. 2021. "Time Harms: Disabled Faculty Navigating the Accommodations Loop." *South Atlantic Quarterly* 120 (2): 257–77.

———. 2024. *Crip Spacetime: Access, Failure, and Accountability in Academic Life*. Durham, NC: Duke University Press.

Puar, Jasbir K. 2017. *The Right to Maim: Debility, Capacity, Disability*. ANIMA: Critical Race Studies Otherwise. Durham, NC: Duke University Press.

Russell, Marta, and Ravi Malhotra. 2002. "Capitalism and Disability." *Socialist Register* 38:211–28. https://socialistregister.com.

Sloane, Mona, and Jordan Kraemer. *Terra Incognita NYC: Mapping New York City's New Digital Public Spaces during the COVID-19 Outbreak*. New Public, December 2020, https://newpublic.org.

Solis, Marie. 2020. "Coronavirus Is the Perfect Disaster for 'Disaster Capitalism.'" *Vice*, March 13, 2020. www.vice.com.

Starks, Briana 2021. "The Double Pandemic: Covid 19 and White Supremacy." *Qualitative Social Work* 20 (1–2): 222–24. https://journals.sagepub.com/doi/full/10.1177/1473325020986011.

Thompson, Vilissa. 2021. "Understanding the Policing of Black, Disabled Bodies." Center for American Progress, February 10, 2021. www.americanprogress.org.

Thrasher, Steven 2022. *The Viral Underclass: The Human Toll When Inequality and Disease Collide*. New York: Macmillan.

Wong, Alice. 2022. "High-Risk Pandemic Stories: A Syllabus." *Disability Visibility Project*, January 9, 2022. https://disabilityvisibilityproject.com.

World Health Organization. 2020. "WHO/Europe Discusses How to Deal with Pandemic Fatigue." October 7, 2020. www.who.int.

WWHIVDD Collective. 2020. *What Does a COVID-19 Doula Do?* http://hivdoula.work.

Yong, Ed. 2020. "America Should Prepare for a Double Pandemic." *The Atlantic*, July 15, 2020. www.theatlantic.com.

———. 2021. "Long-Haulers Are Fighting for Their Future." *The Atlantic*, September 1, 2021. www.theatlantic.com.

ACKNOWLEDGMENTS

Our work has been shaped by countless conversations with fellow disability activists, scholars, journalists, artists, librarians, and many others whose work addresses the urgent and ongoing concerns raised by the COVID-19 pandemic.

This book grew out of a broader documentation project called the "Disability Covid Chronicles." For the first two years of the pandemic, the editors and many of the authors in this volume were fortunate to have regular online meetings to discuss research and archiving, as well as the personal effects of COVID-19 and the social and political shifts it wrought. In these meetings, we were grateful to remotely welcome several guests from a range of allied projects, including the following:

- Alexandra Juhasz, Pato Hebert, Jason DaSilva, and Neta Alexander of the Long Hauling series for ArtsEverywhere
- Megan Moodie, who organized the University of California Humanities Research Initiative working group "How We Make It: Imagining Disability Justice after Covid's Long Haul," which also included Alexandra Juhasz and Pato Hebert
- Sharon Daniel, who discussed her interactive documentary *Exposed*
- Kate Mason and Sarah Willen of the Pandemic Journaling Project
- Marianne Hirsch, Diana Taylor, Laura Wexler, and Lorie Novak of the Zip Code Memory Project
- Lucy Treishman and Maya Goldman of the Breaking Point Project
- Zachary Gillespie, Julie Livingston, and Thuy Linh Tu of the NYU Prison Education Program
- Rachel Kuo, Mon Mohapatra, and Matilda Sabal of Sick of It!
- Scott Knowles and Jacob Steere-Williams of COVIDCalls

In addition to the several graduate students who contributed chapters to the book, we also thank Victoria Netanus Grubbs and Sarah

Vázquez-Xu, who were members of our research team; Indyara Morais, who joined our regular meetings while on a Fulbright fellowship in New York City; and Sasha Kurlenkova, Stephanie Farmer, and Bella Ruhl, who contributed to our website's "Fieldnotes." Similarly, we thank Shannon O'Neill (curator for Tamiment-Wagner Collections), Nicole Greenhouse (web archivist for NYU Libraries), Anna McCormick (NYU librarian for archival arrangement and description), and Laura Chen-Schultz and the other organizers of A/P/A Voices: A COVID-19 Public Memory Project, for providing us with much-needed guidance on the ethics and practicalities of archiving oral histories and digital materials. And we are uniquely indebted to the ME activist and writer Molly Freedenberg for introducing us to Ed Yong, and to Rick Heumann for graciously giving us permission to reprint his late sister Judy Heumann's commencement speech to New York University graduates of 2020–21, when she received an honorary doctorate.

We also thank staff who assisted with the budget, hires, and website—and in countless other ways. These include Muna Diaz, Meesh Fradkin, and Destiny Lopez from NYU's Center for Disability Studies; JoJo Karlin, Marii Nyrop, and Jonathan Greenberg from the NYU Libraries and Digital Humanities Initiative; DeSandra Torbor and Mary McShane from the NYU Steinhardt School; and Myriam Bonilla, Jess Cayer, Latia McAlister, Dani Resto, Carlisa Robinson, and Kenny Yi from NYU's Department of Media, Culture, and Communication.

Additionally, we are grateful to funders who made this book and its related projects possible: an NYU COVID-19 Research Catalyst grant, which included an initial partnership with our colleague Art Caplan, professor of bioethics at the New York University Grossman School of Medicine; a National Science Foundation grant (#2043833); and an NYU Digital Humanities Seed Grant. We are especially appreciative of the guidance we received from NSF Science and Technology Studies program directors Wenda Bauchspies, Frederick Kronz, and Christine Leuenberger.

Our gratitude goes out to the astute readers for NYU Press who took time and care to comment on different versions of the manuscript, offering incisive suggestions for improvement and heartening encouragement, including Alexandra Juhasz and anonymous reviewers. Cara Ryan provided skilled and timely indexing, for which we are grateful.

Additionally, the artist duo Brothers Sick (Ezra and Noah Benus) generously worked with us to adapt their 2020 work "Masks" for the book's cover image.

We also feel extremely fortunate to have had the support, enthusiasm, and thoughtful guidance of our editors, Eric Zinner, editor in chief of NYU Press, and editorial assistant Furquan Sayeed, who carefully shepherded this project to publication.

Finally, we could not have completed this project without the enormous generosity of everyone who shared their pandemic experiences with us—whether credited by name or not—through interviews, preserving ephemera, and in countless other ways. This book is a testament to disability expertise and solidarity.

ABOUT THE EDITORS

MARA MILLS is Associate Professor of Media, Culture, and Communication at New York University. She cofounded and directs the NYU Center for Disability Studies. She is also a founding editorial board member of *Catalyst: Feminism, Theory, Technoscience*. She is recently coeditor of *Crip Authorship: Disability as Method* (NYU Press, 2023) and a 2024 volume of *Osiris* titled "Disability and the History of Science."

HARRIS KORNSTEIN is Assistant Professor of Public and Applied Humanities at the University of Arizona. As an interdisciplinary scholar and artist, their work focuses on digital culture, drag, surveillance, artificial intelligence (AI), media arts and activism, disability, and queer theory. Their research and essays have appeared in journals like *Surveillance & Society* and *Curriculum Inquiry*, several edited books, and popular outlets like *The Guardian*, *Wired*, and *Salon*.

FAYE GINSBURG, David Kriser Professor of Anthropology, is cofounder with Mara Mills, of NYU's Center for Disability Studies; she directs the NYU Center for Media, Culture, and History. She is the author or editor of four award-winning books, and her 2024 book *Disability Worlds* is coauthored with Rayna Rapp. An adviser for the ReelAbilities Film Festival since its inception, she is in her second decade as President of the Familial Dysautonomia Foundation.

RAYNA RAPP is Professor Emerita of Anthropology at NYU and affiliate of the Center for Disability Studies. She has written or edited four award-winning books and published widely on the politics of reproduction, gender at the intersections, and disability. She joins Faye Ginsburg in the research and writing of their 2024 book *Disability Worlds*.

ABOUT THE CONTRIBUTORS

TOMMASO BARDELLI is Director of Research and Popular Education at Worth Rises, an advocacy organization dedicated to dismantling the prison industry. Before joining Worth Rises, Tommaso was a Postdoctoral Fellow at NYU, where he cofounded the NYU Prison Education Program Research Lab. With Andrew Ross and Aiyuba Thomas, he is the author of *Abolition Labor*, examining the experiences of incarcerated workers and chronicling the movement to end slavery and involuntary servitude in US prisons and jails. Tommaso holds a PhD in political science from Yale University.

SALONEE BHAMAN is an interdisciplinary scholar who researches, writes, and teaches about social movements, feminist politics, and economic inequality in the twentieth-century United States. Her current book project explores the political economy of care work and queer subjectivity during the first decades of the HIV/AIDS epidemic in New York City. She holds a PhD in history with a certificate in women, gender, and sexuality studies from Yale University. She is a Faculty Fellow in the program for Interdisciplinary Humanities and Social Engagement (XE) at New York University.

DYLAN BROWN, a graduate of NYU Gallatin School of Individualized Study, is an educator and Associate Director of the NYU Prison Education Program.

BOJANA COKLYAT is Associate Manager of Access Programs and Initiatives at the Whitney Museum of American Art. She is a disabled artist, 2019–20 J. William Fulbright alumna, and previous project leader at the New York City Museum Arts and Culture Access Consortium (MAC). In 2019, she curated *Crip Imponderabilia*, the first gallery exhibit at NYU centering disabled artists and disability culture. Around that time, she began collaborating with Finnegan Shannon on the Alt-Text as Poetry project. This has included facilitating workshops for Twitter, Google, and MIT. Recently, Coklyat has taken on the position of associate producer on a film funded by the American Foundation for the Blind, featuring a variety of different people in the blind community. Coklyat is also currently teaching a class on access and design at the New School.

RACHEL FISH is Associate Professor in the Department of Education and Child Study at Smith College. She uses multiple methods to examine racialized and gendered constructions of disability and giftedness, how these processes are shaped by school context, and how they relate to educational inequality.

CHANCEY FLEET is Assistive Technology Coordinator for the New York Public Library. In that role, she curates accessible technology at the Andrew Heiskell Braille and Talking Book Library, collaborates across the NYPL system to improve equity of access, and coordinates a diverse team of staff and volunteers who provide one-to-one tech coaching and group workshops, free of charge and open to all. Through a 2017 NYPL Innovation grant, she founded and maintains the Dimensions Project, a free open lab for the exploration and creation of accessible images, models, and data representations through tactile graphics, 3-D models, and nonvisual approaches to coding, CAD, and "visual" arts. She was recognized as a 2017 Library Journal Mover and Shaker and in 2018–19 was a Data and Society Fellow.

ALEXANDRA FREIDUS is Assistant Professor of Educational Leadership at the University of Connecticut. Her ethnographic research examines how community stakeholders conceptualize student diversity, how administrators enact educational policy, and how these social and political contexts relate to teaching and learning. Her recent book (published by NYU Press) explores the opportunities and limits of diversity as an approach to educational justice in New York City schools.

YAN GRENIER is Postdoctoral Research Fellow with the Department of Anthropology and the Center for Disability Studies at New York

University. Funded by the Fonds de recherche du Québec Société et Culture (2020–23) and the Social Sciences and Humanities Research Council (2024–25), his ethnographic research focuses on the situated interactions between disabled New Yorkers and the city's transportation infrastructure and services and how these relations are contributing to producing emergent modalities of existence within the city arrangement. He is teaching the first francophone class in critical disability at l'Université St-Paul. Recently, he has taken the role of Associate Professor in the department of Social Work and Criminology at l'Université Laval, where he teaches disability studies.

RACHEL KUO is Assistant Professor of Gender and Women's Studies and Asian American Studies at the University of Wisconsin-Madison. She studies race, social movements, media, and technology. She is a cofounder of the Asian American Feminist Collective, an author of 8 to Abolition, and cocreator of Sick of It!

SHUTING LI is a PhD candidate in sociocultural anthropology, pursuing a certificate in culture and media at New York University. Her doctoral project explores how care robots will shape elder-care practices in the Chinese family by investigating the entanglement of robotic technology, the state, and elder-care practices in the Chinese family in a transnational context. She is the director of the ethnographic documentary *Chang Jiu Yuan / Year after Year*, which was selected for the 2023 19th Chinese American Film Festival and the 2024 17th German International Ethnographic Film Festival.

NADIA MBONDE is a PhD candidate in sociocultural anthropology at New York University. Her research interests lie at the intersection of medical anthropology, disability studies, mad studies, and Black feminist theory. Her dissertation project addresses how perinatal mental health disparities contribute to the ongoing Black maternal mortality and morbidity crisis in the United States.

MON MOHAPATRA is an abolitionist researcher, poet, and spadeworker living on ancestral Canarsee land. Her work focuses on national and local jail moratoriums, supporting an end to caste apartheid, antisurveillance obfuscation practices, and building intergenerational, interclass organizing capacity for abolitionist work in the so-called US and beyond. She is an author of 8 to Abolition, a cofounder of the No New Jails Network, cocreator of Sick of It!, and a member of Critical Resistance and Survived and Punished.

AMANDA MORRIS is a disability reporter for the *Washington Post* who has trailblazed on this beat. Before joining the *Post* in 2022, she was the inaugural disability reporting fellow for the *New York Times* and previously covered science, politics, and national news for outlets like the *Arizona Republic*, the Associated Press, and NPR. A graduate of New York University, she uses her experiences as a hard-of-hearing woman with two deaf parents to inform her coverage.

YVES TONG NGUYEN is a queer and disabled Vietnamese cultural worker, sex worker, and death doula whose organizing home is with Survived & Punished NY and Red Canary Song. They are personally concerned with supporting survivors of all forms of violence through organizing and informal community support.

EMILY LIM ROGERS is Assistant Professor of Cultural Anthropology at Duke University. Her work has appeared in *Medical Anthropology Quarterly* and in the edited volume *Crip Authorship*, among others. Her first book project, *Clinical Proximities: ME/CFS and Biomedicine's Binds*, is an archival and ethnographic excavation of myalgic encephalomyelitis/chronic fatigue syndrome (ME/CFS) in the United States, looking at its history of dismissal and the ways that patient activists have pushed back.

CARA RYAN is an anthropologist who received her PhD from New York University in 2023. Her research has explored autistic communities in New York and France. Her dissertation, supported by the Franco-American Fulbright Commission and the Wenner-Gren Foundation for Anthropological Research, focuses on changing categories of autism in France and autism in the French university system. She is currently an affiliated researcher with the Projekt Design and Social Innovation laboratory at the University of Nîmes (France).

J.C. SALYER is Associate Professor of Practice in Anthropology and Human Rights and is Director of the Human Rights Program at Barnard College, Columbia University. He is also a staff attorney for the Arab-American Family Support Center, a community-based organization in Brooklyn, where he runs the organization's immigration clinic. His recent book, *Court of Injustice: Law without Recognition in U.S. Immigration*, combines anthropological and legal analysis to understand how the US immigration law operates and how immigrants and their attorneys navigate this often-hostile system.

HEENA SHARMA is a facilitator, youth worker, and political educator based in Lenapehoking. She is focused on abolitionist liberatory efforts in her work building grassroots resources and providing direct support to disabled, LGBTQ, and incarcerated BIPOC communities. She is a member of Survived & Punished NY and works at Project LETS.

AIYUBA THOMAS is a justice-impacted researcher, advocate, and educator. With Andrew Ross and Tommaso Bardelli, he is the author of *Abolition Labor*, examining the experiences of incarcerated workers and chronicling the movement to end slavery and involuntary servitude in US prisons and jails. He holds an MA from NYU Gallatin School of Individualized Study and currently serves as Project Manager for "Movements against Mass Incarceration" at Columbia University.

ERICA O. TURNER is Associate Professor of education policy at the University of Wisconsin–Madison. Her research examines racism and inequity—and diverse stakeholders' efforts to challenge those—in education policy and practice.

EMILY WATLINGTON is an art critic, curator, and senior editor at *Art in America*. Her writing focuses on disability arts and work at the intersections of art and science. She is a Fulbright scholar with a master's degree in art history from MIT and the recipient of such awards as the Theorist Award from C/O Berlin and the Vera List Writing Prize for Visual Arts.

ED YONG is a science writer. For his coverage of the COVID-19 pandemic, he won the Pulitzer Prize in explanatory journalism, among other honors. He is the author of two *New York Times* best-sellers: *I Contain Multitudes* and *An Immense World*, which won the Carnegie Medal for Excellence in Nonfiction.

INDEX

Page numbers in italics indicate Figures.

abandonment, organized, 345
ableism, 336, 345
   in immigration law and policy, 65, 167, 169, 255
   racial, 350–51
acceptable loss, 335
access
   friction, 20–21, 201–2
   to masks, 70
   to public transportation, 100–115
   remote, 18, 27, 102, 111, 157, 351
   for work/workers, 111–14
#AccessibilityForAbleds, 112
activism
   AIDS, 8–11, 21–25, 83, 87–88, 201, 337
   art and, 292–93, *293*, *295*, 309–10, *310*, 311, *311*
   disability, 105, *105*, 112, *112*
   Long Covid, 201–9, *207*, *208*
   ME/CFS, 191, 198, 200, 201–9, *204*, *207*, *208*
   Rise and Resist, 105, *105*
   timeline for New York City pandemic and disability, 329–32
ACT UP, 87–88, 201–2. *See also* AIDS activism
ADA. *See* Americans with Disabilities Act
ADAPT New York, 103, 112, *112*
AEDPA. *See* Antiterrorism and Effective Death Penalty Act
Afrofuturism, 272, 284

aging, 102, 228, 231–33, 242–47. *See also* elderly people
   nursing homes and, 1, 4, 6–7, 13, 30, 34nn7–8, 112, 135, 167–71
   social distancing and, 229, 230, 296
   successful, 234–41
AIDA. *See* Anger into Direct Action
AIDS activism, 8–11, 21–25, 83, 87–88, 201, 337
Albence, Matthew T., 72
allocation of healthcare resources, during pandemic, 18, 45–61, 69–71, 120, 147, 278–81
   Criteria for Mechanical Ventilator Triage Following Proclamation of Mass-Casualty Respiratory Emergency, 122
   ECMO machines and, 134
   Glasgow Coma Scale, 143
   Guidance for the Ethical Allocation of Scarce Resources, 122
   New York State Task Force on Life and the Law, 123–25, 131
   SOFA scoring and, 13
   ventilators and, 121–46
American Rescue Plan Act of 2021, 221
American Sign Language mural, 12, *12*
Americans with Disabilities Act (ADA) of 2021, 88, 96, 104
Anderson, Tanisha, 273
Anger into Direct Action (AIDA), 87–88, 97

anti-Asian racism, 22–23, 28, 229, 237–39, 251–69, 263, 268
anti-Black racism, 22, 28, 69, 143, 259, 262–67, 271, 272–75, 279
Anti-Oppression Resource and Training Alliance (AORTA), 336, 336
Antiterrorism and Effective Death Penalty Act (AEDPA) of 1996, 70
AORTA. *See* Anti-Oppression Resource and Training Alliance
Arbery, Ahmaud, 272
"An Army of the Sick Can't Be Defeated" (Brothers Sick art), 9
Arroyo, Quemuel, 108
art/artists. *See also* films; performance art
 activism and, 292–93, 293, 295, 309–12, 310, 311
 American Sign Language mural, 12, 12
 Asian American Feminist Antibodies, 23–24, 24, 257
 bed rest and, 308–17
 Brothers Sick, 9, 145
 Eraso, 313, 314
 Gossiaux, 315, 315–17, 316
 ISO:, 311, 311
 I Think We're Alone Now (Host), 309–10, 310
 memorial, 101, 101
 Poets of Course, 181, 182, 186
 Reality Poets, 169, 170–71, 185, 185
 Sins Invalid, 10, 74, 128, 150
 SiQ, 26, 26–27, 27, 333
 Washington Square Park vigil, 268, 268
Asch, Adrienne, 6, 127, 133
Asian American Feminist Antibodies (artwork), 23–24, 24, 257
Asian American Feminist Collective, 268, 268
Atlanta shooting, 268, 268
autism, 157–58, 160, 172, 173, 289–300, 304–6
 La Bulle! association for, in France, 301–3
 for queer and trans people, 323

Bagenstos, Samuel, 122
Barbarin, Imani, 3–14, 17
BCID. *See* Brooklyn Center for Independence of the Disabled
Being Heumann (Heumann), 325, 326
Be My Eyes (app), 19
Berne, Patty, 10, 144, 342
Bérubé, Michael, 173
The Biggest Obstacle (documentary film), 108, 111, 115
bioethics, 13, 123–25, 129–33
birthing, pregnancy, and postpartum, 273, 276–84
Birthing under Investigation (Schiavenato), 280
Black disabled queer and trans people, 12, 304
Black Futurity, 271–85
Black Lives Matter protests, 23, 219–20, 273, 275, 291–93, 309
Black maternal mental health crisis, xi, 12, 28, 271–85
Bland, Sandra, 273
blindness/blind people, 27, 56–57, 127, 214–27, 315, 323
 app for, 19
Blue and Yellow Tapestry (Eraso), 314, 314
Brea, Jennifer, 198
Bronx, New York City, 4, 34, 45, 51, 68–69, 134, 142, 151, 176, 275, 279
Brooklyn, New York City, 31, 60, 105, 109, 172, 174, 196, 232, 256, 280, 326
Brooklyn Bridge memorial, 31
Brooklyn Center for Independence of the Disabled (BCID), 103, 105, 105
Brothers Sick (artists), 9, 145
La Bulle! (The bubble) (association), 301–3
Butler, Octavia, 272, 284, 285n2

Café Asperger (online community), 301–6
California Care Rationing Coalition press conference, 121

Callahan v. Carey, 92–86
capitalism, 350, 351–52
Caplan, Arthur, 13, 146n6
CARES Act of 2020, 28, 275, 292
carewashing, 5–8
care work. *See* work
Carrington, Leonora, 308
Center for Independence of the Disabled New York (CIDNY), 103, 105, *105*
Chang, Yoonmee, 244
Charlton, James, 33n1
children. *See* disabled children; education; parenting
Chinese immigrants, elderly (*qilao*), 228–47
Chinese words, glossary of, 249–50
chronic fatigue syndrome. *See* Myalgic Encephalomyelitis
CIDNY. *See* Center for Independence of the Disabled New York
Coalition for the Homeless, 81, 87, 89, 91
Coler Nursing Home, 34n7, 169, 170
congregate settings
    homeless shelters, 81–97
    housing for people with disabilities and, 169–71
    migrant detention centers and, 63–77
    nursing homes for elderly and, 1, 4, 6–7, 13, 30, 34n8, 112, 135, 167–71
    prisons and, 45–63
Consolidated Appropriations Act of 2021, 292
Cook County Jail, 256
court cases. *See* legal cases
COVID-19 doula, 337–38
COVID-19 Hate Crimes Act of 2021, 251, 262
COVID-19 Maternity Task Force, 280
COVID-19 pandemic. *See specific topics*
COVID-19 Preparation for People Living with Chronic Illnesses in the U.S., 3, 202
COVID-19 trauma, 338

COVID exceptionalism, 335, 337
Crimp, Douglas, 8
Crip Camp (documentary film), 325–26
crip crisis competencies, 340–41
crip doulaing. *See* disability doulaing
crip family recipes, 338–39
Crip Fund (mutual-aid campaign), 3, 304
cripistemologies of crisis, 340
crip kinship, 167, 179, 181, 184
crip pandemic cultural production, 5–8, 25, 27, 144–45, 197, 202–6, 218–19, 222, 225, 227, 228, 252–59, 268
crip pandemic theorizing, 28, 335
crip spacetime (concept), 339–40
Crip Spacetime (Price), 339
crisis
    cripistemologies of, 340
    methods, 341
crisis standards of care guidelines (CSCs), 121–24, *124*, *125*, *127*, 143
Cristian A.R. v. Decker, 74
CSCs. *See* crisis standards of care guidelines
cultural production, pandemic. *See* crip pandemic cultural production
Cummings, Tommy, 90

DaBaron, Shams, 94–97
Dalí, Salvador, 308
dance, 308
Danner, Deborah, 273
Deaf NYC (virtual panel), 20, *20*
deaf people, 19–20, *20*, 21, 323, 326
death plan, disability cliff and, 173–79
debility, 195, 209, 230, 241–46, 252, 279–80
DHS. *See* New York City Department of Homeless Services
DIA. *See* Disabled in Action
digital public spaces, 341–42
disability. *See specific topics*
disability cliff, 173–79
disability dialectic, 4, 16–21, 33n1, 123
disability doulaing, 21–25, *127*, 337–38, 342

Disability Equity in the Time of COVID-19 (research team), 289
disability expertise, 2–3, 8, 11, 16, 194
disability justice, 2, 22–25, 31, 33, 96, 120, 128, 142–46, 201, 205, 209, 226, 252–66, 281, 305, 309, 342, 350, 352
    immigration law and, 74–76
    material needs and, 290–99
Disability Justice Culture Club, 120
disability politics, 114–15
disability reporters, reflections from, 319–23
disability rights, by state, 124, *124*
disabled, privileged, 349–50
disabled children, 68, 75, 151–64, 167–86, 223, 225, 243, 298, 321–24. *See also* education; parenting
Disabled in Action (DIA), 103, 104, 105, *105*
disinformation, defined, 342
disposability, 342
DOCCS. *See* New York Department of Corrections and Community Supervision
Dokumaci, Arseli, 100, 107
double pandemic, 271–85, 289–99, 342
doulas, 21–25, 127, 337–38, 342

Eastern Correctional Facility, 60
ECMO machines. *See* extracorporeal membrane oxygenation machines
education
    of disabled children during pandemic, 151–64, 298
    IDEA and, 159
    IEP and, 155, 170
    NCLB and, 156
    special education, 152, 155, 160–62, 167
8 to Abolition, 253
elderly people, 2, 31, 53, 56, 128, 312
    Chinese immigrants (*qilao*), 228–47
    nursing homes in congregate settings and, 1, 4, 6–7, 13, 30, 34nn7–8, 112, 135, 167–71

    social distancing and, 229, 230, 296
Elisofon, Marguerite, 173–74
end of pandemic, sociological production of, 352
Eraso, Francisco echo, 313–14, *314*, 317
essential workers. *See* work
exceptionalism, COVID, 335, 337
Excluded Workers Fund, 68
extracorporeal membrane oxygenation (ECMO) machines, 134

films
    The Biggest Obstacle, 108, 111, 115
    Crip Camp, 325–26
    Fire Through Dry Grass, 169–71, 185, *185*
    Isolation Nation, 169, 180–82
    Unrest, 198
Fire Through Dry Grass (film), 169–71, 185, *185*
Fisher, Morleen, 92
Fisher v. The City of New York, 82
Fishkill Green Haven Correctional Facility, 52
Floyd, George, 23, 220, 272, 275, 292
Ford, Ezell, 273
France, 299–303
Free Them All for Public Health (campaign), 253, 255–56, 258
Friedner, Michele, 4–5
FutureCenteredCare (disability initiative), 183–84

Garland-Thomson, Rosemarie, 107, 244
Glasgow Coma Scale, 143
Gossiaux, Emilie L., *315*, 315–17, *316*
Graeber, David, 305
graves, 4, 33n2
"the great resignation," 171–72
Guidance for the Ethical Allocation of Scarce Resources, 122

Hand Movie (performance art), 308
Hart Island, 4, 33n2

hate crimes, 251, 262
    Stop AAPI Hate coalition on, 238–39
Hedva, Johanna, 206, 309
Heiskell Braille and Talking Book Library (at NYPL), 214–15, 221
Hernandez, Ralph, 87–90
Heumann, Judith, 28, 325–28
Hick, John, 131
Hickson, Michael, 122
HideAway series (SiQ poster), *333*
hierarchy, 83, 261, 350
    class, 76
    of disability vulnerability, 6–7, 25
    of harm, 95–97
hinterland of disability, vii, 22, 42, 183, 184, 343
HIV/AIDS, 1, 7, 12, 71, 81–82, 84–86, 89–97, 154, 195, 198, 352
    activism, 8–11, 21–25, 83, 87–88, 201, 337
home building, virtual, 352–53
homelessness, 3, 7, 12, 15, 25, 81–97, 100, 156, 221, 251, 263
housing
    congregate, for people with disabilities, 169–71
    as health care, 81–97
"How to Have Promiscuity in an Epidemic" (Crimp), 8
How to Have Theory in an Epidemic (Treichler), 8

ICE. *See* Immigration and Customs Enforcement
#ICUgenics, 144, 342. *See also* allocation of healthcare resources, during pandemic
I/DD. *See* intellectual/developmental disabilities
IDEA. *See* Individuals with Disabilities Education Act
IEP. *See* Individual Education Plan

Illegal Immigration Reform and Immigrant Responsibility Act (IIRIRA) of 1996, 70
Illich, Ivan, 279
illness methodology, 343–44
immigrants with disabilities, 63–76, 169, 229–30, 232–33, 237–44
immigration
    ableism in, law and policy, 65, 167, 169, 255
    detention, 64, 69–76, 269
Immigration Act of 1882, 65
Immigration and Customs Enforcement (ICE), 67, 70, 72–74, 269
inaccessibility. *See* access
incarceration. *See* prisons and jails
Individual Education Plan (IEP), 155, 170
Individuals with Disabilities Education Act (IDEA), 159
"In Praise of Laziness" (Stilinović), 308
intellectual/developmental disabilities (I/DD), 157, 161, 167–69, 171, 174–75, 179, 181, 183
ISO: (Salerno), 311, *311*
Isolation Nation (film), 169, 180–82
I Think We're Alone Now (Host) (Zavitsanos), 309–10, *310*

jails. *See* prisons and jails
James, Cathy, 181–83
JobPath, 181, 182, 186
justice. *See* court cases; disability justice

Kafai, Shayda. *See* crip kinship
Kafer, Alison, 182, 284
Kahlo, Frida, 308
Kim, Jina, 244
Kleinman, Allison, 183–84

labor, and disability, 23, 262, 266, 290–95
labor/laborers. *See* work/workers
Lee, Christina Yuna, 263, *263*

legal cases
- Callahan v. Carey, 92–86
- Cristian A.R. v. Decker, 74
- Fisher v. The City of New York, 82
- Mixon v. Grinker, 82–85, 87–92

Littlefield, Tyler, 219

lockdown, 8, 15–18, 33, 34n8, 109, 158, 176, 181, 271, 278–79, 309
- for blind people, 215–18, 223, 226
- PAUSE Program and, 13–14, *14*, 34n6, 101, 167, 174, 214
- in prisons and jails, 50–55
- for *qilao*, 231–32, 237–38
- term origins, 14

Long Covid, vii–xi, 5, 10, 22, 27, 31, 33, 134, 191–200, 210, 258, 320–21, 323, 327
- activism around, 201–9, *207*, *208*

Lucerne Hotel, New York City, 93–96

The Machine Consumes the Faceless Workers (Porche), 295

Man, Chella, 12, *12*

Manhattan, 1, 103, 134, 171, 173, 176, 183, 228–46, 291, 298, 315

masks, 3, 174, 214, 216–17, 224, 323
- access to, 70
- deaf people and, 20, 21
- hoarding of, 5–6
- prisons and, 47, 49, 54, 59–61
- public transportation and, 29–30, *30*
- *qilao* and, 228–29, 231, 242
- in schools, 320, 321

mass disabling event, vii, 4, 5, 33, 191, 193, 209
- Barbarin and, 3–14, 17

mass grave, 4, 33n2

Maternity Task Force, COVID-19, 280

Matilda's Law, 34n6, 102

Mauldin, Laura, vii–viii, 19

#MEAction, 191, 198, 200, 201–8, *204*, *207*

ME/CFS. *See* Myalgic Encephalomyelitis

media, 2, 7–8, 18, 100, 103, 156, 162, 191–93, 199, 202, 233, 272, 304, 305
- news reporting and, vii–xi, 3–4, 121, 126, 151–52, 157, 159, 161, 224, 229, 319–24
- social media and, 3, 103, 110, 144, 178, 201, 205, 219, 259, 273, 295, 310, 348, 352

medical gaslighting, 344

Medical Providers Network, 71

memorials
- anti-Asian violence, 263, *263*, 268, *268*
- Brooklyn Bridge, *31*
- MTA, 101, *101*
- NTL, 32

mental health, 138, 175, 179–80, 183, 196, 260. *See also* trauma
- Black mothers and, xi, 12, 28, 271–85
- Chinese immigrants and, 237, 239
- health care workers and, 22
- homelessness and, 94–95
- immigration detention and, 69, 75, 84, 92
- incarceration and, 55, 255
- policing and, 252
- public transportation and, 15–16

Metropolitan Transit Authority (MTA), New York City, 25, *30*, 100–101, 103–5, 108, 110–11, 116
- memorial, 101, *101*

migrant detention centers. *See* immigration

Milbern, Stacey Park, 21, 120–21, *121*

Minerva (Hedva), 309

Mingus, Mia, 2, 168, 181, 260

Mixon, Kenneth, 87

Mixon v. Grinker, 82–85, 87–92

Molina, Andres "Jay," 169–70

mothers
- disabled children and vigilante, 159–62
- mental health and Black, xi, 12, 28, 271–85
- pregnancy, birthing, and postpartum for, 273, 276–84
- trauma and, 277, 278, 279, 281, 283–84

movies. *See* films
MTA. *See* Metropolitan Transit Authority, New York City
mutual aid, 127, 134, 144, 146, 201, 226, 251–69, 283 289–98, 307
  conclusions, 303–6
  Crip Fund campaign for, 3, 304
  developing networks of, 299–303
Myalgic Encephalomyelitis (ME/CFS), vii–ix, 8–9, 11, 24, 191–200. *See also* Long Covid
  activism around, 191, 198, 200, 201–9, *204, 207, 208*
#MyDisabledLifeIsWorthy, 17

Naming the Lost Memorials (NTL), 32
National Council for the Training of Journalists, 320
National Federation of the Blind (NFB), 19
National Institute of Allergy and Infectious Diseases (NIAID), 200
National No New Jails Network, 200
necropolitics, 344
Ne'eman, Ari, 122–24, 127, 142, 143, 148
neoliberalism, pandemic parenting and, 281–83
Neophytides, Alexis, 169, 185, *185*. See also *Fire Through Dry Grass*
news media reporting, vii–xi, 3–4, 121, 126, 151–52, 157, 159, 161, 224, 229, 319–24
New York City
  Bronx, 4, 34, 45, 51, 68–69, 134, 142, 151, 176, 275, 279
  Brooklyn, 31, 60, 105, 109, 172, 174, 196, 232, 256, 280, 326
  COVID-19 deaths by zip code in, *15*
  DHS, 81, 84, 92–95
  Hart Island, 4, 33n2
  immigrants with disabilities in, 63–76
  inaccessibility and, 103–5

Lucerne Hotel, 93–96
Manhattan, 1, 103, 134, 171, 173, 176, 183, 228–46, 291, 298, 315
pandemic and disability activism timeline in, *329–32*
pandemic overview in, 63–64
public transportation, 25, 100–101, 103–5, 108, 110–11, 116
Queens, 4, 5, 69, 109, 140, 172, 232, 237, 258, 267, 274
support of disabled people in, 67–68
New York City Department of Homeless Services (DHS), 81, 84, 92–95
New York Department of Corrections and Community Supervision (DOCCS), 45–47, 49, 52–53
  COVID-19 memoranda from, *46, 47, 48*
New York Immigrant Family Unity Project (NYIFUP), 72
New York Public Library (NYPL), 5, 27
  Heiskell Braille and Talking Book Library, 214–15, 221
New York State
  ADAPT in, 103, 112, *112*
  PAUSE Program of, 13–14, *14*, 34n6, 101, 167, 174, 214
  Task Force on Life and the Law, 123–25, 131
  ventilator allocation in, 121–46
NFB. *See* National Federation of the Blind
NIAID. *See* National Institute of Allergy and Infectious Diseases
nihilism, pandemic, 346
#NoBodyIsDisposable, 141, 342
Nortz, Shelly, 81, 82, 84
NTL. *See* Naming the Lost Memorials
nursing homes, 1, 4, 6–7, 13, 30, 34nn7–8, 112, 135, 167–71
NYIFUP. *See* New York Immigrant Family Unity Project
NYPD Hate Crimes Task Force, 262
NYPL. *See* New York Public Library

O'Laughlin, Daniel, 131
On a Good Day You Can Feel My Love for You (Gossiaux), 315, *315*
On-Demand E-Hail, 110
organized abandonment, 345
Otisville Correctional Facility, 53–57, 59, 81
Outside Voices Theater Company, 180–81

Pagan, Raphael Hernandez, 87
pandemic. *See specific topics*
pandemic ableism, 336, 345
pandemic cultural production. *See* crip pandemic cultural production
pandemic fatigue, 346
pandemic nihilism, 346
pandemic profiteering, 346–47
pandemic revisionism, 347
pandemic rollbacks, 5, 27, 224–27, 347–48
pandemic solutionism, 348
pandemic theorizing, 349
Parable of the Sower (Butler), 272, 284, 285n2
parenting. *See also* disabled children; mothers
    immunocompromised children during pandemic, 321–22
    neoliberalism and pandemic, 281–83
    remote learning and, 151–64, 298
Parts of Some Sextets (Rainer), 308
PAUSE Program (New York State), 13–14, *14*, 34n6, 101, 167, 174, 214
pedagogy of unwellness, 349
performance art, 308
    Outside Voices Theater Company, 180–81
    Tian shi dao zhi qiang play, 229
perinatal period, healthier, 283–84
personal protective equipment (PPE), 70, 141, 195, 258, 347. *See also* masks
Philips, Wayne. *See* Anger into Direct Action
Piepzna-Samarasinha, Leah Lakshmi, 3, 21, 33, 260, 304–6

Poets of Course (writing group), 181, 182, 186
police/policing, 15, 26, 91, 94, 251–53, 262–65, 267, 274
    police brutality and, 22–23, 271–72
population management, 7
Porche, Amanda, 295
post-pandemic, 116, 163, 283
    rollbacks, 5, 27, 224–27, 347–48
postpartum, birthing, and pregnancy, 273, 276–84
postviral affects, 197–201
PPE. *See* personal protective equipment
pregnancy, birthing, and postpartum, 273, 276–84
Price, Margaret, 339
prisons and jails
    carceral care contradictions in, 58–60
    Cook County Jail, 256
    COVID-19 memoranda, *46, 47, 48*
    Eastern Correctional Facility, 60
    Fishkill Green Haven Correctional Facility, 52
    incarceration in, 4, 10–12, 14, 16, 25, 45–61, 63–77, 140, 251–53, 255–58, 265–67
    medical care in, 55–58
    National No New Jails Network and, 200
    New York DOCCS, 45–47, *46, 47, 48, 49,* 52–53
    Otisville Correctional Facility, 53–57, 59, 81
    Rikers Island, 49, 51–52, 253, 256
    San Quentin State Prison, 49, 256
    social distancing in, 49, 50–55, 59, 61
    Wallkill Correctional Facility, 45–46, 51–52, 54
    Wende Correctional Facility, 47, 49
privileged disabled, 349–50
profiteering, pandemic, 346–47
Project Renewal, 93
Prude, Daniel, 273
Puar, Jasbir, 252, 312, 344

public charge, 65–68, 75–76, 241
public spaces, digital, 341–42
public transportation. *See* transportation
Pulrang, Andrew, 4

qilao. *See* Chinese immigrants, elderly
Queens, New York City, 4, 5, 69, 109, 140, 172, 232, 237, 258, 267, 274
queer and trans people, 3, 8, 12, 144, 180, 264, 267
    autism and, 323
    Black disabled, 12, 304
    Facebook group for, 310–11

racial ableism, 350–51
racism
    anti-Asian, 22–23, 28, 229, 237–39, 251–69, 263, 268
    anti-Black, 22, 28, 69, 143, 259, 262–67, 271, 272–75, 279
Rainer, Yvonne, 308
Reality Poets (artist collective), 169–71, 185, *185*
Red and Yellow Tapestry (Eraso), 314, *314*
Red Canary Song (sex workers collective), 253, 257–58, 267, 268, *268*
remote access, 18, 27, 102, 111, 157, 351
remote work, 3, 21, 34–35n11, 196, 226, 283–84
reporters, disability, 319–23
rest, 192, 203–4, 257, 284, 308–17
revisionism, pandemic, 347
Riccobono, Mark, 19
right to shelter, 85–92, 96
Rikers Island, 49, 51–52, 253, 256
Rise and Resist (activists), 105, *105*
risk, disproportionate, 84–85
rollbacks, 5, 27, 224–27, 347–48
Russell, Marta, 7, 83, 95
Ryan White CARE Act, 88

safety, shelter and, 81–97
Salerno, Alex Dolores, 144, 310–17, *311*

San Quentin State Prison, 49, 256
Schalk, Sami, 244, 284
Schiavenato, Stephanie, 280
schooling. *See* education
Sequential Organ Failure Assessment (SOFA scoring), 13
sex workers. *See* work
shelter
    homelessness and, 81–97, 221
    right to, 85–92, 96
    safety and, 81–97
Shepard-Byrd Hate Crimes Prevention Act of 2009, 251
Sick in Quarters (SiQ), 23, 26, 26–27, *27*, 333
Sick of It! A Disability Inside/Outside Project (magazine), 23, 252–53, *254*
"Sick Woman Theory" (Hedva), 206, 309
sign language, 12, *12*
Singer, Merrill, 95
Sins Invalid (arts organization), 10, 74, 128, 150
SiQ. *See* Sick in Quarters
Snyder, Michael, 87
social distancing, viii, 172
    elderly and, 229, 230, 296
    immigrant detention centers and, 71, 73–74
    mental health and, 92
    in prisons and jails, 49, 50–55, 59, 61
    in schools, 152, 160–61
social media, 3, 103, 110, 144, 178, 201, 205, 219, 259, 273, 295, 348, 352
    support on, 310–11
social murder, 351–52
sociological production, of end of pandemic, 352
SOFA scoring. *See* Sequential Organ Failure Assessment
solidarity, xi, 201, 252–53, 255, 262, 269, 300
    artists and, 311
    crip doulaing and, 21–25, 127
    disability politics and, 114–15
solutionism, pandemic, 348

S&P NY. *See* Survived and Punished New York
state, CSCs by, 124, *124*
state abandonment, 345
Staten Island, 258
Stay Safe—COVID-19 Protest Resources (SiQ brochure), 23, 26, *26*
Stilinović, Mladen, 308
stimulus. *See* American Rescue Plan Act of 2021; Consolidated Appropriations Act of 2021
Stop AAPI Hate (coalition), 238–39
stop Asian hate (discourse), 251, 262
#StopRestPace (campaign), 203–4, *204*
Stramondo, Joseph, 123
Survived and Punished New York (S&P NY), 253
syndemic, 95, 272, 343

Talk Description to Me (podcast), 219–20
Taylor, Breonna, 272, 275, 292
testing, COVID, 19, 29, 49, 51–54, 60, 70, 100, 174, 195, 214, 225, 279–80, 296, 320
theorizing, pandemic, 349
Tian shi dao zhi qiang (Written in the walls) (play), 229
timeline, *329–32*
trans people. *See* queer and trans people
transportation
  access to, 100–115
  busses, 106, 108, 109–10
  masks and, 29–30, *30*
  New York City MTA and, 25, 30, 100–101, *101*, 103–5, 108, 110–11, 116
  On-Demand E-Hail, 110
trauma, 71, 94–95, 157, 260–61, 341
  COVID-19, defined, 338
  incarceration and, 255
  maternal, 277, 278, 279, 281, 283–84
Treichler, Paula, 8, 10
True Love (Gossiaux), 316, *316*

Unrest (documentary film), 198

vaccines, x, 5, 18–19, 29–30, 130–31, 135, 140, 319
  poster on hoarding of, *145*
ventilator. *See* allocation of healthcare resources, during pandemic
View of Protest Traveling Down Park Row (photograph), *293*
viral underclass, 352
virtual home building, 352–53

Walensky, Rochelle, 17
Wallace, Walter, Jr., 273
Wallkill Correctional Facility, 45–46, 51–52, 54
Washington Square Park vigil, 268, *268*
Welfare Reform Act of 1996, 66–77
Wende Correctional Facility, 47, 49
Wiberg, Hans Jorgen, 19
Wilder, Terri, 193–94, 196, 199–200, 202–4, 206
Williams, Kate, 112
Williams, Tamara, 84
Wong, Alice, 33, 169–70, 260
work/workers
  access for, 111–14
  care, 9, 92, 151–64, 167–86, 226, 229, 232, 237, 321
  disabled, 101, 106, 107, 215, 225
  essential, 69, 136, 241
  "the great resignation" and, 171–72
  health care, 22, 136–38, 141–42, 195, 257, 274
  sex, 253, 257–58, 262, 265–68, *268*
Written in the walls (*Tian shi dao zhi qiang*) (play), 229

Yong, Ed, xvii–xi, 22, 28, 183, 343. *See also* hinterland of disability

Zavitsanos, Constantina, 305, 309–10, *310*

www.ingramcontent.com/pod-product-compliance
Lightning Source LLC
Chambersburg PA
CBHW061228070526
44584CB00030B/4032